AN LEABF

Co٧ʎ١ST٠

=

Foundations of Organizational Strategy

Michael C. Jensen

FOUNDATIONS OF ORGANIZATIONAL STRATEGY

Harvard University Press

Cambridge, Massachusetts

London, England · 1998

Library of Congress Cataloging-in-Publication Data

Jensen, Michael C.
    Foundations of organizational strategy / Michael C. Jensen.
        p.   cm.
    Includes bibliographical references and index.
    ISBN 0-674-64342-9 (alk. paper)
    1. Organizational behavior.   I. Title.
    HD58.7.J463   1998
    658.4'012—dc21   98-20215

To the memory of William H. Meckling,
my close friend, coauthor, and scholar

Contents

Preface

There are three main elements in an organization's total strategy: its competitive strategy, its organizational strategy, and its human strategy. This volume contains twelve articles written over the last twenty-five years which deal with a firm's organizational strategy. In these articles my coauthors (noted in each chapter) and I lay out the foundations of a theory of organizations that is both integrated and powerful. The development of this material had its genesis in the early 1970s at the University of Rochester, where two complementary initiatives spurred this effort. One was the research that William H. Meckling and I began on agency theory in 1973, which opened up a new set of insights into the behavior of managers and firms. The second was the course development effort that Meckling and I began at that same time, which has led to major courses at both Rochester and Harvard.

In our course at Harvard Business School, entitled "Coordination, Control, and the Management of Organizations" (CCMO), my colleagues (George Baker, Carliss Baldwin, Karen Wruck, and Malcolm Salter) and I apply the concepts to a wide range of management and organizational problems. The course, one of the most successful in the second year of the MBA program, attracts about 600 students each year. The history of the course is summarized in "Organizations and Markets at the Harvard Business School, 1984–1996," by Michael C. Jensen, George Baker, Carliss Baldwin, and Karen H. Wruck, in *The Intellectual Venture Capitalist: John H. McArthur and the Work of the Harvard Business School 1980–1995*, edited by Thomas K. McCraw and Jeffrey L. Cruikshank (Harvard Business School Press, 1998). This article and a complete description of the CCMO course, including the course syllabus, reading list, course notes, and practice questions, are available in four electronic documents on the Internet from the Social Science Research Network Electronic Library at:

http://papers.ssrn.com/paper.taf?abstract_id=58704

I am indebted to many people for stimulation and help in developing these ideas and this book. The book would not have happened without the devoted attention and effort of Janet Montgomery, who has prepared the manuscript from beginning to end, checked and rechecked it for accuracy and consistency, and continually tolerated my idiosyncrasies. My assistant, June Hayes, has patiently aided in this process as well, as did many before her including Kathleen Measer at the University of Rochester, who for years managed the production of my joint work with William H. Meckling. The research on which this work is based has been supported by the University of Rochester Simon School of Business and the Harvard Business School Division of Research. I owe my deepest debt to William H. Meckling, who was the Dean at the University of Rochester when I arrived there as an assistant professor in 1967. We became friends and coauthors as well as colleagues, and his influence on me and others in the profession has been truly profound. He has been crucial in the creation of the Rochester School and all that it has brought to the science and practice of management and economics.

In May 1998, after this preface was first written, William Meckling passed away at his home in Rancho Sante Fe, California. The world lost a great scholar. Without Bill, much of the work in this volume would not have been done. I dedicate this book to him and our friendship.

Michael C. Jensen
July 1998

Foundations of Organizational Strategy

Introduction

The twelve chapters in this volume lay out the foundations of an integrated theory of organizations. The theory assumes that organizations are equilibrium systems that, like markets, can be influenced, but cannot be told what to do; that human beings are rational and self-interested; and that information is costly to produce and transfer among agents. The theory also treats organizations as entities existing in a system of markets (including financial, product, labor, and materials markets) that must be taken into account in the formulation of organizational strategy and structure. I concentrate here on the microanalytic foundations of the theory, and leave for a forthcoming volume analysis of the principles of organizational governance systems.

Economists have historically concentrated on the analysis of markets while treating the organizations in them as black boxes that act as profit-maximizing entities. On the other hand, behavioral organization theorists have largely focused on the internal aspects of organizations, ignoring the forces of markets in which those organizations exist. It could be argued that treating organizations and markets as separate entities was justifiable as long as organizational boundaries were well defined and the preponderance of market transactions were simple and stylized. Today, however, technological and historical developments (including the development of high-speed information analysis and transfer technologies, as well as the emergence of modern high-capacity capital markets) are blurring the boundaries and making the relationship between organizations and markets much more complex. Any rigorous and useful theory of organizations must now be embedded in an understanding of both human behavior *and* markets.

In developing the theory, I have focused in particular on four interrelated areas:

1. the fundamental building blocks of this new theory of organizations, including

   a. the nature of human beings and their behavior,
   b. the costs of transferring information among agents,
   c. the agency costs generated by cooperative behavior among individuals, and
   d. the organizational rules of the game that play such a major role in determining organizational success or failure;
2. residual claims and the critical role they play in determining organizational form and behavior;
3. compensation; and
4. divisional performance measurement and total quality management as applications of the theory.

I begin with a discussion of the nature of human beings: those unusual, complicated, self-interested, and emotional creatures who populate the organizations that business people seek to manage, inspire, and guide. I move on to a discussion of the critical importance of the costs of moving information between people in the economy and in organizations. Because all information cannot be moved to a central decision maker, whether a central planner in the economy or the CEO in a firm, most decision rights must be delegated to those people who have the relevant information.

Thus, the cost of moving information between people creates the necessity for decentralizing some decision rights in organizations and the economy. This decentralization in turn leads to systems to mitigate the control problem that results from the fact that self-interested people (with their own self-control problems) who exercise decision rights as agents on behalf of others will not behave as perfect agents. I call the systems that arise to resolve these control problems the "organizational rules of the game." Capitalist market economies solve these control problems through the institution of alienable decision rights. Because organizations by definition suppress the alienability of decision rights, they must devise substitute mechanisms that perform the functions of alienability. Analysis of how alienability solves the control problem posed by agency costs in capitalist economies leads to an understanding of the three major functions that must be provided in other ways inside organizations. They are: (1) a system for allocating decision rights among agents in the firm, (2) a system for measuring and evaluating performance in the firm, and (3) a system for rewarding and punishing individuals for their performance. Figure 1 depicts the principles of the

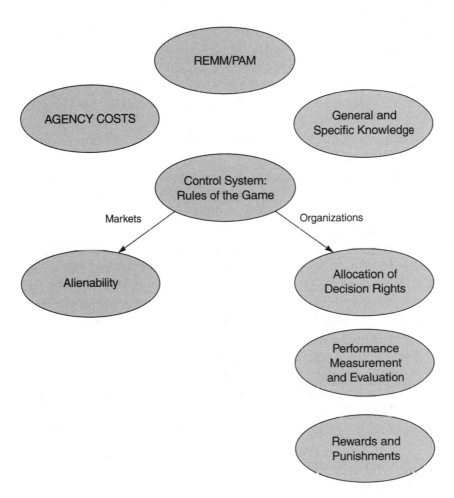

Figure 1 Fundamental conceptual building blocks that form the foundations of organizational strategy. REMM and PAM are the components of the Dualistic Model of human behavior on which the integrated theory of organizations is based. Because specific knowledge is costly to transfer among agents, facilitating its use in organizations and society means that decision rights must be delegated to the agents who possess the specific knowledge relevant to the decisions. Self-control problems and the conflicts of interest among self-interested individuals then create agency problems when decision rights are delegated to agents with the relevant specific knowledge. Alienable decision rights solve this control problem in capitalist societies, but since alienability of decision rights is not delegated to agents inside organizations, they must create substitute control systems that accomplish the control that alienability provides in the economy as a whole. This substitute control system, the "organizational rules of the game," consists of three systems that (1) allocate decision rights to those agents with the relevant specific knowledge for their exercise, (2) measure and evaluate the performance of the decision agents, and (3) reward and punish agents for their performance.

integrated theory and their relations to one another. A more detailed discussion of these principles is given in the following sections.

The model of human behavior. I begin by exploring the rational side of human behavior, which many years ago William Meckling and I labeled "REMM," for Resourceful, Evaluative, Maximizing Model. One of the most important aspects of this model is the proposition that people are inherently self-interested and systematically make substitutions, and although they may well be more or less altruistic, there are nevertheless no "perfect agents" in the real world. In other words, no one so thoroughly embodies the preferences of another that he or she can be that person's perfect agent.

Interestingly, people regularly resist this rational characterization of humans as being too simple, yet there is an enormous amount of evidence on human behavior in the aggregate (and in the long run even for individuals) that is consistent with it. It is, however, incomplete as a description of the totality of human behavior. In recent years I have been concentrating on understanding and integrating the nonrational aspects of human behavior into this integrated theory of organizations—what I have labeled the Pain Avoidance Model (PAM) of human behavior. These two seemingly inconsistent views of human behavior (REMM and PAM) can be integrated into a single framework through what I call the Dualistic Model of human behavior, which describes people as being in one of two regimes at any moment in time. The two regimes are the rational (REMM) and the nonrational (PAM), and the variable that determines which of these two regimes is active at any moment is fear. When frightened, people regularly switch into the PAM regime, in which they systematically make decisions and take actions that harm themselves, their organizations, and the people around them. Because this work on PAM and the Dualistic Model is still in an early stage of development, I have not included it in this volume.

The cost of transferring knowledge. The second major building block of the theory of organizations is the cost of transferring knowledge between agents. The central proposition I put forward, based on work in the 1940s by Friedrich von Hayek, is that certain kinds of knowledge (which I label "specific" knowledge) are very costly to transmit. In such cases, the common managerial tactic of moving the knowledge to the decision maker is not likely to work. Instead, we must *place the decision rights for which that knowledge is valuable in the hands of the person with the knowledge.* (This is the real economic advantage inherent in the modern empowerment movement.) We can then also move the "general" knowledge (defined as that knowledge which can be moved at lower transfer costs) to that decentralized decision maker.

Because vast amounts of knowledge are specific, centralized decision making is likely to fail in most situations. This is why the failure of the world's socialist and communist centrally planned systems was virtually inevitable. Moreover, we can say much about how control systems and the nature of specific knowledge and its location can change with technology, uncertainty, and so on, so that we can make substantive propositions about how such decision rights should be allocated. In addition, we can simply sidestep as irrelevant the age-old debate over centralization versus decentralization. Because some bodies of specific knowledge reside at the top of the organization, while others reside in the middle or at the bottom, the real issue is *which* decision rights to decentralize, and which to centralize.

Agency costs. Having established the fact that a completely centralized solution will seldom, if ever, be optimal, we are then led to confront the difficulties caused by the fact that human beings are self-interested and otherwise imperfect agents. This raises the specter of agency costs and the control problem: the problem associated with limiting the costs due to conflicts of interest with others and with ourselves.

Alienability and the organizational rules of the game. The institutional device that allows a free-market capitalist system to solve the control problem is alienable decision rights. A decision right is the right to choose an action and to take an action, in a context where the police powers of the state will be used to ensure the party's ability to take the action. An *alienable* decision right is one that can be sold or exchanged by the owner, with the owner pocketing the proceeds offered in exchange. For example, if Harry owns the alienable decision rights in a machine, no one can use or sell that machine without his permission. More important, alienable decision rights enable exchange to occur. Exchange, in turn, works to ensure that those who have the specific knowledge and talents valuable to the exercise of a particular right will have a mechanism for gaining possession of that right (by peaceful means). Anyone with better information or talents regarding the use of

Harry's machine can make an offer to purchase it; if they have better information they are likely to value it more highly than he does, and the exchange will tend to occur.

Thus, alienability creates an automatic and decentralized system for partitioning and assigning decision rights to those who value them most highly. In addition, the prices that are determined in these voluntary exchanges provide an effective measure of performance of the party who owns the rights. Assuming there are no externalities, the performance measure yielded by prices incorporates the total current and future value implications of the owner's actions with the decision rights (to the full extent that the contracting parties can anticipate them). Continuing with the present example, if Harry fails to maintain the machine and thereby reduces its present and future productivity, the sale price of the machine will be lower. Finally, since alienability allows the owner of the right to capture the proceeds offered in the exchange, it automatically rewards and punishes the owner for his performance with the rights. It does so by capitalizing the entire present value of the future costs and benefits of the owner's actions onto his shoulders.

I call these three dimensions of system design—the allocation of decision rights, performance measurement, and rewards and punishments—the "organizational rules of the game." They are of particular interest and importance to managers because the defining characteristic of firms is that they do not assign alienable decision rights to agents, but they reserve alienability (the right to pocket the proceeds) to the organization (or, more precisely, to the residual claimants). When General Motors delegates a decision right to an individual (say, the use of a machine), that individual is not given the right to sell that machine to the highest bidder and allowed to capture the proceeds of the sale. If such alienability were granted, it is clear there would be nothing left for the residual claimants of the firm. Therefore the alienability is held by the board of directors, and any sale price inures to the firm itself, not the individual manager. Thus, firms are like lumps in cake batter: they disable the very system that so effectively solves the control and rights-assignment problems in the economy at large.

Obviously, firms must also get *benefits* from suppressing alienability, or they could not survive. These benefits come from two sources: (1) the advantages of specialized risk bearing, made possible by separating the running of an enterprise from the bearing of its risks by stockholders and bondholders, and (2) the gains that come from better coordination across units of the firm that would otherwise lead to externalities in a market solution. Put simply, this latter point means that when managers can coordinate production and exchange better than arm's-length transactions in a market, firms can arise to create value for their owners and society.

Like a compass needle swinging to the north, the analysis now points us to a key consideration: what managers must do when they disable the important functions of alienability. The answer is that they must provide managerial substitutes for the "rules of the game." In other words, they must provide systems that (1) partition decision rights among agents so as to maximize their value, (2) measure and evaluate the performance of agents with respect to those decision rights, and (3) reward and punish agents on the basis of their performance in ways that motivate them to move toward efficiency in their actions.

The building blocks of the theory, simple as they are, are now complete. These concepts can be applied to all kinds of for-profit and nonprofit organizations; to large and small organizations; to partnerships and corporations; and to government and military organizations (such as the Tactical Air Command). My colleagues and I have also applied these concepts in a wide range of management actions and activities: compensation of line workers and CEOs; financial decisions on dividends, capital, and ownership structure; leveraged buyouts; conflicts with unions; downsizing; leveraged growth; total quality management programs; decisions involving the use of cost centers versus profit centers; and so on. Finally, in a forthcoming volume I apply these concepts to the top-level governance systems (including boards of directors) of corporate organizations and limited partnerships, and use the concepts to understand the broad industrial trends of the past forty years, as well as the conflicts these trends have engendered among social classes, and between the developed and underdeveloped nations of the world.

PART I   **Fundamental Building Blocks
of the Theory**

1 | The Nature of Man

Understanding human behavior is fundamental to understanding how organizations function, whether they are profit-making firms in the private sector, nonprofit enterprises, or government agencies intended to serve the "public interest." Much policy disagreement among managers, scientists, policy makers, and citizens arises from substantial, though usually implicit, differences in the way we think about human nature[1]—about the strengths, frailties, intelligence, ignorance, honesty, selfishness, generosity, and altruism of individuals.

The usefulness of any model of human nature depends on its ability to explain a wide range of social phenomena; the test of such a model is the degree to which it is consistent with observed human behavior. A model that explains behavior only in one small geographical area, or only for a short period in history, or only for people engaged in certain pursuits, is not very useful. For this reason we must use a limited number of general traits to characterize human behavior. Greater detail limits the explanatory ability of a model because individual people differ so greatly. Therefore, we seek a set of characteristics that captures the essence of human nature, but no more.

Although this may sound abstract and complex, it is neither. Each of us has in mind and uses models of human nature every day. We all understand, for example, that people are willing to make trade-offs among things that they want. Our spouses, partners, children, friends, business associates, or perfect strangers can be induced to make substitutions of all kinds. We offer to go out to dinner Saturday night instead of to the concert tonight. We offer to substitute a bicycle for a stereo as a birthday gift. We allow an employee to go home early today if the time is made up next week.

If our model specified that individuals were never willing to substitute

By Michael C. Jensen and William H. Meckling; originally published in *Journal of Applied Corporate Finance* 7, no. 2 (Summer 1994), pp. 4–19.

some amount of a good for some amounts of other goods, it would quickly run aground on inconsistent evidence. It could not explain much of the human behavior we observe. While it may sound silly to characterize individuals as unwilling to make substitutions, that view of human behavior is not far from models that are widely accepted and used by many social scientists (for example, Maslow's [1943] hierarchy of human needs and sociologists' models portraying individuals as cultural role players or social victims).

We investigate five alternative models of human behavior that are used frequently enough (though usually implicitly) in the social science literature and in public discussion to merit attention. For convenience, we label the models as follows:

1. The Resourceful, Evaluative, Maximizing Model (or REMM)
2. The Economic (or Money Maximizing) Model
3. The Sociological (or Social Victim) Model
4. The Psychological (or Hierarchy of Needs) Model
5. The Political (or Perfect Agent) Model

These alternative models are pure types characterized in terms of only the barest essentials. We are sensitive to the dangers of creating straw men and concede that our characterization of these models fails to represent the complexity of the views of scientists in each of these fields. In particular, these models do not describe what all individual economists, sociologists, psychologists, and other social scientists use as their models of human behavior. Nevertheless, we believe that enough use is made of such admittedly reductive models throughout the social sciences, and by people in general, to warrant our treatment of them in this chapter.

1.1 The Resourceful, Evaluative, Maximizing Model: REMM

Although the term "REMM" is new, the concept is not. REMM is the product of over 200 years of research and debate in economics, the other social sciences, and philosophy. As a result, REMM is now defined in very precise terms, but we offer here only a bare-bones summary of the concept. Many specifics can be added to enrich its descriptive content without sacrificing the basic foundation provided here.

POSTULATE I. Every individual cares; he or she is an evaluator.

(a) The individual cares about almost everything: knowledge, independence, the plight of others, the environment, honor, interpersonal relationships, status, peer approval, group norms, culture, wealth, rules of conduct, the weather, music, art, and so on.

(b) REMM always allows for trade-offs and substitutions. Each individual is always willing to give up some sufficiently small amount of any particular good (oranges, water, air, housing, honesty, or safety) for some sufficiently large quantity of other goods. Furthermore, valuation is relative in the sense that the value of a unit of any particular good decreases as the individual enjoys more of it relative to other goods.

(c) Individual preferences are transitive—that is, if A is preferred to B, and B is preferred to C, then A is preferred to C.

POSTULATE II. Each individual's wants are unlimited.

(a) If we designate those things that REMM values positively as "goods," then the individual prefers more goods to less. Goods can be anything from art objects to ethical norms.

(b) REMM cannot be satiated. The individual always wants more of some things, whether they are material goods such as art, sculpture, castles, and pyramids; or intangible goods such as solitude, companionship, honesty, respect, love, fame, and immortality.

POSTULATE III. Each individual is a maximizer.

He or she acts so as to enjoy the highest level of value possible. Individuals are always constrained in satisfying their wants. Wealth, time, and the laws of nature are all important constraints that affect the opportunities available to any individual. Individuals are also constrained by the limits of their own knowledge about various goods and opportunities; their choices of goods or courses of action will reflect the costs of acquiring the knowledge or information necessary to evaluate those choices.[2]

The notion of an opportunity set provides the limit on the level of value attainable by any individual. The opportunity set is usually regarded as something that is given and external to the individual. Economists tend to represent it as a wealth or income constraint and a set of prices at which the individual can buy goods. But the notion of an individual's opportunity set can be generalized to include the set of activities he or she can perform during a 24-hour day—or in a lifetime.

POSTULATE IV. The individual is resourceful.

Individuals are creative. They are able to conceive of changes in their environment, foresee the consequences thereof, and respond by creating new opportunities.

Although an individual's opportunity set is limited at any instant in time by his or her knowledge and the state of the world, that limitation is not immutable. Human beings are not only capable of learning about new opportunities, they also engage in resourceful, creative activities that expand their opportunities in various ways.

The kind of highly mechanical behavior posited by economists—that is, assigning probabilities and expected values to various actions and choosing the action with the highest expected value—is formally consistent with the evaluating, maximizing model defined in Postulates I through III. But such behavior falls short of the human capabilities posited by REMM; it says nothing about the individual's ingenuity and creativity.

1.2 REMMs at Work

One way of capturing the notion of resourcefulness is to think about the effects of newly imposed constraints on human behavior. These constraints might be new operating policies in a corporation or new laws imposed by governments. No matter how much experience we have with the response of people to changes in their environment, we tend to overestimate the impact of a new law or policy intended to constrain human behavior. Moreover, the constraint or law will almost always generate behavior that was never imagined by its sponsors. Why? Because of the sponsors' failure to recognize the creativity of REMMs.

REMMs' response to a new constraint is to begin searching for substitutes for what is now constrained, a search that is not restricted to existing alternatives. REMMs will invent alternatives that did not previously exist.

An excellent illustration of how humans function as REMMs is the popular response to the 1974 federal imposition of a 55-mile-per-hour speed limit in all states under penalty of loss of federal transportation and highway moneys. The primary reason offered for this law was the conservation of gasoline and diesel fuel (for simplicity, we ignore the benefits associated with the smaller number of accidents that occur at slower speeds).[3]

The major cost associated with slower driving is lost time. At a maximum speed of 55 mph instead of 70 mph, trips take longer. Those who argue that lost time is not important must recognize that an hour of time consumed is just as irreplaceable as—and generally more valuable than—a gallon of gasoline consumed. On these grounds, the law created inefficiencies, and the behavior of drivers is consistent with that conclusion.[4]

If we calculate the dollar benefits of fuel saved by the 55 mph speed limit and the value of these savings per additional hour of driving time, we can then compare these dollar savings to the value of the driver's time. Suppose driving at 55 mph instead of 70 mph saves 10% on gasoline consumption, so that, for example, if gasoline mileage is 14 mpg at 70 mph, it will be 15.4 mpg at 55 mph. To travel 70 miles at 55 mph will take 1.273 hours instead of 1 hour at 70 mph. The gasoline consumed is 4.545 gallons at 55 mph instead of 5 gallons at 70 mph. This means that for every additional hour of travel time required by the slower speed, a driver saves 1.665 gallons of gasoline = (5.0 − 4.545) divided by (1.273   1.0).

At a price of $1.20 per gallon for gasoline, the driver saves $2.00 per hour of additional travel time—a sum significantly less than the minimum wage. If there are two occupants in the car, they each save $1.00 per hour; and the rate sinks to 66¢ per hour per person if there are three occupants. Therefore, the law requires that drivers and their passengers spend time in an activity that earns them about $2.00 per hour or less, depending on the particular car, the driver's habits, and the number of passengers.

Judging from the widespread difficulties that state authorities have had in enforcing the law, drivers understand the value of their time quite well. People responded in REMM-like fashion to this newly imposed constraint in a number of ways. One was to reduce their automobile, bus, and truck travel, and, in some cases, to shift to travel by other means such as airplanes and trains. Another response was to defy the law by driving at speeds exceeding the 55 mph maximum. Violating the speed limit, of course, exposes offenders to potential costs in the form of fines, higher insurance rates, and possible loss of driver's licenses. This, in turn, provides incentives for REMMs to search out ways to reduce such costs.

The result has been an entire new industry, and the rapid growth of an already existing one. Citizen's Band radios (CBs), which had been used primarily by truckers, suddenly became widely used by passenger car drivers and almost all truckers. There were about 800,000 FCC CB radio licenses outstanding throughout the period 1966–1973. By the end of 1977, there were 11.25 million licensed CBs in use.[5] These two-way radios with relatively short ranges (under 15 miles) allowed drivers to inform each other about the location of police cars, radar traps, unmarked cars, and so on. They significantly reduced the likelihood of arrest for speeding. REMMs by the millions were willing to pay from $50 to $300 for radios to save time and avoid speeding tickets.

CB radios have now been largely replaced by radar detectors that warn drivers of the presence of police radar. These devices have become so common that police have taken countermeasures, such as investing in more expensive and sophisticated radar units that are less susceptible to detection. Manufacturers of radar detectors retaliated by manufacturing increasingly sophisticated units, and some states responded by enacting laws prohibiting the use of radar detectors within their borders.

The message is clear: people who drive value their time at more than $2.00 per hour. When the 55 mph maximum speed limit was imposed, few would have predicted the ensuing chain of events. One seemingly modest constraint on REMMs created a new electronic industry designed to avoid the constraint. And such behavior shows itself again and again in a variety of contexts. Other examples include

- taxpayers' continuous search for, and discovery of, "loopholes" in income tax laws;
- the development of so-called clubs with private liquor stock in areas where serving liquor at public bars is prohibited;
- the ability of General Dynamics' CEO George Anders and his management team, when put under a lucrative incentive compensation plan tied to shareholder value, to quadruple the market value of the company even as the defense industry was facing sharp cutbacks;

- the growth in the number of hotel courtesy cars and gypsy cabs in cities where taxicab licensing results in monopoly fares.

These examples are typical of behavior consistent with the REMM model, but not, as we shall see, with other models that prevail in the social sciences. The failure of the other models is important because the individual stands in relation to organizations as the atom is to mass. From small groups to entire societies, organizations are composed of individuals. If we are to have a science of such organizations, it will have to be founded on building blocks that capture as simply as possible the most important traits of humans. Although clearly not a complete description of human behavior, REMM is the model of human behavior that best meets this criterion.[6]

1.3   REMM Means There Are No "Needs"

REMM implies that there is no such thing as a need, a proposition that arouses considerable resistance. The fallacy of the notion of needs follows from Postulate I-b, the proposition that the individual is always willing to make trade-offs. That proposition means that individuals are always willing to substitute—that is, *they are always willing to give up a sufficiently small amount of any good for a sufficiently large amount of other goods.*[7] Failure to take account of substitution is one of the most frequent mistakes in the analysis of human behavior.

George Bernard Shaw, the famous playwright and social thinker, reportedly once claimed that while on an ocean voyage he met a celebrated actress on deck and asked her whether she would be willing to sleep with him for a million dollars. She was agreeable. He followed with a counterproposal: "What about ten dollars?" "What do you think I am?" she responded indignantly. He replied, "We've already established that—now we're just haggling over price."

Like it or not, individuals are willing to sacrifice a little of almost anything we care to name, even reputation or morality, for a sufficiently large quantity of other desired things, and these things do not have to be money or even material goods. Moreover, the fact that all individuals make trade-offs (or substitute in virtually every dimension imaginable) means that there are no such things as human "needs" in the sense in which that word is often used. There are only human wants, desires, or, in the economist's language, demands. If something is more costly, less will be wanted, desired, or demanded than if it were cheaper.

Using the word "need" as an imperative is semantic trickery. The media and press are filled with talk about housing needs, education needs, food needs, energy needs, and so on. Politicians and others who use that language understand that the word "need" carries emotional impact. It implies a requirement at any cost; if the need is not met, some unspecified disaster will take place. Such assertions have a far different impact if restated to reflect the facts. The proposition that "people want more housing if they can get it cheaply enough" does not ring out from the podium or over the airwaves with the same emotional appeal as "people *need* more housing."

If individuals are required to specify what they mean by need, the emotional specter of the unexamined catastrophe that lies behind the need simply becomes another cost. Needs would be exposed for what they are—desires or wants—and discussion would focus on alternatives, substitutes, and costs in a productive manner.

1.4   Economists, Politicians, and Bureaucrats as REMMs

National Planning and Needs

While economists generally profess fidelity to REMM, their loyalty is neither universal nor constant. Their economic models of human behavior often fall short of REMM—as, for example, when they characterize the individual as a pure money-income maximizer. Moreover, in matters of public policy, there is a systematic relationship between the policies espoused and the degree of infidelity to REMM. One of the better-known members of the economics profession and a recipient of the Nobel Prize, Wassily Leontieff, was featured as a proponent of "national economic planning" in a *New York Times* advertisement that said: "No reliable mechanism in the modern economy relates needs to available manpower, plant and material . . . The most striking fact about the way we organize our economic life is that we leave so much to chance. We give little thought to the direction in which we would like to go" (March 16, 1975). Notice that the emotional content and force of the statement are considerably strengthened by the writer's use of the word "needs" rather than "desires" or "wants."

But let's examine this statement more closely. If by "needs" the authors mean *individual* preferences, wants, or desires, the first sentence is simply false. There *is* a mechanism that relates such needs or wants to "manpower, plant, and material," and it is central to the study of economics: namely, the price system. What the authors are saying is that no one organization or group of individuals *directs* (not plans) production in such a way that what is actually produced is what the advertisement's authors would define as needs. When they go on to say, "We give little thought to the direction in which we would like to go," the antecedent of "we" is meant to be "we, the general public." But, of course, we as individuals (and REMMs) give a great deal of thought to where we want to study and work, how much we will save, where we will invest our savings, what we will buy, what we will produce, and so on.

Leontieff's reputation rests largely on his work on input-output models. It is not surprising that he is enthusiastic about planning, for input-output models generally ignore most of the adjustment processes (that is, price changes and substitutions) that serve to balance supply and demand in a market economy. His input-output models specify fixed relations between inputs like labor, materials, and capital—and outputs like tons of steel. More or less steel can be produced only by adding or subtracting inputs in fixed proportions. There are no resourceful, evaluative maximizers in Leontieff's models. Like ants in an ant colony, his individuals possess productive capacities but very limited adaptability. In a society consisting of such dolts, planning (or, more accurately, directing) appears unavoidable. In the words of another Nobel Prize winner, Frederick A. Hayek, the real planning issue is not *whether* individuals should plan their affairs, but rather *who* should plan their affairs.[8]

The implication of input-output models, then, is that people are incapable of planning and thus require the direction and leadership of "planners." This import has not escaped the notice of bureaucrats, politicians, and managers, who themselves behave as REMMs when they recognize the value of models and theories that imply an increased demand for their services. By their very framing of the issue, Leontieff and politicians assume the answer to Hayek's question: planning does not exist unless the government does it.

For example, politicians are likely to see the value of an energy industry input-output model which, given projections of future energy "needs" (no prices and no substitutions here), tells how many nuclear energy plants must be built, how many strip mines should be opened, and how many new coal cars must be produced in order to become independent of foreign oil sources. The model suggests that, without extensive government intervention, the country cannot achieve energy independence. Such intervention, of course, implies an increase in politicians' power.

It is worth noting that the "we" in the Leontieff-endorsed planning statement is a common but generally unrecognized debating trick. It is standard practice in the political arena to label one's own preferences as "the people's preferences" or "the public's preferences," and to label the policies one supports as "in the public interest." But organizations or groups of individuals cannot have preferences; only individuals can have preferences. One could supply content to terms like "the people's preferences" or "the public interest" by making them synonymous with other concepts—for example, with what a majority would support or what every voter would approve in a referendum. But the typical user would then find the terms far less persuasive, therefore less attractive, and in the case of a complete consensus, never relevant.

Self-Interest and the Demand for Disequilibrium

Bureaucrats and politicians, like many economists, are also predisposed to embrace the concept of market "failure" or "disequilibrium" with the same enthusiasm they have shown for input-output models, and for the same reasons. If something is in disequilibrium, government action is required to bring about equilibrium.

Generally, economists tend to identify equilibrium with stable prices and quantities: a market is in equilibrium when there are no forces causing changes in the price or the quantity exchanged. Yet it is reasonable to argue that all markets are always in equilibrium, and all forces must always be in balance at all times—just as there is an equilibrium rate of heat transfer when heat is applied to one end of a steel bar. This is simply another way of saying that sophisticated, rational individuals always adapt to their opportunity set, where the opportunity set is defined to take account of the cost of adapting. That is, all voluntary exchanges will take place that will make both parties better off (taking all costs into account).

The view that markets are always in equilibrium does not depend on the stability of prices; prices and quantities can change dramatically. Their rate of change, however, is controlled by individual behavior—a balance is struck between the cost of change and the benefits. For example, if the dollar price of a good is prevented by law from changing, the opposing forces are balanced by the introduction of other costs such as queues and waiting time, or by the introduction of other goods as a consideration in the exchange.[9]

Although it is a tautology, the view that markets are always in equilibrium has important advantages. It focuses attention on interesting adjustment phenomena, on information and search costs and how they affect behavior, and on qualitative characteristics of the exchanges that arise to balance the opposing forces. If markets are always in equilibrium, the task of the scientist is to explain how the equilibrium is brought about.

In contrast, the word "disequilibrium" has strong emotional content. It denotes something unnatural, unsightly, and certainly undesirable that requires "corrective action." A market—whether for labor, energy, sugar, health care, or derivative securities—described as being "in disequilibrium" is generally regarded as something bad, and we are immediately led to think about the desirability of some form of government intervention (for example, price controls, embargoes, subsidies, or output restrictions) to eliminate the assumed problem.

One popular pursuit of bureaucrats—making projections of supply and demand—is the outgrowth of their preoccupation with disequilibrium. Such projections usually consist of estimates of numbers of physicists, doctors, mining engineers, barrels of oil, or tons of steel "required and/or available" at some future date, again without reference to prices. Not surprisingly, the projections invariably imply a disequilibrium (a shortage or surplus) whose correction requires government action.

But if these supply and demand projections are interpreted as forecasts of the quantities *and* prices that will prevail in a future economy in equilibrium, they lose all interest for policy makers. None of the usual policy implications follow—no subsidies, taxes, or constraints on individual behavior are called for, nor can any governmental enterprise be justified. Yet the practice of making projections goes on because politicians and bureaucrats, as REMMs, find them useful tools for expanding the role of government and the market for their services.

1.5   The Economic Model of Human Behavior

The economic model is a reductive version of REMM. This individual is an evaluator and maximizer who has only one want: money income. He or she is a short-run *money maximizer* who does not care for others, art, morality, love, respect, or honesty. In its simplest form, the economic model characterizes people as unwilling to trade current money income for future money income, no matter what rate of return they could earn.

The economic model is, of course, not very interesting as a model of human behavior. People do not behave this way. In most cases, use of this model reflects economists' desire for simplicity in modeling; the exclusive pursuit of wealth or money income is easier to model than the complexity of the actual preferences of individuals. As a consequence, however, noneconomists often use this model as a foil to discredit economics, that is, to argue that economics is of limited use because economists focus only on a single characteristic of behavior—and one of the least attractive at that, the selfish desire for money.

1.6   The Sociological Model of Human Behavior

In the sociological model, individuals are viewed as the product of their cultural environment. Humans are not evaluators any more than ants, bees, or termites are evaluators. They are conventional and conformist, and their behavior is determined by the taboos, customs, mores, and traditions of the society in which they were born and raised. In this model, individuals are also often viewed as *social victims,* a concept that has gained widespread acceptance in many quarters (see Sykes 1992).

By contrast, REMM is an evaluator. The REMM model recognizes that customs and mores serve as important constraints on human behavior, and that individuals who violate them incur costs in many forms. But REMMs compare the consequences of alternative courses of action, including those that involve the flouting of social norms, and consciously choose actions that lead to their preferred outcome. Moreover, if the costs or benefits of alternative courses of action change, REMMs change their behavior. In the sociological model individuals do not.

To be sure, social practices, customs, and mores play an important role in determining the attitudes and actions of individuals at any point in time. They represent a major force for teaching, disciplining, and rewarding members of a group, organization, or society. They serve as an external memory device that aids in the storage of knowledge about optimal behavior. But if the group or organization is to prosper—and, indeed, if the society itself is to survive—these cultural practices or values must adapt to approximate optimal behavior given the costs and benefits implied by the opportunity set faced by individuals in the society.

Changes in knowledge, technology, or the environment change the opportunity set. Therefore, a scientist who uses REMM to model behavior would predict that changes in knowledge, technology, and the environment that alter the costs or benefits of actions of large numbers of people will result in changes over time in social customs and mores. In contrast, the sociological model leaves social scientists with no explanation of changes in social customs, mores, taboos, and traditions.

For example, social scientists who use the sociological model would look to changes in morals and social attitudes to explain the increase in sexual activity and the simultaneous decline in birth rates over the past several decades. By contrast, a social scientist using REMM to explain the same phenomena would place greater emphasis on advances in birth control techniques. Why? One major cost of sexual intercourse is the cost associated with bearing and rearing a child. By making it possible for those who do not want children to avoid conception more effectively, better birth control techniques substantially reduce the cost of sexual intercourse.

In addition, extramarital sex and cohabitation of unmarried couples are more acceptable now than prior to the introduction of effective birth control techniques. In this sense, the culture has adapted to the changes in optimal behavior implied by changes in the costs of sexual activity. At the same time, however, one can predict that increases in the costs of sexual activity through the appearance of new untreatable sexually transmitted diseases will cause a resurgence of puritan ethics and a renewed emphasis on the family. This is consistent with the changes occurring as a result of the AIDS epidemic.

But the cultural changes brought about by the new birth control technology go well beyond the family and changes in sexual mores. By allowing women more control over the timing of childbirth, the new technology increases their labor market choices substantially. The lag in cultural and institutional practices in reflecting this newly optimal behavior is both inefficient and a major catalyst for the feminist movement. But the changes required to adjust to optimal behavior under the new cost conditions are unavoidable. Inefficient practices such as discrimination against women in hiring provide profit opportunities for those REMMs with the vision to perceive and act upon the gap between current and optimal practices.[10]

There is a crucial distinction, then, between the REMM model's recognition that cultural factors are *reflected* in human behavior and the sociological model's assertion that cultural factors *determine* human behavior. If behavior is completely determined by acculturation, as the sociological model suggests, then choice, purpose, and conscious adaptation are meaningless. If humans are endowed with little originality, have no ability to evaluate, and simply imitate what they see and do what they are told, it is not clear how *any* social change could take place.

The REMM model, in contrast, explains the evolution of customs and mores as the reflection in habits, unquestioned beliefs, and religion of behavior patterns that reflect optimal responses to the costs and benefits of various actions. When the underlying costs and benefits of various actions change, individuals are faced with a conflict between new, optimal forms of behavior and culturally accepted but inefficient forms. In this situation there will be social conflict. And if the new behavior patterns are indeed optimal, the population will—through experience, education, and death—gradually accommodate the new behavior in the culture.

Consider, for example the clash of economic reality with cultural values that lies behind the decision by IBM's top management to abandon its longstanding (and socially revered) policy of lifetime employment. Beginning with the postwar prosperity of the 1950s and lasting well into the restructuring wave of the 1980s, the concept of lifetime employment by large U.S. corporations became a social expectation—an "implicit contract"—and top executives who resorted to layoffs just to maintain profitability (that is, unless threatened by bankruptcy or extinction) were harshly criticized by the media, if not ostracized by their communities.

Although vigorous social criticism of layoffs persisted throughout the restructurings of the '80s, corporate America has been forced by increasing global competition to recognize that lifetime employment ends up debilitating rather than strengthening companies. But because the expectation of long-term job security became so ingrained in the culture, it has been much more difficult for companies to adjust their practices. In the meantime, Japanese and European companies—traditionally far more committed to lifetime employment than their U.S.

counterparts—are also being forced to rethink the policy while confronting their own problems of chronic industrial overcapacity and the resulting inefficiencies.[11]

Because of its ability to explain such remarkable shifts in cultural values, REMM also provides the foundation for thinking about how to change corporate culture. The shared beliefs, attitudes, customs, and values of people within an organization can be a critical determinant of success or failure. And although an organization's culture constitutes a barrier to valuable innovation at any given moment, culture can be molded through conscious, coordinated effort over time. The values and attitudes of people within an organization will respond over time to view positively those actions which are rewarded in the organization and negatively those actions which are punished. It will also respond to selection policies designed to bring into the company people with values and attitudes consistent with the desired culture.

The sociological model, then, has serious shortcomings as the basis for a body of theory about social behavior. With its near-exclusive focus on cultural continuity, it cannot account for the enormous diversity of human behavior at any given time. Nor can it explain dramatic changes in behavior such as those brought about by improved birth control and other technological advances. The model also ignores the process of conscious deliberation by individuals and organizations when contemplating different courses of action.

Given Its Limitations, Why Is the Sociological Model So Popular?

The popularity of the sociological model can be traced to the relationship between models of human behavior and policy positions, as well as the human tendency to deny personal causal responsibility. If people's behavior is largely determined by factors beyond their control, they are victims and therefore cannot be held responsible for their actions or the state of their lives.

The appeal of such a theory to those who find themselves in trouble or wanting in any way is obvious; the extent to which this theory is played out every day in the media, courtrooms, families, and organizations is discussed at length by Charles Sykes in *A Nation of Victims* (1992). Several all-too-common examples from the book (p. 3) include the following: an employee fired for repeatedly late arrival sues his employer, arguing that he is a victim of "chronic lateness syndrome";

an FBI agent is reinstated after being fired for embezzling funds to re-pay his gambling debts because the court rules that gambling with the money of others is a "handicap" and hence protected under federal law.

Under the social victim model, if an individual steals, it is only be-cause society has made him or her a thief, not because he or she has chosen that activity. And the solution is not to punish the individual for such actions, because no thief chooses to be a thief. In this model, raising the costs of thievery can have no effect on the amount of thiev-ery. The solution is to educate and rehabilitate.

Although education and rehabilitation programs can help to change people, they alone are unlikely to reduce criminal behavior significantly. As these programs become more widespread, and as they are accompa-nied by a reduction in the penalties and other "costs" of criminal behav-ior, we should not be surprised to find that REMMs more frequently choose to be criminals.

For the same reason, it is not surprising from the viewpoint of REMM that Singapore has no drug problem. Arrivals to the country must sign a statement recognizing that possession or sale of drugs is punishable by death. And the population is well aware of these policies; as illustrated by the recent caning of an American for vandalism, pun-ishment for infraction of Singapore law is carried out swiftly and pub-licly.

Educating people about the effects of their choices does, of course, affect behavior; and it takes time for cultural attitudes to change. A complete programmatic attack on crime would include the use of both formal punishments and rewards as well as education and consensus building among the population. Properly carried out, such education and consensus building can tap social rejection and approval as addi-tional (and decentralized) sources of punishments and rewards to rein-force sanctions against criminal or otherwise undesirable behavior.

As another illustration of the workings of the sociological model, consider the current debate over the causes of homelessness. The very use of the term "homeless" suggests no choice on the part of street people (who are therefore victims of the system); it also carries little or none of the social disapprobation of "vagrant," a now unfashionable label. This change in language and attitudes reduces the decentralized sources of social or cultural punishment for being a street person—again, something the REMM model predicts would result in an increase in this socially undesirable behavior. New York City now spends in excess of a half billion dollars a year on subsidies for the homeless, and the problem shows no signs of going away, even with the improvement in the economy. (And the "de-institutionalizing" of the mentally ill, a common explanation, by no means accounts for the vast increase in the numbers of street people.)

The sociological model suggests that if an individual's income and wealth are small, this is entirely the result of cultural factors, environmental adversity, or bad luck—not of conscious effort, the choice of leisure over work, the choice of a particular type of work, or the failure to invest in learning. Therefore, "justice" requires that we confiscate the wealth of the more fortunate to recompense the unfortunate.

Of course, the higher the recompense, the more attractive it is to be poor, and REMMs will respond by taking more leisure, by choosing occupations in which employment is more unstable, and by investing less in learning. The REMM model predicts that if we make the payoff high enough, we can attract an arbitrarily large number of people to become poor or unemployed—or at least to meet the established criteria for those programs. This describes important aspects of our welfare and unemployment systems.

Politicians, bureaucrats, and special interest groups understand that public policy choices are affected by the concept that individuals are responsible for their own fates. Strong popular support for the principle that individuals ought to be rewarded or punished in accordance with their own behavior means that measures that aim to redistribute wealth, or to rehabilitate criminals rather than punish them, would encounter strong opposition. But resourceful politicians and others who want to put such measures into effect can neutralize public opposition by persuading people that everything we do is forced on us by our cultural environment—we are social victims, and thus neither our behavior nor our status is a product of deliberate choice. By undermining the link between choice and consequences, they can overcome the resistance that stems from beliefs that individuals are responsible for their own behavior.

In addition, individuals constantly face a conflict when attempting to help others who are experiencing difficulty, especially those related through family or other ties. The conflict is between the desire to ease or eliminate the difficulties of others through gifts or charity, and the reluctance to distort the incentives of people to take charge of their own lives—say, by investing in education and making other efforts to improve their condition. All parents face such trade-offs when deciding how much help to give their children, and the choices are not easy. The short-term pain associated with denying help to a loved one is very difficult to bear. But casual observation together with evidence of the futility of various social programs seems to indicate that people systematically underestimate the counterproductive long-run effects on individuals of actions that we take to shield them from the consequences of their own choices.[12]

The Sociological Model and Marxism

A discussion of the sociological model would be incomplete without touching upon the use of that concept by Marxists, socialists, and other groups around the world. Marxist politicians understand that the sociological model is the foundation for the centralization of power. Marxism has received wide support in Europe. It has also had substantial support among the Catholic clergy and American academics. Recent evidence on the widespread failure of Russian, Eastern European, and other economies dominated by Marxist thought has revealed the shortcomings of this view and has diminished, but not eliminated, support for it. Ironically, as many formerly socialist Eastern European and Asian countries are moving toward capitalism, the United States is moving toward more socialistic regulatory and political policies.

Socialism is supported by a philosophy that idolizes the state. The urge to subordinate the individual to the organization has ancient roots going back at least to Plato. In portraying his ideal state, Plato says:

> . . . [T]here is common property of wives, of children, and of all chattels. And everything possible has been done to eradicate from our life everywhere and in every way all that is private and individual. So far as it can be done, even those things which nature herself has made private and individual have somehow become the common property of all. Our very eyes and ears and hands seem to see, to hear, and to act, as if they belonged not to individuals but to the community. All men are molded to be unanimous to the utmost degree in bestowing praise and blame, and they even rejoice and grieve about the same things, and at the same time . . .
>
> Nor should the mind of anybody be habituated to letting him do anything at all on his own initiative, neither out of zeal, nor even play-

fully . . . But in war and in the midst of peace—to his leader he shall direct his eye, and follow him faithfully. And even in the smallest matters he should stand under leadership. For example, he should get up, or move, or wash, or take his means . . . only if he has been told to do so. . . . In a word, he should teach his soul, by long habit, never to dream of acting independently, and to become utterly incapable of it.[13]

Plato's ideal state is an example of the most extreme anti-individualist position, one which makes the organization itself the ultimate end. The state is treated as a living organism; it is the overriding value. Individual purpose is not only unimportant, it is an evil that must be stamped out.

Plato's views are not very different from those of most Marxists. The role of the individual poses a dilemma for Marxists. Avowed Marxist states around the world such as the former Soviet Union, China, and Cuba display an attitude with respect to individual citizens that is close to Plato's utopia. Party doctrine denounces individualistic motivation and invokes the common good. In intellectual discourse, Marxist theorists press for an organizational or social class approach to the study of society. In Marxist theory, the worker and the capitalist play out their roles regardless of the costs and benefits of their actions. Capitalists are what they are and do what they do because they are capitalists, and so too for workers. In the Marxist model, individuals do not evaluate, choose, or maximize; they behave according to the sociological model.

The sociological model is devoid of prescriptive content, yet it is commonly used for normative purposes. If humans are not evaluators (they only play the roles given to them by the culture), it is meaningless to talk about making people better off. Although Marxists reject the Western economic tradition of considering the individual as the basic unit of analysis, they also express great concern for the plight of the less fortunate and make much of concepts such as class conflict and exploitation.

Thus, these concerns for the welfare of people (primarily the workers or underclass) exhibit an obvious and fatal inconsistency. Unless we attribute preferences to the individual, language that describes differences in an individual's well-being makes no sense. Notions like equality and justice are popular among those who employ the sociological model of humanity, but such ethical norms are not internally meaningful because they imply that individuals care about their condition—that is, that they are evaluators, they experience envy, and they choose.

Furthermore, if the state is all that matters, as Marxist doctrine maintains, concern for the plight of the individual is irrelevant at best and can be inimical to the general good. Concepts such as exploitation and conflict can be used in a group context to refer to more than one individual, but such language has meaning only in terms of individuals. Organizations cannot be exploited any more than machines or rocks can be exploited. Only individuals can be exploited, can suffer, can make war; only individuals can be objects of compassion. Organizations are purely conceptual artifacts, even when they are assigned the legal status of individuals. In the end, we can do things *to* and *for* individuals only.

1.7   The Psychological Model of Human Behavior

The psychological model is a step up the evolutionary ladder from the sociological model. As in REMM, humans in this model are resourceful; they care; they have wants and drives. But the individual's wants are viewed essentially as absolutes that are largely independent of one another. Therefore, substitutions or trade-offs are not part of individual human behavior. In effect, the individual is said to have "needs" in the sense of that word which we have already rejected.

Perhaps the best-known formulation of what we call the psychological model was provided by A. H. Maslow. "Human needs," wrote Maslow in 1943, "arrange themselves in hierarchies of prepotency. That is to say, the appearance of one need usually rests on the prior satisfaction of another more prepotent need."[14] Maslow's needs, in order of their "prepotency" from high to low, are physiological (food, water), safety, love, and self-actualization.

In contrast to REMM, in Maslow's *hierarchy of needs* model the individual is unwilling to give up any food for any amount of safety until his or her food needs are satisfied. Only after the food needs are completely satisfied will he or she be concerned about safety. What Maslow and his followers have done is to confuse two entirely different issues: how an individual allocates resources among alternative goods at a given level of wealth, and how that allocation pattern varies as an individual's wealth rises.

Maslow himself, in the latter part of his famous article, qualifies his early statements that deny substitution. He argues that he did not mean that literally 100 percent of a person's food need had to be satisfied in order for that individual to begin to satisfy the safety needs, and so on.[15]

Although most of Maslow's followers have ignored his qualifications, these latter statements show him moving toward the notion of substitution and the income elasticity of demand, a relationship known to economists for many years and incorporated in REMM.[16]

Moreover, ample evidence of human behavior contradicts Maslow's hierarchy of needs model. We see astronauts, skiers, and car racers accepting less safety in return for wealth, fame, and just plain thrills. Poets, artists, and gurus go without material comforts to devote their time to contemplation and art, and, to us, these pursuits sound closer to self-actualization than physiological goods.

The psychological model, like the sociological model, is not satisfactory for describing the behavior of individuals in the study of social phenomena. Yet there is some valid content in Maslow's model. His ordering of wants probably corresponds to how most people would allocate a $1,000 increment of wealth on expenditures at increasing levels of wealth. Wealthier people will tend to spend less of their additional wealth on goods satisfying physiological wants, and more on each of the categories of goods that are higher in Maslow's hierarchy.[17] Nevertheless, inconsistent with Maslow's model, individuals at any level of wealth are willing to sacrifice some amount of any good for sufficiently large amounts of all other goods.

Thus, while Maslow's ordering of categories of human wants tends to describe how expenditures increase with increased wealth, it is neither a hierarchy nor does it describe needs. It is difficult to infer much else about social behavior from the hierarchy of needs model that is not trivial or false. The psychological model predicts that if the cost of any good rises, the individual will reduce outlays on whatever is the highest-ranking good he or she currently buys, a behavioral reaction that is clearly contradicted by actual consumer behavior. When the price of one good rises relative to other goods, consumers react by reducing purchases of the good whose price has risen, not the purchases of goods that are highest on Maslow's list.

Once substitution is ruled out, the individual's attempt to maximize by reconciling wants with means is largely ignored, and attention focuses instead on the study of individual wants (or classes of wants). Examples from the field of organizational behavior (OB) are numerous. One general problem (an extremely important one) is how to get employees to be more productive. The general answer under the psychological model is to reward them by satisfying their needs.

The OB literature does not generally recognize that the employer's problem is one of designing an overall employment package that takes into account the potential for trade-offs. Instead, each good that the employer can provide the employee is considered in isolation. Job enrichment and the quality of the working environment are examples. More of each is always taken to be better than less, and not only is the optimality criterion seldom applied to determine the correct level of job enrichment or quality of the environment, but optimality itself is seldom discussed.

The prevalence of Maslow's model in the behavioral science field is, we believe, a major reason for the failure of the field to develop a unified body of theory. Theory erected on the basis of individuals who are driven by wants, but who cannot or will not make substitutions, will necessarily consist of a series of independent propositions relating particular drives to actions and will never be able to capture the complexity of human behavior.

1.8   The Political Model of Human Behavior

While resourceful and, in a certain sense, evaluators and maximizers, individuals under the political model are assumed to evaluate and maximize in terms of other individuals' preferences rather than their own. In contrast to REMM, the individual is a *perfect agent* seeking to maximize "the public good" rather than his or her own welfare.

It is important to distinguish between altruism (that is, a willingness to sacrifice some of one's own goods, time, or welfare for the benefit of others) and the political model. Altruists do not behave according to the political model. Since they have their own preferences, they cannot be perfect agents. A perfect agent is a person who will maximize with respect to the preferences of the principal while, if necessary, denying his or her own. Perfect agents would be equally satisfied working to save the whales, feed the poor, make computers, or care for the musical interests of the rich through the local symphony orchestra at the bidding of their employers. Altruist that she was, Mother Teresa's devotion to caring for the poor of Calcutta did not make her a perfect agent. It is highly doubtful that she would have agreed to (or effectively) represent the interests of someone who wished to save the whales, or make computers. Like all REMMs, she had her own preferences and exercised her choice over whom or what cause she devoted her time to helping.

The logic in which the political model figures so prominently is simple, though it will not withstand careful scrutiny. Whenever individuals acting on their own behalf will not bring about the "desired" outcome, government must take a hand. If consumers might be misled by deceptive advertising, have government regulate advertising. If sellers might market products that are harmful to consumers, have government regulate consumer product safety. If consumers might not understand the terms of lending contracts, have government regulate the language that can be used in such contracts. These solutions serve two powerful interests: first, the strong tendency of people to avoid taking responsibility for themselves, and second, the degree to which these solutions increase the power and reach and, therefore, the self-interest of politicians and bureaucrats.

The fatal flaw in the above propositions is their assumption that when politicians intervene, they act to accomplish the desired result—that is, they act in the public interest. Those who argue for such government intervention simply assume that politicians can and will behave in accord with the desires of the electorate.

The political or perfect agent model lies at the heart of virtually all campaigns that purport to solve problems by creating a governmental agency or appointing a political body. Worried about too many dangerous drugs or injuries in coal mines? Establish a Food and Drug Administration (FDA) to regulate drug testing and to grant approval for the marketing of new drugs. To reduce injuries in coal mines, pass a mine safety law with the Department of Mines to administer it. Unfortunately, the results of such programs do not lend support to the political model. After the 1962 amendments regulating the efficacy of new drugs, the number of new drugs approved in the United States fell by half.[18] Moreover, between 1966 and 1970, more than 2,000 small nonunion coal mines closed down with no measurable reduction of injuries or death rates in coal mines.[19]

These results occur—and are indeed predictable—because the people who enact and administer the laws are REMMs. The bureaucrats in the FDA, for instance, face high costs if they err and allow a drug that has injurious side effects (such as thalidomide) to be marketed. On the other hand, the people who suffer and die because FDA procedures have kept a new drug bottled up in the testing laboratories for several years (or perhaps never let it on the market) usually don't even know that they have been harmed. Patients now able to get efficacious drug treatments in Europe that are not available in the United States are becoming aware of the consequences of FDA regulations, but their number is small. Political action by AIDS patients and their advocates has persuaded the FDA to relax restrictions limiting access to promising AIDS treatments before they have satisfied all normal FDA regulations for public use.

The mine safety law that closed down many nonunion mines was passed after active lobbying by both the United Mine Workers Union and the Bituminous Coal Operators Association (which represents the mining firms unionized by the United Mine Workers). Both of these groups faced competition from small mines that were generally staffed by nonunion labor. The costs imposed on these mines by the law were so onerous that many of them were driven out of business.

Allegiance to the political model has been a major deterrent to the development of a body of theory that could explain with reasonable accuracy how the political system operates. Social scientists, especially political scientists, have been aware of the strong desire that politicians exhibit to be reelected, and they have usually tacitly assumed that this induces them to behave in accord with the wishes of the majority. But this model of the legislative process is incapable of explaining what actually occurs.

We know that legislators consistently vote for measures that cannot possibly be in the interest of a majority of their constituents.[20] With the exception of Wisconsin (and even there it is doubtful), there surely is no state in the Union where a majority benefits from government sponsorship of a cartel among milk producers. Other examples are tariffs on TV sets, oil import quotas, "voluntary" quotas on foreign automobiles, and punitive tariffs on flat-panel computer screens, to name just a few.

Elected officials who are REMMs sense that they have the opportunity to become entrepreneurs. They have access at relatively low cost to mass advertising via television, radio, newspapers, and magazines. Resourceful politicians also ally themselves with organized groups that get media attention and encourage the organization of new groups. Indeed, now that the general nature of the process and the payoff to such organizations have been perceived, popular fronts have proliferated, each vying for publicity, even to the point of using violence to demonstrate their sincerity.

Individually and collectively, legislators have an interest in enlarging the role of the state, and, as REMMs, they engage in continuous marketing of programs to achieve that end. If crises do not exist, they create them, or at least the illusion of crises. Then they rescue their constituents from disaster with legislation that sacrifices the general welfare to benefit special interests.

For example, in recent years members of the Clinton administration and associated special interest groups have campaigned to create the public impression of a health care crisis and hence support for legislation to "reform" the U.S. health care system (Stelzer 1994). The proposed changes would result in massive new regulation and centralization of the system. In so doing, it would transfer substantial control over an additional 14% of the U.S. gross national product to the government, with obvious implications for the power base of the bureaucracy.

Almost as clear, unfortunately, is the import of these changes for the efficiency and quality of U.S. health care. The proposed changes would result in a centralization and cartelization of the health care industry in the hands of government and newly proposed private bodies. This is exactly the wrong way to go with this industry. Because the specific knowledge of each case lies with the doctor and the patient, decision making in the health care industry, to be effective, must be decentralized and thus kept in the hands of the doctor and patient. The proposed centralized process for deciding on patient treatment and care will inevitably result in large declines in the quality of health care. Even ignoring the effects of the centralization, the administration's original plan to take $150 billion of annual costs (and therefore real resources) out of the system while adding as many as 37 million people to it would reduce the quality and timeliness of future care; it would also create shortages and lead to rationing.

There is a U.S. health care *cost* problem, to be sure; but it does not stem from too little regulation and too few subsidies. Rather, it comes from our third-party insurance system that effectively removes responsibility for the costs from the most important decision maker—that is, the patient. The key to solving this problem is to impose the financial consequences of their medical decisions on patients through greater use of co-pay insurance with larger deductibles that place first-dollar costs on patients while protecting them against catastrophic illness.

The Political Model in the Private Sector

The political (or perfect agent) model is also widely used by managers of private organizations in managing their employees. Corporate managers often wish to believe that people are perfect agents with no preferences of their own. If there is a problem in part of the organization with a manager who is making the wrong decisions, the problems must come from having a "bad" person in the job. The solution is then to fire the manager and replace him or her with a new person. Tell that person (who is assumed to be a perfect agent) what you want done, and then wait for it to happen.

In contrast, managers using the REMM model would predict that if the manager has the proper talents and training, it is the organizational structure and incentives that are at the root of the problem. The solution would then be not to fire the manager, but to reform the organizational policies.

Problems in organizations often arise because managers are rewarded for doing things that harm the organization—for example, empire building or maximizing market share at the expense of shareholder value. In compensating managers according to negotiated budgets, many companies effectively induce line managers to negotiate budget targets that are well below the level that would maximize the value of the organization. The managers do this, of course, to ensure they can easily meet the target.

In a related problem, large public corporations also regularly retain and tend to waste large amounts of free cash flow—that is, cash flow in excess of that required to fund all profitable projects of the firm. Spending the cash on acquisitions or other unprofitable projects (undertaken with the aid of unrealistically high forecasts of future profitability) gives management a bigger company to run, thereby increasing managers' power and prestige in the community. Because managerial pay tends to be positively related to the size of the company, these actions generally increase their compensation as well. In addition, keeping the cash in the firm gives them a cushion for spending during tough times, whether it is economic or not. Retaining the excess cash also makes it easier to avoid closing plants, laying off employees, cutting charitable contributions, and making the other hard choices associated with freeing up underutilized resources. Yet it is important for managers to make these difficult choices so that the resources can be put to higher-valued uses in the rest of society.[21]

1.9   Conclusions

We argue that the explanatory power of REMM, the resourceful, evaluative, maximizing model of human behavior, dominates that of all the other models summarized here. To be sure, each of the other models captures an important aspect of behavior, while failing in other respects. REMM incorporates the best of each of these models.

From the economic model, REMM takes the assumptions that people are resourceful, self-interested maximizers but rejects the notion that they are interested only in money income or wealth.

From the psychological model, REMM takes the assumption that the income elasticity of demand for various goods has certain regularities the world over. Nevertheless, in taking on this modified notion of a hierarchy of needs, it does not violate the principle of substitution by assuming that people have "needs."

From the sociological model, REMM takes the assumption that "society" imposes costs on people for violating social norms, which in turn affect behavior; but it also assumes that individuals will depart from such norms if the benefits are sufficiently great. Indeed, this is how social change takes place.

From the political model, REMM takes on the assumption that people have the capacity for altruism. They care about others and take their interests into account while maximizing their own welfare. REMM rejects, however, the notion that people are perfect agents.

In using REMM, detail must be added (as we have done implicitly in the examples above) to tailor the model to serve as a decision guide in specific circumstances. We must specify more about people's tastes and preferences that are relevant to the issue at hand—for example, by making explicit assumptions that people have a positive rate of discount for future as opposed to present goods and that they value leisure as well as intangibles such as honor, companionship, and self-realization. Finally, combining these assumptions with knowledge of the opportunity set from which people are choosing in any situation (that is, the rates at which people can trade off or substitute among various goods) leads to a powerfully predictive model.

REMM is the basic building block that has led to the development of a more or less unified body of theory in the social sciences. For example, some economists, like the recent Nobel laureate Gary Becker, have applied REMM in fields previously reserved to sociologists such as discrimination, crime, marriage, and the family.[22] Political scientists in company with economists have also employed utility-maximizing models of political behavior to explain voter behavior and the behavior of regulators and bureaucrats.[23] Still others are using REMM to explain organizational problems inside firms.[24]

For all its diversity, this growing body of research has one common message: Whether they are politicians, managers, academics, professionals, philanthropists, or factory workers, individuals are resourceful, evaluative maximizers. They respond creatively to the opportunities the environment presents to them, and they work to loosen constraints that prevent them from doing what they wish to do. They care about not only money, but almost everything—respect, honor, power, love, and the welfare of others. The challenge for our society, and for all organizations within it, is to establish rules of the game and educational procedures that tap and direct the creative energy of REMMs in ways that increase the effective use of our scarce resources.

2 | Self-Interest, Altruism, Incentives, and Agency Theory

2.1   Introduction

In "Incentives, Rationality, and Society" Michael Brennan (1994) attacks the use of incentives for executive compensation and, indirectly, for use in society in general. He argues that economics views rational behavior as self-interested and that this proposition is wrong both in a positive sense (that is, people don't behave that way) and in a normative sense (because if they did behave in a self-interested way, the world would be a more brutish and undesirable place). Brennan is correct that people do not always behave in a rational way, but this fact provides no support for his opposition to incentives, or his opposition to self-interest.

Brennan's arguments, although popular in many quarters, are, I believe, logically and empirically incorrect. Underlying his argument is a strong aversion to incentives, an opposition that reveals itself in several places to be primarily, if not wholly, an antagonism to the use of monetary incentives. (He cites approvingly the incentives provided by awards banquets and small prizes.) He is also not fond of the agency model, concluding that the model is incorrect and, moreover, that "if we go on hammering into our students the mistaken notion that rationality is identical with self-interest we shall make our agency models come true, but at the cost of producing a society that will not function" (p. 39). These views are held by many people and therefore are worthy of further discussion. I shall deal first with the issue of incentives and then move on to self-interest, nonrational behavior, and the theory of agency.

Originally published in the *Journal of Applied Corporate Finance* 7, no. 2 (Summer 1994).

2.2   The Meaning and Role of Incentives in the Logic of Choice

Brennan argues disapprovingly that economic man "will never perform without incentives" (p. 34). He appears to desire a world in which there are no incentives, and at times seems to believe that action in the absence of incentives is the natural and, therefore, desirable state of affairs. Many managers, policy makers, and religious leaders share this view.

It is inconceivable that purposeful action on the part of human beings can be viewed as anything other than responses to incentives. Indeed, the issue of incentives goes to the heart of what it means to maximize or optimize, in fact to the very core of what it means to choose. Rational individuals always choose the option that makes them better off as they see it. This is, by definition, what we mean by purposeful action—the attempt to accomplish some end. And it is the difference in (expected) well-offness between taking one action as opposed to another that provides incentives and results in choice.

As I said, much anti-incentive reasoning seems to be based on the notion of a natural state of affairs in which there are no incentives and no conflicts of interest. For there to be no incentives, all alternative courses of action or choices must promise the same degree of utility as viewed by the individual. Such a world is virtually inconceivable (and would certainly be uninteresting if it did exist). It does not exist in the state of nature: not all land is equally fertile, nor are all paths equally level or unobstructed by water or other hurdles. Thus, even primitive man faced incentives to cultivate one piece of land rather than another, or to choose one path over another. Incentives exist (whether we like it or not) in all cases in which people have real choice. This is true in organizations as well as in nature.

Managers in every organization, even one with no pay-for-performance, face incentives—including incentives to do bad as well as good. The issue for any organization is not whether to introduce incentives to motivate its employees. There are always incentives; the issue is simply which incentives we want to encourage and which we want to suppress.

Optimal decisions often meet with opposition and retribution from colleagues, employees, communities, policy makers, regulators, and others with conflicting interests—thereby providing managers with incentives to forsake them. To increase the chances that managers will take the best actions possible, we must ensure that the incentives (that is, the trade-offs) they face encourage them to move in the correct direction. This means that we must strive to ensure that the culture of the organization, and any other variables under our control, reward proper, as opposed to improper, action.

The main advantage of monetary incentives in this mosaic of organizational incentives is that general purchasing power is valued by almost everyone (because it is a claim on all resources), and it can be easily varied with performance. On the other hand, it often is difficult, and in some cases impossible, to vary other aspects of the organizational setting in a way that relates to organizational, group, or individual performance.

I hasten to add that, for a variety of reasons, monetary incentives are not the best way to motivate every action. Because monetary incentives are so strong, and because it is sometimes difficult to specify the proper performance measure, monetary incentives are often dominated by other approaches. But in the end, where money incentives are required, they are required precisely because people are motivated by things other than money.

2.3   Self-Interest, Altruism, and Perfect Agents

History provides much evidence on the adverse consequences that follow from failing to understand the proper role of self-interest, how self-interest is consistent with altruistic concerns for the welfare of others, and how increased attention to self-interest or rational behavior would make the world a better, not worse, place to live. Brennan is correct in his observation that people do not always behave in a rational manner. But when they do so, contrary to Brennan's beliefs, and consistent with his examples of soldiers and managers, people invariably make themselves and those around them worse off.

Brennan (1994, p. 34) defines economic man in a way often used as a caricature to discredit economics, and I agree with him that his characterization of economic man is not descriptive of human behavior. (Although I do not believe it characterizes the way most economists view human behavior, I shall not belabor the point here.) People do care about failure and success, they do have emotions and care about honor and self-esteem, and they do feel shame and pride. In Chapter 1 William Meckling and I have discussed at length the minimal characterization of human beings capable of capturing this complexity. We call this model

REMM—for the Resourceful, Evaluative, Maximizing Model of human behavior—and argue that these three characteristics are very powerful for describing the rational behavior of human beings. The model is powerful in the sense that it leads to good predictions of how human beings will actually behave.

Brennan and others err when they include altruism in the category of non-self-interested behavior. Self-interested behavior in Brennan's view means that people care only about themselves and not at all about others; they have no altruistic tastes in that they are unwilling to sacrifice any of their own time or resources for the betterment of others. This is neither logically implied by the assumption of self-interest nor empirically correct. He cites two sorts of evidence that indicate the self-interested model of human behavior is wrong: (1) that people do show concern for the welfare of others, and (2) that people often do not show concern for their own welfare. I have no disagreement with the evidence.

As Meckling and I made clear in Chapter 1, there is nothing inconsistent between self-interested and altruistic behavior. More important, Brennan implicitly takes the existence of altruistic behavior to mean that individuals are perfect agents for others. But the willingness to sacrifice some of one's own time, energy, and resources for the benefit of others by no means indicates that a person is a perfect agent—a common and dangerous fallacy. By a perfect agent I mean someone who makes decisions with no concern for his or her own preferences, but only for those of another, including an employer or principal. As we pointed out in Chapter 1, there is vast evidence that people do have altruistic motives, and there is equally vast evidence that people are not perfect agents. To find extensive evidence of altruism, we need only look to the willingness of people to give to charity, and to help family, neighbors, and even strangers.

To see equally vast evidence that people are seldom perfect agents for any interest, we need look no farther than the conflict and abuse in families, the sexual abuse of youthful parishioners by some Catholic priests, and the general failure of organizational control systems (including recent abuses by the officers and board of the United Way charity). In spite of this plentiful evidence, Brennan, arguing in favor of the perfect agent model, says: "we are also capable of rising above our own narrow self-interest, and we are more likely to do so the greater is our responsibility for the welfare of others" (p. 37). In the extreme, it appears only too easy for men such as Hitler or the Romanian dictator Ceausescu to impose huge costs on the populations with whose welfare they are nominally vested. Unfortunately, as the media coverage illustrates in these days of race wars and regional violence, such atrocities are all too common. The abusive cases aside, Meckling and I have argued that even Mother Teresa was not a perfect agent because she would have been unwilling to devote her time and energy to arbitrarily chosen ends of an employer. Her preferences evidenced a strong desire to help the poor of Calcutta over all sorts of alternatives, and to that extent she was self-interested although altruistic. In this sense we are all alike in that we have our own preferences. And as I suggest in the following section, greater attention to self-interest or rational behavior would make the world a better, not worse, place to live.

2.4 Nonrational Behavior

Brennan cites several examples from an article by Postrel and Rumelt (1992) of soldiers and managers behaving in ways that are clearly inconsistent with their own near-term self-interest. The soldiers fail to take obvious steps (such as keeping their helmets and arms, and digging foxholes) to maintain their own protection and fighting capability, while the managers routinely mistreat customers. Such self-damaging behavior is not unique, and economists viewing the world through their lens of rationality generally fail to see that such behavior is common to virtually everyone.

While Postrel, Rumelt, and Brennan are correct that people do not always act in their own-self interest, this provides no support for Brennan's call for suppression of incentives. In fact, Postrel and Rumelt correctly see the import of their stories as calling for even more precise use of incentives to address self-control problems—for example, by paying attention to the timing and context of rewards and punishments to help individuals resist self-destructive impulses.

REMM provides great predictive power and a solid basis for policy decisions in business as well as personal and public life, but it is not complete. The problem is the essentially dualistic nature of human behavior: people evidence both rational and nonrational behaviors, and these behaviors coexist in inherent contradiction. These contradictions are not aberrations from normality, but rather an integral part of normality itself. The soldier example illustrates behavior that contradicts

REMM, but the contradiction goes far beyond the extreme conditions of war. Clinical psychological records as well as everyday observations of family, organizational, and social action abound with examples of nonrational behavior.

By nonrational I do not mean random or unexplainable; I mean non-functional behavior that systematically harms the individual. But this nonrational behavior can be modeled, and I believe it is possible to integrate it with REMM, and thereby to increase vastly the predictive power of our analytical apparatus.[1]

I postulate a Pain Avoidance Model (PAM) to complement REMM. PAM describes nonrational human behavior that arises under conditions of fear. While attempting (generally subconsciously) to avoid the pain associated with recognizing personal error, people often put themselves in a position where they incur far more pain, and end up making themselves worse off than if they had just recognized their error in the first place.

Unfortunately, these nonrational behaviors are systematic, not random. Recent brain research indicates that these virtually universal human defensive responses are founded in the biological and chemical structure of the brain—responses that are intimately involved with the brain's "fight or flight" response.[2] What is surprising about this defensive behavior is the seemingly trivial events or challenges that frighten humans, and that while they are experiencing this fright, these same individuals are commonly unaware of it. This frequently occurs, for example, when people are faced with evidence or theories that threaten to change the lens through which they view reality, including not only the world around them, but their view of themselves.

We commonly observe people refusing to learn or to change, even when the personal consequences of this refusal are negative—for example, the common tendency of managers to refuse to adapt to changes in the competitive environment in the absence of a major organizational crisis. Even scholars, whose business is the creation of new theories and knowledge, commonly react negatively (and sometimes with much personal anger) to those new theories and evidence. It is as if old ideas form ruts in our brains that prevent change.

The primary result of defensiveness is a reluctance to learn and an inability to adjust behavior to serve better our own interests. These nonrational responses are evident throughout organizations and society. Examples include the tendency of people to systematically overrate themselves in rankings of their peers, the infrequent use of pay-for-performance compensation systems, the common refusal of people to welcome feedback on their errors, and the systematic tendency for corporate managers to overpay for acquisitions.[3] These nonrational responses lie, for example, at the heart of the failure of the internal control systems in corporations that has led to the waste of hundreds of billions of dollars and the failure of a number of the crown jewels of corporate America over the last two decades. (See Jensen 1993.)

While grounded in the fight or flight response—a mechanism that has contributed to survival for millions of years—the human responses to emotional or psychic pain are apparently highly counterproductive in our densely populated and complex modern industrial world. This phenomenon causes people to become stuck, unchanging, and unchangeable. They become wedded to the theories in their brains in ways that make them systematically worse off. And to make these challenges more difficult to deal with, the biological structure of the brain generally makes the individual blind to his or her own behavior. For this reason, learning in these situations is both very difficult and slow.

An interesting aspect of this nonrational behavior is the universal tendency for humans to hold views of themselves and their behavior—"espoused theories" in the language of Argyris (1990, 1991, 1993)—that are false. They are false because they are inconsistent with the theories on which the individuals act—what Argyris calls their "theories in use." Discovering these violations of our own principles and beliefs amounts to discovering our "irrationality," and this is highly threatening to an individual's self-esteem. The brain's fear response and the associated anxiety then severely limit our ability to perceive when our espoused theories are false. It is obviously difficult to change incorrect behavior under such circumstances.

The common disconnection between espoused theories and theories in use undermines the premise of Brennan's argument for limiting students' ability to learn that people generally behave in self-interested ways. He asserts, in his opening paragraph, that people's espoused theories determine their behavior. "Self-image is a major determinant of behaviour . . . If I think of myself as an honest person, I shall behave in an honest way" (p. 31). The evidence contradicting this theory is observable around us every day.

The combination of REMM and PAM leads to a much richer positive description of behavior. Even more important, this dualistic model will lead to much more effective normative propositions, programs, and devices for helping people minimize the nonrational, nonfunctional aspects of their behavior.

Note that these tendencies for individuals to act in ways that are inconsistent with their self-interest are another source of conflicts with employees, employers, partners, mates, colleagues, and so on. Therefore, they are another source of agency costs that must be addressed in any cooperative effort. And this, in turn, leads us to a structure for thinking about how to use group processes and organizational procedures to limit the counterproductive effects of this behavior.

In this expanded view of human behavior, REMM becomes more than a purely *positive* description of human behavior—it becomes a *normative* model that says this is how humans should behave. Consistent with this view, the solutions suggested by the psychological and psychiatric professions are best interpreted as helping people learn to correct their "mistakes" in order to behave in more REMM-like ways.[4]

The problem is not, therefore, to persuade people to avoid acting in their own self-interest, as Brennan argues, but to help them learn to avoid the systematic mistakes that make themselves, and those around them, worse off. I am not advocating that people learn to behave in an unbridled selfish way in which they do not care for the welfare of others, honesty, or honor. Without honor, there can be no trust, and without trust many beneficial activities and exchanges will not occur. Honesty, honor, and trust are therefore in the self-interest of all humans. In short, self-interest does not mean selfish.

2.5   Agency Theory

I now turn to agency theory, its definition, and the opposition to it from Brennan and others. In the end, of course, the usefulness of any theory depends on its ability to describe the world. No theory, including agency, is perfect, but I am surprised by the opposition that is based on a patriarchal fear that if we let the masses find out how people really behave it will further corrupt them. Let me take a moment to review briefly the modern history of this topic as I have witnessed it.

In the early 1970s William Meckling and I wrote an article on the theory of agency whose purpose was to open up the black box in economics and finance called the firm.[5] (See Chapter 3.) Our point was to show that firms were highly unlikely to behave in the value-maximizing way that was common to so much of the modeling and analysis in economics and finance. In opening up the box, we provided a structure within which we could begin to analyze the conflicts of interest between the involved human beings and the resulting equilibrium behavior of the organizations. Judging by the subsequent theoretical and empirical use of these concepts, the profession has found the approach a productive one.

We opened that original paper with the famous statement from Adam Smith in which he called attention to the conflicts of interest between the owners of joint stock companies and their managers and directors. Although he did not use the language of agency costs, he clearly understood the problem and in a sense was the original agency theorist. Smith believed so strongly in the power of self-interest and the conflicts it generates that he was extremely pessimistic about the ability of the joint stock company to survive in any but the simplest of activities where management's behavior could be easily monitored.

> Without a monopoly . . . a joint stock company, it would appear from experience, cannot long carry on any branch of foreign trade. To buy in one market, in order to sell, with profit, in another, when there are many competitors in both; to watch over, not only the occasional variations in the demand, but the much greater and more frequent variations in the competition . . . is a species of warfare . . . which can scarce ever be conducted successfully, without such an unremitting exertion of vigilance and attention, as cannot long be expected from the directors of a joint stock company. (Smith, 1776, p. 460)

Smith observed the failure of dozens of stock companies in his day, and concluded that the only activities a joint stock company could carry on successfully without a state-granted monopoly were those which were easily monitored—in his words, in which "all the operations are capable of being reduced to what is called a routine, or to such a uniformity of method as admits of little or no variation" (p. 461). In his opinion, this limited joint stock companies to banking, fire and marine insurance, canals, and municipal water supply. Smith did not, obviously, anticipate the evolution of governance mechanisms that have enabled the corporation to survive and even to thrive in a plethora of economic activities throughout the world.

Agency theory postulates that because people are, in the end, self-interested they will have conflicts of interest over at least some issues any time they attempt to engage in cooperative endeavors. This cooperation includes not only commerce through partnerships, and corporations, but also interaction in families and other social organizations. We focused our analysis in our original article on the conflicts of interest between stockholders and managers in the public corporation, not only because of the vast extent of the resources now controlled by such organizations, but also because those conflicts of interest are obvious and easily observed in the world around us. Similarly, each of us can observe the conflicts in families, and in the social and other organizations we associate with, and the structure of our analysis applies to each of them. The conflicts are so ubiquitous and so familiar that they have almost become invisible.

Meckling and I argued that because conflicts of interest cause problems and therefore losses to the parties involved, the parties themselves have strong motivation to minimize the agency costs (as we labeled them) of such cooperation. This *conservation of value principle* is the basic force that motivates both principal and agent, or partners, to minimize the sum of the costs of writing and enforcing (implicit and explicit) contracts through monitoring and bonding, and the residual loss incurred because it will not pay to enforce all contracts perfectly. The theory provides the structure within which to model and understand a vast array of human organizational arrangements, including incentive compensation, auditing, and bonding arrangements of all kinds. That literature is large and continues to grow.

Constrained at the time by our economists' view of rationality, Meckling and I discussed only one source of agency costs, that which emanates from the conflicts of interest between people. There is clearly a second major source of agency costs, the costs incurred as a result of the self-control problems discussed above—that is, the actions that people take that harm themselves as well as those around them—what Richard Thaler years ago characterized as agency problems with one's self.[6]

It is now time to take the next logical step. We have as a profession broken open the black box called the *firm* and are fully cognizant that, because of the inherent conflicts of interest among the parties to the firm, it does not maximize in any simple sense.[7] The next step is to break open the black box called the *individual* and similarly recognize that, because of self-control problems that lead to nonfunctional behavior, the individual cannot be said to maximize in the simple sense we economists have assumed for two hundred years. Indeed, some of the apparent contradictions evident in Adam Smith's work, especially that between *The Wealth of Nations* and his *Theory of Moral Sentiments,* may well reflect this conflicting, dualistic nature of humanity. As my discussion in this chapter indicates, self-control problems are much more important than most economists have perceived. I predict they will receive vastly increased attention in the future—attention that will result in better models and policies, both public and private.

2.6   Conclusions

Michael Brennan laments that the teaching of agency theory and the use of incentives will somehow "coarsen" humanity and make the world we live in a less hospitable place. Although this issue is worthy of careful research, it does not follow logically from the content of the theory, nor does his conjecture fit with my observations from twenty years of teaching this material.

When I teach agency theory, I do not find students surprised at the existence of conflicts. They live in the midst of them—and those conflicts which are not experienced personally can be shared in the daily torrent of offerings from the world's media. Because of the universality of conflict, the danger is that we may take it for granted and thus fail to see it at all.

I find that students and business people are excited by the central proposition of agency theory, and that central proposition is *not* that people are self-interested, or that conflicts exist. The central proposition of agency theory is that rational self-interested people *always* have incentives to reduce or control conflicts of interest so as to reduce the losses these conflicts engender. They can then share the gains. Moreover, the theory provides a general structure to point the way to a variety of classes of solutions to these problems.

Perhaps Brennan and others object to the fact that agency theory holds out no encouragement that human nature can be improved, and that society, organizations, and even individuals themselves could rid themselves of these costly conflicts of interest. The reality, however, is that even if we could instill more altruism in everyone, agency problems would not be solved. Put simply, altruism, the concern for the well-being of others, does not turn people into perfect agents who do the bidding of others.

I am skeptical of our ability to change human nature. Thousands of years of effort by all great religions of the world have failed to eradicate the reality of self-interest. Instead, I place my bets on the institutional structures, contracts, and informal arrangements that we create to reduce conflict, to govern our relations, and to increase the extent of cooperation and the benefits we reap from it. Such efforts, which arise from self-interest, are privately rewarding and improve the quality of life in our society.

3 Theory of the Firm: Managerial Behavior, Agency Costs, and Ownership Structure

The directors of such [joint-stock] companies, however, being the managers rather of other people's money than of their own, it cannot well be expected, that they should watch over it with the same anxious vigilance with which the partners in a private copartnery frequently watch over their own. Like the stewards of a rich man, they are apt to consider attention to small matters as not for their master's honour, and very easily give themselves a dispensation from having it. Negligence and profusion, therefore, must always prevail, more or less, in the management of the affairs of such a company.

—Adam Smith, *The Wealth of Nations*

3.1   Introduction

In this chapter we draw on recent progress in the theory of (1) property rights, (2) agency, and (3) finance to develop a theory of ownership structure[1] for the firm. In addition to tying together elements of the theory of each of these three areas, our analysis casts new light on and has implications for a variety of issues in the professional and popular literature including the definition of the firm, the "separation of ownership and control," the "social responsibility" of business, the definition of a "corporate objective function," the determination of an optimal capital structure, the specification of the content of credit agreements, the theory of organizations, and the supply side of the completeness of markets problems.

Our theory helps explain:

1. why an entrepreneur or manager in a firm which has a mixed financial structure (containing both debt and outside equity claims) will choose a set of activities for the firm such that the total value of the firm is *less* than it would be if he were the sole

By Michael C. Jensen and William H. Meckling; originally published in *Journal of Financial Economics* 3, no. 4 (October 1976), pp. 305–360.

owner, and why this result is independent of whether the firm operates in monopolistic or competitive product or factor markets;

2. why his failure to maximize the value of the firm is perfectly consistent with efficiency;

3. why the sale of common stock is a viable source of capital even though managers do not literally maximize the value of the firm;

4. why debt was relied upon as a source of capital before debt financing offered any tax advantage relative to equity;

5. why preferred stock would be issued;

6. why accounting reports would be provided voluntarily to creditors and stockholders, and why independent auditors would be engaged by management to testify to the accuracy and correctness of such reports;

7. why lenders often place restrictions on the activities of firms to whom they lend, and why firms would themselves be led to suggest the imposition of such restrictions;

8. why some industries are characterized by owner-operated firms whose sole outside source of capital is borrowing;

9. why highly regulated industries such as public utilities or banks will have higher debt equity ratios for equivalent levels of risk than the average nonregulated firm;

10. why security analysis can be socially productive even if it does not increase portfolio returns to investors.

Theory of the Firm: An Empty Box?

While the literature of economics is replete with references to the "theory of the firm," the material generally subsumed under that heading is not actually a theory of the firm but rather a theory of markets in which firms are important actors. The firm is a "black box" operated so as to meet the relevant marginal conditions with respect to inputs and outputs, thereby maximizing profits, or more accurately, present value. Except for a few recent and tentative steps, however, we have no theory which explains how the conflicting objectives of the individual participants are brought into equilibrium so as to yield this result. The limitations of this black box view of the firm have been cited by Adam Smith and Alfred Marshall, among others. More recently, popular and professional debates over the "social responsibility" of corporations, the separation of ownership and control, and the rash of reviews of the literature on the "theory of the firm" have evidenced continuing concern with these issues.[2]

A number of major attempts have been made during recent years to construct a theory of the firm by substituting other models for profit or value maximization, with each attempt motivated by a conviction that the latter is inadequate to explain managerial behavior in large corporations.[3] Some of these reformulation attempts have rejected the fundamental principle of maximizing behavior as well as rejecting the more specific profit-maximizing model. We retain the notion of maximizing behavior on the part of all individuals in the analysis that follows.[4]

Property Rights

An independent stream of research with important implications for the theory of the firm has been stimulated by the pioneering work of Coase, and extended by Alchian, Demsetz, and others.[5] A comprehensive survey of this literature is given by Furubotn and Pejovich (1972). While the focus of this research has been "property rights,"[6] the subject matter encompassed is far broader than that term suggests. What is important for the problems addressed here is that specification of individual rights determines how costs and rewards will be allocated among the participants in any organization. Since the specification of rights is generally affected through contracting (implicit as well as explicit), individual behavior in organizations, including the behavior of managers, will depend upon the nature of these contracts. We focus in this chapter on the behavioral implications of the property rights specified in the contracts between the owners and managers of the firm.

Agency Costs

Many problems associated with the inadequacy of the current theory of the firm can also be viewed as special cases of the theory of agency relationships, in which there is a growing literature.[7] This literature has developed independently of the property rights literature even though the problems with which it is concerned are similar; the approaches are in fact highly complementary to each other.

We define an agency relationship as a contract under which one or more persons—the principal(s)—engage another person—the agent—

to perform some service on their behalf which involves delegating some decision-making authority to the agent. If both parties to the relationship are utility maximizers, there is good reason to believe that the agent will not always act in the best interests of the principal. The *principal* can limit divergences from his interest by establishing appropriate incentives for the agent and by incurring monitoring costs designed to limit the aberrant activities of the agent. In addition, in some situations it will pay the *agent* to expend resources (bonding costs) to guarantee that he will not take certain actions which would harm the principal or to ensure that the principal will be compensated if he does take such actions. However, it is generally impossible for the principal or the agent at zero cost to ensure that the agent will make optimal decisions from the principal's viewpoint. In most agency relationships the principal and the agent will incur positive monitoring and bonding costs (nonpecuniary as well as pecuniary), and in addition there will be some divergence between the agent's decisions[8] and those decisions which would maximize the welfare of the principal. The dollar equivalent of the reduction in welfare experienced by the principal as a result of this divergence is also a cost of the agency relationship, and we refer to this latter cost as the "residual loss." We define *agency costs* as the sum of:

1. the monitoring expenditures by the principal,[9]
2. the bonding expenditures by the agent,
3. the residual loss.

Note also that agency costs arise in any situation involving cooperative effort (such as the coauthoring of this chapter) by two or more people even though there is no clear-cut principal-agent relationship. Viewed in this light, it is clear that our definition of agency costs and their importance to the theory of the firm bears a close relationship to the problem of shirking and monitoring of team production which Alchian and Demsetz (1972) raise in their paper on the theory of the firm.

Since the relationship between the stockholders and the managers of a corporation fits the definition of a pure agency relationship, it should come as no surprise to discover that the issues associated with the "separation of ownership and control" in the modern diffuse ownership corporation are intimately associated with the general problem of agency. We show below that an explanation of why and how the agency costs generated by the corporate form are borne leads to a theory of the ownership (or capital) structure of the firm.

Before moving on, however, it is worthwhile to point out the generality of the agency problem. The problem of inducing an "agent" to behave as if he were maximizing the "principal's" welfare is quite general. It exists in all organizations and in all cooperative efforts—at every level of management in firms,[10] in universities, in mutual companies, in cooperatives, in governmental authorities and bureaus, in unions, and in relationships normally classified as agency relationships such as those common in the performing arts and the market for real estate. The development of theories to explain the form which agency costs take in each of these situations (where the contractual relations differ significantly), and how and why they are borne, will lead to a rich theory of organizations which is now lacking in economics and the social sciences generally. We confine our attention in this chapter to only a small part of this general problem—the analysis of agency costs generated by the contractual arrangements between the owners and top management of the corporation.

Our approach to the agency problem here differs fundamentally from most of the existing literature. That literature focuses almost exclusively on the normative aspects of the agency relationship; that is, how to structure the contractual relation (including compensation incentives) between the principal and agent to provide appropriate incentives for the agent to make choices which will maximize the principal's welfare, given that uncertainty and imperfect monitoring exist. We focus almost entirely on the positive aspects of the theory. That is, we assume individuals solve these normative problems, and given that only stocks and bonds can be issued as claims, we investigate the incentives faced by each of the parties and the elements entering into the determination of the equilibrium contractual form characterizing the relationship between the manager (i.e., agent) of the firm and the outside equity and debt holders (i.e., principals).

General Comments on the Definition of the Firm

Ronald Coase (1937) in his seminal paper entitled "The Nature of the Firm" pointed out that economics had no positive theory to determine the bounds of the firm. He characterized the bounds of the firm as that range of exchanges over which the market system was suppressed and where resource allocation was accomplished instead by authority and direction. He focused on the cost of using markets to effect contracts and exchanges and argued that activities would be included within the firm whenever the costs of using markets were greater than the costs of using direct authority. Alchian and Demsetz (1972) object to the notion that activities within the firm are governed by authority, and correctly emphasize the role of contracts as a vehicle for voluntary exchange. They emphasize the role of monitoring in situations in which there is joint input or team production.[11] We are sympathetic to the importance they attach to monitoring, but we believe the emphasis that Alchian and Demsetz place on joint input production is too narrow and therefore misleading. Contractual relations are the essence of the firm, not only with employees but with suppliers, customers, creditors, and so on. The problem of agency costs and monitoring exists for all of these contracts, independent of whether there is joint production in their sense; that is, joint production can explain only a small fraction of the behavior of individuals associated with a firm.

It is important to recognize that most organizations are simply *legal fictions*[12] *which serve as a nexus for a set of contracting relationships among individuals.* This includes firms, nonprofit institutions such as universities, hospitals, and foundations, mutual organizations such as mutual savings banks and insurance companies and cooperatives, some private clubs, and even governmental bodies such as cities, states, and the federal government, government enterprises such as TVA, the Post Office, transit systems, and so forth.

The private corporation or firm is simply one form of *legal fiction which serves as a nexus for contracting relationships and which is also characterized by the existence of divisible residual claims on the assets and cash flows of the organization which can generally be sold without permission of the other contracting individuals.* Although this definition of the firm has little substantive content, emphasizing the essential contractual nature of firms and other organizations focuses attention on a crucial set of questions—why particular sets of contractual relations arise for various types of organizations, what the consequences of these contractual relations are, and how they are affected by changes exogenous to the organization. Viewed this way, it makes little or no sense to try to distinguish those things that are "inside" the firm (or any other organization) from those things that are "outside" of it. There is in a very real sense only a multitude of complex relationships (i.e., contracts) between the legal fiction (the firm) and the owners of labor, material, and capital inputs and the consumers of output.[13]

Viewing the firm as the nexus of a set of contracting relationships among individuals also serves to make it clear that the personalization of the firm implied by asking questions such as "what should be the objective function of the firm?" or "does the firm have a social responsibility?" is seriously misleading. *The firm is not an individual.* It is a legal fiction which serves as a focus for a complex process in which the conflicting objectives of individuals (some of whom may "represent" other organizations) are brought into equilibrium within a framework of contractual relations. In this sense the "behavior" of the firm is like the behavior of a market, that is, the outcome of a complex equilibrium process. We seldom fall into the trap of characterizing the wheat or stock market as an individual, but we often make this error by thinking about organizations as if they were persons with motivations and intentions.[14]

Overview of the Chapter

We develop our theory in stages. Sections 3.2 and 3.4 provide analyses of the agency costs of equity and debt respectively. These form the major foundation of the theory. In Section 3.3 we pose some questions regarding the existence of the corporate form of organization and examine the role of limited liability. Section 3.5 provides a synthesis of the basic concepts derived in Sections 3.2–3.4 into a theory of the corporate ownership structure which takes account of the trade-offs available to the entrepreneur-manager between inside and outside equity and debt. Some qualifications and extensions of the analysis are discussed in Section 3.6, and Section 3.7 contains a brief summary and conclusions.

3.2   The Agency Costs of Outside Equity

Overview

In this section we analyze the effect of outside equity on agency costs by comparing the behavior of a manager when he owns 100 percent of the residual claims on a firm with his behavior when he sells off a portion of those claims to outsiders. If a wholly-owned firm is managed by the owner, he will make operating decisions that maximize his utility. These decisions will involve not only the benefits he derives from pecuniary returns but also the utility generated by various non-pecuniary aspects of his entrepreneurial activities, such as the physical appointments of the office, the attractiveness of the office staff, the level of employee discipline, the kind and amount of charitable contributions, personal relations ("friendship," "respect," and so on) with employees, a larger than optimal computer to play with, or purchase of production inputs from friends. The optimum mix (in the absence of taxes) of the various pecuniary and non-pecuniary benefits is achieved when the marginal utility derived from an additional dollar of expenditure (measured net of any productive effects) is equal for each non-pecuniary item and equal to the marginal utility derived from an additional dollar of after-tax purchasing power (wealth).

If the owner-manager sells equity claims on the corporation which are identical to his own (i.e., which share proportionately in the profits of the firm and have limited liability), agency costs will be generated by the divergence between his interest and those of the outside shareholders, since he will then bear only a fraction of the costs of any non-pecuniary benefits he takes out in maximizing his own utility. If the manager owns only 95 percent of the stock, he will expend resources to the point where the marginal utility derived from a dollar's expenditure of the firm's resources on such items equals the marginal utility of an additional 95 cents in general purchasing power (i.e., *his* share of the wealth reduction) and not one dollar. Such activities, on his part, can be limited (but probably not eliminated) by the expenditure of resources on monitoring activities by the outside stockholders. But as we show below, the owner will bear the entire wealth effects of these expected costs so long as the equity market anticipates these effects. Prospective minority shareholders will realize that the owner-manager's interests will diverge somewhat from theirs; hence the price which they will pay for shares will reflect the monitoring costs and the effect of the divergence between the manager's interest and theirs. Nevertheless, ignoring for the moment the possibility of borrowing against his wealth, the owner will find it desirable to bear these costs as long as the welfare increment he experiences from converting his claims on the firm into general purchasing power[15] is large enough to offset them.

As the owner-manager's fraction of the equity falls, his fractional claim on the outcomes falls and this will tend to encourage him to appropriate larger amounts of the corporate resources in the form of perquisites. This also makes it desirable for the minority shareholders to expend more resources in monitoring his behavior. Thus, the wealth costs to the owner of obtaining additional cash in the equity markets rise as his fractional ownership falls.

We shall continue to characterize the agency conflict between the owner-manager and outside shareholders as deriving from the manager's tendency to appropriate perquisites out of the firm's resources for his own consumption. However, we do not mean to leave the impression that this is the only or even the most important source of conflict. Indeed, it is likely that the most important conflict arises from the fact that as the manager's ownership claim falls, his incentive to devote significant effort to creative activities such as searching out new profitable ventures falls. He may in fact avoid such ventures simply because it requires too much trouble or effort on his part to manage or to learn about new technologies. Avoidance of these personal costs and the anxieties that go with them also represent a source of on-the-job utility to him, and it can result in the value of the firm being substantially lower than it otherwise could be.

A Simple Formal Analysis of the Sources of Agency Costs of Equity and Who Bears Them

In order to develop some structure for the analysis to follow, we make two sets of assumptions. The first set (permanent assumptions) are those which will carry through almost all of the analysis in Sections 3.2–3.4. The effects of relaxing some of these are discussed in Section 3.6. The second set (temporary assumptions) are made only for expositional purposes and are relaxed as soon as the basic points have been clarified.

Permanent assumptions
(P.1) All taxes are zero.
(P.2) No trade credit is available.
(P.3) All outside equity shares are non-voting.
(P.4) No complex financial claims such as convertible bonds or preferred stock or warrants can be issued.
(P.5) No outside owner gains utility from ownership in a firm in any way other than through its effect on his wealth or cash flows.
(P.6) All dynamic aspects of the multiperiod nature of the problem

are ignored by assuming there is only one production-financing decision to be made by the entrepreneur.

(P.7) The entrepreneur-manager's money wages are held constant throughout the analysis.

(P.8) There exists a single manager (the peak coordinator) with ownership interest in the firm.

Temporary assumptions

(T.1) The size of the firm is fixed.

(T.2) No monitoring or bonding activities are possible.

(T.3) No debt financing through bonds, preferred stock, or personal borrowing (secured or unsecured) is possible.

(T.4) All elements of the owner-manager's decision problem involving portfolio considerations induced by the presence of uncertainty and the existence of diversifiable risk are ignored.

Define:

X = $\{x_1, x_2, \ldots, x_n\}$ = vector of quantities of all factors and activities within the firm from which the manager derives non-pecuniary benefits;[16] the x_i are defined such that his marginal utility is positive for each of them;

$C(X)$ = total dollar cost of providing any given amount of these items;

$P(X)$ = total dollar value to the firm of the productive benefits of X;

$B(X)$ = $P(X) - C(X)$ = net dollar benefit to the firm of X ignoring any effects of X on the equilibrium wage of the manager.

Ignoring the effects of X on the manager's utility and therefore on his equilibrium wage rate, the optimum levels of the factors and activities X are defined by X^* such that

$$\frac{\partial B(X^*)}{\partial X^*} = \frac{\partial P(X^*)}{\partial X^*} - \frac{\partial C(X^*)}{\partial X^*} = 0.$$

Thus for any vector $X \geq X^*$ (i.e., where at least one element of X is greater than its corresponding element of X^*), $F \equiv B(X^*) - B(X) > 0$ measures the dollar cost to the firm (net of any productive effects) of providing the increment $X - X^*$ of the factors and activities which generate utility to the manager. We assume henceforth that for any given level of cost to the firm, F, the vector of factors and activities on

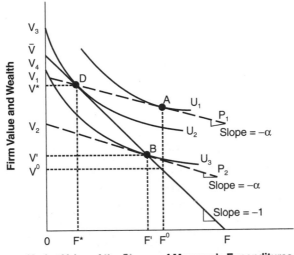

Figure 3.1 The value of the firm *(V)* and the level of non-pecuniary benefits consumed *(F)* when the fraction of outside equity is $(1-\alpha)V$, and $U_j(j = 1,2,3)$ represents the owner's indifference curves between wealth and non-pecuniary benefits.

which *F* is spent are those, $\hat{X}$, which yield the manager maximum utility. Thus $F \equiv B(X^*) - B(\hat{X})$.

We have thus far ignored in our discussion the fact that these expenditures on X occur through time and therefore there are trade-offs to be made across time as well as between alternative elements of X. Furthermore, we have ignored the fact that the future expenditures are likely to involve uncertainty (i.e., they are subject to probability distributions) and therefore some allowance must be made for their riskiness. We resolve both of these issues by defining C, P, B, and F to be the *current market values* of the sequence of probability distributions on the period-by-period cash flows involved.[17]

Given the definition of F as the current market value of the stream of manager's expenditures on non-pecuniary benefits, we represent the constraint which a single owner-manager faces in deciding how much non-pecuniary income he will extract from the firm by the line $\overline{V}F$ in Figure 3.1. This is analogous to a budget constraint. The market value of the firm is measured along the vertical axis and the market value of the manager's stream of expenditures on non-pecuniary benefits, *F,* is measured along the horizontal axis. $O\overline{V}$ is the value of the firm when the amount of non-pecuniary income consumed is zero. By definition $\overline{V}$ is the maximum market value of the cash flows generated by the firm for a given money wage for the manager when the manager's consumption of non-pecuniary benefits is zero. At this point all the factors and activities within the firm which generate utility for the manager are at the level X^* defined above. There is a different budget constraint $\overline{V}F$ for each possible scale of the firm (i.e., level of investment, I) and for alternative levels of money wage, W, for the manager. For the moment we pick an arbitrary level of investment (which we assume has already been made) and hold the scale of the firm constant at this level. We also assume that the manager's money wage is fixed at the level W^* which represents the current market value of his wage contract[18] in the optimal compensation package which consists of both wages, W^*, and non-pecuniary benefits, F^*. Since one dollar of current value of non-pecuniary benefits withdrawn from the firm by the manager reduces the market value of the firm by \$1, by definition, the slope of $\overline{V}F$ is -1.

The owner-manager's tastes for wealth and non-pecuniary benefits is represented in Figure 3.1 by a system of indifference curves, U_1, U_2, and so on.[19] The indifference curves will be convex as drawn as long as the owner-manager's marginal rate of substitution between non-pecuniary benefits and wealth diminishes with increasing levels of the benefits. For the 100 percent owner-manager, this presumes that there are not perfect substitutes for these benefits available on the outside, that is, to some extent they are job-specific. For the fractional owner-manager this presumes that the benefits cannot be turned into general purchasing power at a constant price.[20]

When the owner has 100 percent of the equity, the value of the firm will be V^* where indifference curve U_2 is tangent to $\overline{V}F$, and the level of non-pecuniary benefits consumed is F^*. If the owner sells the entire equity but remains as manager, and if the equity buyer can, at zero cost, force the old owner (as manager) to take the same level of non-pecuniary benefits as he did as owner, then V^* is the price the new owner will be willing to pay for the entire equity.[21]

In general, however, we could not expect the new owner to be able to enforce identical behavior on the old owner at zero costs. If the old owner sells a fraction of the firm to an outsider, he, as manager, will no longer bear the full cost of any non-pecuniary benefits he consumes. Suppose the owner sells a share of the firm, $1-\alpha$, $(0 < \alpha < 1)$ and retains for himself a share, α. If the prospective buyer believes that the owner-manager will consume the same level of non-pecuniary benefits as he did as full owner, the buyer will be willing to pay $(1-\alpha)V^*$ for a fraction $(1-\alpha)$ of the equity. Given that an outsider now holds a claim to $(1-\alpha)$ of the equity, however, the *cost* to the owner-manager of consuming \$1 of non-pecuniary benefits in the firm will no longer be \$1. Instead, it will be $\alpha \times \$1$. If the prospective buyer actually paid $(1-\alpha)V^*$ for his share of the equity, and if thereafter the manager could choose whatever level of non-pecuniary benefits he liked, his budget constraint would be V_1P_1 in Figure 3.1 and has a slope equal to $-\alpha$. Including the payment the owner receives from the buyer as part of the owner's post-sale wealth, his budget constraint, V_1P_1, must pass through D, since he can if he wishes have the same wealth and level of non-pecuniary consumption he enjoyed as full owner.

But if the owner-manager is free to choose the level of perquisites, F, subject only to the loss in wealth he incurs as a part owner, his welfare will be maximized by increasing his consumption of non-pecuniary benefits. He will move to point A where V_1P_1 is tangent to U_1 representing a higher level of utility. The value of the firm falls from V^*, to V^0, that is, by the amount of the cost to the firm of the increased non-pecuniary expenditures, and the owner-manager's consumption of non-pecuniary benefits rises from F^* to F^0.

If the equity market is characterized by rational expectations, the buyers will be aware that the owner will increase his non-pecuniary consumption when his ownership share is reduced. If the owner's response function is known or if the equity market makes unbiased estimates of the owner's response to the changed incentives, the buyer will not pay $(1-\alpha)V^*$ for $(1-\alpha)$ of the equity.

Theorem. For a claim on the firm of $(1-\alpha)$ the outsider will pay only $(1-\alpha)$ times the value he expects the firm to have given the induced change in the behavior of the owner-manager.

Proof. For simplicity we ignore any element of uncertainty introduced by the lack of perfect knowledge of the owner-manager's response function. Such uncertainty will not affect the final solution if the equity market is large as long as the estimates are rational (i.e., unbiased) and the errors are independent across firms. The latter condition assures that this risk is diversifiable and therefore that equilibrium prices will equal the expected values.

Let W represent the owner's total wealth after he has sold a claim equal to $1-\alpha$ of the equity to an outsider. W has two components. One is the payment, S_o, made by the outsider for $1-\alpha$ of the equity; the rest, S_i, is the value of the owner's (i.e., insider's) share of the firm, so that W, the owner's wealth, is given by

$$W = S_o + S_i = S_o + \alpha V(F, \alpha),$$

where $V(F, \alpha)$ represents the value of the firm given that the manager's fractional ownership share is α and that he consumes perquisites with current market value of F. Let V_2P_2, with a slope of $-\alpha$, represent the trade-off the owner-manager faces between non-pecuniary benefits and his wealth after the sale. Given that the owner has decided to sell a claim $1-\alpha$ of the firm, his welfare will be maximized when V_2P_2 is tangent to some indifference curve such as U_3 in Figure 3.1. A price for a claim of $(1-\alpha)$ on the firm that is satisfactory to both the buyer and the seller will require that this tangency occur along $\overline{VF}$, that is, that the value of the firm must be V'. To show this, assume that such is not the case—that the tangency occurs to the left of the point B on the line $\overline{VF}$. Then, since the slope of V_2P_2 is negative, the value of the firm will be larger than V'. The owner-manager's choice of this lower level of consumption of non-pecuniary benefits will imply a higher value both to the firm as a whole and to the fraction of the firm $(1-\alpha)$ which the outsider has acquired; that is, $(1-\alpha)V' > S_o$. From the owner's viewpoint, he has sold $1-\alpha$ of the firm for less than he could have, given the (assumed) lower level of non-pecuniary benefits he enjoys. On the other hand, if the tangency point B is to the right of the line $\overline{VF}$, the owner-manager's higher consumption of non-pecuniary benefits means the value of the firm is less than V', and hence $(1-\alpha)V(F, \alpha) < S_o = (1-\alpha)V'$. The outside owner then has paid more for his share of the equity than it is worth. S_o will be a mutually satisfactory price if and only if $(1-\alpha)V' = S_o$. But this means that the owner's post-sale wealth is equal to the (reduced) value of the firm V', since

$$W = S_o + \alpha V' = (1-\alpha)V' + \alpha V' = V'.$$

Q.E.D.

The requirement that V' and F' fall on $\overline{VF}$ is thus equivalent to requiring that the value of the claim acquired by the outside buyer be equal to the amount he pays for it, and conversely for the owner. *This means that the decline in the total value of the firm $(V^* - V')$ is entirely* *imposed on the owner-manager.* His total wealth after the sale of $(1-\alpha)$ of the equity is V' and the decline in his wealth is V^*-V'.

The distance V^*-V' is the reduction in the market value of the firm engendered by the agency relationship and is a measure of the "residual loss" defined earlier. In this simple example the residual loss represents the total agency costs engendered by the sale of outside equity because monitoring and bonding activities have not been allowed. The welfare loss the owner incurs is less than the residual loss by the value to him of the increase in non-pecuniary benefits $(F'-F^*)$. In Figure 3.1 the difference between the intercepts on the Y axis of the two indifference curves U_2 and U_3 is a measure of the owner-manager's welfare loss due to the incurrence of agency costs,[22] and he would sell such a claim only if the increment in welfare he achieved by using the cash amounting to $(1-\alpha)V'$ for other things was worth more to him than this amount of wealth.

Determination of the Optimal Scale of the Firm

The case of all equity financing. Consider the problem faced by an entrepreneur with initial pecuniary wealth, W, and monopoly access to a project requiring investment outlay, I, subject to diminishing returns to scale in I. Figure 3.2 portrays the solution to the optimal scale of the firm taking into account the agency costs associated with the existence of outside equity. The axes are as defined in Figure 3.1 except we now plot on the vertical axis the total wealth of the owner, that is, his initial wealth, W, plus $V(I)-I$, the net increment in wealth he obtains from exploitation of his investment opportunities. The market value of the firm, $V = V(I, F)$, is now a function of the level of investment, I, and the current market value of the manager's expenditures of the firm's resources on non-pecuniary benefits, F. Let $\overline{V}(I)$ represent the value of the firm as a function of the level of investment when the manager's expenditures on non-pecuniary benefits, F, are zero. The schedule with intercept labeled $W + [\overline{V}(I^*)-I^*]$ and slope equal to -1 in Figure 3.2 represents the locus of combinations of post-investment wealth and dollar cost to the firm of non-pecuniary benefits which are available to the manager when investment is carried to the value maximizing point, I^*. At this point $\Delta\overline{V}(I)-\Delta I = 0$. If the manager's wealth were large enough to cover the investment required to reach this scale of operation, I^*, he would consume F^* in non-pecuniary benefits and have

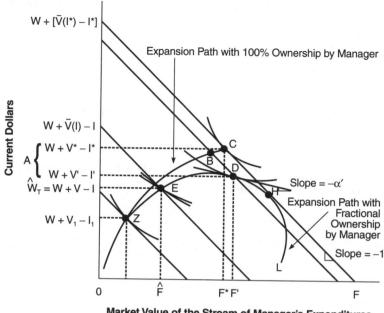

Figure 3.2 Determination of the optimal scale of the firm in the case where no monitoring takes place. Point C denotes optimum investment, I^*, and non-pecuniary benefits, F^*, when investment is 100% financed by the entrepreneur. Point D denotes optimum investment, I', and non-pecuniary benefits, F', when outside equity financing is used to help finance the investment and the entrepreneur owns a fraction α' of the firm. The distance A measures the gross agency costs.

pecuniary wealth with value $W + V^* - I^*$. However, if outside financing is required to cover the investment he will not reach this point if monitoring costs are non-zero.[23]

The expansion path $OZBC$ represents the equilibrium combinations of wealth and non-pecuniary benefits, F, which the manager could obtain if he had enough personal wealth to finance all levels of investment up to I^*. It is the locus of points such as Z and C which present the equilibrium position for the 100 percent owner-manager at each possible level of investment, I. As I increases we move up the expansion path to the point C where $V(I) - I$ is at a maximum. Additional investment beyond this point reduces the net value of the firm, and as it does the equilibrium path of the manager's wealth and non-pecuniary benefits retraces (in the reverse direction) the curve $OZBC$. We draw the path as a smooth concave function only as a matter of convenience.

If the manager obtained outside financing and if there were zero costs to the agency relationship (perhaps because monitoring costs were zero), the expansion path would also be represented by $OZBC$. Therefore, this path represents what we might call the "idealized" solutions, that is, those which would occur in the absence of agency costs.

Assume that the manager has sufficient personal wealth to completely finance the firm only up to investment level I_1, which puts him at point Z. At this point $W = I_1$. To increase the size of the firm beyond this point he must obtain outside financing to cover the additional investment required, and this means reducing his fractional ownership. When he does this he incurs agency costs, and the lower his ownership fraction, the larger are the agency costs he incurs. However, if the investments requiring outside financing are sufficiently profitable his welfare will continue to increase.

The expansion path $ZEDHL$ in Figure 3.2 portrays one possible path of the equilibrium levels of the owner's non-pecuniary benefits and wealth at each possible level of investment higher than I_1. This path is the locus of points such as E or D where (1) the manager's indifference curve is tangent to a line with slope equal to $-\alpha$ (his fractional claim on the firm at that level of investment), and (2) the tangency occurs on the "budget constraint" with slope $= -1$ for the firm value and non-pecuniary benefit trade-off at the same level of investment.[24] As we move along $ZEDHL$ his fractional claim on the firm continues to fall as he raises larger amounts of outside capital. This expansion path represents his complete opportunity set for combinations of wealth and non-pecuniary benefits, given the existence of the costs of the agency relationship with the outside equity holders. Point D, where this opportunity set is tangent to an indifference curve, represents the solution which maximizes his welfare. At this point, the level of investments is I', his fractional ownership share in the firm is α', his wealth is $W+V'-I'$, and he consumes a stream of non-pecuniary benefits with current market value of F'. The gross agency costs (denoted by A) are equal to $(V^*-I^*)-(V'-I')$. Given that no monitoring is possible, I' is the socially optimal level of investment as well as the privately optimal level.

We can characterize the optimal level of investment as that point, I' which satisfies the following condition for small changes:

$$\Delta V - \Delta I + \alpha'\Delta F = 0. \tag{1}$$

$\Delta V - \Delta I$ is the change in the net market value of the firm, and $\alpha'\Delta F$ is the dollar value to the manager of the incremental fringe benefits he consumes (which cost the firm ΔF dollars); see note 25 for the proof and Eq. (2).[25] Furthermore, recognizing that $V = \overline{V} - F$, where $\overline{V}$ is the value of the firm at any level of investment when $F = 0$, we can substitute into the optimum condition to get

$$(\Delta\overline{V} - \Delta I) - (1 - \alpha')\Delta F = 0 \tag{3}$$

as an alternative expression for determining the optimum level of investment.

The idealized or zero agency cost solution, I^*, is given by the condition $(\Delta\overline{V} - \Delta I) = 0$, and since ΔF is positive the actual welfare maximizing level of investment I' will be less than I^*, because $(\Delta\overline{V} - \Delta I)$ must be positive at I' if (3) is to be satisfied. Since $-\alpha'$ is the slope of the indifference curve at the optimum and therefore represents the manager's demand price for incremental non-pecuniary benefits, ΔF, we know that $\alpha'\Delta F$ is the dollar value to him of an increment of fringe benefits costing the firm ΔF dollars. The term $(1-\alpha')\Delta F$ thus measures the dollar "loss" to the firm (and himself) of an additional ΔF dollars spent on non-pecuniary benefits. The term $\Delta\overline{V} - \Delta I$ is the gross increment in the value of the firm ignoring any changes in the consumption of non-pecuniary benefits. Thus, the manager stops increasing the size of the firm when the gross increment in value is just offset by the incremental "loss" involved in the consumption of additional fringe benefits due to his declining fractional interest in the firm.[26]

The Role of Monitoring and Bonding Activities in Reducing Agency Costs

In the above analysis we have ignored the potential for controlling the behavior of the owner-manager through monitoring and other control activities. In practice, it is usually possible by expending resources to alter the opportunity the owner-manager has for capturing non-pecuniary benefits. These methods include auditing, formal control systems, budget restrictions, the establishment of incentive compensation systems which serve to identify the manager's interests more closely with those of the outside equity holders, and so forth. Figure 3.3 portrays the effects of monitoring and other control activities in the simple situation portrayed in Figure 3.1. Figures 3.1 and 3.3 are identical except for the curve BCE in Figure 3.3, which depicts a "budget constraint" derived when monitoring possibilities are taken into account. Without monitor-

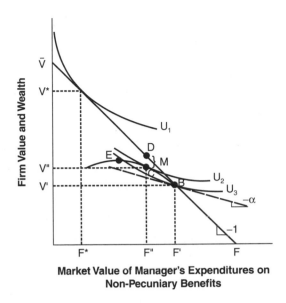

Figure 3.3 The value of the firm *(V)* and level of non-pecuniary benefits *(F)* when outside equity is $(1-\alpha)$, U_1, U_2, U_3 represent the owner's indifference curves between wealth and non-pecuniary benefits, and monitoring (or bonding) activities impose opportunity set *BCE* as the trade-off constraint facing the owner.

ing, and with outside equity of $(1-\alpha)$, the value of the firm will be V' and non-pecuniary expenditures F'. By incurring monitoring costs, M, the equity holders can restrict the manager's consumption of perquisites to amounts less than F'. Let $F(M, \alpha)$ denote the maximum perquisites the manager can consume for alternative levels of monitoring expenditures, M, given his ownership share α. We assume that increases in monitoring reduce F, and reduce it at a decreasing rate, that is, $\partial F/\partial M < 0$ and $\partial^2 F/\partial M^2 > 0$.

Since the current value of expected future monitoring expenditures by the outside equity holders reduces the value of any given claim on the firm to them dollar for dollar, the outside equity holders will take this into account in determining the maximum price they will pay for any given fraction of the firm's equity. Therefore, given positive monitoring activity, the value of the firm is given by $V = \overline{V} - F(M,\alpha) - M$, and the locus of these points for various levels of M and for a given level of α lie on the line *BCE* in Figure 3.3. The vertical difference between the $\overline{V}F$ and *BCE* curves is M, the current market value of the future monitoring expenditures.

If it is possible for the outside equity holders to make these monitoring expenditures and thereby to impose the reductions in the owner-manager's consumption of F, he will voluntarily enter into a contract with the outside equity holders which gives them the rights to restrict his consumption of non-pecuniary items to F''. He finds this desirable because it will cause the value of the firm to rise to V''. Given the contract, the optimal monitoring expenditure on the part of the outsiders, M, is the amount $D-C$. The entire increase in the value of the firm that accrues will be reflected in the owner's wealth, but his welfare will be increased by less than this because he forgoes some non-pecuniary benefits he previously enjoyed.

If the equity market is competitive and makes unbiased estimates of the effects of monitoring expenditures on F and V, potential buyers will be indifferent between the following two contracts:

1. Purchase of a share $(1-\alpha)$ of the firm at a total price of $(1-\alpha)V'$ and no rights to monitor or control the manager's consumption of perquisites.
2. Purchase of a share $(1-\alpha)$ of the firm at a total price of $(1-\alpha)V''$ and the right to expend resources up to an amount equal to $D-C$ which will limit the owner-manager's consumption of perquisites to F''.

Given the contract (2) the outside shareholders would find it desirable to monitor to the full rights of their contract because it will pay them to do so. However, if the equity market is competitive the total benefits (net of the monitoring costs) will be capitalized into the price of the claims. Thus, not surprisingly, the owner-manager reaps all the benefits of the opportunity to write and sell the monitoring contract.[27]

An analysis of bonding expenditures. We can also see from the analysis of Figure 3.3 that it makes no difference who actually makes the monitoring expenditures—the owner bears the full amount of these costs as a wealth reduction in all cases. Suppose that the owner-manager could expend resources to guarantee to the outside equity holders that he would limit his activities which cost the firm F. We call these expenditures "bonding costs," and they would take such forms as contractual guarantees to have the financial accounts audited by a public accountant, explicit bonding against malfeasance on the part of the manager, and contractual limitations on the manager's decision-making power (which impose costs on the firm because they limit his ability to take full advantage of some profitable opportunities as well as limiting his ability to harm the stockholders while making himself better off).

If the incurrence of the bonding costs were entirely under the control of the manager and if they yielded the same opportunity set BCE for him in Figure 3.3, he would incur them in amount $D-C$. This would limit his consumption of perquisites to F'' from F', and the solution is exactly the same as if the outside equity holders had performed the monitoring. The manager finds it in his interest to incur these costs as long as the net increments in his wealth which they generate (by reducing the agency costs and therefore increasing the value of the firm) are more valuable than the perquisites given up. This optimum occurs at point C in both cases under our assumption that the bonding expenditures yield the same opportunity set as the monitoring expenditures. In general, of course, it will pay the owner-manager to engage in bonding activities and to write contracts which allow monitoring as long as the marginal benefits of each are greater than their marginal cost.

Optimal scale of the firm in the presence of monitoring and bonding activities. If we allow the outside owners to engage in (costly) monitoring activities to limit the manager's expenditures on non-pecuniary benefits and allow the manager to engage in bonding activities to guarantee to the outside owners that he will limit his consumption of F, we get an expansion path such as that illustrated in Figure 3.4 on which Z and G lie. We have assumed in drawing Figure 3.4 that the cost functions involved in monitoring and bonding are such that some positive levels of the activities are desirable, that is, yield benefits greater than their cost. If this is not true, the expansion path generated by the expenditure of resources on these activities would lie below ZD and no such activity would take place at any level of investment. Points Z, C, and D and the two expansion paths they lie on are identical to those portrayed in Figure 3.2. Points Z and C lie on the 100 percent ownership expansion path, and points Z and D lie on the fractional ownership, zero monitoring, and bonding activity expansion path.

The path on which points Z and G lie is the one given by the locus of equilibrium points for alternative levels of investment characterized by the point labeled C in Figure 3.3, which denotes the optimal level of

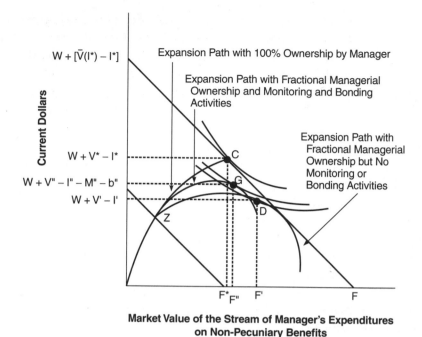

Figure 3.4 Determination of optimal scale of the firm allowing for monitoring and bonding activities. Optimal monitoring costs are M'' and bonding costs are b'', and the equilibrium scale of firm, manager's wealth, and consumption of non-pecuniary benefits are at point G.

monitoring and bonding activity and the resulting values of the firm and non-pecuniary benefits to the manager given a fixed level of investment. If any monitoring or bonding is cost-effective, the expansion path on which Z and G lie must be above the non-monitoring expansion path over some range. Furthermore, if it lies anywhere to the right of the indifference curve passing through point D (the zero monitoring-bonding solution) the final solution to the problem will involve positive amounts of monitoring and/or bonding activities. On the basis of the discussion above, we know that as long as the contracts between the manager and outsiders are unambiguous regarding the rights of the respective parties, the final solution will be at that point where the new expansion path is just tangent to the highest indifference curve. At this point the optimal levels of monitoring and bonding expenditures are M'' and b''; the manager's post-investment-financing wealth is given by $W + V'' - I'' - M'' - b''$ and his non-pecuniary benefits are F''. The total gross agency costs, A, are given by $A(M'', b'', \alpha'', I'') = (V^* - I^*) - (V'' - I'' - M'' - b'')$.

Pareto Optimality and Agency Costs in Manager-Operated Firms

In general we expect to observe both bonding and external monitoring activities, and the incentives are such that the levels of these activities will satisfy the conditions of efficiency. They will not, however, result in the firm being run in a manner so as to maximize its value. The difference between V^*, the efficient solution under zero monitoring and bonding costs (and therefore zero agency costs), and V'', the value of the firm given positive monitoring costs, is the total gross agency costs defined earlier in the introduction. These are the costs of the "separation of ownership and control" which Adam Smith focused on in the passage quoted at the beginning of this chapter and which Berle and Means (1932) popularized 157 years later. The solutions outlined above to our highly simplified problem imply that agency costs will be positive as long as monitoring costs are positive—which they certainly are.

The reduced value of the firm caused by the manager's consumption of perquisites outlined above is "non-optimal" or inefficient only in comparison to a world in which we could obtain compliance of the agent to the principal's wishes at zero cost or in comparison to a *hypothetical* world in which the agency costs were lower. But these costs (monitoring and bonding costs and "residual loss") are an unavoidable result of the agency relationship. Furthermore, since they are borne entirely by the decision maker (in this case the original owner) responsible for creating the relationship, he has the incentives to see that they are minimized (because he captures the benefits from their reduction). Furthermore, these agency costs will be incurred only if the benefits to the owner-manager from their creation are great enough to outweigh them. In our current example these benefits arise from the availability of profitable investments requiring capital investment in excess of the original owner's personal wealth.

In conclusion, finding that agency costs are non-zero (i.e., that there are costs associated with the separation of ownership and control in the corporation) and concluding therefrom that the agency relationship is non-optimal, wasteful, or inefficient is equivalent in every sense to comparing a world in which iron ore is a scarce commodity (and therefore costly) to a world in which it is freely available at zero resource costs, and concluding that the first world is "non-optimal"—a perfect example of the fallacy criticized by Coase (1964) and what Demsetz (1969) characterizes as the "Nirvana" form of analysis.[28]

Factors Affecting the Size of the Divergence from Ideal Maximization

The magnitude of the agency costs discussed above will vary from firm to firm. It will depend on the tastes of managers, the ease with which they can exercise their own preferences as opposed to value maximization in decision making, and the costs of monitoring and bonding activities.[29] The agency costs will also depend upon the cost of measuring the manager's (agent's) performance and evaluating it, the cost of devising and applying an index for compensating the manager which correlates with the owner's (principal's) welfare, and the cost of devising and enforcing specific behavioral rules or policies. Where the manager has less than a controlling interest in the firm, it will also depend upon the market for managers. Competition from other potential managers limits the costs of obtaining managerial services (including the extent to which a given manager can diverge from the idealized solution that would obtain if all monitoring and bonding costs were zero). The size of the divergence (the agency costs) will be directly related to the cost of replacing the manager. If his responsibilities require very little knowledge specialized to the firm, if it is easy to evaluate his performance, and if replacement search costs are modest, the divergence from the ideal will be relatively small and vice versa.

The divergence will also be constrained by the market for the firm itself, that is, by capital markets. Owners always have the option of selling their firm, either as a unit or piecemeal. Owners of manager-operated firms can and do sample the capital market from time to time. If they discover that the value of the future earnings stream to others is higher than the value of the firm to them given that it is to be manager-operated, they can exercise their right to sell. It is conceivable that other owners could be more efficient at monitoring or even that a single individual with appropriate managerial talents and with sufficiently large personal wealth would elect to buy the firm. In this latter case the purchase by such a single individual would completely eliminate the agency costs. If there were a number of such potential owner-manager purchasers (all with talents and tastes identical to the current manager), the owners would receive in the sale price of the firm the full value of the residual claimant rights including the capital value of the eliminated agency costs plus the value of the managerial rights.

Monopoly, competition, and managerial behavior. It is frequently argued that the existence of competition in product (and factor) markets will constrain the behavior of managers to idealized value maximization, that is, that monopoly in product (or monopsony in factor) markets will permit larger divergences from value maximization.[30] Our analysis does not support this hypothesis. The owners of a firm with monopoly power have the same incentives to limit divergences of the manager from value maximization (i.e., the ability to increase their wealth) as do the owners of competitive firms. Furthermore, competition in the market for managers will generally make it unnecessary for the owners to share rents with the manager. The owners of a monopoly firm need only pay the supply price for a manager.

Since the owner of a monopoly has the same wealth incentives to minimize managerial costs as would the owner of a competitive firm, both will undertake that level of monitoring which equates the marginal cost of monitoring to the marginal wealth increment from reduced consumption of perquisites by the manager. Thus, the existence of monopoly will not increase agency costs.

Furthermore, the existence of competition in product and factor markets will not eliminate the agency costs due to managerial control problems, as has often been asserted (see Friedman 1970). If my competitors all incur agency costs equal to or greater than mine, I will not be eliminated from the market by their competition.

The existence and size of the agency costs depend on the nature of the monitoring costs, the tastes of managers for non-pecuniary benefits, and the supply of potential managers who are capable of financing the entire venture out of their personal wealth. If monitoring costs are zero, agency costs will be zero, or if there are enough 100 percent owner-managers available to own and run all the firms in an industry (competitive or not) then agency costs in that industry will also be zero.[31]

3.3   Some Unanswered Questions Regarding the Existence of the Corporate Form

The analysis to this point has left us with a basic puzzle: Why, given the existence of positive costs of the agency relationship, do we find the usual corporate form of organization with widely diffuse ownership so widely prevalent? If one takes seriously much of the literature regarding the "discretionary" power held by managers of large corporations, it is difficult to understand the historical fact of enormous growth in equity in such organizations, not only in the United States, but throughout the world. To paraphrase Alchian (1968): How does it happen that millions of individuals are willing to turn over a significant fraction of their wealth to organizations run by managers who have so little interest in their welfare? What is even more remarkable, why are they willing to make these commitments purely as residual claimants, that is, on the anticipation that managers will operate the firm so that there will be earnings which accrue to the stockholders?

There is certainly no lack of alternative ways that individuals might invest, including entirely different forms of organizations. Even if consideration is limited to corporate organizations, there are clearly alternative ways capital might be raised, for example, through fixed claims of various sorts, bonds, notes, or mortgages. Moreover, the corporate income tax seems to favor the use of fixed claims since interest is treated as a tax-deductible expense. Those who assert that managers do not behave in the interest of stockholders have generally not addressed a very important question: Why, if non-manager-owned shares have such a serious deficiency, have they not long since been driven out by fixed claims?[32]

Some Alternative Explanations of the Ownership Structure of the Firm

The role of limited liability. Manne (1967) and Alchian and Demsetz (1972) argue that one of the attractive features of the corporate form vis-à-vis individual proprietorships or partnerships is the limited liability feature of equity claims in corporations. Without this provision each and every investor purchasing one or more shares of a corporation would be potentially liable to the full extent of his personal wealth for the debts of the corporation. Few individuals would find this a desirable risk to accept, and the major benefits to be obtained from risk reduction through diversification would be to a large extent unobtainable. This argument, however, is incomplete because limited liability does not eliminate the basic risk, it merely shifts it. The argument must rest ultimately on transaction costs. If all stockholders of GM were liable for GM's debts, the maximum liability for an individual shareholder would be greater than it would be if his shares had limited liability. However, given that many other stockholders also existed and that each was liable for the unpaid claims in proportion to his ownership, it is highly unlikely that the maximum payment each would have to make would be large in the event of GM's bankruptcy since the total wealth of those stockholders would also be large. However, the existence of unlimited liability would impose incentives for each shareholder to keep track of both the liabilities of GM and the wealth of the other GM owners. It is easily conceivable that the costs of so doing would, in the aggregate, be much higher than simply paying a premium in the form of higher interest rates to the creditors of GM in return for their acceptance of a contract which grants limited liability to the shareholders. The creditors would then bear the risk of any non-payment of debts in the event of GM's bankruptcy.

It is also not generally recognized that limited liability is merely a necessary condition for explaining the magnitude of the reliance on equities, not a sufficient condition. Ordinary debt also carries limited liability.[33] If limited liability is all that is required, why don't we observe large corporations, individually owned, with a tiny fraction of the capital supplied by the entrepreneur, and the rest simply borrowed?[34] At first this question seems silly to many people (as does the question regarding why firms would ever issue debt or preferred stock under conditions where there are no tax benefits obtained from the treatment of interest or preferred dividend payments).[35] We have found that this question is often misinterpreted to mean why do firms obtain capital. The issue is not why they obtain capital, but why they obtain it through the particular forms we have observed for such long periods of time. The fact is that no well-articulated answer to this question currently exists in the literature of either finance or economics.

The "irrelevance" of capital structure. In their pathbreaking article on the cost of capital, Modigliani and Miller (1958) demonstrated that in the absence of bankruptcy costs and tax subsidies on the payment of interest, the value of the firm is independent of the financial structure. They later (1963) demonstrated that the existence of tax subsidies on interest payments would cause the value of the firm to rise with the amount of debt financing by the amount of the capitalized value of the tax subsidy. But this line of argument implies that the firm should be financed almost entirely with debt. Realizing the inconsistency with observed behavior, Modigliani and Miller comment (1963, p. 442):

> It may be useful to remind readers once again that the existence of a tax advantage for debt financing . . . does not necessarily mean that corporations should at all times seek to use the maximum amount of debt in their capital structures . . . there are as we pointed out, limitations imposed by lenders . . . as well as many other dimensions (and kinds of costs) in real-world problems of financial strategy which are not fully comprehended within the framework of static equilibrium models, either our own or those of the traditional variety. These additional considerations, which are typically grouped under the rubric of "the need for preserving flexibility," will normally imply the maintenance by the corporation of a substantial reserve of untapped borrowing power.

Modigliani and Miller are essentially left without a theory of the determination of the optimal capital structure, and Fama and Miller, commenting on the same issue (1972, p. 173), reiterate this conclusion: "And we must admit that at this point there is little in the way of convincing research, either theoretical or empirical, that explains the amounts of debt that firms do decide to have in their capital structure."

The Modigliani-Miller theorem is based on the assumption that the probability distribution of the cash flows to the firm is independent of the capital structure. It is now recognized that the existence of positive costs associated with bankruptcy and the presence of tax subsidies on corporate interest payments will invalidate this irrelevance theorem precisely because the probability distribution of future cash flows changes as the probability of the incurrence of the bankruptcy costs changes, that is, as the ratio of debt to equity rises. We believe the existence of agency costs provides stronger reasons for arguing that the probability distribution of future cash flows is *not* independent of the capital or ownership structure.

While the introduction of bankruptcy costs in the presence of tax subsidies leads to a theory which defines an optimal capital structure,[36] we argue that this theory is seriously incomplete because it implies that no debt should ever be used in the absence of tax subsidies if bankruptcy costs are positive. Since we know debt was commonly used prior to the existence of the current tax subsidies on interest payments, this theory does not capture what must be some important determinants of the corporate capital structure.

In addition, neither bankruptcy costs nor the existence of tax subsidies can explain the use of preferred stock or warrants which have no tax advantages, and there is no theory that tells us anything about what determines the fraction of equity claims held by insiders as opposed to outsiders, which our analysis in Section 3.2 indicates is so important. We will return to these issues later after analyzing in detail the factors affecting the agency costs associated with debt.

3.4   The Agency Costs of Debt

In general, if the agency costs engendered by the existence of outside owners are positive, the absentee owner (i.e., shareholders) can gain by selling out to an owner-manager who can avoid these costs.[37] This could be accomplished in principle by having the manager become the sole equity holder by repurchasing all of the outside equity claims with funds obtained through the issuance of limited liability debt claims and the use of his own personal wealth. This single-owner corporation would not suffer the agency costs associated with outside equity. Therefore there must be some compelling reasons why we find the diffuse-owner corporate firm financed by equity claims so prevalent as an organizational form.

An ingenious entrepreneur eager to expand has open to him the opportunity to design a whole hierarchy of fixed claims on assets and earnings, with premiums paid for different levels of risk.[38] Why don't we observe large corporations individually owned with a tiny fraction of the capital supplied by the entrepreneur in return for 100 percent of the equity and the rest simply borrowed? We believe there are a number of reasons: (1) the incentive effects associated with highly leveraged firms; (2) the monitoring costs these incentive effects engender; and (3) bankruptcy costs. Furthermore, all of these costs are simply particular aspects of the agency costs associated with the existence of debt claims on the firm.

The Incentive Effects Associated with Debt

We do not find many large firms financed almost entirely with debt-type claims (i.e., non-residual claims) because of the effect such a financial structure would have on the owner-manager's behavior. Potential creditors will not loan $100,000,000 to a firm in which the entrepreneur has an investment of $10,000. With that financial structure the owner-manager will have a strong incentive to engage in activities (investments) which promise very high payoffs if successful even if they have a very low probability of success. If they turn out well, he captures most of the gains; if they turn out badly, the creditors bear most of the costs.[39]

To illustrate the incentive effects associated with the existence of debt and to provide a framework within which we can discuss the effects of monitoring and bonding costs, wealth transfers, and the incidence of agency costs, we again consider a simple situation. Assume we have a manager-owned firm with no debt outstanding in a world in which there are no taxes. The firm has the opportunity to take one of two mutually exclusive equal cost investment opportunities, each of which yields a random payoff, $\overline{X}_j$, T periods in the future ($j = 1,2$). Production and monitoring activities take place continuously between time 0 and time T, and markets in which the claims on the firm can be traded are open continuously over this period. After time T the firm has no productive activities, so the payoff $\overline{X}_j$ includes the distribution of all remaining assets. For simplicity, we assume that the two distributions are log-normally distributed and have the same expected total payoff, $E(\overline{X})$, where $\overline{X}$ is defined as the logarithm of the final payoff. The distributions differ only by their variances with $\sigma_1^2 < \sigma_2^2$. The systematic or covariance risk of each of the distributions, β_j, in the Sharpe (1964)–Lintner (1965) capital asset pricing model, is assumed to be identical. Assuming that asset prices are determined according to the capital asset pricing model, the preceding assumptions imply that the total market value of each of these distributions is identical, and we represent this value by V.

If the owner-manager has the right to decide which investment program to take, and if after he decides this he has the opportunity to sell part or all of his claims on the outcomes in the form of either debt or equity, he will be indifferent between the two investments.[40]

However, if the owner has the opportunity to *first* issue debt, then to decide which of the investments to take, and then to sell all or part of his remaining equity claim on the market, he will not be indifferent between the two investments. The reason is that by promising to take the low variance project, selling bonds, and then taking the high variance project, he can transfer wealth from the (naive) bondholders to himself as equity holder.

Let X^* be the amount of the "fixed" claim in the form of a non-coupon bearing bond sold to the bondholders such that the total payoff to them R_j ($j = 1, 2$, denotes the distribution the manager chooses) is

$$R_j = X^*, \text{ if } \overline{X}_j \geqslant X^*,$$
$$= X_j, \text{ if } \overline{X}_j \leqslant X^*.$$

Let B_1 be the current market value of bondholder claims if investment 1 is taken, and let B_2 be the current market value of bondholder claims if investment 2 is taken. Since in this example the total value of the firm, V, is independent of the investment choice and also of the financing decision, we can use the Black-Scholes (1973) option pricing model to determine the values of the debt, B_j, and equity, S_j, under each of the choices.[41]

Black and Scholes derive the solution for the value of a European call option (one that can be exercised only at the maturity date) and argue that the resulting option pricing equation can be used to determine the value of the equity claim on a leveraged firm. That is, the stockholders in such a firm can be viewed as holding a European call option on the total value of the firm with exercise price equal to X^* (the face value of the debt), exercisable at the maturity date of the debt issue. More simply, the stockholders have the right to buy the firm back from the bondholders for a price of X^* at time T. Merton (1973, 1974) shows that as the variance of the outcome distribution rises the value of the stock (i.e., call option) rises, and since our two distributions differ only in their variances, $\sigma_2^2 > \sigma_1^2$, the equity value S_1 is less than S_2. This implies $B_1 > B_2$, since $B_1 = V - S_1$, and $B_2 = V - S_2$.

Now if the owner-manager could sell bonds with face value X^* under the conditions that the potential bondholders believed this to be a claim on distribution 1, he would receive a price of B_1. After selling the bonds, his equity interest in distribution 1 would have value S_1. But we know S_2 is greater than S_1, and thus the manager can make himself better off by changing the investment to take the higher variance distribution 2, thereby redistributing wealth from the bondholders to himself. All this assumes of course that the bondholders could not prevent him from changing the investment program. *If the bondholders cannot do so, and if they perceive that the manager has the opportunity to take distribution 2, they will pay the manager only B_2 for the claim X^*, realizing that his maximizing behavior will lead him to choose distribution 2. In this* event there is no redistribution of wealth between bondholders and stockholders (and in general with rational expectations there never will be) and no welfare loss. It is easy to construct a case, however, in which these incentive effects do generate real costs.

Let cash flow distribution 2 in the previous example have an expected value, $E(X_2)$, which is lower than that of distribution 1. Then we know that $V_1 > V_2$, and if ΔV, which is given by

$$\Delta V = V_1 - V_2 = (S_1 - S_2) + (B_1 - B_2),$$

is sufficiently small relative to the reduction in the value of the bonds, the value of the stock will increase.[42] Rearranging the expression for ΔV, we see that the difference between the equity values for the two investments is given by

$$S_2 - S_1 = (B_1 - B_2) - (V_1 - V_2),$$

and the first term on the right-hand side, $(B_1 - B_2)$, is the amount of wealth "transferred" from the bondholders and $V_1 - V_2$ is the reduction in overall firm value. Since we know $B_1 > B_2$, $S_2 - S_1$ can be positive even though the reduction in the value of the firm, $V_1 - V_2$, is positive.[43] Again, the bondholders will not actually lose as long as they accurately perceive the motivation of the equity-owning manager and his opportunity to take project 2. They will presume that he will take investment 2, and hence will pay no more than B_2 for the bonds when they are issued.

In this simple example the reduced value of the firm, $V_1 - V_2$, is the agency cost engendered by the issuance of debt[44] and it is borne by the owner-manager. If he could finance the project out of his personal wealth, he would clearly choose project 1 since its investment outlay was assumed equal to that of project 2 and its market value, V_1, was greater. This wealth loss, $V_1 - V_2$, is the "residual loss" portion of what we have defined as agency costs, and it is generated by the cooperation required to raise the funds to make the investment. Another important part of the agency costs is monitoring and bonding costs, and we now consider their role.

The Role of Monitoring and Bonding Costs

In principle it would be possible for the bondholders, by the inclusion of various covenants in the indenture provisions, to limit the managerial behavior that results in reductions in the value of the bonds. Provisions which impose constraints on management's decisions regarding such things as dividends, future debt issues,[45] and maintenance of working capital are not uncommon in bond issues.[46] To completely protect the bondholders from the incentive effects, these provisions would have to be incredibly detailed and cover most operating aspects of the enterprise including limitations on the riskiness of the projects undertaken. The costs involved in writing such provisions, the costs of enforcing them, and the reduced profitability of the firm (induced because the covenants occasionally limit management's ability to take optimal actions on certain issues) would likely be non-trivial. In fact, since management is a continuous decision-making process it will be almost impossible to completely specify such conditions without having the bondholders actually perform the management function. All costs associated with such covenants are what we mean by monitoring costs.

The bondholders will have incentives to engage in the writing of such covenants and in monitoring the actions of the manager to the point where the "nominal" marginal cost to them of such activities is just equal to the marginal benefits they perceive from engaging in them. We use the word "nominal" here because debtholders will not in fact bear these costs. As long as they recognize their existence, they will take them into account in deciding the price they will pay for any given debt claim,[47] and therefore the seller of the claim (the owner) will bear the costs just as in the equity case discussed in Section 3.2.

In addition, the manager has incentives to take into account the costs imposed on the firm by covenants in the debt agreement which directly affect the future cash flows of the firm since they reduce the market value of his claims. Because both the external and the internal monitoring costs are imposed on the owner-manager, it is in his interest to see that the monitoring is performed in the lowest-cost way. Suppose, for example, that the bondholders (or outside equity holders) would find it worthwhile to produce detailed financial statements such as those contained in the usual published accounting reports as a means of monitoring the manager. If the manager himself can produce such information at lower costs than they (perhaps because he is already collecting much of the data they desire for his own internal decision-making purposes), it would pay him to agree in advance to incur the cost of providing such reports and to have their accuracy testified to by an independent outside auditor. This is an example of what we refer to as bonding costs.[48]

Bankruptcy and Reorganization Costs

We argue in Section 3.5 that as the debt in the capital structure increases beyond some point, the marginal agency costs of debt begin to dominate the marginal agency costs of outside equity, and the result of this is the generally observed phenomenon of the simultaneous use of both debt and outside equity. Before discussing these issues, however, we consider here the third major component of the agency costs of debt which helps to explain why debt doesn't completely dominate capital structures—the existence of bankruptcy and reorganization costs.

It is important to emphasize that bankruptcy and liquidation are very different events. The legal definition of bankruptcy is difficult to specify precisely. In general, it occurs when the firm cannot meet a current payment on a debt obligation,[49] or when one or more of the other indenture provisions providing for bankruptcy is violated by the firm. If the total value of the firm is less than the creditors' claims the stockholders have lost all claims on the firm,[50] and the remaining loss, the difference between the face value of the fixed claims and the market value of the firm, is borne by the debtholders. Liquidation of the firm's assets will occur only if the market value of the future cash flows generated by the firm is less than the opportunity cost of the assets, that is, the sum of the values that could be realized if the assets were sold piecemeal.

If there were no costs associated with the event called bankruptcy, the total market value of the firm would not be affected by increasing the probability of its incurrence. However, it is costly, if not impossible, to write contracts representing claims on a firm which clearly delineate the rights of holders for all possible contingencies. Thus even if there were no adverse incentive effects in expanding fixed claims relative to equity in a firm, the use of such fixed claims would be constrained by the costs inherent in defining and enforcing those claims. Firms incur obligations daily to suppliers, to employees, to different classes of investors, and so forth. So long as the firm is prospering, the adjudication of claims is seldom a problem. When the firm has difficulty meeting some of its obligations, however, the issue of the priority of those claims can pose serious problems. This is most obvious in the extreme case where the firm is forced into bankruptcy. If bankruptcy were costless, the reorganization would be accompanied by an adjustment of the claims of various parties and the business could, if that proved to be in the interest of the claimants, simply go on (although perhaps under new management).[51]

In practice, bankruptcy is not costless, but generally involves an adjudication process which itself consumes a fraction of the remaining value of the assets of the firm. Thus the cost of bankruptcy will be of concern to potential buyers of fixed claims in the firm because their existence will reduce the payoffs to them in the event of bankruptcy. These are examples of the agency costs of cooperative efforts among individuals (although in this case perhaps "non-cooperative" would be a better term). The price buyers will be willing to pay for fixed claims will thus be inversely related to the probability of the incurrence of these costs, that is, to the probability of bankruptcy. Using a variant of the argument employed above for monitoring costs, it can be shown that the total value of the firm will fall, and the owner-manager equity holder will bear the entire wealth effect of the bankruptcy costs as long as potential bondholders make unbiased estimates of their magnitude at the time they initially purchase bonds.[52]

Empirical studies of the magnitude of bankruptcy costs are almost nonexistent. Warner (1975) in a study of 11 railroad bankruptcies between 1930 and 1955 estimates the average costs of bankruptcy[53] as a fraction of the value of the firm three years prior to bankruptcy to be 2.5% (with a range of 0.4% to 5.9%). The average dollar costs were $1.88 million. Both of these measures seem remarkably small and are consistent with our belief that bankruptcy costs themselves are unlikely to be the major determinant of corporate capital structures. It is also interesting to note that the annual amount of defaulted funds has fallen significantly since 1940 (see Atkinson 1967). One possible explanation for this phenomenon is that firms are using mergers to avoid the costs of bankruptcy. This hypothesis seems even more reasonable if, as is frequently the case, reorganization costs represent only a fraction of the costs associated with bankruptcy.

In general the revenues or the operating costs of the firm are not independent of the probability of bankruptcy and thus the capital structure of the firm. As the probability of bankruptcy increases, both the operating costs and the revenues of the firm are adversely affected, and some of these costs can be avoided by merger. For example, a firm with a high probability of bankruptcy will also find that it must pay higher salaries to induce executives to accept the higher risk of unemployment. Furthermore, in certain kinds of durable-goods industries the demand function for the firm's product will not be independent of the probability of bankruptcy. The computer industry is a good example. There, the buyer's welfare is dependent to a significant extent on the ability to maintain the equipment, and on continuous hardware and software development. Furthermore, the owner of a large computer often receives benefits from the software developments of other users. Thus if the manufacturer leaves the business or loses his software support and development experts because of financial difficulties, the value of the equipment to his users will decline. The buyers of such services have a continuing interest in the manufacturer's viability not unlike that of a bondholder, except that their benefits come in the form of continuing services at lower cost rather than principal and interest payments. Service facilities and spare parts for automobiles and machinery are other examples.

In summary, then, the agency costs associated with debt[54] consist of:

- the opportunity wealth loss caused by the impact of debt on the investment decisions of the firm;
- the monitoring and bonding expenditures by the bondholders and the owner-manager (i.e., the firm);
- the bankruptcy and reorganization costs.

Why Are the Agency Costs of Debt Incurred?

We have argued that the owner-manager bears the entire wealth effects of the agency costs of debt, and he captures the gains from reducing them. Thus, the agency costs associated with debt discussed above will tend, in the absence of other mitigating factors, to discourage the use of corporate debt. What are the factors that encourage its use?

One factor is the tax subsidy on interest payments. (This will not explain preferred stock where dividends are not tax-deductible.)[55] Modigliani and Miller (1963) originally demonstrated that the use of riskless perpetual debt will increase the total value of the firm (ignoring the agency costs) by an amount equal to τB, where τ is the marginal and average corporate tax rate and B is the market value of the debt. Fama and Miller (1972, chap. 4) demonstrate that for the case of risky debt the value of the firm will increase by the market value of the (uncertain) tax subsidy on the interest payments. Again, these gains will accrue entirely to the equity and will provide an incentive to utilize debt to the point where the marginal wealth benefits of the tax subsidy are just equal to the marginal wealth effects of the agency costs discussed above.

However, even in the absence of these tax benefits, debt would be utilized if the ability to exploit potentially profitable investment opportunities is limited by the resources of the owner. If the owner of a project cannot raise capital, he will suffer an opportunity loss represented by the increment in value offered to him by the additional investment opportunities. Thus even though he will bear the agency costs from selling debt, he will find it desirable to incur them to obtain additional capital as long as the marginal wealth increments from the new investment projects are greater than the marginal agency costs of debt, and these agency costs are in turn less than those caused by the sale of additional equity discussed in Section 3.2. Furthermore, this solution is optimal from the social viewpoint. However, in the absence of tax subsidies on debt these projects must be unique to this firm[56] or they would be taken by other competitive entrepreneurs (perhaps new ones) who possessed the requisite personal wealth to fully finance the projects[57] and therefore would be able to avoid the existence of debt or outside equity.

3.5   A Theory of the Corporate Ownership Structure

In the previous sections we discussed the nature of agency costs associated with outside claims on the firm—both debt and equity. Our purpose here is to integrate these concepts into the beginnings of a theory of the corporate ownership structure. We use the term "ownership structure" rather than "capital structure" to highlight the fact that the crucial variables to be determined are not just the relative amounts of debt and equity but also the fraction of the equity held by the manager. Thus, for a given size firm we want a theory to determine three variables:[58]

S_i: inside equity (held by the manager),
S_o: outside equity (held by anyone outside of the firm),
B: debt (held by anyone outside of the firm).

The total market value of the equity is $S = S_i + S_o$, and the total market value of the firm is $V = S + B$. In addition, we also wish to have a theory which determines the optimal size of the firm, that is, its level of investment.

Determination of the Optimal Ratio of Outside Equity to Debt

Consider first the determination of the optimal ratio of outside equity to debt, S_o/B. To do this let us hold the size of the firm constant. V, the actual value of the firm for a given size, will depend on the agency costs incurred; hence we use as our index of size V^*, the value of the firm at a given scale when agency costs are zero. For the moment we also hold the amount of outside financing $(B+S_o)$ constant. Given that a specified amount of financing $(B+S_o)$ is to be obtained externally, our problem is to determine the optimal fraction $E^* \equiv S_o^*/(B + S_o)$ to be financed with equity.

We argued above that: (1) as long as capital markets are efficient (i.e., characterized by rational expectations) the prices of assets such as debt and outside equity will reflect unbiased estimates of the monitoring costs and redistributions which the agency relationship will engender, and (2) the selling owner-manager will bear these agency costs. Thus from the owner-manager's standpoint the optimal proportion of outside funds to be obtained from equity (versus debt) *for a given level of internal equity* is that E which results in minimum total agency costs.

Figure 3.5 presents a breakdown of the agency costs into two separate components: Define $A_{So}(E)$ as the total agency costs (a function of E) associated with the "exploitation" of the outside equity holders by the owner-manager, and $A_B(E)$ as the total agency costs associated with the presence of debt in the ownership structure. $A_T(E) = A_{So}(E) + A_B(E)$ is the total agency cost.

Consider the function $A_{So}(E)$. When $E \equiv S_o/(B+S_o)$ is zero, that is, when there is no outside equity, the manager's incentive to exploit the outside equity is at a minimum (zero) since the changes in the value of the *total* equity are equal to the changes in *his* equity.[59] As E increases to 100 percent his incentives to exploit the outside equity holders increase and hence the agency costs $A_{So}(E)$ increase.

The agency costs associated with the existence of debt, $A_B(E)$, are composed mainly of the value reductions in the firm and monitoring costs caused by the manager's incentive to reallocate wealth from the bondholders to himself by increasing the value of his equity claim. They are at a maximum where all outside funds are obtained from debt, that is, where $S_o = E = 0$. As the amount of debt declines to zero these costs also go to zero because as E goes to 1, the manager's incentive to reallocate wealth from the bondholders to himself falls. These incentives

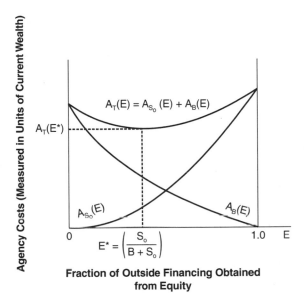

Figure 3.5 Total agency costs, $A_T(E)$, as a function of the ratio of outside equity to total outside financing, $E \equiv S_o/(B+S_o)$, for a given firm size V^* and given total amounts of outside financing $(B+S_o)$. $A_{So}(E) \equiv$ agency costs associated with outside equity. $A_B(E) \equiv$ agency costs associated with debt, B. $A_T(E^*) =$ minimum total agency costs at optimal fraction of outside financing E^*.

fall for two reasons: (1) the total amount of debt falls, and therefore it is more difficult to reallocate any given amount away from the debtholders, and (2) his share of any reallocation that is accomplished is falling since S_o is rising and therefore $S_i/(S_o+S_i)$, his share of the total equity, is falling.

The curve $A_T(E)$ represents the sum of the agency costs from various combinations of outside equity and debt financing, and as long as $A_{So}(E)$ and $A_B(E)$ are as we have drawn them, the minimum total agency cost for a given size firm and outside financing will occur at some point such as $A_T(E^*)$ with a mixture of both debt and equity.[60]

A caveat. Before proceeding further we wish to point out that the issue regarding the exact shapes of the functions drawn in Figure 3.5 and several others discussed below is essentially an open question at this time. In the end, the shape of these functions is a question of fact and can only be settled by empirical evidence. We outline some a priori arguments which we believe lead to some plausible hypotheses about the behavior of the system, but confess that we are far from understanding the many conceptual subtleties of the problem. We are fairly confident of our arguments regarding the signs of the first derivatives of the functions, but the second derivatives are also important to the final solution, and much more work (both theoretical and empirical) is required before we can have much confidence regarding these parameters. We anticipate the work of others as well as our own to cast more light on these issues. Moreover, we suspect the results of such efforts will generate revisions to the details of the material that follows. We believe it is worthwhile to delineate the overall framework in order to demonstrate, if only in a simplified fashion, how the major pieces of the puzzle fit together into a cohesive structure.

Effects of the Scale of Outside Financing

In order to investigate the effects of increasing the amount of outside financing, $B+S_o$, and therefore reducing the amount of equity held by the manager, S_i, we continue to hold the scale of the firm, V^*, constant. Figure 3.6 presents a plot of the agency cost functions $A_{So}(E)$, $A_B(E)$ and $A_T(E) = A_{So}(E) + A_B(E)$, for two different levels of outside financing. Define an index of the amount of outside financing to be

$$K = (B + S_o)/V^*,$$

and consider two different possible levels of outside financing K_o and K_1 for a given scale of the firm such that $K_o < K_1$.

As the amount of outside equity increases, the owner's fractional claim on the firm, α, falls. He will be induced thereby to take additional non-pecuniary benefits out of the firm because his share of the cost falls. This also increases the marginal benefits from monitoring activities and therefore will tend to increase the optimal level of monitoring. Both of these factors will cause the locus of agency costs $A_{So}(E;K)$ to shift upward as the fraction of outside financing, K, increases. This is depicted in Figure 3.6 by the two curves representing the agency costs of equity, one for the low level of outside financing, $A_{So}(E;K_o)$, the other for the high level of outside financing, $A_{So}(E;K_1)$. The locus of the latter lies above the former everywhere except at the origin, where both are zero.

The agency cost of debt will similarly rise as the amount of outside financing increases. This means that the locus of $A_B(E;K_1)$ for high outside financing, K_1, will lie above the locus of $A_B(E;K_o)$ for low outside

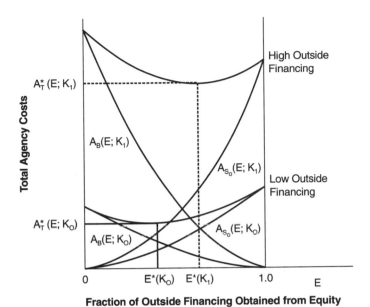

Figure 3.6 Agency cost functions and optimal outside equity as a fraction of total outside financing, $E^*(K)$, for two different levels of outside financing. K, for a given size firm, $V^* : K_1 > K_o$.

financing, K_o, because the total amount of resources which can be reallocated from bondholders increases as the total amount of debt increases. However, since these costs are zero when the debt is zero for both K_o and K_1 the intercepts of the $A_B(E;K)$ curves coincide at the right axis.

The net effect of the increased use of outside financing given the cost functions assumed in Figure 3.6 is: (1) to increase the total agency costs from $A_T(E^*;K_o)$ to $A_T(E^*;K_1)$, and (2) to increase the optimal fraction of outside funds obtained from the sale of outside equity. We draw these functions for illustration only and are unwilling to speculate at this time on the exact form of $E^*(K)$ which gives the general effects of increasing outside financing on the relative quantities of debt and equity.

The locus of points $A_T(E^*;K)$ where agency costs are minimized (not shown in Figure 3.6) determines $E^*(K)$, the optimal proportions of equity and debt to be used in obtaining outside funds as the fraction of outside funds, K, ranges from 0 to 100 percent. The solid line in Figure 3.7 is a plot of the minimum total agency costs as a function of the amount of outside financing for a firm with scale V_0^*. The dotted line

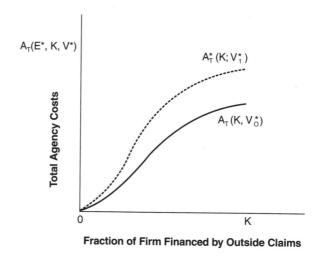

Figure 3.7 Total agency costs as a function of the fraction of the firm financed by outside claims for two firm sizes, $V_1^* > V_0^*$.

shows the total agency costs for a larger firm with scale $V_1^* > V_0^*$. That is, we hypothesize that the larger the firm becomes, the larger are the total agency costs because it is likely that the monitoring function is inherently more difficult and expensive in a larger organization.

Risk and the Demand for Outside Financing

The model we have used to explain the existence of minority shareholders and debt in the capital structure of corporations implies that the owner-manager, if he resorts to any outside funding, will have his entire wealth invested in the firm. The reason is that he can thereby avoid the agency costs that additional outside funding imposes. This suggests that he would not resort to outside funding until he had invested 100 percent of his personal wealth in the firm—an implication which is not consistent with what we generally observe. Most owner-managers hold personal wealth in a variety of forms, and some have only a relatively small fraction of their wealth invested in the corporation they manage.[61] Diversification on the part of owner-managers can be explained by risk aversion and optimal portfolio selection.

If the returns from assets are not perfectly correlated, an individual can reduce the riskiness of the returns on his portfolio by dividing his wealth among many different assets, that is, by diversifying.[62] Thus a manager who invests all of his wealth in a single firm (his own) will generally bear a welfare loss (if he is risk-averse) because he is bearing more risk than necessary. He will, of course, be willing to pay something to avoid this risk, and the costs he must bear to accomplish this diversification will be the agency costs outlined above. He will suffer a wealth loss as he reduces his fractional ownership because prospective shareholders and bondholders will take into account the agency costs. Nevertheless, the manager's desire to avoid risk will contribute to his becoming a minority stockholder.

Determination of the Optimal Amount of Outside Financing, K^*

Assume for the moment that the owner of a project (i.e., the owner of a prospective firm) has enough wealth to finance the entire project himself. The optimal scale of the corporation is then determined by the condition that $\Delta V - \Delta I = 0$. In general, if the returns to the firm are uncertain, the owner-manager can increase his welfare by selling off part of the firm as either debt or equity and reinvesting the proceeds in other assets. If he does this with the optimal combination of debt and equity (as in Figure 3.6), the total wealth reduction he will incur is given by the agency cost function, $A_T(E^*,K;V^*)$ in Figure 3.7. The functions $A_T(E^*,K;V^*)$ will be S-shaped (as drawn) if total agency costs for a given scale of firm increase at an increasing rate at low levels of outside financing, and at a decreasing rate for high levels of outside financing as monitoring imposes more and more constraints on the manager's actions.

Figure 3.8 shows marginal agency costs as a function of K, the fraction of the firm financed with outside funds assuming the total agency cost function is as plotted in Figure 3.7, and assuming the scale of the firm is fixed. The demand by the owner-manager for outside financing is shown by the remaining curve in Figure 3.8. This curve represents the marginal value of the increased diversification which the manager can obtain by reducing his ownership claims and optimally constructing a diversified portfolio. It is measured by the amount he would pay to be allowed to reduce his ownership claims by a dollar in order to increase his diversification. If the liquidation of some of his holdings also influences the owner-manager's consumption set, the demand function plotted in Figure 3.8 also incorporates the marginal value of these effects. The intersection of these two schedules determines the optimal frac-

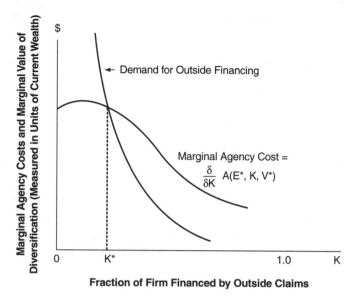

Figure 3.8 Determination of the optimal amount of outside financing, K^*, for a given scale of firm.

tion of the firm to be held by outsiders, and this in turn determines the total agency costs borne by the owner. This solution is Pareto-optimal; there is no way to reduce the agency costs without making someone worse off.

Determination of the Optimal Scale of the Firm

While the details of the solution of the optimal scale of the firm are complicated when we allow for the issuance of debt, equity, and monitoring and bonding, the general structure of the solution is analogous to the case where monitoring and bonding are allowed for the outside equity example (see Figure 3.4 on p. 72).

If it is optimal to issue any debt, the expansion path taking full account of such opportunities must lie above the curve ZG in Figure 3.4. If this new expansion path lies anywhere to the right of the indifference curve passing through point G, debt will be used in the optimal financing package. Furthermore, the optimal scale of the firm will be determined by the point at which this new expansion path touches the highest indifference curve. In this situation the resulting level of the owner-manager's welfare must therefore be higher.

3.6 Qualifications and Extensions of the Analysis

Multiperiod Aspects of the Agency Problem

We have assumed throughout our analysis that we are dealing only with a single investment-financing decision by the entrepreneur and have ignored the issues associated with the incentives affecting future financing-investment decisions which might arise after the initial set of contracts are consummated between the entrepreneur-manager, outside stockholders, and bondholders. These are important issues which are left for future analysis.[63] Their solution will undoubtedly introduce some changes in the conclusions of the single decision analysis. It seems clear, for instance, that the expectation of future sales of outside equity and debt will change the costs and benefits facing the manager in making decisions which benefit himself at the (short-run) expense of the current bondholders and stockholders. If he develops a reputation for such dealings, he can expect this to influence unfavorably the terms at which he can obtain future capital from outside sources. This will tend to increase the benefits associated with "sainthood" and will tend to reduce the size of the agency costs. Given the finite life of any individual, however, such an effect cannot reduce these costs to zero, because at some point these future costs will begin to weigh more heavily on his successors and therefore the relative benefits to him of acting in his own best interests will rise.[64] Furthermore, it will generally be impossible for him to fully guarantee to outside interests that his successor will continue to follow his policies.

The Control Problem and the Outside Owner's Agency Costs

The careful reader will notice that nowhere in the analysis thus far have we taken into account many of the details of the relationship between the part owner-manager and the outside stockholders and bondholders. In particular, we have assumed that all outside equity is nonvoting. If such equity does have voting rights, then the manager will be concerned about the effects on his long-run welfare of reducing his fractional ownership below the point where he loses effective control of the corporation—that is, below the point where it becomes possible for the outside equity holders to fire him. A complete analysis of this issue will require a careful specification of the contractual rights involved on both sides, the role of the board of directors, and the coordination (agency) costs borne by the stockholders in implementing policy changes. This latter point involves consideration of the distribution of the outside ownership claims. Simply put, forces exist to determine an equilibrium distribution of outside ownership. If the costs of reducing the dispersion of ownership are lower than the benefits to be obtained from reducing the agency costs, it will pay some individual or group of individuals to buy shares in the market to reduce the dispersion of ownership. We occasionally witness these conflicts for control which involve outright market purchases, tender offers, and proxy fights. Further analysis of these issues is left to the future.

A Note on the Existence of Inside Debt and Some Conjectures on the Use of Convertible Financial Instruments

We have been asked[65] why debt held by the manager (i.e., "inside debt") plays no role in our analysis. We have as yet been unable to incorporate this dimension formally into our analysis in a satisfactory way. The question is a good one and suggests some potentially important extensions of the analysis. For instance, it suggests an inexpensive way for the owner-manager with both equity and debt outstanding to eliminate a large part (perhaps all) of the agency costs of debt. If he binds himself contractually to hold a fraction of the total debt equal to his fractional ownership of the total equity, he would have no incentive whatsoever to reallocate wealth from the debtholders to the stockholders. Consider the case where

$$B_i/S_i = B_o/S_o, \tag{4}$$

where S_i and S_o are as defined earlier, B_i is the dollar value of the inside debt held by the owner-manager, and B_o is the debt held by outsiders. In this case, if the manager changes the investment policy of the firm to reallocate wealth between the debt and equity holders, the net effect on the total value of his holdings in the firm will be zero. Therefore, his incentives to perform such reallocations are zero.[66]

Why then do we not observe practices or formal contracts which accomplish this elimination or reduction of the agency costs of debt? Maybe we do for smaller privately held firms (we have not attempted to obtain this data), but for large, diffuse owner corporations the practice does not seem to be common. One reason for this, we believe, is that in some respects the claim that the manager holds on the firm in the form of his wage contract has some of the characteristics of debt.[67] If true, this implies that even with zero holdings of formal debt claims he still has positive holdings of a quasi-debt claim, and this may accomplish the satisfaction of condition (4). The problem here is that any formal analysis of this issue requires a much deeper understanding of the relationship between formal debt holdings and the wage contract; that is, how much debt is it equivalent to?

This line of thought also suggests some other interesting issues. Suppose the implicit debt characteristics of the manager's wage contract result in a situation equivalent to

$$B_i/S_i > B_o/S_o.$$

Then he would have incentives to change the operating characteristics of the firm (i.e., reduce the variance of the outcome distribution) to transfer wealth from the stockholders to the debtholders, which is the reverse of the situation we examined in Section 3.4. Furthermore, this seems to capture some of the concern often expressed regarding the fact that managers of large publicly held corporations seem to behave in a risk-averse way to the detriment of the equity holders. One solution to this would be to establish incentive compensation systems for the manager or to give him stock options which in effect give him a claim on the upper tail of the outcome distribution. This also seems to be a commonly observed phenomenon.

This analysis also suggests some additional issues regarding the costs and benefits associated with the use of more complicated financial claims such as warrants, convertible bonds, and convertible preferred stock which we have not yet formally analyzed. Warrants, convertible bonds, and convertible preferred stock have some of the characteristics of non-voting shares, although they can be converted into voting shares under some terms. Alchian and Demsetz (1972) provide an interesting analysis regarding the use of non-voting shares. They argue that some shareholders with strong beliefs in the talents and judgments of the manager will want to be protected against the possibility that some other shareholders will take over and limit the actions of the manager (or fire him). Given that the securities exchanges prohibit the use of non-voting shares by listed firms, the use of the option-type securities might be a substitute for these claims.

In addition, warrants represent a claim on the upper tail of the distribution of outcomes, and convertible securities can be thought of as securities with nondetachable warrants. It seems that the incentive effect of warrants would tend to offset to some extent the incentive effects of the existence of risky debt because the owner-manager would be sharing part of the proceeds associated with a shift in the distribution of returns with the warrant holders. Thus, we conjecture that potential bondholders will find it attractive to have warrants attached to the risky debt of firms in which it is relatively easy to shift the distribution of outcomes to expand the upper tail of the distribution to transfer wealth from bondholders. It would also then be attractive to the owner-manager because of the reduction in the agency costs which he would bear. This argument also implies that it would make little difference if the warrants were detachable (and therefore saleable separately from the bonds) since their mere existence would reduce the incentives of the manager (or stockholders) to increase the riskiness of the firm (and therefore increase the probability of bankruptcy). Furthermore, the addition of a conversion privilege to fixed claims such as debt or preferred stock would also tend to reduce the incentive effects of the existence of such fixed claims and therefore lower the agency costs associated with them. The theory predicts that these phenomena should be more frequently observed in cases where the incentive effects of such fixed claims are high than when they are low.

Monitoring and the Social Product of Security Analysts

One of the areas in which further analysis is likely to lead to high payoffs is that of monitoring. We currently have little work that could be glorified by the title of a "Theory of Monitoring," and yet this is a crucial building block of the analysis. We would expect monitoring activities to become specialized to those institutions and individuals who possess comparative advantages in these activities. One of the groups who seem to play a large role in these activities is composed of the security analysts employed by institutional investors, brokers, and investment advisory services as well as the analysis performed by individual investors in the normal course of investment decision making.

A large body of evidence exists which indicates that security prices incorporate in an unbiased manner all publicly available information and much of what might be called "private information."[68] There is also a large body of evidence which indicates that the security analysis ac-

tivities of mutual funds and other institutional investors are not reflected in portfolio returns, that is, they do not increase risk-adjusted
portfolio returns over a naive random selection buy-and-hold strategy.[69]
Therefore, some have been tempted to conclude that the resources ex-
pended on such research activities to find under- or over-valued securities is a social loss. In an earlier paper (Jensen 1975) I argued that this
conclusion cannot be unambiguously drawn because there is a large
consumption element in the demand for these services.

Furthermore, the analysis of this chapter would seem to indicate that
to the extent that security analysis activities reduce the agency costs
associated with the separation of ownership and control, they are indeed socially productive. Moreover, if this is true, we expect the major
benefits of the security analysis activity to be reflected in the higher
capitalized value of the ownership claims to corporations and *not* in the
period-to-period portfolio returns of the analyst. Equilibrium in the
security analysis industry requires that the private returns to analysis
(i.e., portfolio returns) must be just equal to the private costs of such
activity,[70] and this will not reflect the social product of this activity
which will consist of larger output and higher *levels* of the capital value
of ownership claims. Therefore, the argument implies that if there is
a non-optimal amount of security analysis being performed, it is too
much,[71] not too little (since the shareholders would be willing to pay
directly to have the "optimal" monitoring performed), and we do not
seem to observe such payments.

Specialization in the Use of Debt and Equity

Our previous analysis of agency costs suggests at least one other testable hypothesis: namely, that in those industries where the incentive
effects of outside equity or debt are widely different, we would expect
to see specialization in the use of the low agency cost financing arrangement. In industries where it is relatively easy for managers to lower the
mean value of the outcomes of the enterprise by outright theft, special
treatment of favored customers, ease of consumption of leisure on the
job, and so forth (for example, the bar and restaurant industry), we
would expect to see the ownership structure of firms characterized by
relatively little outside equity (i.e., 100 percent ownership of the equity
by the manager) with almost all outside capital obtained through the
use of debt.

The theory predicts that the opposite would be true where the incentive effects of debt are large relative to the incentive effects of equity. Firms like conglomerates, in which it would be easy to shift outcome distributions adversely for bondholders (by changing the acquisition or divestiture policy), should be characterized by relatively lower utilization of debt. Conversely, in industries where the freedom of management to take riskier projects is severely constrained (for example, regulated industries such as public utilities), we should find more intensive use of debt financing.

The analysis suggests that in addition to the fairly well understood role of uncertainty in the determination of the quality of collateral, there is at least one other element of great importance—the ability of the owner of the collateral to change the distribution of outcomes by shifting either the mean outcome or the variance of the outcomes. A study of bank lending policies should reveal these to be important aspects of the contractual practices observed there.

Application of the Analysis to the Large Diffuse Ownership Corporation

While we believe that the structure outlined in the preceding pages is applicable to a wide range of corporations, it is still in an incomplete state. One of the most serious limitations of the analysis is that, as it stands, we have not worked out its application to the very large modern corporation whose managers own little or no equity. We believe our approach can be applied to this case, but the details must await future work.

The Supply Side of the Incomplete Markets Question

The analysis of this chapter is also relevant to the incomplete market issue considered by Arrow (1964a, 1964b), Diamond (1967), Hakansson (1974a, 1974b), Rubinstein (1974a, 1974b), Ross (1974), and others. The problems addressed in this literature derive from the fact that whenever the available set of financial claims on outcomes in a market fails to span the underlying state space (see Arrow 1964a, 1964b; Debreu 1959), the resulting allocation is Pareto-inefficient. A disturbing element in this literature surrounds the fact that the inefficiency conclusion is generally drawn without explicit attention in the analysis to the costs of creating new claims or of maintaining the expanded set of markets called for to bring about the welfare improvement.

The demonstration of a possible welfare improvement from the expansion of the set of claims by the introduction of new basic contingent claims or options can be thought of as an analysis of the demand conditions for new markets. Viewed from this perspective, what is missing in the literature on this problem is the formulation of a positive analysis of the supply of markets (or the supply of contingent claims). That is, what is it in the maximizing behavior of individuals in the economy that causes them to create and sell contingent claims of various sorts?

The analysis in this chapter can be viewed as a small first step in the direction of formulating an analysis of the supply of markets issue, which is founded in the self-interested maximizing behavior of individuals. We have shown why it is in the interest of a wealth-maximizing entrepreneur to create and sell claims such as debt and equity. Furthermore, as we have indicated, it appears that extensions of these arguments will lead to a theory of the supply of warrants, convertible bonds, and convertible preferred stock. We are not suggesting that the specific analysis offered above is likely to be sufficient to lead to a theory of the supply of the wide range of contracts (both existing and merely potential) in the world at large. However, we do believe that framing the question of the completeness of markets in terms of the joining of both the demand and supply conditions will be very fruitful instead of implicitly assuming that new claims spring forth from some (costless) wellhead of creativity unaided or unsupported by human effort.

3.7   Conclusions

The publicly held business corporation is an awe-inspiring social invention. Millions of individuals voluntarily entrust billions of dollars, francs, pesos, and so on of personal wealth to the care of managers on the basis of a complex set of contracting relationships which delineate the rights of the parties involved. The growth in the use of the corporate form as well as the growth in market value of established corporations suggests that, at least up to the present, creditors and investors have by and large not been disappointed with the results, despite the agency costs inherent in the corporate form.

Agency costs are as real as any other costs. The level of agency costs depends, among other things, on statutory and common law and human ingenuity in devising contracts. Both the law and the sophistication of contracts relevant to the modern corporation are the products of a historical process in which there were strong incentives for individuals to minimize agency costs. Moreover, there were alternative organizational forms available, and opportunities to invent new ones. Whatever its shortcomings, the corporation has thus far survived the market test against potential alternatives.

4 | Specific and General Knowledge and Organizational Structure

4.1   Introduction

In this chapter we analyze the institutional devices through which decision-making rights are assigned in markets and within firms and the devices used to motivate agents to make proper decisions. We focus on how the costs of transferring information between agents influence the organization of markets and firms.

Specific and General Knowledge

We define *specific knowledge* as knowledge that is costly to transfer among agents and *general knowledge* as knowledge that is inexpensive to transmit. Because it is costly to transfer, getting specific knowledge used in decision making requires decentralizing many decision rights both in the economy and in firms. Such delegation, in turn, creates two problems: the rights assignment problem (determining who should exercise a decision right), and the control or agency problem (how to ensure that self-interested decision agents exercise their rights in a way that contributes to the organizational objective).

Capitalist economic systems solve the rights assignment and control problems by granting *alienability* of decision rights to decision agents. A right is alienable if its owner has the right to sell a right and capture the proceeds offered in the exchange. Indeed, we define ownership to mean possession of a decision right along with the right to alienate that right, and we believe that when people use the word "ownership" that is what is meant. This combination of a decision right with the right to alienate that right is also what is generally meant by the term "property right" so frequently used in economics (see, for example, Coase 1960;

By Michael C. Jensen and William H. Meckling; originally published in *Contract Economics*, ed. Lars Werin and Hans Wijkander (Oxford: Blackwell, 1992).

Alchian and Allen 1983, p. 91). In contrast to markets, organizations generally do not delegate both decision rights and the alienability of those rights to the agent. A machine operator might be delegated the rights to operate and maintain a machine, but not the rights to sell it and pocket the proceeds. In the absence of alienability, organizations must solve both the rights assignment and control problems by alternative systems and procedures. We will discuss the critical role that alienability plays in the market system and some of the substitute control mechanisms used in firms.

Colocation of Knowledge and Decision Authority

F. A. Hayek was an early proponent of the importance of knowledge and its distribution to a well-functioning economy. In his seminal article entitled "The Use of Knowledge in Society," Hayek (1945, pp. 519ff.) argues that most economists, as well as advocates of centralized planning, misunderstand the nature of the economic problem. "The economic problem of society is . . . not merely a problem of how to allocate 'given' resources—if 'given' is taken to mean given to a single mind . . . It is rather a problem of how to secure the best use of resources known to any of the members of society . . . a problem of the utilization of knowledge which is not given to anyone in its totality." Hayek's insight was that an organization's performance depends on the colocation of decision-making authority with the knowledge important to those decisions.[1] He argues that the distribution of knowledge in society calls for decentralization:

> If we agree that the economic problem of society is mainly one of rapid adaptation to changes in the particular circumstances of time and place, decisions must be left to the people who are familiar with these circumstances, who know directly of the relevant changes and of the resources immediately available to meet them. We cannot expect that this problem will be solved by first communicating all this knowledge to a central board which, after integrating all knowledge, issues its orders. We must solve it by some form of decentralization. (Hayek 1945, p. 524)

Hayek's pioneering work provides a point of departure for analyzing how the distribution of knowledge affects organizational structure and its critical role in the development of a theory of organization. Hayek presumes that markets automatically move decision rights to the agents with the relevant knowledge, and that those agents will use the decision rights properly. Unfortunately, he never discusses how this occurs. We show how understanding this issue provides insights into the organizational and managerial problems of firms.

In Section 4.2 we discuss the limits of human mental capacities and their implications for the costs of transferring knowledge. Section 4.3 defines the characteristics of decision rights and rights systems. Section 4.4 discusses the functions of alienability, its role in solving the rights assignment and control problems in markets, and the implications of the market solution for the internal problems faced by organizations that cannot use alienability to solve the rights assignment and control problem. Section 4.5 analyzes the problems of the firm in colocating decision rights and specific knowledge, and Section 4.6 discusses the technology for partitioning decision rights within the firm. Section 4.7 deals with internal control systems, and Section 4.8 concludes the chapter.

4.2   Knowledge

Limitations on Human Sensory and Mental Faculties

The opportunity set confronting an individual or a firm is a function of the individual's knowledge. Decision makers have limited knowledge at two levels. "Technological feasibility" reflects currently limited human knowledge about physical laws. Economic analysis reflects this limitation in the statement that knowledge is given and depends on the state of technology at the time.

The second limitation on knowledge, and the one of more concern here, is due to physical limitations specific to each individual, what March and Simon (1958) labeled "bounded rationality" (see also Simon 1955, 1959). Humans have limited mental capability. The computers and sensory systems with which we are individually endowed are a scarce resource with limited storage and processing capability, as well as limited input and output channels. The limitations on human mental and sensory faculties mean that storing, processing, transmitting, and receiving knowledge are costly activities. This limited capacity of the brain means that knowledge possessed by any individual decision maker or group of decision makers is thereby limited to a minuscule subset of the knowledge known to humanity. While decision makers seldom, if ever, possess all available knowledge, they are constantly creating new knowledge. In maximizing their objective functions, decision makers deliberately seek out knowledge (including knowledge about what decisions to consider).

When knowledge is valuable in decision making, there are benefits to colocating decision authority with the knowledge that is valuable to those decisions. There are two ways to colocate knowledge and decision rights. One is by moving the knowledge to those with the decision rights; the other is by moving the decision rights to those with the knowledge. The process for moving knowledge to those with decision rights has received much attention from researchers and designers of management information systems. But the process for moving decision rights to those with the relevant knowledge has received relatively little attention in either economics or management.

In a market system, colocation of decision rights and knowledge occurs either when those with decision rights expend resources to acquire the knowledge or when those with knowledge buy the decision rights. When the cost of moving knowledge is higher than the cost of moving decision rights, knowledge holders will value the decision rights more highly and will purchase them. Therefore, optimizing behavior on the part of individuals causes the distribution of decision-making rights in the economy to reflect the limitations of human mental and sensory systems.

Knowledge and the Cost of Transfer

Although knowledge has many characteristics of potential interest, we concentrate here only on the cost of transferring knowledge between people. The cost of transferring knowledge depends on factors such as the nature of the knowledge, the organizational environment, and technology. We use the terms "specific" and "general" knowledge to distinguish between knowledge at the extremes of the continuum measuring transfer costs. The more costly knowledge is to transfer, the more specific it is, and the less costly the knowledge is to transfer the more general it is.

Transfer, as we use it, means effective transfer, not merely communication. The recipient of knowledge is presumed to understand the message well enough to act on it. The simple purchase of a physics book is not sufficient to transfer the knowledge to the purchaser (as evidenced by students who regularly pay thousands of dollars for help in acquiring such knowledge). Thus, transfer involves the use of storage and processing capacity as well as input/output channels of the human brain. Moreover, knowledge transfers are not instantaneous; it takes people time to absorb information. These delays are costly, and for some decisions such cost can be high, including even the complete loss of opportunities.

Hayek (1945) takes the distribution of knowledge in the economy as given and thus never mentions the cost of transferring or producing knowledge, even though it is logically the foundation of his analysis.[2] Writing during the 1940s British debate over central planning, he attacks central planners on grounds that they will make bad decisions because they will not (indeed cannot) have knowledge of "particular circumstances of time and place." As examples of such knowledge he cites a not-fully-employed machine, someone's particular skills, surplus stock, empty or half-filled freighters, temporary opportunities in real estate, and commodity price differences. Hayek points out that conveying knowledge of particular circumstances to a central authority in statistical form is impossible.

Even though it is costly, we do observe situations in which colocation is achieved by transferring knowledge. Formal educational programs and the collection, analysis, and dissemination of data are obvious examples. Some firms, such as United and American Airlines, achieved a major competitive advantage with computerized reservation and pricing systems that reduced the cost of transferring knowledge about prices, empty seats, and schedules (see Copeland and McKenney 1990). Particularly challenging information transfer problems arise in situations where optimal decision making requires integration of specific knowledge located in widely separate individuals. Integrating the specific knowledge of marketing, manufacturing, and R&D personnel to design and bring a new product to the market is an example.

While the general applicability of scientific knowledge distinguishes it from idiosyncratic knowledge, it is costly to transfer between agents and, therefore, also falls in the category of specific knowledge. Science creates order out of chaos by excising particulars and providing general rules of cause and effect relations. Scientific knowledge is an essential ingredient in decisions, because it provides the basis for predicting the outcomes of alternative courses of action. At the level of the firm, scientific knowledge plays a central role in the resolution of the key questions that economists address—what to produce and how to produce it. For example, the design and development of products from machinery and buildings to household appliances and drugs depend critically on scientific knowledge.

In addition to scientific and idiosyncratic knowledge, knowledge produced by assembling and analyzing knowledge of particular circumstances (through time and/or across circumstances such as location, income, education, age) is a significant input to decision making. For example, the entrepreneur who wants to capitalize on a particular half-filled freighter must be able to identify the freighter, its location, its cargo capability, and so forth. On the other hand, someone deciding whether to become an agent to increase the utilization of freighters will want to assemble knowledge about how many partially filled freighters there are, what routes they follow, what kinds of cargo capacity they have, and so on—knowledge that abstracts from the particular circumstances crucial to utilizing fully a particular freighter. Assembled knowledge includes, but is not limited to, that generated by formal statistical methods.

Assembled knowledge also includes knowledge gleaned from experience. Examples include the exercise of skills such as machine operation, writing, mathematics, or statistics. Knowledge of law, of accounting practices, of contracting practices, of the rules that govern the operation of organized exchanges, and the like is also an important input to decision making. Assembled knowledge can be either general (as is likely to be true of the output of statistical manipulation of basic data) or specific (as is likely to be true of experiential knowledge).

4.3   Rights Systems

A decision right is the right to decide on and to take an action. Decision rights are the basis for saying that individuals have the "power" to make decisions and to take actions with resources. Power means that a decision made by a party will be operative. In modern societies the ultimate source of this power is the police powers—the threat of physical violence by the state. An entity has the right to take an action with a specific object, if the police powers of the state will be used to help ensure its ability to take the action. The right to choose what action will be taken is an important part of possessing a right. The word "right" in this context has no normative content.

In any developed social system the right to take actions with specific physical objects, including our persons, is assigned to specific individuals or organizations. In a private-property capitalist system most of these rights are assigned to private individuals or organizations. In a socialist or communist system most of these rights are assigned to the state or the governing party.

Although it is not commonly emphasized,[3] the usual economic analysis of the price system is founded on the existence of a system of privately "owned" rights. There are two actions of special importance that are an integral part of ownership of a right in a resource: the right to sell the resource (more accurately, to sell rights in the resource) and the right to capture the proceeds of the sale.[4] Thus, the objects of exchange in markets are not physical articles per se, but bundles of rights attached to those articles.[5] It is this system of *alienable rights* (almost universally characterized erroneously in our profession as "the price system") that extends the efficient utilization of resources beyond the capacity of any single mind. It provides incentives to make individuals take appropriate actions without anyone having to direct them.[6] This is what Adam Smith (1776) called the "invisible hand," and his point was that control of human behavior is inherent in markets. The assignment of decision-making rights in modern societies is largely a matter of law.[7] But once assigned, rights are regularly reshuffled by contracts, by purchase and sale, and by managerial assignment within firms. In the case of the United States, the body of law that spells out the assignment of rights is the product of hundreds of years of law-making of three sorts: court decisions (common law), legislative enactments (statutory law, including constitutions), and administrative decrees (administrative law).

The private-property capitalist mechanism is the product of thousands of years of evolution. It is highly complex and embraces a multitude of actions, objects, and individuals. Most important, however, is the fact that it functions as a free-standing system. It is automatic; there is no central direction. With minor exceptions, rights to take almost all conceivable actions with virtually all physical objects are fixed on identifiable individuals or firms at every instant of time. The books are kept up to date despite the burden imposed by dynamic forces, such as births and deaths, dissolutions, and new technology. Disputes arise, but evolution has provided a sophisticated arbitration service, the courts, to deal with that problem as well. The extent to which the legal system enforces property rights (the security of decision rights and the right to alienate them) is a major determinant of the effectiveness of markets.

The failure of socialist and communist economies (whose distinguishing characteristic is the absence of private rights) is now the topic of headlines throughout the world. The difficulties that Eastern bloc countries are having in attempting to establish capitalist market systems to replace their failed systems is testimony to the complexity and value of market systems.[8] These economies provide vivid evidence on the inefficiency and poverty that result from the waste of specific knowledge and the lack of control in the absence of alienable decision rights. Without the assignment of private alienable rights there can be no true market system. Thus, given their failure to establish alienable private rights in resources, it is not surprising that many of these countries are failing in their attempt to create effective market systems.

4.4   The Functions of Alienability

The alienability of rights deserves special attention in analyzing both markets and organizations because understanding the function of alienability in markets clarifies several critical functions that must be performed in organizations. The analysis thereby focuses attention on the critical issues to be resolved by scholars and practicing managers in their efforts to understand and manage organizations.

Alienability is the effective combination of two rights: the right to sell or transfer rights and the right to capture the proceeds of exchange.[9] Alienability is not only a necessary condition to exchange, it is the foundation of markets and the institutional device through which markets colocate knowledge with decision rights and control decision makers.

Alienability solves the rights assignment problem. When decision rights are alienable, voluntary exchange creates a process in which the purchase and sale of rights by maximizing individuals colocates knowledge and decision rights. It does so by conveying decision rights to the site of knowledge. In a market system, decision rights are acquired through exchange by those who have knowledge. Voluntary exchange ensures that decision rights will tend to be acquired by those who value them most highly, and this will be those who have specific knowledge and abilities that are most valuable to the exercise of the right.

Control is the process and rules governing the measures of performance, and the rewards and punishments meted out in response to individual actions. Control and knowledge are complements in the analysis of organizations. Knowledge and the decision rights possessed by the individual, as well as the state of the world, define the opportunity set from which individual decision makers can choose. The control system plays a major role in determining which choices individuals make from their opportunity sets.

Alienability solves the control problem. By colocating decision rights with rights to their capital value, alienability provides both a measure of performance for individual decision makers and rewards and punishments to motivate them to use those decision rights efficiently. Market prices for alienable rights reveal the value of assets in alternative uses to current rights holders as well as to potential rights holders. Where resources produce future flows of revenue or consumption services, and rights to those flows are alienable, prices represent the present value of claims to those future flows. These capitalized values perform two important functions in controlling human behavior:

1. They provide a measure of the performance of the parties who have the rights to decide how the asset or assets will be used.
2. They provide the reward or punishment that accrues to the owners of the rights as a result of their decisions.

The colocation of decision rights with rights to their capital value accomplished by alienability thus both measures the performance of individuals and capitalizes the wealth consequences of an individual's decisions upon that person. The decision maker who chooses an action that lowers the value of rights assigned to him or her bears the costs. When the decision maker chooses actions that enhance the value of the rights, he or she captures the increased value. The major problems with the market control system occur when the legal or technological environments create externalities by not allowing for the definition and assignment of rights that cause an individual to bear the full costs or to capture the full rewards of his or her actions. Pollution or nonpatentable inventions are good examples of situations in which decision makers do not bear the full costs or benefits of their actions.

The problems that arose in organizing in Eastern bloc countries without alienability highlight the significance of alienability to organizational structure and efficiency. But the internal organization of the capitalist firm is also an instance of the absence of alienable decision rights.

Indeed, we distinguish activities within the firm from activities between the firm and the rest of the world by whether alienability is transferred to agents along with the decision rights. In this view, transfers of decision rights without the right to alienate those rights are intra-firm transactions. While firms can sell assets, workers in firms generally do not receive the rights to alienate their positions or any other assets or decision rights under their control. They cannot pocket the proceeds. This means that there is no automatic decentralized process which tends to ensure that decision rights in the firm migrate to the agents that have the specific knowledge relevant to their exercise, and that there is no automatic performance measurement and reward system that motivates agents to use their decision rights in the interest of the organization. Explicit managerial direction and the creation of mechanisms to substitute for alienability are required.

The Existence of Firms

Pushed to its logical extreme, our focus on specific knowledge implies more or less complete atomization of the economy. There is no room for the firm. Firms as we know them would not exist if alienability of all decision rights were granted to each agent along with the rights. There would be nothing left over for the residual claimants in the enterprise, be they entrepreneurs, partners, or stockholders.

Firms must obtain advantages from the suppression of alienability that are large enough to offset the costs associated with its absence, or they could not survive open competition with independent agents. Such advantages could come from economies of scale or scope, or the reduction of transaction costs that could not be obtained by independent contracting agents.

Knowledge considerations are one cause for the emergence of firms. Indeed, Demsetz (1988, p. 159) argues that "conservation of expenditures on knowledge" determines the vertical boundaries of the firm. Bringing diverse knowledge together to bear on decisions significantly expands the opportunity set because no one person is likely to possess the set of knowledge relevant to a particular decision. In principle, an entrepreneur could assemble the relevant knowledge by individual exchanges, and knowledge transfer on a quid pro quo basis is not an uncommon phenomenon. Consulting and legal services provide obvious examples, and so do the network organizations growing in the United States that contract out most internal functions common to organizations (see Kensinger and Martin 1991).

Where the production, transfer, and application of knowledge are the primary goods being offered, however, exchanges tend to take the form of long-term relationships, and the most common of these is employment contracts. Such contracts tend to be general in nature—the contents of the exchange are not precisely specified—and they seldom are alienable. The transaction costs emphasized by Coase (1937) and Williamson (1975) are one reason such contracts emerge. Single proprietors who contract on a case-by-case basis for production and application of all knowledge would soon find themselves swamped by transaction costs in all but the smallest-scale firms.

The value of proprietary knowledge to competitors or potential competitors is another reason for long-term employment relationships. Longer-term contracts reduce the costs of restricting the flow of valuable knowledge to outsiders. Finally, longer-run relationships encourage individual participants to invest in firm-specific knowledge that has little or no value except within the particular organization

The suppression of alienability, while required for the existence of a firm, does impose costs, and we believe that those costs can be reduced by thorough understanding and analysis of the functions performed by alienability.

The franchise organization, a rapidly growing sector of the American economy, is a good example of a mixture of firm and market systems that uses alienability of rights as part of the control system. A franchise contract sells the right to manage a divisional profit center to a manager for a franchise fee. The manager receives the capital value right to the residual cash flows, subject to an annual royalty payment and contractual provisions limiting his decision rights in various areas.[10] Most important for our purposes, the manager receives the right to alienate the franchise contract by sale to others. The contract often restricts alienation rights in various ways, for example by the right of the franchiser to approve the purchaser. Alienability's advantage as a control device is that it rewards and punishes agents by imposing on them the capitalized value of the future costs and benefits of their decisions. In the absence of arm's-length transactions, this is difficult to implement inside a firm. Nevertheless, mechanisms do exist to provide the functions that alienability normally provides in markets. We turn now to a discussion of these substitute mechanisms and how they help to solve the organizational problems of the firm.

4.5 The Organizational Problems of the Firm: Trade-offs between Costs Owing to Poor Information and Agency Costs

We have seen how alienability solves the rights assignment and control problems in the economy. Recognizing that firms, by definition, can make relatively little internal use of alienability enables us to see clearly the problems faced by every firm in constructing substitute mechanisms. The assignment and enforcement of decision rights in organizations are a matter of organizational policy and practice, not voluntary exchange among agents. In principle the modern corporation vests all decision rights in the board of directors and the chief executive's office. Decision rights are partitioned out to individuals and to organizational units by the rules established by top-level management and the board of directors. The chief executive's office enforces the rules by rewarding and punishing those who follow or violate the rules. These assignment and enforcement powers are constrained in important ways by the laws and regulations of the state and by social custom.

Every chief executive officer (CEO), including a benevolent despot with the power to direct the economy, confronts the rights assignment and control problems of organizational structure discussed above. The limitations of his or her own mental and communication abilities make it impossible for the CEO to gather the requisite information to make every detailed decision personally. Any CEO attempting to do so in a large, complex organization will commit major errors. In delegating authority to maximize survival, the CEO wants to partition the decision rights out among agents in the organization so as to maximize their aggregate value. Ideally, this means colocating decision responsibility with the knowledge that is valuable in making particular decisions. This requires consideration of the costs of generating and transferring knowledge in the organization, and how the assignment of decision rights influences incentives to acquire information.

In assigning decision rights, the CEO confronts a second problem. Because they are ultimately self-interested, the agents to whom the CEO delegates authority have objective functions that diverge from his or her own. The costs resulting from such conflicts of interest in cooperative behavior are commonly called agency costs. (See Chapter 3.) Because agency costs inevitably result from the delegation of decision rights, the CEO must devise a control system (a set of rules) that fosters desirable behavior. It is, however, generally impossible to structure an incentive and control system that will cause agents to behave exactly as the CEO wishes. In addition, control and incentive systems are costly to design and implement. Agency costs are the sum of the costs of designing, implementing, and maintaining appropriate incentive and control systems and the residual loss resulting from the difficulty of solving these problems completely.

Figure 4.1 provides an intuitive way to think about the trade-offs associated with assigning a particular decision right to different levels in the organization's hierarchy. The vertical axis measures costs and the horizontal axis measures the distance of the decision right from the CEO's office (measured by levels of hierarchy) in a simple, hierarchically structured organization. For simplicity, this figure abstracts from the decision regarding where the right is assigned within a given level of the hierarchy,[11] and thus deals with the age-old centralization/decentralization debate in organizations.

Determining the optimal level of decentralization requires balancing the costs of bad decisions owing to poor information and those owing to inconsistent objectives. The costs owing to poor information plotted in Figure 4.1 measure the costs of acquiring information plus the costs of poor decisions made because it is too expensive to acquire all relevant information. In the extreme case of a completely centralized organization (located at the origin on the horizontal axis) the costs owing to poor information are high while the agency costs owing to inconsistent objectives are zero.[12]

The costs owing to poor information fall as the CEO delegates the decision right to lower levels in the organization. They fall because the decision right is exercised by agents that have more specific knowledge relevant to the decision. We assume for simplicity that the hierarchy and both cost functions are continuous. We assume that the costs owing to inconsistent objectives increase monotonically and at an increasing rate as the right is assigned to lower levels, and that these costs are conditioned on optimal controls at each alternative rights assignment. We

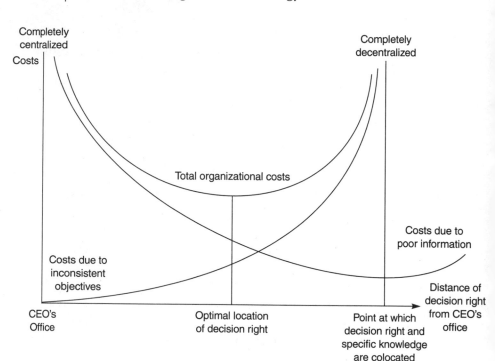

Figure 4.1 The trade-off between costs owing to inconsistent objectives and costs owing to poor information as a decision right is moved further from the CEO's office in the hierarchy.

also assume that the cost owing to poor information has a unique minimum. By definition this minimum must occur where the right is colocated with the specific knowledge relevant to the decision.

Total organizational costs plotted in Figure 4.1 are the sum of the costs owing to poor information and the costs owing to inconsistent objectives. They are high at the completely centralized allocation and decline as the right is moved down in the hierarchy to where more relevant specific knowledge is located. The vertical line in the figure marks the optimal location of the decision right. It occurs where the decrease in the cost owing to poor information just offsets the increase in the cost owing to inconsistent objectives (the point where the absolute values of the slopes of the two curves are equal).

Specific knowledge exists at all levels of the organization, not just at lower levels. For example, a machine operator often has specific knowledge of a particular machine's operating idiosyncrasies, but the chief financial officer is likely to have the specific knowledge relevant to the capital structure decision. The CEO may often have the best specific knowledge of the strategic challenges and opportunities facing the firm. The key to efficiency is to assign decision rights to each agent at each level to minimize the sum of the costs owing to poor information and the costs owing to inconsistent objectives. Figure 4.1 illustrates that even at the optimum an organization will be making poor decisions owing to both poor information and the conflicts that arise from inconsistent objectives.

The optimal degree of decentralization depends on factors like the size of the organization, information technology (including computers, communications, and travel), the rate of change in the environment, government regulation, and the control technology. In general, as the size of a firm increases, the sum of the cost owing to poor information and the cost owing to inconsistent objectives rises. When the marginal costs owing to poor information rise more rapidly with size than the marginal costs owing to inconsistent objectives, the optimal degree of decentralization rises. Changes in information technology have an ambiguous impact on the optimal degree of decentralization. The direction of the effect depends on which information is most affected. When improved technology makes it easier to transfer specific knowledge effectively from lower to higher levels in the organization, there will be a shift toward centralization.[13] When improved technology makes it easier to transfer to lower levels in the organization information that formerly was specific to higher levels in the organization, there will be a shift toward decentralization.[14]

Increased governmental regulation tends to increase centralization. It does so by increasing the amount of specific knowledge in the headquarters office dealing with the regulatory agency. Improvements in control technology, such as communication and measurement techniques that reduce the marginal agency costs associated with delegating decision rights, will tend to increase decentralization in an organization.

Our characterization of decision rights so far has been overly simple. It is relatively uncommon in large organizations for agents to have the total rights to make any major decision in the way we normally think about decisions. Instead, as Fama and Jensen (1983a, 1983b) argue, decisions are normally made by a process in which individuals are assigned decision management and decision control rights. Decision management rights are the rights to initiate and implement recommendations for resource allocations. Decision control rights are the rights to ratify initiatives and to monitor the implementation of resource commitments. Although we cannot pursue the issue here, the analysis portrayed in Figure 4.1 can be applied to the assignment of both decision management and decision control rights. When, for example, the relevant specific knowledge for decision control (as for the performance measurement, evaluation, and bonus process for lower-level managers) lies at a lower level in the organization, some decentralization of control rights is optimal.

In sum, the CEO in the typical firm cannot generally use alienability to solve the firm's organizational problems. He cannot delegate the alienability of decision rights to decision agents without thereby converting them into independent firms. Organizational problems within the firm must therefore be solved by substitute means. This is accomplished by devising a set of rules of the game for the firm, which:

1. Partition out the decision-making rights to agents throughout the organization.
2. Create a control system that
   a. provides measures of performance;
   b. specifies the relationship between rewards and punishments and the measures of performance.

This is a simple but remarkably powerful list. While there are many factors that determine the behavior of any individual organization, our empirical observations indicate that knowledge of these rules of the game enables one to make good predictions about an organization's behavior and effectiveness. We now consider common organizational devices for implementing these organizational rules of the game.

4.6   The Technology for Partitioning Decision Rights in the Firm

The techniques available for structuring activities within the firm are a product of evolution, as is the system of rights for the economy as a whole. What has evolved is a complex body of managerial technology that is employed in partitioning decision rights and in controlling behavior within the firm. Scientific understanding of that technology is rudimentary, but we can describe some of its major components and their use.

Job Descriptions and Internal Common Law

Decision rights are allocated to agents within firms in various ways. Many are allocated directly to individuals or positions through job descriptions, and these descriptions are often the best source of written documentation of the assignment of decision rights in an organization. Examples include the right to make pricing, hiring, or promotion decisions, the rights to initiate recommendations for resource allocation, to ratify or monitor the initiatives of others, or to implement particular programs.[15] The allocations of decision rights to individuals evolve over time as the organization and individuals change. These rights assignments occur both formally and informally, and are associated with committee memberships and project assignments as well as the organization's internal "regulatory" and "common law" traditions.

Budgeting

Physical and monetary budgets are common techniques for partitioning decision rights in firms. Agents can be given decision rights over the use of physical resources, such as capital equipment or building space. The rights allocated through such physical budgets are less complete and therefore more constraining than are decision rights allocated by grant of monetary budgets. Dollar budget authorizations tend to be used when the intent is to grant some discretion in the choice of inputs. When rights are allocated through monetary budgets without side constraints, decision agents have the opportunity to sell or exchange, and therefore to substitute among assets. The organization is better off to the extent that managers use their specific knowledge to make substitutions that increase the efficiency of the organization. Such substitution is generally not possible with pure physical allocations of assets.

Budgets denominated in money terms are frequently constrained in ways that deny managers the opportunity to substitute. These line budgets (commonly used in government as well as industry) are broken down in great detail, and the recipient is specifically forbidden to transfer funds from one category to another. Under such budgets the manager's ability to use his or her specific knowledge to increase efficiency is obviously restricted. Such restrictions can be optimal if the specific knowledge relevant to making these substitutions lies at a higher level in the organization.[16]

Budgets can be fixed or variable. They are fixed if the amount of authorized spending is independent of the level of activity or of performance. Under a variable performance budget, spending authority is a specified function of performance or activity levels, for example a fraction of revenues.[17] While variable budget allocations have substantial incentive effects (because most agents prefer to have control over more resources), these incentive effects often seem to be ignored in practice.

Budgets are usually accompanied by side-constraints. Physical resource budgets, for example, are commonly restricted to use rights; the recipient is not allowed to sell the resources and retain the proceeds. Diversion of dollars or physical resources to personal use (except that specified as compensation) is also prohibited. Manpower or head count limitations that are independent of the dollars available are another example of a separate constraint.

Rules, Regulations, or Fiat

The rules and regulations that accompany budgets are examples of regulatory constraints on behavior that exist because employees are self-interested. Such constraints imposed by fiat are the most primitive form of control technology. Like line budgets, they control by circumscribing in advance the opportunity set from which a decision maker can choose. Unless the regulator is omniscient, such rules will eliminate superior, as well as inferior, courses of action because they are made without the specific knowledge that lies at the local level. In this sense, control by regulation tends to disregard the advantage of colocating knowledge and decision rights at the local level. Regulations are efficient control devices when the budget office has the relevant specific knowledge or where the prohibited behavior is virtually never consistent with the objectives of the CEO, for example theft or embezzlement.

4.7   The Control System

Because all individuals in a firm are self-interested, simply delegating decision rights to them and dictating the objective function that each is to maximize is not sufficient to accomplish the objective. A control system that ties the individual's interest more closely to that of the organization is required. The control system specifies (a) the performance measurement and evaluation system for each subdivision of the firm and each decision agent, and (b) the reward and punishment system that relates individuals' rewards to their performance. In a real sense, specification of the performance measurement and evaluation system *is* specification of the objective function, but it is not generally viewed this way. Self-interest motivates individuals to discover and understand the performance measures and evaluation system on which their rewards and punishments depend. It does not take them long to discover when the rewarded objective is different from that which is stated.

Cost Centers and Profit Centers as Performance Measurement Systems

Cost centers and profit centers embody two widely used divisional performance measurement rules. Cost centers are subdivisions that are directed to minimize the total cost of providing a specified quantity of service. Manufacturing divisions are frequently organized as cost centers. Mathematically, and in the absence of information or agency problems, minimizing total cost for a given quantity of output is equivalent to maximizing output for a given total cost. In addition, both are consistent with maximizing the value of the firm if the correct output constraint is chosen. Given information and agency problems, however, the two formulations are not equivalent. Minimizing cost for given total output often seems to degrade into a system where managers are rewarded for minimizing average cost per unit of output.

Note that measuring performance by average cost per unit of output will virtually never be consistent with firm value maximization in the absence of a quantity constraint. The decision manager with such an objective will strive to achieve the output quantity that minimizes average cost even though it bears no relation to the value-maximizing quantity. Chapter 12 discusses these issues in more detail.

The tendency of firms to divisionalize along product lines appears to be influenced by control considerations. Product subdivisions are often operated as profit centers where the measure of performance is the difference between some measure of revenues and costs. Profit centers are more independent than cost centers; their budgets are more likely to be variable than those of cost centers, and this generally means fewer knowledge demands on the CEO. The scale of operations of the center then varies directly with revenues, and does not require the same fore-casting accuracy as a fixed dollar budget would require. The reduction in knowledge required to monitor the division is particularly evident where the products are sold in outside markets. Here the CEO can use competition in outside markets as a part of the control system. Competition and the ability of the division's customers to purchase from others provide the CEO with a performance measure for the product division (profits) that incorporates consumer assessment of quality, timeliness, and value. Internal transfer pricing systems in which buyers have the right to purchase from any source also allow the CEO to decentralize to the buyers an important part of the control system. Such decentralization is optimal to the extent that specific knowledge of product and service quality lies with the buyers and is costly to observe from higher in the hierarchy.

Neither profit centers nor cost centers are panaceas for the CEO's organizational problems. Cost centers, for example, tend to lead to problems of quantity and quality control. Measured on the cost of output for a fixed quantity, division managers are motivated to reduce cost by reducing quality. Preventing this requires quality to be cheaply observable from higher in the hierarchy. To the extent that quality is easily observable, cost centers will tend to be more desirable. Divisions where quantity is difficult or impossible to measure (such as computer services) are difficult to run as cost centers, because the manager can simply reduce the quantity of service in order to lower cost.

Strategic business planning is a widely used but ill-defined term. Strategic planning as implemented in its heyday at General Electric in the United States was a budget-target system in which performance is measured by how close the results are to a plan. In this form strategic business planning is the private organizational version of central planning in the market system. It poses problems because its success depends critically on setting correct plans or targets for each division and decision agent. This in turn imposes enormous knowledge requirements on the central staff that must do the planning. When much of the required specific knowledge is located at lower levels in the organization and involves high cost to transfer to the central planning staff, strategic business planning will be inefficient. When such knowledge is important the result of centrally devised targets will be poor plans and strategic business planning will generate large organizational costs. This is consistent with the failure of large central planning staffs in many American corporations over the past two decades (see Kiechel 1982; Hayes 1985, 1986).

The Role of Budgets in Performance Measurement

Budgets are related to performance measurement in several ways. Budgets are sometimes used to delegate decision rights, but they are also used as targets in the performance measurement system, for example as expenditure or revenue targets. In these cases the amount by which expenditures are less than the targets and by which revenues exceed targets are favorable performance measures. In the most general form (that is, strategic planning), deviations on either side of the target are unfavorable measures of performance. When budgets are used to delegate decision rights, measures of violations of budgeted expenditures must be part of performance measurement if expenditure limits are to have meaning. Indeed, violations of any rules, regulations, or fiat must affect performance measures and rewards and punishments if the constraints are to affect behavior.

Measuring, Rewarding, and Punishing Individual Performance

The performance measurements discussed previously are group measures. But the CEO's measurement problem is not simply one of measuring group performance. In the end, he or she must reward and punish individuals. For a sizable organization, the CEO cannot literally either review the performance of every individual or decide on his or her specific rewards. Inevitably, the CEO will delegate much of the responsibility for measuring and rewarding performance and will promulgate rules or policies that control the decisions of those to whom authority is delegated. The CEO can, for example, tie individual rewards to individual performance by direct pay-for-performance systems (and here the sensitivity of the relation between pay and performance is a major decision variable), or by promotions that depend on performance. Individual rewards can be tied to group performance by creating bonus pools that are a function of group performance or by profit-sharing plans, employees' stock ownership plans, stock option plans, or phantom stock plans. The tendency for large organizations to avoid pay-for-performance incentive plans and to rely instead on promotion-based rewards is an interesting phenomenon that is as yet poorly understood by economists. (These issues are discussed at length by Baker et al. 1988 and in Chapter 8).

4.8   Conclusions

In this chapter we have analyzed the relations between knowledge, control, and organizational structure, both in the market system as a whole and in private organizations. The limited capacity of the human mind and the costs of producing and transferring knowledge mean that knowledge relevant to all decisions can never be located in a single individual or body of experts. Thus, if knowledge valuable to a particular decision is to be used in making that decision, there must be a system for assigning decision rights to individuals who have the knowledge and abilities or who can acquire or produce them at low cost. In addition, self-interest on the part of individual decision makers means that a control system is required to motivate individuals to use their specific knowledge and decision rights properly.

The problem of rights assignment and control is solved in a capitalist economy by a system of voluntary exchange founded on a system of alienable decision rights. Voluntary exchange of alienable decision rights tends to ensure that the agent with the relevant knowledge and abilities, who therefore values a decision right most highly, will acquire it. This solves the rights assignment problem of colocating decision rights and specific knowledge.

In the absence of externalities, alienable decision rights also solve the control problem; they motivate individual decision agents to use their decision rights efficiently. Alienability does this by providing an effective system, the market price or capital value of the right, that measures the performance of any individual's use of a decision right. Alienability also means that the individual can capture the value of the right in exchange. Thus, alienability also provides an effective reward and punishment system that capitalizes the costs and benefits of an individual's actions onto his or her own shoulders.

Alienable rights cannot generally solve the control problem in firms because firms cannot usually assign alienability along with the decision rights without turning each individual agent into an independent firm. Indeed, the absence of alienability is one of the major distinctions between firms and markets.

Because of the limited computational capacity, storage, and input/output channels of the human mind, it is often desirable for groups of individuals to exercise decision rights jointly. Private organizations are widespread examples of such joint exercise of decision rights. In such organizations independent individuals coordinate their actions through contracts with the legal fiction that serves as the firm's nexus. The bundle of decision rights owned in the name of such an organization is vested nominally in its board of directors and CEO, and the rights are then partitioned out among decision agents in the organization. Those organizations that accomplish this partitioning in a fashion that maximizes their value will tend to win out in the competition for survival. The characteristic that distinguishes such organizations from markets is the fact that alienability of the rights is not delegated to individual decision agents in the organization.

The inalienability of decision rights within an organization means that the exchange mechanisms that partition decision rights to colocate them with the relevant knowledge and skill are not operative. Furthermore, the inalienability of rights within an organization means that the control problems must be solved by alternative means. Organizations solve these problems by establishing internal rules of the game that provide:

1. A system for partitioning decision rights out to agents in the organization.
2. A control system that provides:
   a. a performance measurement and evaluation system;
   b. a reward and punishment system.

In general, because of their inability to simulate true capital value claims, these substitute rules of the game will not perform as effectively as alienable rights in a market system. Therefore, survival requires that the firm must realize offsetting benefits from the joint exercise of rights that are large enough to offset the disadvantages incurred by sacrificing alienability. Economies of scale and scope, information advantages, and specialization are potential sources of such benefits.

The creation of a science of organizations is still in its infancy. We believe that the structure outlined in this chapter provides a view of organizations that yields important insights for both social scientists and managers. Knowledge of an organization's rules of the game and a surprisingly small amount about its technology or opportunity set enables one to make accurate predictions of its behavior. Such predictions are of great value both to managers and to social scientists.

5 | Organization Theory and Methodology

5.1 Introduction

A major challenge facing social scientists is the development of a body of theory to explain why organizations take the form they do and why they behave as they do. My objective is to outline some aspects of this emerging line of research on organizations and to call attention to a number of related methodological issues that play an important role in this research: the relation between positive and normative theories, the importance to the research effort of the choice of tautologies and definitions, the nature of evidence, and the role of mathematics. I conclude with a brief discussion of the two literatures of agency theory.

I have two basic propositions that directly bear on accounting:

1. accounting is an integral part of the structure of every organization;
2. a fundamental understanding of why accounting practices evolve as they do and how to improve them requires a deeper understanding about organizations than now exists in the social sciences.

By way of background, I shall digress briefly to discuss the relation between positive and normative research.

5.2 Positive and Normative Theory and Decision Making

In the period prior to the mid-1970s, accounting theory was predominantly normative. It focused on policy prescriptions for management or public policy—questions involving the appropriate treatment of infla-

Originally published in *The Accounting Review* 58, no. 2 (April 1983), pp. 319–339.

tion, exchange rates, inventories, leases, and so on. These policy questions are, of course, both interesting and important, and they are best answered with knowledge of a wide range of positive theory—that is, knowledge about how the world behaves. For example, accountants have been justifiably concerned with the effects of General Price Level Adjusted accounting (GPLA) on accounting numbers. But a manager interested in maximizing the value of his firm also must estimate either explicitly or implicitly how such accounting procedures will affect firm value. And how GPLA affects firm value is a purely positive issue in the sense that the term is used in the social sciences.[1] Normative questions take the form: "How should price level changes be reflected in the accounting statements?" Positive questions take the form: "How does GPLA affect the value of the firm?" Answers to normative questions always depend on the choice of the criterion or objective function, which is a matter of values. Therefore, normative propositions are never refutable by evidence. Answers to positive questions, on the other hand, involve discovery of some aspect of how the world behaves and are always potentially refutable by contradictory evidence.

Considerable discussion and disagreement have occurred over methodological issues associated with the emerging literature on positive accounting theory, and my purpose here is to try to clarify some of these issues. In the end, of course, we are all interested in normative questions; a desire to understand how to accomplish goals motivates our interest in these methodological topics and in positive theories.

An interesting relationship between normative and positive issues often goes unrecognized. Consider the general structure of a decision problem:

$$\max_{\{X_i\}} V = V(Y_1, Y_2, \ldots, Y_N; Z_1, Z_2, \ldots, Z_L)$$

Subject to the following constraints:

$$\left[\begin{array}{l} \text{Accounting and other} \\ \text{identities (such as budget} \\ \text{constraints, time} \\ \text{constraints, etc.)} \end{array} \right]$$

Positive theories

$$
\begin{bmatrix}
Y_1 = f_1(X_1, X_2, \ldots, X_K; Y_2, Y_3, \ldots, Y_N; Z_1, Z_2, \ldots, Z_{L)} \\
Y_2 = f_2(X_1, X_2, \ldots, X_K; Y_1, Y_3, \ldots, Y_N; Z_1, Z_2, \ldots, Z_L \\
\cdot \\
\cdot \\
\cdot \\
Y_N = f_N(X_1, X_2, \ldots, X_K; Y_1, Y_2, \ldots, Y_{N-1}; Z_1, Z_2, \ldots, Z_L
\end{bmatrix}
$$

where V is the objective function to be maximized, the X's are the decision variables, the Y's are the arguments of the objective function that are determined within the system (the "endogenous" variables), and the Z's are the variables determined outside the system (the "exogenous" variables).

The constraints of the problem are of great interest here, and we can break them into two general categories. The first category contains all accounting and other identities (such as budget constraints, time constraints [24 hours in a day], and so on). The second category of constraints given by the functions, f_i, determine how the decision variables, X, and the exogenous variables, Z, affect the values of the endogenous variables, Y, in the objective function.

The second set of constraints is made up of positive theories about the way the world works:[2] for example, how decisions on accounting practices, organizational structure, advertising, pricing, and production policies combine with physical laws affecting production and the exogenous variables such as weather, interest rates, governmental regulatory policies, and human behavior to determine the endogenous variables, Y, that affect the value of the firm. Suppose the value of the firm is a function of expected net cash flows, their riskiness, and the interest rate. To choose among alternative accounting policies, a manager desiring to maximize the value of the firm wants to know how those alternative choices affect the expected net cash flows and their riskiness. Answers to such questions require positive theories.

Positive theory enters the decision process in one more way. While the choice of the objective or maximand (firm value in our example) is a value judgment and therefore a normative issue, knowledge of the valuation function itself (that is, the function that relates the value of the maximand to the values of the endogenous and exogenous variables) is a positive issue and requires a theory.

It is obvious from the logical structure of decision making that purposeful decisions cannot be made without the implicit or explicit use of positive theories. You cannot decide what action to take and expect to meet your objective if you have no idea about how alternative actions affect the desired outcome—and that requires positive theory. Furthermore, using incorrect positive theories or ignoring important constraints leads to decisions that have unexpected and undesirable outcomes. This is equally true for the manager, the auditor, the FASB, or the governmental regulatory body.

The history of operations research provides an interesting example of the importance of positive theories. I believe that a major reason for the early successes of operations research and its later failure to live up to the promise offered by those successes can be traced to the nature of the theories given emphasis in those efforts. The operations research literature seems to evidence careful attention to the constraints that positive physical or engineering theories impose on decision making. When such physical phenomena are the dominant constraining force, ignoring other constraints given by market forces, information costs, and the peculiarities of human behavior can still lead to highly successful results—witness the successes in using linear programming to help run oil refineries or to solve feed-mixture problems. In these problems, prices could reasonably be taken as fixed because of the competitive nature of the markets involved. Furthermore, the fact that human beings do not always do what they are told or even do what they agree to do is less important in a highly mechanized process. In this sense refining and diet problems, where most of the important constraints involve chemical or other physical phenomena, are very special. The application of operations research to marketing and finance and to the management of people has been less successful. The paucity of successful applications in these areas stems not from deficiencies in the techniques or lack of technical expertise, but from the fact that researchers generally ignored the task of developing and incorporating as constraints in their problems robust positive theories of the market, organizational and human behavioral phenomena that were important to the problems.[3] This is also the reason why as scientists we cannot successfully use a straightforward operations research approach to choose accounting procedures or accounting standards; we do not know the necessary positive theories well enough to predict the effects of alternative choices.

All purposeful actions must (at least implicitly) involve positive theory, that is, a presumption that the chosen action will bring about the desired results. However, it is not necessary to presume that these positive theories are explicitly contemplated by the agents we study. In fact, as Alchian (1950) long ago pointed out, we need not even assume that agents are engaged in purposeful activity for our models to work. As an extreme case, suppose agents do not learn from observation and randomly choose strategies and actions. Suppose also that the environment rewards with survival those who happen to select strategies that are closer to optimal and grants extinction to those who are unlucky enough to choose dominated strategies or actions. In such an environment, observed behavior and institutions will tend toward the optimal because those far from it will continually tend toward extinction. In the less extreme and more realistic case where agents learn from empirical observation and engage in purposeful action, we can expect surviving institutions and practices to be an even better source of information to the scientist seeking to discover the relevant positive theories. Finally, science itself can affect the world. As our scientific understanding of the world is improved, our ability to relate actions to desired outcomes is improved. Pareto (1935, sec. 1785) summarizes the point quite succinctly:

> In the Middle Ages master-masons built marvelous edifices by rules of thumb, by empiricism, without the remotest knowledge of any theory as to the resistance capacities of building materials—merely by trying and trying again, rectifying mistakes as they went along. Now thanks to such theories, modern engineers not only eliminate the losses incident to the old mistakes, but erect buildings that the master-masons and other artisans of the past centuries could not possibly have built. Practice had taught physicians certain remedies that were oftentimes better than those recommended by quacks or alchemists. Sometimes again they were altogether worthless. Nowadays chemical theories have eradicated not all, but a very large number, of those mistakes, and biology has made it possible to make better use of many substances that chemistry places at the disposal of medicine. Only a few years back, in making cast iron in a blast-furnace it was wiser to follow the directions of an empiricist than the prescriptions of theory. Today the iron industry is no longer carried on without consultant chemists and other theorists. The same may be said of the dyeing industry and of many others.

As a result of the subtle interactions of the continual striving by purposeful individuals and the natural selection properties of the environment, extremely complicated and sophisticated institutions and practices can arise. And, as Hayek (1979, pp. 153ff.) emphasizes, most of the complex and sophisticated phenomena that make up human culture (markets and mores are examples) were never consciously invented by any individual. Indeed, much of human culture is still not well understood.

The general decision structure delineated above also clarifies the criteria for accepting or rejecting theories. Theories are not rejected in a vacuum. If a theory predicts poorly but still better than the best available alternative, it will not be abandoned by the decision maker because doing so will reduce his welfare. As the old saying goes, "You can only beat a theory with another theory." The choice among competing theories will be based on which is expected to yield the highest value of the objective function when used for decision making. Single observations inconsistent with a theory will not necessarily bring rejection, nor is there a "natural" significance level such as 5% that brings rejection. Thus, care must be taken in interpreting the significance tests often used by scientists who are not in a decision-making capacity and therefore do not have a well-defined objective function to use for deciding among contending theories.

How does one go about developing a positive theory of accounting, one that will ultimately aid in normative choices? I start by focusing on the relationship between organizational form and accounting practice—to recognize formally that accounting is a basic part of the structure of every organization. I then discuss the emerging research on an economic theory of organization.

5.3   Accounting and Organizational Form

Accountants have long recognized the importance accounting has played in the stewardship or control of organizations, and this is consistent with the notion that accounting is a basic part of organizational structure and that accounting practice and organizational form are related. Accounting practices clearly differ across organizations—profit versus nonprofit, for example. Frequently nonprofits do not record capital assets on their balance sheets and do not calculate depreciation. Fund accounting, of course, is very different from the usual for-profit system. Satisfactory explanations of these differences do not exist.[4] But this is not surprising, considering that social scientists have not generated satisfactory explanations for why nonprofit organizations exist and why they seem to dominate some activities like education and religion and not others like manufacturing.[5] Taxes are not sufficient to explain their existence, because nonprofits existed long before income taxes became important. Moreover, many other types of organizational forms exist and tend to be related to the type of production activities the organization undertakes. Publicly held or open corporations are dominant in large, complex, capital-intensive activities like manufacturing. Partnerships are dominant in sensitive service activities like law and public accounting, and nonprofits in religion, education, and classical music.

Moreover, within broad organizational categories, specific organizations differ along many dimensions such as performance evaluation, compensation, budgeting, costing, pricing, capital structure, distribution, and sales practices. There is little scientific understanding about why organizations of a given general type differ along these dimensions. And if accounting practices are significantly affected by an organization's structure, then without a fundamental understanding of why organizations differ we have no fundamental understanding about why accounting policies differ across organizations.[6]

Consider, for example, the use of profit centers versus cost centers as the basis for defining divisions of an organization. Although economists and accountants have analyzed both of these organizational devices, no satisfactory theory exists that will predict when an activity within an organization will be organized as a cost center and when as a profit center.[7] Though the accounting procedures employed for each type of organization are well known, the relation of the accounting procedures to the development of the firm's organization is worthy of research. In addition, there is evidence in Chandler's work (1962, pp. 61, 145ff.) that the organizational innovations that led to the large, integrated, multi-divisional American firms in the early 1900s were accompanied by substantial innovations in accounting practices.

We are almost as ignorant regarding why financial reporting practices differ among organizations. Again, to the extent that little theory exists to explain why organizations differ in their financial reporting practices and what the effects of those different practices are, little scientific basis exists to advise management, the FASB, or the SEC on how to improve such practices through changes in accounting standards or regulation.[8] This brings me back to my main topic, the emerging research in economics that is related to organizations.

5.4   The Impending Revolution in Organization Theory

I believe that a revolution will take place over the next decade or two in our knowledge about organizations. This process will involve accounting researchers as well as economists and other social scientists. Accounting theory has benefited greatly from advances in our knowledge of finance and financial markets over the last two decades—advances in which accounting researchers have played an important role. I foresee advances in organization theory which will have an even larger impact on accounting research, and the effects will extend beyond accounting to finance, economics, and management education and practice.

The last decade has been marked by a growing interest in organizations within the economics profession. The work of several dozen scholars comes to mind, and I am sure there is much work unknown to me.[9] The science of organizations is still in its infancy, but the foundation for a powerful theory of organizations is being put into place. In a parallel development, there is a growing body of accounting literature addressing related problems that generally goes under the label of positive research in accounting.[10] The existence of empirical regularities between the choice of accounting procedures and organizational characteristics such as size and capital structure is beginning to be documented in that literature. A healthy and prospering journal, the *Journal of Accounting and Economics,* has been founded by Ross Watts and Jerold Zimmerman to further encourage the development of a positive accounting literature.

The Dimensions of Organizations

William Meckling and I have spent a half-dozen years investigating the application of the principles of economics to the analysis of organizations and in the process have developed a new course entitled "Coordination and Control in Organizations." One of the frustrating aspects of that effort has been the difficulty associated with developing an understanding and definition of the relevant dimensions to use in characterizing the structure of an organization. Organizations are complex systems. If we are to make progress in understanding them, we must order that complexity. We must find and articulate a set of organizational characteristics which can explain why various organizations function as they do.

In developing our coordination and control course, we have arrived at a three-part taxonomy to characterize organizations (see Chap. 4):

- the performance measurement and evaluation system,
- the reward and punishment system,
- the system for partitioning and assigning decision rights among participants in the organization.

A full discussion of this classification scheme is beyond the scope of this chapter, but it is important to note that the accounting and control system plays a major role in all three dimensions. Viewing the organization from this perspective helps provide structure to the notion of the stewardship role of accounting in the organization. Furthermore, differences in these three dimensions across organizations are highly likely to result in differences in accounting systems. This also indicates that accounting is an integral part of the structure of every organization and that a thorough understanding of organizational forces is important to a theory of accounting.

In addition to the requirement for a better understanding of the relevant dimensions of organizations, progress in the development of a theory of organizations will also be aided by understanding why economics has not already yielded such a theory.

Limitations of the Economic Theory of the Firm

Unfortunately, the vast literature in economics that falls under the label of "Theory of the Firm" is not a positive theory of the firm, but rather a theory of markets. The organization or firm in that theory is little more than a black box that behaves in a value- or profit-maximizing way. In most economic analyses, the firm is modeled as an entrepreneur who maximizes profits in an environment in which all contracts are perfectly and costlessly enforced. In this firm there are no "people" problems or information problems, and as a result the research based on this model has no implications for how organizations are structured or how they function internally. The firm is, in effect, assumed to be an elementary component of the analysis even though in fact it is an exceedingly complex subsystem. This is not necessarily wrong. When it is appropriate for a scientist to treat a complex subsystem as an elementary component is a subtle and difficult issue. Herbert Simon's article entitled "The

Architecture of Complexity" contains an excellent analysis of this issue. As Simon (1962, p. 469) poses the problem:

> In most systems in nature, it is somewhat arbitrary as to where we leave off the partitioning, and what subsystems we take as elementary. Physics makes much of the concept of "elementary particle" although particles have a disconcerting tendency not to remain elementary very long. Only a couple of generations ago, the atoms themselves were elementary particles; today, to the nuclear physicist they are complex systems. For certain purposes of astronomy, whole stars, or even galaxies, can be regarded as elementary subsystems. In one kind of biological research, a cell may be treated as an elementary subsystem; in another, a protein molecule; in still another, an amino acid residue.

Just as astronomers can usefully abstract from the complexities inside a star or a galaxy for certain purposes, the classical economic notion of the firm has usefully abstracted from the internal complexities of organizations. This has yielded a robust theory of markets that is of great value. However, precisely because the definition of the firm abstracts from most of the real problems and complexities of organizations, it provides no insights to the construction of a theory of organizations. The concepts of marginal analysis, competition, opportunity cost, and equilibrium that have been useful in the development of a theory of markets will also be valuable in the development of a theory of organizations. They are not, however, enough to accomplish the job. This raises the question of what we use to replace the black box view of the firm.

5.5 The Nexus of Contracts View of Organizations

I believe it is productive to define an organization as a legal entity that serves as a nexus[11] for a complex set of contracts (written and unwritten) among disparate individuals (see Chapter 3, Section 3.1). The multilateral contracts between agents that characterize market relations are supplanted within an organization by a system in which the relationships among the cooperating agents are largely effected through unilateral contracts with the legal entity that serves as the contracting nexus. These contracts specify the rules of the game within the organization, including the three critical dimensions outlined above: the performance evaluation system, the reward system, and the assignment of decision rights. This view of organizations focuses attention on the nature of the contractual relations among the agents who come together in an organization—including suppliers of labor, capital, raw materials, risk-bearing services, and customers.

The nexus of contracts view helps us to see organizations in a way that can provide useful insights. It leads to inquiry about why certain contractual relations arise and how those relations respond to changes in the environment. For example, it leads us to see the shopping center as an organizational form that is an interesting alternative to a collection of independently owned stores grouped together in a shopping district or as an alternative to a large department store where there is no independent ownership of individual departments. The department store is an organizational device that internalizes the externalities generated by locating certain types and qualities of stores together and providing certain services centrally—so too is a supermarket. On the other hand, as such organizations grow in size, shirking problems grow larger and so do other problems associated with providing department managers, buyers, and so on with the correct incentives. The shopping center, with common ownership of buildings and parking facilities coupled with contractual procedures that control such factors as the types of stores in the center and their quality, can also internalize many of the externalities of pure independent ownership. Some of the incentive problems are solved in the shopping center structure by maintaining independent ownership of the individual stores and charging for participation in the organization through a fixed fee rental plus a percentage of revenues or profits.

Although this is not the place to pursue it, it is easy to see how comparisons of such organizational forms lead to questions regarding the factors that give competitive advantages to each of these three organizational types (shopping centers, department stores, and independently owned specialty stores) at various times and at various locations. Such questions are relevant because we know that all three types of organizations continue to compete and survive. Close examination should also reveal differences in accounting systems in these organizations (differences that arise from the problems and opportunities peculiar to each of them) and the role accounting plays in permitting these organizations to survive. Understanding such differences and why they arise will add another set of elements to the theory of accounting.

The nexus of contracts view of organizations also helps to dispel the tendency to treat organizations as if they were persons. Organizations do not have preferences, and they do not choose in the conscious and rational sense that we attribute to people. Anyone who has served on committees understands this fact. Usually no single person on a committee has the power to choose the outcome, and the choices that result from committee processes seldom resemble anything like the reasoned choice of a single individual. The voting paradox examined at length in the political science literature is an example of this point. The old description of the camel as a "horse designed by a committee" also captures the point.

The behavior of the organization is the equilibrium behavior of a complex contractual system made up of maximizing agents with diverse and conflicting objectives. In this sense, the behavior of the organization is like the equilibrium behavior of a market. We do not often characterize the steel market or the wheat market as having preferences and motives or making choices as an individual does, but this mistake is commonly made about General Motors, Peat, Marwick, Mitchell & Co., and so on. Construction of a theory of organizations involves creating a theory that describes the equilibrium behavior of these complex contractual systems where the individual agent is the elementary unit of analysis.[17]

As Simon emphasizes, the definition of the elementary unit of analysis in science is not a matter of "right" or "wrong" but rather one of usefulness. Whether one chooses the "black box" or "nexus of contracts" definition of an organization depends on the question at hand. Some questions, such as how outputs of a firm or industry respond to price changes, are more productively addressed with the former definition. Other questions, such as those involving organizational problems like the choice of accounting practices, are more productively addressed in the nexus of contracts perspective. However, when using the black box approach it is important to remember that it is a convenient abstraction that is appropriate only for analysis of some questions. The danger in its use arises because it further encourages the tendency to personalize organizations by attributing motives and preferences to what is in fact a complex equilibrium system. Such personalization easily leads to uncritical application of the black box approach to questions it cannot handle.

5.6   Some Recent Results on Control

Eugene Fama and I worked for several years to analyze the characteristics that give survival value to different organizational forms. One of our concerns has been to understand the factors that give survival value to organizations like large public corporations characterized by separation of "ownership and control," or, more precisely, separation of the decision management and residual risk-bearing functions. Scholars from Adam Smith (1776) to Berle and Means (1932) have pointed out the inconsistency of interests between managers and outside stockholders and have emphasized the costs these conflicts generate. Yet, even though other organizational forms such as proprietorships, small partnerships, and closed corporations compete with corporations and do so without the handicap of the costs of separation of ownership and control, the evidence is clear: in the production of a wide range of activities, the corporation continues to win the competition for survival.

In fact, the large, publicly held corporation is not unique in its separation of "ownership and control." Separation of decision management and residual risk-bearing characterizes many organizational forms, for example, financial mutuals and large professional partnerships. Nonprofit organizations that have no alienable residual claims constitute the extreme form of separation of ownership from control.

Fama and I conclude that separation of decision management (the initiation and implementation of decisions) from decision control (the ratification and monitoring of decisions) in the organization is the major device that limits the costs due to separation of "ownership and control." The evidence indicates that open corporations, financial mutuals, large partnerships, and nonprofit organizations are all characterized by separation of decision management and decision control functions. Moreover, all these organizations use a common device—boards of directors, trustees, or managing partners—to accomplish such separation at the top level of the organization. These boards have the right to ratify and monitor the decisions that are initiated and implemented by top-level managers. In addition, they always have the power to hire, fire, and set the compensation of the top-level managers. This top-level separation of decision management from decision control and the separation and diffusion of decision management and decision control rights among agents throughout lower levels of the organization are the contractual responses that limit the costs of the separation of "ownership and control" and therefore foster survival of these organizations (see Chapter 7).

Watts and Zimmerman have pointed out that our separation proposition mirrors the standards recommended in the auditing and control literature. Stettler's (1977) auditing text, for example, urges that operations responsibility be separated from accounting responsibility by vesting the two functions in different people.[13] In handling cash, the recommendation is to separate the responsibility for the record-keeping function from the person who receives the cash, and similarly for authorizing and drawing checks in the payout process. These widely practiced principles have evolved from long experience with conflicts of interest and evidently have survival value. Since Fama and I derived our propositions about control in a quite different context, these common practices for handling cash, accounts payable, and so on are encouraging evidence consistent with our thesis. It is exciting that, appropriately generalized, some of the same principles that apply to the conflict of interest problem in the handling of cash also apply to the conflict of interests between managers and stockholders and boards of directors of corporations, financial mutuals, large partnerships, and even nonprofit organizations. This gives hope that the next decade will witness success in the construction of a rich and general theory of control.

5.7   Methodological Issues

Whether the potential to develop a science of organizations will be exploited depends, of course, on many factors. I would like to discuss some important methodological issues, including the importance of tautologies and definitions, the difficulty but desirability of dealing with qualitative institutional evidence, and the role of mathematics.

The Importance of Tautologies

In the language of science, a tautology is a statement that is true by definition and can never be refuted by evidence.[14] Therefore, it is not a hypothesis or a theory. A definition declares that a newly introduced symbol means the same as another combination of symbols whose meaning is already known; it, therefore, likewise cannot be refuted by evidence.

The choice of tautologies or definitions has a large impact on the success or failure of research efforts—a fact that often goes unrecognized. Discussion of new research efforts often meets with resistance on the grounds that the effort is purely definitional, or the propositions are tautological and devoid of empirical content. Yet thorough and careful attention to definitions and tautologies is often extremely productive in the early stages of research, especially if the research represents a radical departure from the past. On the other hand, it is also common to observe talented effort devoted to sterile research on toy problems or characterizations of problems that bear little relation to the world and the rich variety of options that people face. The sterility of this research can often be traced to the choice of definitions and tautologies that focus the effort. Unfortunately, there is no obvious criterion we can apply to help us select more productive rather than less productive tautologies or definitions. Perhaps such choices will remain one of the "artistic" or creative parts of science.

Alfred Whitehead and Bertrand Russell (1910, pp. 11ff.) emphasized the importance of the choice of definitions:

> In spite of the fact that definitions are theoretically superfluous, it is nevertheless true that they often convey more important information than is contained in the propositions in which they are used. This arises from two causes. First, a definition usually implies that the *definiens* [the meaning in terms of the combination of already known symbols] is worthy of careful consideration. Hence the collection of definitions embodies our choice of subjects and our judgment as to what is most important. Secondly, when what is defined is (as often occurs) something already familiar, such as cardinal or ordinal numbers, the definition contains an analysis of a common idea, and may therefore express a notable advance. Cantor's definition of the continuum illustrates this: his definition amounts to the statement that what he is defining is the object which has the properties commonly associated with the word "continuum," though what precisely constitutes these properties had not before been known. In such cases, a definition is a "making definite"; it gives definiteness to an idea which had previously been more or less vague.
>
> For these reasons, it will be found, in what follows, that the definitions are what is most important, and what most deserves the reader's prolonged attention.

The mathematical biologist A. J. Lotka (1956, pp. 3f.) provides another example when he characterizes the enunciation of the survival of the fittest as one of the fundamental advances of science. It is a tautology because the fit is defined to be that which survives. The Coase Theorem (1960) is another important tautology that has helped us to see the importance of transactions costs in a fundamentally different fashion (see Demsetz 1982, chap. 2). The proposition that consumers make choices so as to maximize their utility is also a tautology that has proved useful in understanding human behavior and markets. Another tautology that accountants will agree is important is the proposition that assets equal liabilities plus equity—at least as long as I'm not doing the arithmetic. The usefulness and power of double-entry bookkeeping are testified to by its survival since at least the fifteenth century and its continuing widespread use. Viewing double-entry bookkeeping this way leaves me believing that we still do not thoroughly understand why it is a powerful organizing device. I am so used to thinking of assets and the claims on them, equities and liabilities, as a way of organizing thoughts about companies that it is hard to conceive of alternatives.[15]

The word "tautology" has strong pejorative overtones in our profession—to be accused of stating a tautology is practically the highest of professional insults. Therefore, I hasten to add that while a tautology of one form or another lies at the heart of all useful theory, this does not mean that such theory has no refutable, that is, positive, implications. Darwin and the biologists who followed him as well as economists using the Coase Theorem and utility maximization have thoroughly demonstrated the empirical content of their theories.

The manner in which we use tautologies to develop positive theories is closely related to the nature of the scientific process itself. The process involves the use of the definitions and the underlying tautology (such as the survival of the fittest) and a subset of the available data on surviving and extinct species to develop propositions about the important aspects of the environment and their relation to traits contributing to survival. When successful, the result is a theory that is consistent with the utilized data. This theory can then be tested with as yet unused data. In addition, the theoretical structure can be manipulated to derive additional nonobvious propositions which can also be confronted with new or previously unused data to provide tests. When the data are substantially inconsistent with the predictions, the theory is revised or replaced and the process continues. This is an ongoing process, of course, and takes place over a series of studies and papers.

Finally, note how Whitehead and Russell's emphasis on the importance of definitions applies to the economic notion of the firm. Defining the firm as a black box diverts attention away from what is going on within the firm. The nexus of contracts definition of organizations, on the other hand, focuses attention on the problems that the contracts are intended to solve, that is, on how things get done within the organization. Whether the nexus of contracts view will be as productive as I think it will be is itself an empirical question. However, the relatively recent development of the positive theory of agency lends encouragement to the view that the nexus of contracts approach will be productive.

Two Useful Tautologies: Agency Costs are Minimized and Survival of the Fittest

The positive theory of agency also derives from several definitions and a simple tautology. Cooperative behavior between human beings is viewed as a contracting problem among self-interested individuals with divergent interests. Agency costs are defined as the sum of the costs of structuring, bonding, and monitoring contracts between agents. Agency costs also include the costs stemming from the fact that it doesn't pay to enforce all contracts perfectly. Recognizing that one or more of the contracting parties can capture the benefits from reducing the agency costs in any relationship provides the analytical device, the tautology, that yields implications for the forms of the contracts that evolve[16]— maximizing agents minimize the agency costs in any contracting relationship (see Chapter 3). Notice how conveniently this dovetails with the notion of organizations as a nexus of contracts; its application there implies that the organizational form, its contracts, will be those that minimize the agency costs.

Adding two more elements, (1) the notion that competition is a general phenomenon that takes place over many dimensions, including organizational form, and (2) the survival of the fittest tautology,[17] completes most of the major building blocks of the analytical framework for creating a theory of organizations. The view is one of organizations competing with each other to deliver the activities demanded by customers. Those organizations survive that are able to deliver the activities or products at the lowest price while covering costs. Understanding the survival process involves understanding how the contracts of particular organizations achieve low-cost control of agency problems and how they combine with the production technology of an activity to enable the organization to survive (see Fama and Jensen 1983a, 1983b, 1985).

The Nature of Evidence

Since a theory of organizations is in essence a special case of a general theory of contracting, it is likely that some confusion and disagreement will arise in the profession over the nature of evidence bearing on the theory. Indeed, this disagreement is already becoming evident in the research on organizations and in positive research in accounting.

Economists, financial economists, accounting researchers, and behavioral scientists are well indoctrinated in the methodology associated with the use of quantitative evidence in the testing of theories. We have been fortunate, for example, that the theory of efficient markets yields direct predictions about the characteristics of the probability distributions of asset price changes and returns—predictions for which a rich variety of data and statistical theory are conveniently available for testing purposes. However, many important predictions of the research on positive organization theory and positive accounting theory will be characterizations of the contracting relations, and much of the best evidence on these propositions will be qualitative and institutional evidence, that is, evidence on the forms of the contracts, their provisions, and on other organizational and accounting practices. By its nature, much of this institutional evidence cannot be summarized by measures using real numbers. We simply do not know how to aggregate such evidence, nor can we calculate formal measures of central tendency and standard errors of estimate. This means, of course, that regression equations cannot be estimated, and this will not bring comfort to those empiricists who clutch regression equations to their breasts like security blankets. Statisticians and econometricians are likely to react because this violates a long and venerable tradition of formal testing.

Whenever feasible, of course, it is desirable to obtain quantitative predictions of a form amenable to the usual testing procedures. However, since the theory is aimed at explaining the contract structures and practices of organizations, it seems unwise to ignore evidence on such structures in testing the theory. It seems especially unwise in the early stages of development, because any theory that is likely to be useful and worthy of detailed consideration should not be vastly inconsistent with the readily available institutional evidence. Not all such theories will, however, be acceptable, and herein lies a serious inference problem. The fact is that a well-developed theory of inference for dealing with quantitative data exists, and it is of great value. Such a theory is not nearly as well developed for dealing with the qualitative institutional data that characterize the organizational field, and therefore the likelihood of misuse of data and incorrect inferences is higher.

Nonparametric statistics provide only limited help in dealing with institutional evidence because these procedures generally presume independence in sample observations—a condition seldom satisfied. In addition, it is often difficult to know what procedures were followed in selecting a sample of institutional evidence, and this raises serious questions about the existence of selection bias and therefore about the inferences to be made from the evidence. Finally, because institutional evidence consists of noncommensurable items we do not know how to formally weight the individual pieces of evidence; they cannot be simply counted or added up. Yet this does not mean the observations are not evidence, and most people intuitively understand this when it comes to the issues considered in a criminal trial. With the help of statisticians and philosophers, perhaps some progress will be made in resolving these inference problems.

Meanwhile, it is unwise to ignore important institutional evidence while paying great attention to unimportant quantitative evidence simply because its dimensions are more familiar. The practice of using pejorative labels such as "casual," "anecdotal," or "ad hoc" to describe such institutional or qualitative evidence is counterproductive to the research process. Such labels suggest uncaring or sloppy methods or unimportant evidence. The terms "readily available" or "institutional" evidence are reasonable substitutes for these emotion-laden terms, while the terms "incomplete" or "inappropriate" evidence are reasonable descriptive labels to use when the researcher's methods are in fact uncaring or sloppy. Not all institutional evidence is readily available: much of it requires a great deal of effort to gather. On the one hand, stock price data, accounting data, and national income data are readily available to the scientist, but they are not given pejorative labels such as "casual." For several carefully executed and useful studies using institutional evidence, I recommend the study of the covenants in bond indentures by Smith and Warner (1979), the Mayers and Smith work (1981, 1982a, 1982b) on organizations and contractual practices in the insurance industry, the study of the market for accounting theories by Watts and Zimmerman (1979), and the study of private specification of accounting procedures by Leftwich (1983).

The Role of Mathematics

Mathematics is a very useful language, but not universally so. It is often useful in the derivation of nonobvious implications that are difficult to develop by other techniques. The propositions of portfolio theory and asset pricing are examples. The unaided human mind and the English language are not well suited to handling the complexities of the notion of a covariance matrix and solutions to sets of simultaneous equations. Without the help of the language of mathematics, the insights of portfolio theory and asset pricing along with many others would likely remain unknown.

Sometimes, however, the use of mathematics is counterproductive in the research process. This is especially true in dealing with new and uncharted areas such as organization theory and accounting theory. As implied by the previous discussion of definitions and tautologies, a great deal of work has to be done in a new area of analysis that represents a radical departure from current knowledge before the dimensionality of the problem and the major variables can be defined. Mathematics seems to be useless for solving these problems. My impression is that attempts to use it at such an early stage in the development of an area are often counterproductive because authors are led to assume the problem away or to define sterile "toy" problems that are mathematically tractable.

Unfortunately, there exists in the profession an unwarranted bias toward the use of mathematics even in situations where it is unproductive or useless. One manifestation of this is the common use of the terms "rigorous" or "analytical" or even "theoretical" as identical with "mathematical." None of these links is, of course, correct. Mathematical is not the same as rigorous, nor is it the same as analytical or theoretical. Propositions can be logically rigorous without being mathematical, and analysis does not have to take the form of symbols and equations. The English sentence and paragraph will do quite well for many analytical purposes. In addition, the use of mathematics does not prevent the commission of errors—even egregious ones.

There will always be some people who think and produce better in one language than another. And there will be problems and problem areas where one language or analytical approach is more productive than another. Nevertheless, some researchers take the attitude that analysis is worthwhile and important only if accomplished through the language of mathematics. Others are antagonistic toward analysis that uses mathematics. We can hope that as the profession matures, more tolerance, understanding, and consideration of these issues will prevail. As our knowledge of organizations and accounting theory grows I expect to see increased productive use of mathematics.

5.8   The Two Agency Literatures

Since the original papers by Spence and Zeckhauser (1971) and Ross (1973), substantial attention has been given to the development of the theory of agency. Interestingly, that development has resulted in two almost entirely separate and valuable literatures that nominally address the same problem. However, the two literatures differ in many respects, and they reference each other less than one might expect given the closeness of their topics. Being actively involved in one of these efforts and a neophyte in the other, I am not the best person to provide an unbiased comparison of them, but some discussion seems appropriate at this point.

Earlier, I briefly discussed one of the agency literatures—what I have labeled the "positive theory of agency." The other literature has acquired the label "principal-agent."[18] Both literatures address the contracting problem between self-interested maximizing parties, and both use the same agency cost minimizing tautology (although not necessarily stated in that form). They differ, however, in many respects. The principal-agent literature is generally mathematical and non-empirically-oriented, while the positive agency literature is generally non-mathematical and empirically oriented (although neither literature is entirely so).

The principal-agent literature has generally concentrated on modeling the effects of three factors on contracts between parties interacting in the hierarchical fashion suggested by the term "principal-agent": (1) the structure of the preferences of the parties to the contracts, (2) the nature of uncertainty, and (3) the informational structure in the environment. Attention is generally focused on risk sharing and the form of the optimal contract between principal and agent, and on welfare comparisons of the equilibrium contracting solutions in the presence of information costs vis-à-vis the solutions in the absence of such costs.

The positive agency literature has generally concentrated on modeling the effects of additional aspects of the contracting environment and the technology of monitoring and bonding on the form of the contracts and organizations that survive. Capital intensity, degree of specialization of assets, information costs, capital markets, and internal and external labor markets are examples of factors in the contracting environment that interact with the costs of various monitoring and bonding practices to determine the contractual forms.[19]

Each of the agency literatures has its strong and weak points, and on occasion tension has surfaced between them. In some sense the reasons are understandable. Part is due to the "tyranny of formalism" that develops when mathematically inclined scholars take the attitude that if the analytical language is not mathematics, it isn't rigorous, and if a problem cannot be solved with the use of mathematics, the effort should be abandoned. Part is due to the belief that the lack of the use of mathematics in the positive agency literature results in ex post facto theorizing that assures the hypotheses will not be rejected. Part is also due to the problems associated with the use of qualitative and institutional evidence, discussed earlier.

Though much of the principal-agent literature seems to be produced in the normative mode, most of it can be interpreted in a positive fashion. However, some believe that so little is put into the current principal-agent models that there is little hope of producing results that will explain much of the rich variety of observed contracting practices. Tractability problems seem to limit the richness of the input to the principal-agent models, especially when it comes to analyzing the effects of markets on the contracting process—for example, capital and labor markets and the market for control. It also seems difficult to analyze within the principal-agent models the effects of complex equilibrium systems in the contracting milieu, for example, mutual monitoring systems like the collegial system so familiar to academics.

The issue boils down to an empirical question regarding how useful the preference, stochastic structure, and information structure variables are in explaining observed contracting practices. The positive agency literature proceeds on the implicit assumption that the variables emphasized in the principal-agent literature are relatively unimportant in understanding the observed phenomenon when compared with richer specifications of information costs, other aspects of the environment, and the monitoring and bonding technology.

On the other hand, the methods of the positive agency literature justifiably seem to some to be unconstrained and often perilously close to tautological. In part this arises from a misunderstanding by some of the nature of the scientific process—the manner in which we use tautologies to develop positive theories. At the risk of oversimplifying, the ideal process proceeds by using the agency definitions and the cost-minimizing tautology described earlier and a subset of the observed contract structures to develop propositions about the important aspects of the environment and the monitoring and bonding technology—that is, to derive a theory that is consistent with those contracts. If successful, that effort provides a structure that can be manipulated to derive additional nonobvious positive propositions, i.e., hypotheses. Confronting these propositions with previously unknown or unused data provides a test of the theory. If the data are substantially inconsistent with the predictions, the theory is then revised or replaced with a new alternative, and the process continues. This is the scientific process. In the initial stages we should take care to avoid requiring researchers to accomplish all this in a single study or paper—an undesirable requirement from the standpoint of the progress of science. It is important that we, as colleagues, referees, and editors, avoid applying standards to individual papers that are appropriately applied only to the scientific process as a whole.

On the other hand, it is appropriate to be suspicious of results obtained from "too much" fishing in the data—including the institutional data—although it is often difficult to tell how much of that has taken place. The appropriate response is to treat the results of early studies as more like a set of relatively untested hypotheses than a well-tested and surviving theory.

As a result of the continued gradual development of our empirical and conceptual knowledge, I expect to see the two agency literatures become closer, partly because the intellectual efforts devoted by both groups will result in a clearer understanding of the definitions of the important concepts and the relevant dimensions upon which to order the complexity of the world. Mathematics will then be of great help in the generation of nonobvious testable propositions and as a language for use in communicating the important aspects of the theoretical structure.

In the end, competition in research is as important to innovation and progress as competition in the product markets. Scholars will make their own judgments of what are currently useful results and where the productive and exciting research approaches and opportunities are. I have little doubt that with the passage of time, the "fit" (that is, the productive and useful results and approaches) will "survive."

PART II

Residual Claims and Organizational Forms

Agency Problems and Residual Claims

6.1 Introduction

Organizational Survival

Social and economic activities, such as religion, entertainment, education, research, and the production of other goods and services, are carried on by different types of organizations, for example, corporations, proprietorships, partnerships, mutuals, and nonprofits. Most goods and services can be produced by any form of organization, and there is competition among organizational forms for survival in any activity. In the absence of fiat, the form of organization that survives in an activity is the one that delivers the product demanded by customers at the lowest price while covering costs. This is the telling dimension on which the economic environment chooses among organizational forms.

An important factor in the survival of organizational forms is control of agency problems. These problems arise because contracts are not costlessly written and enforced. Agency costs include the costs of structuring, monitoring, and bonding a set of contracts among agents with conflicting interests, plus the residual loss incurred because the cost of full enforcement of contracts exceeds the benefits.[1] In this chapter we explain the special features of the residual claims of different organizational forms as efficient approaches to controlling special agency problems. We analyze only private organizations. In related papers we have examined other features of the contract structures of different organizational forms that contribute to their survival: in particular, (1) the control of agency problems in the class of organizations characterized by separation of "ownership" and "control," and (2) the effects of special

By Eugene F. Fama and Michael C. Jensen; originally published in *Journal of Law and Economics* 26 (June 1983).

characteristics of residual claims on decision rules for resource allocation.[2]

Residual Claims: General Discussion

The contract structures of organizations limit the risks undertaken by most agents by specifying either fixed payoffs or incentive payoffs tied to specific measures of performance. The residual risk—the risk of the difference between stochastic inflows of resources and promised payments to agents—is borne by those who contract for the rights to net cash flows. We call these agents the residual claimants or residual risk bearers.

The characteristics of residual claims distinguish organizations from one another and help explain the survival of organizational forms in specific activities. We first analyze and contrast the relatively unrestricted residual claims of open corporations with the restricted residual claims of proprietorships, partnerships, and closed corporations. We then turn to the more specialized residual claims of professional partnerships, financial mutuals, and nonprofits.

6.2 Open Corporations

Most large nonfinancial organizations are open corporations. The common stock residual claims of such organizations are unrestricted in the sense that (1) stockholders are not required to have any other role in the organization, (2) their residual claims are freely alienable, and (3) the residual claims are rights in net cash flows for the life of the organization. Because of the unrestricted nature of the residual claims of open corporations, there is generally almost complete separation and specialization of decision functions and residual risk bearing.

Common Stock versus State Contingent Claims

One can imagine claims that are even less restricted than the common stocks of open corporations. There could be "state contingent claims"—that is, claims of the sort discussed by Arrow (1964b) and Debreu (1959) specifying payoffs for each possible future state of the world. Such state contingent claims allow any (hence generally "less restricted") allocation of risk. They are, nonetheless, fixed payoff promises. To specify the total payoffs to be obtained in all future states, one would need to identify all current and future decisions of an organization through state contingent claim contracts. Given the costs and information requirements this implies, it is not surprising that state contingent claims are not the dominant system for allocating risk.

We can also imagine state contingent claims that are true residual claims. The claim would cover a fraction of the organization's net cash flows in a given state rather than a specified payoff in that state. However, this type of claim generates conflicts among the claim holders of different states because alternative decisions shift payoffs across states and benefit some claim holders at the expense of others. Common stock that represents proportionate claims on the payoffs of all future states eliminates these agency problems, but at the sacrifice of some efficiency in the allocation of risk. Common stock and other common forms of residual claims also avoid most of the costs of defining and verifying states of the world.

The Advantages of Common Stock Residual Claims

1. *Unrestricted Risk Sharing among Residual Claimants.* The common stock of open corporations allows more efficient risk sharing than residual claims that are not separable from decision roles, as, for example, in proprietorships and partnerships where the proprietors and partners are the decision makers and the primary residual claimants. Common stock allows residual risk to be spread across many residual claimants who individually choose the extent to which they bear risk and who can diversify across organizations offering such claims. Other things being equal, portfolio theory implies that such unrestricted risk sharing lowers the cost of risk-bearing services.[3]

2. *Specialized Risk Bearing by Residual Claimants.* The activities of large open nonfinancial corporations are typically complicated, involving contracts with many factors of production, for example, different types of labor, raw materials, and managers. When there is significant variation through time in the probability of default on these contracts, contracting costs increase. In addition, because the human capital of agents is generally employed in a single organization, risk aversion tends to cause them to charge more for any risk they bear than security holders who can diversify risk across many organizations.[4]

Efficient accommodation of large-scale specialized risk bearing by residual claimants is an advantage of corporate common stock. To bond contractual payments to other agents, the common stockholders put up wealth, which is used to purchase assets. If the wealth required to bond promised payments goes beyond the value of inputs optimally purchased rather than rented, common stock proceeds can be used to purchase liquid assets, for example, the securities of other organizations, that have no function except to bond specialization of risk bearing by residual claimants.

3. *Purchase of Organization-specific Assets.* Klein, Crawford, and Alchian (1978) and Jensen and Meckling (see Chapter 3) have argued that because of conflicts of interest with outside owners of organization-specific assets—assets that have lower value to other organizations—rental contracts for such assets generate higher agency costs than outright purchase. Common stock, with its capacity for raising wealth from residual claimants, is an efficient vehicle for financing such purchases in activities where using large amounts of organization-specific risky assets is efficient.

4. *Specialization of Management.* In the complicated production and distribution activities of large open corporations, coordinating the activities of agents, recontracting among them, and initiating and implementing resource allocation decisions are specialized tasks that are important to the survival of the organization and largely fall on its managers. However, managerial skills are not necessarily tied to wealth or willingness to bear risk, and incompetent managers who are important residual claimants can be difficult to remove. Thus, ignoring agency problems in the decision process, the survival of a complex organization is enhanced by common stock residual claims that allow specialization of management—in effect, the absence of a classical entrepreneur who is both decision maker and residual risk bearer.

5. *The Market Value Rule for Investment Decisions.* When common stocks are traded without transactions costs in a perfectly competitive capital market, the stockholders agree that resource allocation decisions should be evaluated according to their contribution to the current market value of their residual claims.[5] The market value rule weighs current against future resources according to the opportunity costs at which resources can be traded across time in the capital market. For example, the market value rule favors expenditures to reduce the current and future costs of delivering products whenever the current market value

of the future cost savings is greater than the current expenditure. Product prices can then be lowered while still covering costs.

In contrast, when the horizon of the residual claims is less than the life of the organization, residual claimants assign zero value to cash flows that occur beyond the horizon.[6] Similarly, when residual claims are not freely alienable or separable from other roles in the organization, it is rational for risk bearers to attribute lower current value to uncertain cash flows than is implied by capital market prices for the future resources.[7] As a consequence, ignoring agency problems in the decision process, organizations with common stock residual claims, investing according to the market value rule which is optimal for their residual claimants, will be able to deliver products at lower prices than organizations with restricted residual claims.

The Agency Problems of Common Stock Residual Claims

The unrestricted nature of the common stock residual claims of open corporations leads to an important agency problem. The decision process is in the hands of professional managers whose interests are not identical to those of residual claimants. This problem of separation of "ownership" and "control"—more precisely, the separation of residual risk bearing from decision functions—has troubled students of open corporations from Adam Smith (1776) to Berle and Means (1932) and Jensen and Meckling (1976). In Chapter 7, "Separation of Ownership and Control," we argue that this agency problem is controlled by decision systems that separate the management (initiation and implementation) and control (ratification and monitoring) of important decisions at all levels of the organization.

Devices for separating decision management and decision control include (1) decision hierarchies in which the decision initiatives of lower-level agents are passed on to higher-level agents, first for ratification and then for monitoring, (2) boards of directors that ratify and monitor the organization's most important decisions and hire, fire, and compensate top-level decision managers, and (3) incentive structures that encourage mutual monitoring among decision agents. The costs of such mechanisms for separating decision management from decision control are part of the price that open corporations pay for the benefits of unrestricted common stock residual claims.

6.3   Restricted versus Unrestricted Residual Claims

The proprietorships, partnerships, and closed corporations observed in small-scale production activities differ in many ways both from one another and from open corporations. For example, proprietorships have a single residual claimant, whereas partnerships and closed corporations have multiple residual claimants. As a consequence, the residual claim contracts in partnerships and closed corporations must specify rights in net cash flows and procedures for transferring residual claims to new agents more explicitly than the residual claims in proprietorships.

However, for control of the agency problems in the decision process, the common characteristic of the residual claims of proprietorships, partnerships, and closed corporations that distinguishes them from open corporations is that the residual claims are largely restricted to important decision agents. This restriction avoids the agency problems between residual claimants and decision agents that arise because of separation of risk-bearing and decision functions in open corporations. Thus, costly mechanisms for separating the management and control of decisions are avoided.[8]

Restricting residual claims to decision makers controls agency problems between residual claimants and decision agents, but at the expense of the benefits of unrestricted common stock. The decision process suffers efficiency losses because decision agents must be chosen on the basis of wealth and willingness to bear risk as well as for decision skills. Residual claimants forgo optimal diversification so that residual claims and decision making can be combined in a small number of agents. Forgone diversification and limited alienability lower the value of the residual claims, raise the cost of risk-bearing services, and lead to less investment in projects with uncertain payoffs than when residual claims are unrestricted. Finally, because decision agents have limited wealth, restricting residual claims to them also limits resources available for bonding contractual payoffs and for acquiring risky organization-specific assets.

An organizational form survives in an activity when the costs and benefits of its residual claims and the approaches it provides to controlling agency problems combine with available production technology to allow the organization to deliver products at lower prices than other organizational forms. The restricted residual claims of proprietorships, partnerships, and closed corporations are more likely to dominate when technology does not involve important economies of scale that lead to large demands for specialized decision skills, specialized risk bearing, and wealth from residual claimants. In these circumstances, the agency costs saved by restricting residual claims to decision agents outweigh the benefits that would be obtained from separation and specialization of decision and risk-bearing functions. On the other hand, unrestricted common stock residual claims are more likely to dominate when there are important economies of scale in production that (1) can be realized only with a complex decision hierarchy that makes use of specialized decision skills throughout the organization, (2) generate large aggregate risks to be borne by residual claimants, and (3) demand large amounts of wealth from residual claimants to purchase risky assets and to bond the payoffs promised to a wide range of agents in the organization. In such complex organizations the benefits of unrestricted common stock residual claims are likely to outweigh the costs of controlling the agency problems inherent in the separation and specialization of decision and risk-bearing functions. In these circumstances, the open corporation is more likely to win the competition for survival.[9]

6.4   Special Forms of Residual Claims

The restriction of residual claims to important decision agents distinguishes the residual claims of proprietorships, partnerships, and closed corporations from the unrestricted residual claims of open corporations. There are, however, other organizational forms, including professional partnerships, financial mutuals, and nonprofits, that offer more unusual residual claims. We explain the special characteristics of the residual claims of these organizations as effective devices for controlling special agency problems.

Professional Partnerships

Like the proprietorships, partnerships, and closed corporations discussed above, the residual claims of the professional partnerships observed in law, public accounting, medicine, and business consulting are restricted to important decision agents. However, in professional partnerships, a partner's share in net cash flows is renegotiated periodically, and his rights in net cash flows are often limited to his period of service in the organization. In effect, a professional partner's residual claim is a flexible and inalienable share of net cash flows for a limited horizon. Flexible sharing rules, inalienability, and limited horizons distinguish the residual claims of professional partnerships from those of the proprietorships, partnerships, and closed corporations observed in other activities. Moreover, these special features of professional partnership residual claims are generally retained when these organizations become professional service corporations for tax purposes.

1. *Decentralized Decision Making and Restricted Residual Claims.* In professional partnerships, large and small, individuals or small teams work on cases, audits, and so on. Because of the importance of specific knowledge about particular clients—knowledge that is costly to transfer among agents—it is efficient for the teams in large partnerships to make most decisions locally. Thus, with respect to the services rendered to customers, decision control takes place within teams, where interaction and mutual monitoring are heaviest. At this level, however, decision management (initiation and implementation) and decision control (ratification and monitoring) are not separate. To control the resulting agency problems, the residual claims in professional partnerships are restricted to the professional agents who are the important team members and who have major decision-making roles. This is consistent with the hypothesis developed in Chapter 7, "Separation of Ownership and Control," that combination of decision management and control functions in one or a few agents leads to restriction of residual claims to the important decision agents.

2. *The Demand for Monitoring, Bonding, and Consulting.* Lawyers, public accountants, physicians, and some business consultants provide services in which one incompetent act can do large damage to a client. As a consequence, certification and pedigree are important to clients. Moreover, even in the largest professional service organizations, services are rendered in individual cases by one or a few professionals. Responsibility for variation in the quality of services is easily assigned to individual agents, and the performance of agents is often well known to clients. In these circumstances, the value of human capital is sensitive to performance. In effect, unlimited liability is imposed on the human capital of professional agents by the market for their services. This gives the professional incentives to purchase monitoring and consulting to help limit losses in the value of human capital.

Since professional services are technical, a lawyer, physician, public accountant, or business consultant is efficiently monitored by others of the same training, who can also provide valuable consulting services. Such mutual monitoring and consulting are encouraged when professional agents agree to pool net cash flows and to share liability for the actions of colleagues. Pooling of net cash flows and liability is attractive because it encourages mutual monitoring and consulting, which in turn improve the quality of services delivered, control liability losses, and enhance the human capital of the partners. Pooling of net cash flows and liability also has risk-sharing advantages.

The analysis is robust to the fact that partnerships sometimes purchase malpractice insurance. Insurance eliminates variability of liability payoffs by substituting a certain insurance premium. However, if premiums are renegotiated to reflect the malpractice experience of the insured, insurance does not destroy the professional's incentives to be monitored or to consult with other professionals.[10] In addition, insurance covers liability to customers but not reductions in the value of human capital caused by incompetent or malfeasant acts.

3. *Large Professional Partnerships and Flexible Sharing Rules.* Some professional partnerships have hundreds and sometimes thousands of partners. Such large partnerships provide portfolios of specialized services that are marketed and delivered over a wide geographical area. They can also provide large bonds to protect clients against losses from malfeasance or incompetence.[11] Large partnerships are also educational organizations, offering young professionals a wide range of opportunities and interaction with other professionals. We are more concerned, though, with the effects of size on the contract structures of these organizations than with explaining why they are large.

Having attained partner status, a professional may be tempted to free-ride on the efforts of colleagues. The residual claims of large partnerships take a direct approach to this agency problem. The residual claim is not generally a fixed share of net cash flows. Rather, a partner's share is renegotiated annually on the basis of past performance and estimates of likely contributions to future net cash flows. In these large partnerships, service to a client is delivered by a small group of professionals who interact and monitor one another intensively. The composition of the teams changes from case to case to match specialized talents to specialized problems. As a result, the professionals develop knowledge of the talents and contributions of a range of colleagues. Flexible sharing rules add to partners' incentives to gather and communicate such knowledge to the renegotiation process.

Given flexible sharing rules and the way payoffs are tied to performance, large professional partnerships can be viewed as associations of proprietors who get together to obtain the benefits from marketing a portfolio of specialized skills both to clients and to young professionals who purchase specialized education. Or, since the partners often work in small teams that shift from case to case, a large partnership can be regarded as a fluid association of small partnerships.

4. *Limited Horizon Residual Claims.* Limitations on the horizon covered by residual claims cause organizations to bias decisions against alternatives that generate net cash flows beyond the horizon. In "Organizational Forms and Investment Decisions"[12] we argue that the limited horizon feature of the residual claims of professional partnerships reflects the relative unimportance of assets that are not effectively capitalized in the human capital of existing partners. There are generally no important patents, specialized assets, or technologies to be passed from one generation of partners to the next. Each partner brings a depleting asset—human capital—to the partnership. The annual readjustments of shares in net cash flows that are typical, especially in large professional partnerships, calibrate a partner's payoffs to reflect the current and expected future contributions of his human capital. When a partner's human capital is used up or withdrawn from the organization, contributions to net cash flows cease, and this is reflected in the termination, without substantial compensation, of his residual claim.

This explanation of the limited horizon feature of the residual claims of professional partnerships gets support from several sources:

1. Professional human capital serves as a bond against malfeasance when its value is sensitive to performance. However, professional human capital cannot be sold to cover liability losses to customers. To satisfy the demand for reimbursement for such losses and to bond their services further, partners generally extend their liability to tangible assets held outside the organization (that is, they contract for unlimited liability), or they purchase insurance against liability losses to clients. Such use of unlimited liability and insurance is consistent with the proposition that the dominant asset in a professional partnership is the inalienable human capital of the partners.

2. Unlike professional partnerships, the proprietorships, partnerships, and closed corporations observed in small-scale production activities commonly have mechanisms for transferring residual claims to the cash flows generated by assets other than human capital. Buy-out

provisions with internal pricing rules for residual claims and first refusal rights are examples of such mechanisms. Moreover, the residual claims of these organizations are similar in other respects to those of professional partnerships, for example, restriction of the residual claims to important decision agents and periodic renegotiation of salaries to reflect variation through time in the contribution of human capital to net cash flows.

3. Most important, professional partners drop the limited horizon feature of their residual claims when there are substantial assets in the organization in addition to the human capital of existing partners. For example, a departing partner is generally compensated for her share in assets, such as cash and accounts receivable. More interesting, professional partnerships sometimes have devices for compensating a retiring partner for information about her clients that she passes along to remaining partners. Such payments for information reduce the incentives of partners to take actions that substitute near-term cash flows for long-term cash flows in a manner that inhibits organizational survival. It is also interesting that organizations in business and financial consulting that were once professional partnerships with limited horizon residual claims are tending to reorganize as open corporations. We hypothesize that this is largely caused by the pressure to transfer the rights to valuable nonhuman capital assets owned within the organization from one generation of residual claimants to the next.

Financial Mutuals

A common form of organization in financial activities is the mutual. In some financial activities, including life insurance, casualty insurance, and personal savings, mutuals exist side by side with open corporations, and there is no obvious tendency for one form of organization to dominate. Mutuals are dominant among investment mutual funds, but commercial banks are always corporations. Our task is to explain why mutuals survive in some financial activities but not in others.

1. *The Control Function of Redeemable Claims.* An unusual characteristic of mutuals is that the residual claimants are customers, for example, the policyholders of mutual insurance companies, the depositors of mutual savings banks, and the shareholders of mutual funds. However, the unique characteristic of the residual claims of mutuals, which is important in understanding their survival value, is that the

residual claims are redeemable on demand. The policyholder, depositor, or shareholder can, at his initiative, turn in his claim at a price determined by a prespecified rule. For example, the shareholder of an open-end mutual fund can redeem his claim for the market value of his share of the fund's assets, while the whole life or endowment insurance policyholder, like the shareholder of a mutual savings bank, can redeem his claim for its specified value plus accumulated dividends.

There is a special form of diffuse control inherent in the redeemable claims of financial organizations. The withdrawal decisions of redeemable claim holders affect the resources under the control of the organization's managers, and they do so in a more direct fashion than customer decisions in nonfinancial organizations. The decision of the claim holder to withdraw resources is a form of partial takeover or liquidation which deprives management of control over assets. This control right can be exercised independently by each claim holder. It does not require a proxy fight, a tender offer, or any other concerted takeover bid. In contrast, decisions of customers in open nonfinancial corporations, and the repricing of the corporation's securities in the capital market, provide signals about the performance of its decision agents, but without further action, either internal or from the corporate takeover market, the judgments of customers and of the capital market leave the assets owned within the organization under the control of the managers.

2. *The Limitations of Redeemable Claims.* Redeemable claims are not an efficient general financing instrument for nonfinancial organizations. Giving every claim holder the right to force contractions of assets would impose substantial costs on nonfinancial activities. For example, nonfinancial corporations typically have large demands for organization-specific assets that have lower value to other organizations. Substantial costs would be incurred in forced sales of such illiquid assets to accommodate redemptions of claims. In contrast, a financial organization purchases and sells financial assets to meet purchases and redemptions of claims. This is accomplished at low cost because financial assets are not organization-specific and can be traded with low transactions costs.

There is a more subtle problem with redeemable residual claims in nonfinancial activities. The pricing rule used to redeem claims preempts development of an outside secondary market for the claims. No one will buy at a price higher than the redemption price or sell at a lower price.

The absence of secondary markets for the redeemable claims of financial organizations is no problem since redemption price rules (for example, the net asset value rule for mutual fund shares) can be based on prices of financial assets quoted in the capital market. In contrast, the residual claims of nonfinancial organizations are claims on uncertain future cash flows. Without a secondary market for the claims, accurate and inexpensive external indexes of their value would not exist, and any internal redemption pricing rule would be costly or arbitrary.

3. *Corporate Financial Organizations.* Our analysis should also explain why some financial organizations are mutuals and others are open corporations. The theory predicts that more of the business of financial mutuals involves management of portfolios of financial assets, whereas corporate financial organizations are more involved in business activities requiring organization-specific assets that are expensive to trade and that generate uncertain future net cash flows that are not easily priced.

Observation of different financial organizations is roughly consistent with these hypotheses. Most investment mutual funds manage portfolios of traded securities. The funds are open-end mutuals with redeemable residual claims, except for a handful of closed-end funds organized as open corporations with nonredeemable common stock residual claims. Consistent with our hypothesis, the closed-end funds often hold assets such as real estate or shares in new ventures that are expensive to value and to trade, though this is not universal.[13]

Commercial banks are required by law to be corporations. Our analysis suggests that they would be corporations even in the absence of the requirement. A major part of bank business is providing transaction services. Depositors pay for these services directly or by forgoing returns on deposits. The primary assets of commercial banks are short-term loans. Granting and renewing these loans involves monitoring the borrowers and certifying credit worthiness—a service for which the borrowers pay. The capital value of the stochastic net cash flows from services to depositors and borrowers would not easily be captured in the internal pricing rule of a redeemable residual claim.

What survives in commercial banking is a contract structure involving deposits that, like all redeemable claims, allow the depositors to affect the resources under management control. Consistent with our model, variation in deposits is met by purchases and sales of government and private bonds traded at low cost in secondary markets. Since depositors do not have residual claims on net cash flows from service and other activities, redemption of deposits does not require internal valuation of these net cash flows. The rights to the residual net cash flows are assigned to common stock. Since the common stock is not redeemable, there are incentives for development of a secondary market. The residual claims against uncertain future net cash flows are then priced more effectively than would be the case with redeemable residual claims for which there would be no secondary market. Such mixed capital structures, with fixed value redeemable claims (policies or deposits) and nonredeemable common stock residual claims, are also characteristic of the savings banks and insurance companies organized as open corporations.

Our analysis should also explain the differences between the corporate and mutual organizations observed in the same financial activity, for example, life insurance or personal saving. Relative to the mutuals, corporate financial organizations should be more involved in business activities other than management of financial assets, and these business activities should involve relatively more nonfinancial assets that can only be varied with large costs. The data on the business receipts (revenues other than interest, dividends, and capital gains) and long-term nonfinancial assets of banks and life insurance companies given in Table 6.1 are consistent with these hypotheses. Corporate commercial banks have more business receipts relative to total receipts and more long-term nonfinancial assets relative to total assets than mutual savings banks or savings and loan associations. More interesting, savings and loans, which are sometimes corporations, have relatively more business receipts and long-term nonfinancial assets than mutual savings banks. Likewise, corporate life insurance companies have higher ratios of business receipts to total receipts and higher ratios of long-term nonfinancial assets to total assets than mutual life insurance companies.[14]

The data for casualty insurance organizations are less supportive. Consistent with our analysis, mutual casualty companies show lower ratios of long-term nonfinancial assets to total assets than corporate casualty companies. However, contrary to our analysis, the mutuals have higher ratios of business receipts to total receipts.[15]

Finally, an interesting organizational experiment is taking place in the banking sector. Although commercial banks are required to be corporations, regulations restricting commercial banks and savings banks to different activities are being relaxed. The direction is toward allowing

Table 6.1   Business Receipts and Long-Term Nonfinancial Assets of Corporate and Mutual Financial Organizations, Selected Years

	1967	1969	1971	1973	1975
Business receipts as a percentage of total receipts:					
Corporate commercial banks	12.6	11.1	14.0	12.0	8.3
Savings and loans	4.7	4.7	6.3	5.4	5.6
Mutual savings banks	2.9	3.0	3.1	2.8	3.1
Corporate life insurance	82.7	82.7	83.0	82.0	81.0
Mutual life insurance	72.9	72.6	72.9	72.1	72.1
Corporate casualty insurance	91.5	89.2	89.7	87.7	87.1
Mutual casualty insurance	94.0	93.0	92.7	92.0	90.1
Long-term nonfinancial assets as a percentage of total assets:					
Corporate commercial banks	2.4	2.7	3.0	3.2	3.0
Savings and loans	2.4	2.4	2.4	2.4	2.4
Mutual savings banks	1.2	1.1	1.2	1.6	1.7
Corporate life insurance	4.9	6.1	5.4	5.4	6.5
Mutual life insurance	2.8	3.1	3.2	3.3	3.5
Corporate casualty insurance	5.3	7.6	9.0	9.5	9.5
Mutual casualty insurance	3.6	3.9	3.7	3.9	3.6

Source: U.S. Internal Revenue Service, computer tape of corporate statistics of income. Business receipts are revenues other than interest, dividends, and capital gains. Policy premiums are included in business receipts for insurance companies.

savings banks to provide services such as checking privileges and short-term business loans, previously restricted to commercial banks. If the dominance of the corporate format in commercial banking is not the consequence of regulation, then as savings banks become involved in the service activities of commercial banking, they will tend to organize as corporations. On the other hand, if commercial banking services can be provided at lower prices with the mutual format, corporate commercial banks will not survive when mutual savings banks are allowed to compete with them.

Nonprofit Organizations

The familiar economic analysis of the entrepreneurial firm is of little help in explaining the dominance of nonprofits in some activities, such as religion, education, research, and classical music, but not in others, including automobile manufacturing, legal services, and popular music. We explain the survival of nonprofits in donor-financed activities as an efficient solution to the special agency problem posed by private donations.

1. *Nonprofit Organizations and Donations.* Donations per se do not imply dominance for the nonprofit form. When donations are applied directly to well-defined units of output, a for-profit producer perceives them as a reduction in variable costs or as an increase in demand and increases output accordingly. In fact, we observe unit subsidies both in activities organized on a nonprofit basis, for example, educational scholarships, and in activities organized on a for-profit basis, such as free tickets to sports events for various groups.

However, some donors wish to provide general donations to particular producers (churches, universities, and so on) rather than unit subsidies. Such unrestricted donations pose agency problems for any organization with residual claimants. Residual claimants contract for rights to net cash flows. When activities are financed in part through donations, part of net cash flow is from resources provided by donors. Contracts that define the share of residual claimants in net cash flows are unlikely to assure donors that their resources are protected from expropriation by residual claimants. One solution to this agency problem is to have no alienable residual claims and to contract with donors to apply all net cash flows to output. Thus, our hypothesis is that the absence of residual claims avoids the donor-residual claimant agency problem and explains the dominance of nonprofits in donor-financed activities.[16]

The absence of alienable residual claims in nonprofits does not mean that residual risk is not borne. When net cash flows are used to expand outputs or to lower the prices of outputs, part of the risk of net cash flows is borne by consumers and part by the factors used to produce the outputs. Thus, residual net cash flows are allocated, but there are no specific residual claimants with alienable property rights in net cash flows. Moreover, the absence of residual claims does not mean that nonprofits make no profits. It means that alienable claims to profits do not exist.

Donations can substitute for the resources provided by residual claimants to purchase assets that are optimally owned rather than rented. When held as endowment, donations also help to bond contracts with other agents in the organization. From a survival viewpoint the advantage of donations over resources provided by residual claimants is that donors forgo claims on their donations and on the returns earned on the donations, and this tends to allow the organization to deliver its products at lower prices.

Our nonprofit hypothesis deals only with activities financed by donations. Such donor-financed activities are dominated by nonprofits, for example, private universities, churches, hospitals, charities, and cultural performing groups (symphony orchestras, ballet companies, and opera companies). However, the limited scope of the hypothesis means that it cannot explain the nonprofits observed in activities where donations play no role, for example, country clubs.

2. *Other Explanations for Nonprofits.* One criticism of our hypothesis about the causal relation from donations to the nonprofit form is that it ignores the difficulty of measuring and selling the outputs of, for example, churches. The inference is that this explains the nonprofit form in these activities. It is difficult to measure all the things one gets from religion, education, research, or cultural activities. However, the same is true of products such as rock music and legal or psychiatric services marketed by organizations that have residual claims. Moreover, if donations disappeared, for-profit organizations, or more precisely organizations that have alienable residual claims, would arise to supply religion, research, and education. Some for-profit organizations supply these services now. For-profit educational organizations and research groups sell definable parts of their outputs; tuition for education and royalties to patents are examples. For-profit churches might sell ordinations, indulgences, or admission to services. Consistent with our hypothesis, when education and research are provided by organizations that have alienable residual claims, these organizations are not also financed with donations.

Some argue that sale of some products and services (for example, religion) is not acceptable and that this explains the nonprofit form in these activities. This is consistent with our hypothesis. When giving outputs away generates more resources through donations than sale, survival dictates the nonprofit form. Thus, universities generally make research freely available because this generates more resources through research grants and other donations than direct sale of the research. Churches usually do not insist on payment of admission charges or member taxes because they attract more total resources through voluntary contributions.

Coldly economic statements like these lead to the criticism that our analysis leaves no room for altruism. The opposite is true. Altruistic internal agents increase the willingness of altruistic customers and donors to provide resources. In our terms, the altruism of internal agents allows low-cost control of agency problems and acts to bond donors and customers against expropriation. Strong tastes for an organization's outputs on the part of internal agents and customers—what we call altruism in the case of nonprofits—contribute to the survival of any organization. All organizations try to develop such brand loyalty, but the nonprofits are especially successful, perhaps because of the nature of their products.

Some researchers claim that donors, customers, and internal agents have tastes for the nonprofit form itself in some activities. To explain the complete dominance of nonprofits in an activity, however, this approach requires uniformity of tastes. If subgroups of customers, internal agents, and donors have no preference for the nonprofit form, we would expect more competition among profit and nonprofit organizations in donor-financed activities.

Finally, tax concessions are important to some nonprofits. However, the major activities dominated by nonprofits, such as religion, private education, research, hospital care, and certain cultural activities, were dominated by nonprofits before taxes were a major issue.[17] Our hypothesis about the relation between unrestricted donations and the nonprofit form provides a more consistent explanation of the historical dominance of nonprofits in these activities. On the other hand, tax exemptions probably explain the nonprofits in activities where private donations are not a factor, including nursing homes, homes for the elderly, and private nursery schools.

3. *The General Control Problem in Nonprofits.* The donors of nonprofits have agency problems with internal decision agents similar to those faced by residual claimants in other organizations, such as open corporations and financial mutuals, where important decision managers do not bear a major share of the wealth effects of their decisions. We argue in the following chapter that, like all other organizations characterized by separation of decision management from residual risk bearing, a nonprofit is on stronger footing in the competition for survival when it has a decision system that separates the management (initiation and implementation) and control (ratification and monitoring) of important decisions. For nonprofits, the survival value of such decision systems is due to the assurances they provide that donations are used effectively and are not easily expropriated.

For example, like open corporations and financial mutuals, donor nonprofits have boards of directors (or trustees) with the power to ratify and monitor important decisions and to hire, fire, and set the compensation of important decision agents. The similarities of the decision control systems of nonprofits, financial mutuals, and open corporations, along with the differences due to special agency problems and special features of residual claims (including the absence thereof), are discussed in Chapter 7.

6.5   Conclusions

Most goods and services can be produced by any form of organization. Organizations compete for survival, and the form of organization that survives in an activity is the one that delivers the product demanded by customers at the lowest price while covering costs.

The characteristics of residual claims are important both in distinguishing organizations from one another and in explaining the survival of specific organizational forms in specific activities. We explain the survival of organizational forms largely in terms of the comparative advantages of characteristics of residual claims in controlling the agency problems of an activity. The analysis identifies the underlying characteristics of activities that determine the organizational forms that survive.

Open Corporations

The common stock residual claims of open corporations are unrestricted in the sense that (1) they are freely alienable, (2) they are rights in net cash flows for the life of the organization, and (3) stockholders are not required to have any other role in the organization. Other things being equal, the open corporation is more likely to survive in an activity

1. the greater the benefits of unrestricted risk sharing,
2. the greater the benefits of specialized management,
3. the greater the amount of organization-specific assets to be purchased,
4. the greater the wealth required to bond contractual payoffs, and
5. the lower the cost of separating decision management (initiation and implementation) from decision control (ratification and monitoring).

For example, these factors favor the open corporate form when the technology in an activity implies economies of scale that involve (a) large aggregate residual risks to be shared among residual claimants, (b) large demands for specialized decision agents throughout the organization, and (c) large demands for wealth from residual claimants to bond contracts and to purchase organization-specific assets. Economies of scale are also likely to imply organizations that are complex in the sense that valuable specific knowledge—knowledge that is expensive to transfer across agents—is widely diffused among agents.[18] Such complexity tends to favor unrestricted common stock residual claims which allow specialization of management and delegation of decision functions to agents with valuable relevant knowledge.

The benefits of unrestricted common stock residual claims in activities where optimal organizations are large and complex offset the agency costs resulting from the separation of decision functions and residual risk bearing. In Chapter 7, "Separation of Ownership and Control," we contend that these agency costs are controlled by decision structures that separate the management and control of important decisions.

Proprietorships, Partnerships, and Closed Corporations

In a fictional world where contracts with decision agents were costlessly written and enforced, separation and specialization of decision and risk-bearing functions would involve no agency costs, and most if not all organizations would have unrestricted residual claims. However, actual organizations can realize the benefits of unrestricted residual claims only by incurring costs to control agency problems between specialized decision agents and specialized residual risk bearers. As a consequence, it is advantageous in some activities to trade the benefits of unrestricted common stock residual claims for the low-cost control of agency problems in the decision process obtained when residual claims are restricted to important decision agents. This restriction is a common characteristic of the residual claims of proprietorships, partnerships, and closed corporations. Other things being equal, these organizations with their restricted residual claims are more likely to survive in activities where the costs of separating decision management from decision control are high. They are also more likely to survive when there are no important economies of scale and thus (a) no large demands for unrestricted risk sharing and specialized decision skills, and (b) no large demands for wealth from residual claimants to bond contracts and purchase organization-specific assets.

Special Forms of Residual Claims

Organizations such as professional partnerships, financial mutuals, and nonprofits have residual claims with unique characteristics that we explain as devices for controlling special agency problems.

1. *Professional Partnerships.* These are characterized by (1) restriction of residual claims to major decision agents, (2) periodic renegotiation of partner shares in net cash flows (flexible sharing rules), and (3) inalienable residual claims in net cash flows with horizons that are often limited to a partner's period of service in the organization. Professional partnerships are more likely to survive in an activity when

1. valuable specific knowledge relevant to both the management and control of decisions is combined and diffused among agents;
2. there are no strong demands for organization-specific tangible assets; and
3. the benefits from consulting and mutual monitoring among decision agents are high.

These characteristics are observed in professional service activities (law, public accounting, and business consulting) where (1) restricting residual claims to important decision agents helps control the agency problems caused by delegating combined decision management and control rights with respect to cases, audits, and so forth to agents with relevant specific knowledge; (2) the primary asset of the activity is professional human capital; and (3) mutual monitoring and consulting among agents are important to maintain the value of human capital, which is sensitive to performance.

2. *Financial Mutuals.* The distinguishing characteristic of the residual claims of financial mutuals is that the policyholder, depositor, or shareholder can sell his claim to the organization on demand at a price determined by a rule. The decision to withdraw resources by the holder of a redeemable claim is a form of partial takeover or liquidation that deprives management of control over assets. This mechanism for decision control can be exercised independently by each claim holder. It does not require a proxy fight, a tender offer, or any other concerted takeover bid. Mutuals are more likely to survive in an activity the lower the cost

1. of expanding and contracting assets, and
2. of obtaining accurate indices of asset values.

These conditions occur in financial organizations where assets are primarily the securities of other organizations. Redeemable residual claims are a low-cost mechanism for controlling agency problems between the residual claimants and the decision agents of financial mutuals because accurate and inexpensive indexes for asset values are available and the assets are traded with low transactions costs. Redeemable claims are a high-cost mechanism for decision control in activities that involve large amounts of assets not traded in secondary markets. Redeemable residual claims are also inefficient in activities that involve large amounts of lumpy or organization-specific assets that can be varied only with large costs.

3. *Nonprofits.* The nonprofit organization is characterized by the absence of alienable residual claims to net cash flows and contractual constraints on the distribution of net cash flows. Inalienable residual claims are vested in a board of trustees, and net cash flows are committed to current and future output. Nonprofits are more likely to survive in an activity

1. the greater the potential supply of donations, and
2. the lower the cost of separating decision management from decision control.

The nonprofit organization is a solution to the agency problem posed by donations. When the activities of an organization are financed in part through donations, part of stochastic net cash flow is due to the resources provided by donors. Contracts that define the share of residual claimants in net cash flows are unlikely to assure donors that their resources are protected against expropriation by residual claimants. One solution to this agency problem between donors and residual claimants is to have no residual claimants and to contract with donors to apply net cash flows to future output. The absence of alienable residual claims means that decision managers in nonprofits do not bear the wealth effects of their decisions. As in other organizations where residual risk bearing and decision management functions are separated, the resulting agency problems in the decision process are controlled by decision structures that separate the management and control of important decisions.

7 | Separation of Ownership and Control

7.1 Introduction

In the absence of fiat, the form of organization that survives in an activity is the one that delivers the product demanded by customers at the lowest price while covering costs.[1] Our goal is to explain the survival of organizations characterized by separation of "ownership" and "control"—a problem that has bothered students of corporations from Adam Smith to Berle and Means and Jensen and Meckling.[2] In more precise language, we are concerned with the survival of organizations in which important decision agents do not bear a substantial share of the wealth effects of their decisions.

We argue that the separation of decision and risk-bearing functions observed in large corporations is common to other organizations such as large professional partnerships, financial mutuals, and nonprofits. We contend that separation of decision and risk-bearing functions survives in these organizations in part because of the benefits of specialization of management and risk bearing but also because of an effective common approach to controlling the agency problems caused by separation of decision and risk-bearing functions. In particular, our hypothesis is that the contract structures of all of these organizations separate the ratification and monitoring of decisions from initiation and implementation of the decisions.

7.2 Residual Claims and Decision Processes

An organization is the nexus of contracts, written and unwritten, among owners of factors of production and customers.[3] These contracts or internal "rules of the game" specify the rights of each agent in

By Eugene F. Fama and Michael C. Jensen; originally published in *Journal of Law and Economics* 26 (June 1983).

the organization, the performance criteria on which agents are evaluated, and the payoff functions they face. The contract structure combines with available production technologies and external legal constraints to determine the cost function for delivering an output with a particular form of organization.[4] The form of organization that delivers the output demanded by customers at the lowest price, while covering costs, survives.

The central contracts in any organization specify (1) the nature of residual claims and (2) the allocation of the steps of the decision process among agents. These contracts distinguish organizations from one another and explain why specific organizational forms survive. We first discuss the general characteristics of residual claims and decision processes. We then present the major hypotheses about the relations between efficient allocations of residual claims and decision functions. The analysis focuses on two broad types of organizations—those in which risk-bearing and decision functions are separated and those in which they are combined in the same agents. We analyze only private organizations that depend on voluntary contracting and exchange.

Residual Claims

The contract structures of most organizational forms limit the risks undertaken by most agents by specifying either fixed promised payoffs or incentive payoffs tied to specific measures of performance. The residual risk—the risk of the difference between stochastic inflows of resources and promised payments to agents—is borne by those who contract for the rights to net cash flows. We call these agents the residual claimants or residual risk bearers. Moreover, the contracts of most agents contain the implicit or explicit provision that, in exchange for the specified payoff, the agent agrees that the resources he provides can be used to satisfy the interests of residual claimants.

Having most uncertainty borne by one group of agents, residual claimants, has survival value because it reduces the costs incurred to monitor contracts with other groups of agents and to adjust contracts for the changing risks borne by other agents. Contracts that direct decisions toward the interests of residual claimants also add to the survival value of organizations. Producing outputs at lower cost is in the interest of residual claimants because it increases net cash flows, but lower costs also contribute to survival by allowing products to be delivered at lower prices.

The residual claims of different organizational forms contain different restrictions. For example, the least restricted residual claims in common use are the common stocks of large corporations. Stockholders are not required to have any other role in the organization; their residual claims are alienable without restriction; and, because of these provisions, the residual claims allow unrestricted risk sharing among stockholders. We call these organizations *open* corporations, to distinguish them from *closed* corporations which are generally smaller and have residual claims that are largely restricted to internal decision agents.[5]

The Decision Process

By focusing on entrepreneurial firms in which all decision rights are concentrated in the entrepreneur, economists tend to ignore analysis of the steps of the decision process. However, the way in which organizations allocate the steps of the decision process across agents is important in explaining the survival of organizations.

In broad terms, the decision process has four steps:

1. *initiation*—generation of proposals for resource utilization and structuring of contracts;
2. *ratification*—choice of the decision initiatives to be implemented;
3. *implementation*—execution of ratified decisions; and
4. *monitoring*—measurement of the performance of decision agents and implementation of rewards.

Because the initiation and implementation of decisions typically are allocated to the same agents, it is convenient to combine these two functions under the term *decision management*. Likewise, the term *decision control* includes the ratification and monitoring of decisions. Decision management and decision control are the components of the organization's decision process or decision system.

7.3 Fundamental Relations Between Risk-Bearing and Decision Processes

We first state and then elaborate the central complementary hypotheses about the relations between the risk-bearing and decision processes of organizations.

1. Separation of residual risk bearing from decision management leads to decision systems that separate decision management from decision control.
2. Combination of decision management and decision control in a few agents leads to residual claims that are largely restricted to these agents.

The Problem

Agency problems arise because contracts are not costlessly written and enforced. Agency costs include the costs of structuring, monitoring, and bonding a set of contracts among agents with conflicting interests. Agency costs also include the value of output lost because the costs of full enforcement of contracts exceed the benefits.[6]

Control of agency problems in the decision process is important when the decision managers who initiate and implement important decisions are not the major residual claimants and therefore do not bear a major share of the wealth effects of their decisions. Without effective control procedures, such decision managers are more likely to take actions that deviate from the interests of residual claimants. An effective system for decision control implies, almost by definition, that the control (ratification and monitoring) of decisions is to some extent separate from the management (initiation and implementation) of decisions. Individual decision agents can be involved in the management of some decisions and the control of others, but separation means that an individual agent does not exercise exclusive management and control rights over the same decisions.

The interesting problem is to determine when separation of decision management, decision control, and residual risk bearing is more efficient than combining these three functions in the same agents. We first analyze the factors that make combination of decision management, decision control, and residual risk bearing efficient; we then analyze the factors that make separation of these three functions efficient.

Combination of Decision Management, Decision Control, and Residual Risk Bearing

Suppose the balance of cost conditions, including both technology and the control of agency problems, implies that in a particular activity the optimal organization is noncomplex. For our purposes, *noncomplex* means that specific information relevant to decisions is concentrated in one or a few agents. (Specific information is detailed information that is costly to transfer among agents.)[7] Most small organizations tend to be noncomplex and most large organizations tend to be complex, but the correspondence is not perfect. For example, research-oriented universities, though often small in terms of assets or faculty size, are nevertheless complex in the sense that specific knowledge, which is costly to transfer, is diffused among both faculty and administrators. On the other hand, mutual funds are often large in terms of assets but are noncomplex in the sense that information relevant to decisions is concentrated in one or a few agents. We take it as given that optimal organizations in some activities are noncomplex. Our more limited goal is to explain the implications of noncomplexity for control of agency problems in the decision process.

If we ignore agency problems between decision managers and residual claimants, the theory of optimal risk bearing tells us that residual claims that allow unrestricted risk sharing have advantages in small as well as in large organizations.[8] However, in a small noncomplex organization, specific knowledge important for decision management and control is concentrated in one or a few agents. As a consequence, it is efficient to allocate decision control as well as decision management to these agents. Without separation of decision management from decision control, residual claimants have little protection against opportunistic actions of decision agents, and this lowers the value of unrestricted residual claims.

A feasible solution to the agency problem that arises when the same agents manage and control important decisions is to restrict residual claims to the important decision agents. In effect, restriction of residual claims to decision agents substitutes for costly control devices to limit the discretion of decision agents. The common stocks of closed corporations are this type of restricted residual claim, as are the residual claims in proprietorships and partnerships. The residual claims of these organizations (especially closed corporations) are also held by other agents whose special relations with decision agents allow agency problems to be controlled without separation of the management and control of decisions. For example, family members have many dimensions of exchange with one another over a long horizon and therefore have advantages in monitoring and disciplining related decision agents. Business associates whose good will and advice are important to the organization are also potential candidates for holding minority residual claims of organizations that do not separate the management and control of decisions.[9]

Restricting residual claims to decision makers controls agency problems between residual claimants and decision agents, but it sacrifices the benefits of unrestricted risk sharing and specialization of decision functions. The decision process suffers efficiency losses because decision agents must be chosen on the basis of wealth and willingness to bear risk as well as for decision skills. The residual claimants forgo optimal risk reduction through portfolio diversification so that residual claims and decision making can be combined in a small number of agents. Forgone diversification lowers the value of the residual claims and raises the cost of risk-bearing services.

Moreover, when residual claims are restricted to decision agents, it is generally rational for the residual claimant–decision makers to assign lower values to uncertain cash flows than residual claimants would in organizations where residual claims are unrestricted and risk bearing can be freely diversified across organizations. As a consequence, restricting residual claims to agents in the decision process leads to decisions (for example, less investment in risky projects that lower the costs of outputs) that tend to penalize the organization in the competition for survival.[10]

However, because contracts are not costlessly written and enforced, all decision systems and systems for allocating residual claims involve costs. Organizational survival involves a balance of the costs of alternative decision systems and systems for allocating residual risk against the benefits. Small noncomplex organizations do not have demands for a wide range of specialized decision agents; on the contrary, concentration of specific information relevant to decisions implies that there are efficiency gains when the rights to manage and control decisions are combined in one or a few agents. Moreover, the risk-sharing benefits forgone when residual claims are restricted to one or a few decision agents are less serious in a small noncomplex organization than in a large organization, because the total risk of net cash flows to be shared is generally smaller in small organizations. In addition, small organizations do not often have large demands for wealth from residual claimants to bond the payoffs promised to other agents and to purchase risky assets. As a consequence, small noncomplex organizations can efficiently control the agency problems caused by the combination of decision management and control in one or a few agents by restricting residual claims to these agents. Such a combining of decision and risk-bearing functions is efficient in small noncomplex organizations because the benefits of unrestricted risk sharing and specialization of decision functions are less than the costs that would be incurred to control the resulting agency problems.

The proprietorships, partnerships, and closed corporations observed in small-scale production and service activities are the best examples of classical entrepreneurial firms in which the major decision makers are also the major residual risk bearers. These organizations constitute evidence in favor of the hypothesis that combination of decision management and decision control in one or a few agents leads to residual claims that are largely restricted to these agents.

We analyze next the forces that make separation of decision management, decision control, and residual risk bearing efficient—in effect, the forces that cause the classical entrepreneurial firm to be dominated by organizational forms in which there are no decision makers in the classical entrepreneurial sense.

Separation of Decision Management, Decision Control, and Residual Risk Bearing

Our concern in this section is with the organizational forms characterized by separation of decision management from residual risk bearing—what the literature on open corporations calls, somewhat imprecisely, separation of ownership and control. Our hypothesis is that all such organizations, including large open corporations, large professional partnerships, financial mutuals, and nonprofits, control the agency problems that result from separation of decision management from residual risk bearing by separating the management (initiation and implementation) and control (ratification and monitoring) of decisions. Documentation of this hypothesis takes up much of the rest of this chapter.

1. *Specific Knowledge and Diffusion of Decision Functions.* Most organizations characterized by separation of decision management from residual risk bearing are *complex* in the sense that specific knowledge relevant to different decisions—knowledge which is costly to transfer across agents—is diffused among agents at all levels of the

organization. Again, we take it as given that the optimal organizations in some activities are complex. Our theory attempts to explain the implications of complexity for the nature of efficient decision processes and for control of agency problems in the decision process.

Since specific knowledge in complex organizations is diffused among agents, diffusion of decision management can reduce costs by delegating the initiation and implementation of decisions to the agents with valuable relevant knowledge. The agency problems of diffuse decision management can then be reduced by separating the management (initiation and implementation) and control (ratification and monitoring) of decisions.

In the unusual cases where residual claims are not held by important decision managers but are nevertheless concentrated in one or a few residual claimants, control of decision managers can in principle be direct and simple, with the residual claimants ratifying and monitoring important decisions and setting rewards.[11] Such organizations conform to our hypothesis, because top-level decision control is separated from top-level decision managers and exercised directly by residual claimants.

However, in complex organizations valuable specific knowledge relevant to decision control is diffused among many internal agents. This generally means that efficient decision control, like efficient decision management, involves delegation and diffusion of decision control as well as separation of decision management and control at different levels of the organization. We expect to observe such delegation, diffusion, and separation of decision management and control below the top level of complex organizations, even in those unusual complex organizations where residual claims are held primarily by top-level decision agents.

2. Diffuse Residual Claims and Delegation of Decision Control. In the more common complex organizations, residual claims are diffused among many agents. Having many residual claimants has advantages in large complex organizations because the total risk of net cash flows to be shared is generally large and there are large demands for wealth from residual claimants to bond the payoffs promised to a wide range of agents and to purchase risky assets. When there are many residual claimants, it is costly for all of them to be involved in decision control and it is efficient for them to delegate decision control. For example, some delegation of decision control is observed even in the large professional partnerships in public accounting and law, where the residual claimants are expert internal decision agents. When there are many partners it is inefficient for each to participate in ratification and monitoring of all decisions.

Nearly complete separation and specialization of decision control and residual risk bearing are common in large open corporations and financial mutuals where most of the diffuse residual claimants are not qualified for roles in the decision process and thus delegate their decision control rights to other agents. When residual claimants have no role in decision control, we expect to observe separation of the management and control of important decisions at all levels of the organization.

Separation and diffusion of decision management and decision control—in effect, the absence of a classical entrepreneurial decision maker—limit the power of individual decision agents to expropriate the interests of residual claimants. The checks and balances of such decision systems have costs, but they also have important benefits. Diffusion and separation of decision management and control have benefits because they allow valuable knowledge to be used at the points in the decision process where it is most relevant, and they help control the agency problems of diffuse residual claims. In complex organizations, the benefits of diffuse residual claims and the benefits of separation of decision functions from residual risk bearing are generally greater than the agency costs they generate, including the costs of mechanisms to separate the management and control of decisions.

3. *Decision Control in Nonprofits and Financial Mutuals.* Most organizations characterized by separation of decision management from residual risk bearing are complex. However, separation of the management and control of decisions contributes to the survival of any organization where the important decision managers do not bear a substantial share of the wealth effects of their decisions—that is, any organization where there are serious agency problems in the decision process. We argue below that separation of decision management and residual risk bearing is a characteristic of nonprofit organizations and financial mutuals, large and small, complex and noncomplex. Thus, we expect to observe separation of the management and control of important decisions even in small noncomplex nonprofits and financial mutuals where, ignoring agency problems in the decision process, concentrated and combined decision management and control would be more efficient.

4. *Common General Features of Decision Control Systems.* Our hypothesis about the decision systems of organizations characterized by separation of decision management and residual risk bearing gets support from the fact that the major mechanisms for diffusing and separating the management and control of decisions are much the same across different organizations.

Decision hierarchies. A common feature of the diffuse decision management and control systems of complex organizations (for example, large nonprofit universities as well as large open corporations) is a formal decision hierarchy with higher-level agents ratifying and monitoring the decision initiatives of lower-level agents and evaluating their performance.[12] Such hierarchical partitioning of the decision process makes it more difficult for decision agents at all levels of the organization to take actions that benefit themselves at the expense of residual claimants. Decision hierarchies are buttressed by organizational rules of the game, for example, accounting and budgeting systems, that monitor and constrain the decision behavior of agents and specify the performance criteria that determine rewards.[13]

Mutual monitoring systems. The formal hierarchies of complex organizations are also buttressed by information from less formal mutual monitoring among agents. When agents interact to produce outputs, they acquire low-cost information about colleagues, information that is not directly available to higher-level agents. Mutual monitoring systems tap this information for use in the control process. Mutual monitoring systems derive their energy from the interests of agents to use the internal agent markets of organizations to enhance the value of human capital.[14] Agents choose among organizations on the basis of rewards offered and potential for development of human capital. Agents value the competitive interaction that takes place within an organization's internal agent market because it enhances current marginal products and contributes to human capital development. Moreover, if agents perceive that evaluation of their performance is unbiased (that is, if they cannot systematically fool their evaluators), then they value the fine-tuning of the reward system that results from mutual monitoring information, because it lowers the uncertainty of payoffs from effort and skill. Since the incentive structures and diffuse decision control systems that result from the interplay of formal hierarchies and less formal mutual monitoring systems are also in the interests of residual claimants, their survival value is evident.

Boards of directors. The common apex of the decision control systems of organizations, large and small, in which decision agents do not bear a major share of the wealth effects of their decisions is some form of board of directors. Such boards always have the power to hire, fire, and compensate the top-level decision managers and to ratify and monitor important decisions. Exercise of these top-level decision control rights by a group (the board) helps to ensure separation of decision management and control (that is, the absence of an entrepreneurial decision maker) even at the top of the organization.[15]

7.4 The Spectrum of Organizations

Organizations in which important decision agents do not bear a major share of the wealth effects of their decisions include open corporations, large professional partnerships, financial mutuals, and nonprofits. We are concerned now with analyzing the data each of these organizations provides to test the hypothesis that separation of decision management functions from residual risk bearing leads to decision systems that separate the management and control of decisions.

To motivate the discussion of specific organizational forms, we also outline a set of more specialized propositions to explain the survival value of the special features of their residual claims. These more specialized hypotheses about the survival of specific organizational forms in specific activities are developed in Chapter 6, "Agency Problems and Residual Claims."

Open Corporations

1. *Unrestricted Common Stock Residual Claims.* Most large nonfinancial organizations are open corporations. The common stock residual claims of such organizations are unrestricted in the sense that stockholders are not required to have any other role in the organization, and their residual claims are freely alienable. As a result of the unrestricted nature of the residual claims of open corporations, there is almost com-

plete specialization of decision management and residual risk bearing. Even managers who own substantial blocks of stock, and thus are residual risk bearers, may elect to sell these shares.

Unrestricted common stock is attractive in complicated risky activities where substantial wealth provided by residual claimants is needed to bond the large aggregate payoffs promised to many other agents. Unrestricted common stock, with its capacity for generating large amounts of wealth from residual claimants on a permanent basis, is also attractive in activities that are more efficiently carried out with large amounts of risky assets owned within the organization rather than rented. Moreover, since decision skills are not a necessary consequence of wealth or willingness to bear risk, the specialization of decision management and residual risk bearing allowed by unrestricted common stock enhances the adaptability of a complex organization to changes in the economic environment. The unrestricted risk sharing and diversification allowed by common stock also contribute to survival by lowering the cost of risk-bearing services.

2. *Control of the Agency Problems of Common Stock.* Separation and specialization of decision management and residual risk bearing lead to agency problems between decision agents and residual claimants. This is the problem of separation of ownership and control that has long troubled students of corporations. For example, potential exploitation of residual claimants by opportunistic decision agents is reflected in the arguments leading to the establishment of the Securities and Exchange Commission and in the concerns of the modern corporate governance movement. Less well appreciated, however, is the fact that the unrestricted nature of common stock residual claims also allows special market and organizational mechanisms for controlling the agency problems of specialized risk bearing.

The stock market. The unrestricted alienability of the residual claims of open corporations gives rise to an external monitoring device unique to these organizations—a stock market that specializes in pricing common stocks and transferring them at low cost. Stock prices are visible signals that summarize the implications of internal decisions for current and future net cash flows. This external monitoring exerts pressure to orient a corporation's decision process toward the interests of residual claimants.

The market for takeovers. External monitoring from a takeover market is also unique to the open corporation and is attributable to the unrestricted nature of its residual claims.[16] Because the residual claims are freely alienable and separable from roles in the decision process, attacking managers can circumvent existing managers and the current board to gain control of the decision process, either by a direct offer to purchase stock (a tender offer) or by an appeal for stockholder votes for directors (a proxy fight).

Expert boards. Internal control in the open corporation is delegated by residual claimants to a board of directors. Residual claimants generally retain approval rights (by vote) on such matters as board membership, auditor choice, mergers, and new stock issues. Other management and control functions are delegated by the residual claimants to the board. The board then delegates most decision management functions and many decision control functions to internal agents, but it retains ultimate control over internal agents—including the rights to ratify and monitor major policy initiatives and to hire, fire, and set the compensation of top-level decision managers. Similar delegation of decision management and control functions, at the first step to a board and then from the board to internal decision agents, is common to other organizations, such as financial mutuals, nonprofits, and large professional partnerships, in which important decision agents do not bear a major share of the wealth effects of their decisions.

However, the existence of the stock market and the market for takeovers, both special to open corporations, explains some of the special features of corporate boards, in particular: (1) why inside manager board members are generally more influential than outside members, and (2) why outside board members are often decision agents in other complex organizations.[17]

Since the takeover market provides an external court of last resort for protection of residual claimants, a corporate board can be in the hands of agents who are decision experts. Given that the board is to be composed of experts, it is natural that its most influential members are internal managers since they have valuable specific information about the organization's activities. It is also natural that when the internal decision control system works well, the outside members of the board are nominated by internal managers. Internal managers can use their knowledge of the organization to nominate outside board members with relevant complementary knowledge: for example, outsiders with expertise in capital markets, corporate law, or relevant technology who provide an important support function to the top managers in dealing with specialized decision problems.

However, the board is not an effective device for decision control unless it limits the decision discretion of individual top managers. The board is the top-level court of appeals of the internal agent market,[18] and as such it must be able to use information from the internal mutual monitoring system. To accomplish this and to achieve effective separation of top-level decision management and control, we expect the board of a large open corporation to include several of the organization's top managers. The board uses information from each of the top managers about his decision initiatives and the decision initiatives and performance of other managers. The board also seeks information from lower-level managers about the decision initiatives and performance of top managers.[19] This information is used to set the rewards of the top managers, to rank them, and to choose among their decision initiatives. To protect information flows to the board, we expect that top managers, especially those who are members of the board, can effectively be fired only with consent of the board and thus are protected from reprisals by other top managers.

The decision processes of some open corporations seem to be dominated by an individual manager, generally the chief executive officer. In some cases, this signals the absence of separation of decision management and decision control, and, in our theory, the organization suffers in the competition for survival. We expect, however, that the apparent dominance of some top managers is more often due to their ability to work with the decision control systems of their organizations than to their ability to suppress diffuse and separate decision control. In any case, the financial press regularly reports instances where apparently dominant executives are removed by their boards.

Corporate boards generally include outside members, that is, members who are not internal managers, and they often hold a majority of seats.[20] The outside board members act as arbiters in disagreements among internal managers and carry out tasks that involve serious agency problems between internal managers and residual claimants, for example, setting executive compensation or searching for replacements for top managers.

Effective separation of top-level decision management and control means that outside directors have incentives to carry out their tasks and do not collude with managers to expropriate the interests of residual claimants. Our hypothesis is that outside directors have incentives to develop reputations as experts in decision control. Most outside directors of open corporations are either managers of other corporations or important decision agents in other complex organizations.[21] The value of their human capital depends primarily on their performance as internal decision managers in other organizations. They use their directorships to signal to internal and external markets for decision agents that (1) they are decision experts, (2) they understand the importance of diffuse and separate decision control, and (3) they can work with such decision control systems. The signals are credible when the direct payments to outside directors are small, but there is substantial devaluation of human capital when internal decision control breaks down and the costly last-resort process of an outside takeover is activated.

Professional Partnerships

1. *Mutual Monitoring, Specific Knowledge, and Restricted Residual Claims.* The residual claims of professional partnerships in activities such as law, public accounting, medicine, and business consulting are restricted to the major professional agents who produce the organization's services. This restriction increases the incentives of agents to monitor each other's actions and to consult with each other to improve the quality of services provided to customers. Such mutual monitoring and consulting are attractive to the professional agents in service activities where responsibility for variation in the quality of services is easily assigned and the value of professional human capital is sensitive to performance. The monitoring and consulting are likely to be effective when professional agents with similar specialized skills agree to share liability for the actions of colleagues.

In both large and small partnerships, individuals or small teams work on cases, audits, and so forth. Because of the importance of specific knowledge about particular clients and circumstances, it is efficient for the teams to make most decisions locally. At this level, however, decision management and decision control are not separate. To control the resulting agency problems, the residual claims in professional partnerships, large and small, are restricted to the professional agents who have the major decision-making roles. This is consistent with our hypothesis that combination of decision management and control functions leads to restriction of residual claims to the agents who both manage and control important decisions.

2. *Large Professional Partnerships.* The partners in large professional partnerships are diffuse residual claimants whose welfare depends on the acts of agents they do not directly control. Thus, these organizations provide a test of our hypothesis that separation of residual risk bearing and decision management leads to decision systems that separate the management and control of important decisions. The major decision control devices of large professional partnerships are similar to those of other organizations with diffuse residual claims. For example, residual claimants in large partnerships delegate to boards the ratification and monitoring of important decisions above the level of individual cases and audits. Moreover, the sharing of liability and residual cash flows among important decision agents (the partners) ensures that large partnerships have strong versions of the mutual monitoring systems that we contend are common to the decision control systems of complex organizations.

The boards of large partnerships have special features that relate to the restriction of the residual claims to important internal agents. The residual claimants are experts in the organization's activities, and they observe directly the effects of actions taken by the board of managing partners. Thus, unlike the stockholders of open corporations, the residual claimants in large partnerships have little demand for outside experts to protect their interests, and their boards are composed entirely of partners.

The board is involved in decisions with respect to the management of the partnership, for example, where new offices should be opened, who should be admitted to the partnership, and who should be dismissed. The board is also involved in renegotiating the shares of the partners. Here, as in other decisions, the boards of large partnerships combine the valuable specific knowledge available at the top level with information from partner–residual claimants. The role of the board is to develop acceptable consensus decisions from this information. Thus, the boards of large professional partnerships are generally called committees of managing partners rather than boards of directors. The idea is that such committees exist to manage agency problems among partners and to study and determine major policy issues in a manner that is less costly than when performed jointly by all partners.

Since the residual claims in a large professional partnership are not alienable, unfriendly outside takeovers are not possible. Inside takeovers by dissident partners are possible, however, because the managing boards of these organizations are elected by the partner–residual claimants.

Financial Mutuals

A common form of organization in financial activities is the mutual. An unusual characteristic of mutuals is that the residual claimants are customers, for example, the policyholders of mutual insurance companies, the depositors of mutual savings banks, and the shareholders of mutual funds. Like the diffuse stockholders of large nonfinancial corporations, most of the diffuse depositors, policyholders, and mutual fund shareholders of financial mutuals do not participate in the internal decision process. Thus, financial mutuals provide another test of our hypothesis that substantial separation of decision management and residual risk bearing leads to decision systems that separate the management and control of decisions.

1. *The Control Function of Redeemable Claims.* For the purpose of decision control, the unique characteristic of the residual claims of mutuals is that they are redeemable on demand. The policyholder, depositor, or shareholder can, on demand, turn in his claim at a price determined by a prespecified rule. For example, the shareholder of an open-end mutual fund can redeem his claim for the market value of his share of the fund's assets, while the whole life or endowment insurance policyholder, like the shareholder of a mutual savings bank, can redeem his claim for its specified value plus accumulated dividends.

The decision of the claim holder to withdraw resources is a form of partial takeover or liquidation which deprives management of control over assets. This control right can be exercised independently by each claim holder. It does not require a proxy fight, a tender offer, or any other concerted takeover bid. In contrast, customer decisions in open nonfinancial corporations and the repricing of the corporation's securities in the capital market provide signals about the performance of its decision agents. Without further action, however, either internal or from the market for takeovers, the judgments of customers and of the capital market leave the assets of the open nonfinancial corporation under the control of the managers.

2. *The Board of Directors.* Like other organizations characterized by

substantial separation between decision management and residual risk bearing, the top-level decision control device in financial mutuals is a board of directors. Because of the strong form of diffuse decision control inherent in the redeemable residual claims of financial mutuals, however, their boards are less important in the control process than the boards of open nonfinancial corporations. The reduced role of the board is especially evident in mutual savings banks and mutual funds, which are not complex even though often large in terms of assets. Moreover, the residual claimants of mutuals show little interest in their boards and often do not have the right to vote for board members.[22] Outside board members are generally chosen by internal managers. Unlike open corporations, the boards of financial mutuals do not often impose changes in managers. The role of the board, especially in the less complex mutuals, is largely limited to monitoring agency problems against which redemption of residual claims offers little protection, for example, fraud or outright theft of assets by internal agents.

Nonprofit Organizations

When an organization's activities are financed in part through donations, part of net cash flows comes from resources provided by donors. Contracts that define the share of residual claimants in net cash flows are unlikely to assure donors that their resources are protected from expropriation by residual claimants. In a nonprofit organization, however, there are no agents with alienable rights in residual net cash flows and thus there are no residual claims. We argue in Chapter 6, "Agency Problems and Residual Claims," that the absence of such residual claims in nonprofits avoids the donor-residual claimant agency problem and explains the dominance of nonprofits in donor-financed activities.[23]

The absence of residual claims in nonprofits avoids agency problems between donors and residual claimants, but the incentives of other internal agents to expropriate donations remain. These agency problems between donors and decision agents in nonprofits are similar to those in other organizations where important decision managers do not bear a major share of the wealth effects of their decisions. Our hypothesis predicts that, like other organizations characterized by separation of decision management from residual risk bearing, nonprofits have decision systems that separate the management (initiation and implementation) and control (ratification and monitoring) of decisions. Such decision systems survive in donor nonprofits because of the assurances they provide that donations are used effectively and are not easily expropriated.

1. *Nonprofit Boards.* In small nonprofits delegation of decision management to one or a few agents is generally efficient. For example, in nonprofit cultural performing groups, an artistic director usually chooses performers, does the primary monitoring of their outputs, and initiates and implements major decisions. Nevertheless, the important decision agents in these organizations are chosen, monitored, and evaluated by boards of directors. Boards with similar decision control rights are common to other small nonprofits characterized by concentrated decision management, such as charities, private museums, small private hospitals, and local Protestant and Jewish congregations. Boards are also observed at the top of the decision control systems of complex nonprofits, such as private universities, in which both decision management and decision control are diffuse.

Although their functions are similar to those of other organizations, nonprofit boards have special features that are due to the absence of alienable residual claims. For example, because of the discipline from the outside takeover market, boards of open corporations can include internal decision agents, and outside board members can be chosen for expertise rather than because they are important residual claimants. In contrast, because a nonprofit lacks alienable residual claims, the decision agents are immune from ouster (via takeover) by outside agents. Without the takeover threat or the discipline imposed by residual claimants with the right to remove members of the board, nonprofit boards composed of internal agents and outside experts chosen by internal agents would provide little assurance against collusion and expropriation of donations. Thus, nonprofit boards generally include few if any internal agents as voting members, and nonprofit boards are often self-perpetuating, that is, new members are approved by existing members. Moreover, nonprofit board members are generally substantial donors who serve without pay. Willingness to provide continuing personal donations of wealth or time is generally an implicit condition for membership on nonprofit boards. Acceptance of this condition certifies to other donors that board members are motivated to take their decision control task seriously.

2. *The Roman Catholic Church.* To our knowledge the only nonprofit organization that is financed with donations but lacks a board

of important continuing donors with effective decision control rights is the Roman Catholic church. Parish councils exist in local Catholic churches, but unlike their Protestant and Jewish counterparts, they are only advisory. The clerical hierarchy controls the allocation of resources, and the papal system does not seem to limit the discretion of the Pope, the organization's most important decision agent.

Other aspects of the contracts of the Catholic clergy in part substitute for the control of expropriation of donations that would be provided by more effective donor-customer constraints on decisions. For example, the vows of chastity and obedience incorporated into the contracts of the Catholic clergy help to bond against expropriation of donations by avoiding conflicts between the material interests of a family and the interests of donor-customers. In addition, the training of a Catholic priest is organization-specific. For example, it involves a heavy concentration on (Catholic) theology, whereas the training of Protestant ministers places more emphasis on social service skills. Once certified, the Catholic priest is placed by the hierarchy. He cannot offer his services on a competitive basis. In exchange for developing such organization-specific human capital, the Catholic priest, unlike his Protestant and Jewish counterparts, gets a lifetime contract that promises a real standard of living. The organization-specific nature of the human capital of the Catholic clergy and the terms of the contract under which it is employed act as a bond to donor-customers that the interests of the Catholic clergy are closely bound to the survival of the organization and thus to the interests of donor-customers.

Although Protestantism arose over doctrinal issues, the control structures of Protestant sects—in particular, the evolution of lay councils with power to ratify and monitor resource allocation decisions—can be viewed as a response to breakdowns of the contract structure of Catholicism, that is, expropriation of Catholic donor-customers by the clergy. The evolution of Protestantism is therefore an example of competition among alternative contract structures to resolve an activity's major agency problem—in this case monitoring important agents to limit expropriation of donations.

There is currently pressure to allow Catholic priests to marry, that is, to drop the vow of chastity from their contracts. We predict that if this occurs, organizational survival will require other monitoring and bonding mechanisms, for example, control over allocation of resources by lay councils similar to those observed in Protestant and Jewish congregations.

3. *The Private University and Decision Systems in Complex Nonprofits.* In complex nonprofits we observe mechanisms for diffuse decision control similar to those of other complex organizations. For example, large private universities, like large open corporations, have complicated decision hierarchies and active internal agent markets with mutual monitoring systems that generate information about the performance of agents. Again, however, the decision control structures of complex nonprofits have special features attributable to the absence of alienable residual claims.

For example, a university's trustees are primarily donors rather than experts in the details of education or research. In ratifying and monitoring decision initiatives presented by internal decision agents (presidents, chancellors, provosts, and so forth) and in evaluating the agents themselves, boards rely on information from the internal diffuse decision system—for example, reports from faculty senates and appointments committees—and on external peer reviews.

Moreover, the structure of internal diffuse decision control systems is a more formal part of a university's contract structure (its charter or by-laws) than in large for-profit organizations such as open corporations. For example, unlike corporate managers, university deans, department heads, provosts, and presidents are generally appointed for fixed terms. The end of a contract period activates a process of evaluation, with search committees chosen according to formal rules and with rules for passing their recommendations on to the board. A more formal structure of diffuse decision management and control is helpful to trustees who do not have specialized knowledge about a university's activities. It also helps to assure donors that the absence of discipline from an outside takeover market is compensated by a strong system for internal decision control.

7.5 Conclusions

The theory developed in this chapter views an organization as a nexus of contracts (written and unwritten). The theory focuses on the contracts that (1) allocate the steps in an organization's decision process, (2) define residual claims, and (3) set up devices for controlling agency problems in the decision process. We focus on the factors that give survival value to organizational forms that separate what the literature imprecisely calls ownership and control.

The Central Hypotheses

An organization's decision process consists of decision management (initiation and implementation) and decision control (ratification and monitoring). Our analysis produces two complementary hypotheses about the relations between decision systems and residual claims:

- Separation of residual risk bearing from decision management leads to decision systems that separate decision management from decision control.
- Combination of decision management and decision control in a few agents leads to residual claims that are largely restricted to these agents.

Combination of Decision Management and Control

When it is efficient to combine decision management and control functions in one or a few agents, it is efficient to control agency problems between residual claimants and decision makers by restricting residual claims to the decision makers. This proposition gets clear support from the proprietorships, small partnerships, and closed corporations observed in small-scale production and service activities. These organizations are all characterized by concentrated decision systems and residual claims that are restricted to decision agents.

Separation of Residual Risk Bearing from Decision Management

1. *The Role of Specific Knowledge.* In contrast, most of the organizations characterized by separation of residual risk bearing from decision management are complex in the sense that specific information valuable for decisions is diffused among many agents throughout the organization. Thus in a complex organization separation of residual risk bearing from decision management arises in part because efficient decision systems are diffuse. Benefits from better decisions can be achieved by delegating decision functions to agents at all levels of the organization

who have relevant specific knowledge, rather than allocating all decision management and control to the residual claimants. Control of the agency problems of such diffuse decision systems is then achieved by separating the ratification and monitoring of decisions (decision control) from initiation and implementation (decision management). The efficiency of such decision systems is buttressed by incentive structures that reward agents both for initiating and implementing decisions and for ratifying and monitoring the decision management of other agents.

2. *The Role of Diffuse Residual Claims.* In most complex organizations, residual claims are diffused among many agents. When there are many residual claimants, it is costly for all of them to be involved in decision control. As a consequence there is separation of residual risk bearing from decision control, and this creates agency problems between residual claimants and decision agents. Separation of decision management and decision control at all levels of the organization helps to control these agency problems by limiting the power of individual agents to expropriate the interests of residual claimants. Thus diffusion and separation of decision management and control have survival value in complex organizations both because they allow valuable specific knowledge to be used at the points in the decision process where it is most relevant and because they help control the agency problems of diffuse residual claims.

3. *Common Features of Decision Control Systems.* What we call separation of residual risk bearing from decision management is the separation of ownership and control that has long bothered students of open corporations. We argue that separation of decision and risk bearing functions is also common to other organizations like large professional partnerships, financial mutuals, and nonprofits. Moreover, our central hypothesis about control of the agency problems caused by separation of residual risk bearing from decision management gets support from the fact that the major mechanisms for separating decision management and decision control are much the same across organizations.

The common central building blocks of the diffuse decision control systems of complex organizations of all types are formal decision hierarchies in which the decision initiatives of lower-level agents are passed on to higher-level agents, first for ratification and then for monitoring. Such decision hierarchies are found in large open corporations, large professional partnerships, large financial mutuals, and large nonprofits.

Formal decision hierarchies are buttressed by less formal mutual monitoring systems that are a by-product of interaction that takes place to produce outputs and develop human capital.

The common apex of the decision control systems of organizations, large and small, in which decision agents do not bear a major share of the wealth effects of their decisions is a board of directors (or trustees, managing partners, and so forth) that ratifies and monitors important decisions and chooses, dismisses, and rewards important decision agents. Such multiple-member boards make collusion between top-level decision management and control agents more difficult, and they are the mechanism that allows separation of the management and control of the organization's most important decisions.

PART III   Compensation

8 | Compensation and Incentives: Practice versus Theory

Economists have grown increasingly interested in the theory of the firm in recent years.[1] These efforts have focused on the relations between markets and hierarchies, the influence of organization-specific assets, corporate governance systems, and the agency problems caused by conflicts of interest among the contracting parties that make up the firm. One of the more important, but least analyzed, factors affecting organizational behavior is the internal incentive structure, which includes the management of human resources in general, and compensation policies in particular. A thorough understanding of internal incentives is critical to developing a viable theory of the firm, since they largely determine how individuals behave in organizations.

Our economic understanding of internal incentive structures is far from complete. There has been an enormous amount of research in the economics of contracting,[2] but this increasingly technical research has generated few empirical implications, and it offers little guidance in understanding actual compensation arrangements in large organizations. There are many common and important features of organizational incentive systems that economists have not studied extensively, including pay systems that are largely independent of performance, the overwhelming use of promotion-based incentive systems, egalitarian pay systems apparently motivated by horizontal equity considerations, the asymmetric effects of rewards and punishments, tenure and up-or-out promotion systems, survey-based and seniority-based pay systems, profit sharing, holiday bonuses, the generally rare observation of bonding and up-front entry fees for jobs, "efficiency wages," and the general reluctance of employers to fire, penalize, or give poor performance evaluations to employees.

By George P. Baker, Michael C. Jensen, and Kevin J. Murphy; originally published in *Journal of Finance* 43, no. 3 (July 1988), pp. 593–616.

In this chapter we discuss aspects of compensation in which current economic theory and actual practice seem particularly disassociated, and we summarize empirical evidence that is inconsistent with traditional economic theories. Typical explanations offered by psychologists, behaviorists, human resource consultants, and personnel executives are distinctly uneconomic—focusing on notions such as fairness, equity, morale, trust, social responsibility, and culture. The challenge to economists is to provide viable economic explanations for these practices or to integrate these alternative notions into the traditional economic model. One promising avenue is to recognize that few decision makers in organizations are one hundred percent owners of the residual claims, and this layering of agency problems can induce serious lapses in the incentives of decision makers to devise and enforce efficient contracts and compensation systems. We return to this issue in the last section.

Our objective is to motivate future theoretical and empirical research that will ultimately change the way in which economists, behaviorists, and practitioners think about incentives, compensation, the management of human resources, and organizational behavior. We believe this is a major growth area for research in management and economics.

8.1   The Absence of Pay-for-Performance Compensation Systems

Economic models of compensation generally assume that higher performance requires greater effort or that it is in some other way associated with disutility on the part of workers. In order to provide incentives, these models predict the existence of reward systems that structure compensation so that a worker's expected utility increases with observed productivity. These rewards can take many different forms, including praise from superiors and co-workers, implicit promises of future promotion opportunities, feelings of self-esteem that come from superior achievement and recognition, and current and future cash rewards related to performance. Economists, while recognizing that nonmonetary rewards for performance can be important, tend to focus on monetary rewards because individuals are willing to substitute nonmonetary for monetary rewards and because money represents a generalized claim on resources and is therefore in general preferred over an equal dollar-value payment in kind.

Table 8.1 Salary Premiums Associated with Performance Ratings, and Frequency Distribution of Performance Ratings, for 7,629 Managers in Two Large Manufacturing Firms

Performance Rating	Salary Premium Relative to Lowest Performance Rating (percent)	Percentage of Sample Receiving Performance Rating
(1)	(2)	(3)
Company A (4,788 managers):		
Not acceptable	0	.2
Acceptable	1.4	5.3
Good	5.3	74.3
Outstanding	7.8	20.2
Company B (2,841 managers):		
Unacceptable	0	0
Minimum acceptance	0	0
Satisfactory	0	1.2
Good	1.8	36.6
Superior	3.6	58.4
Excellent	6.2	3.8

Source: Medoff and Abraham (1980), Tables I and II. Salary premiums are estimated for regressions of log (earnings) on performance-rating dummies and demographic variables.

Evidence from research on compensation plans indicates that explicit financial rewards in the form of transitory performance-based bonuses seldom account for an important part of a worker's compensation. Table 8.1 summarizes results from Medoff and Abraham (1980), who examined the pay of managerial and professional employees in two large manufacturing firms and found small differences in earnings resulting from superior performance.

Column 2 shows that Company A employees ranking lowest on the performance-rating scale are paid only 7.8% less than those ranking highest; low-ranking Company B employees receive only 6.2% less than high-ranking employees. Moreover, column 3 shows that almost 95% of the employees in Company A are classified as "Good" or "Outstanding," and the implied premium for being an "Outstanding" employee rather than a "Good" employee is only 2.5%. Similarly, 95% of the Company B employees are rated "Good" or "Superior," and the premium for being "Superior" instead of "Good" is only 1.8%.

Lawler (1971, p. 158) cites six separate studies of the relationship between pay and performance, and finds that "their evidence indicates that pay is not very closely related to performance in many organizations that claim to have merit increase salary systems . . . The studies suggest that many business organizations do not do a very good job of tying pay to performance. This conclusion is rather surprising in light of many companies' very frequent claims that their pay systems are based on merit. It is particularly surprising that pay does not seem to be related to performance at the managerial level." Thus, the Medoff and Abraham evidence seems to be indicative of general performance measurement and compensation systems, and we have no thorough understanding of the forces responsible for these practices.

Is Pay an Effective Motivator?

The potential benefits of tying pay to performance are obvious, and it is surprising to economists that firms apparently resist introducing bonus-based compensation plans with enough financial "action" to have a major motivational effect. One explanation for the lack of pay-for-performance plans, offered primarily by psychologists and behaviorists, is that monetary rewards are counterproductive. Deci (1972) argues that money actually lowers employee motivation, by reducing the "intrinsic rewards" that an employee receives from the job. Similarly, Slater (1980) concludes that "getting people to chase money . . . produces nothing but people chasing money. Using money as a motivator leads to a progressive degradation in the quality of everything produced." Kohn (1988) in his article "Incentives Can Be Bad for Business" offers three reasons why merit-pay systems are counterproductive. "First, rewards encourage people to focus narrowly on a task, to do it as quickly as possible, and to take few risks . . . Second, extrinsic rewards can erode intrinsic interest . . . [Finally], people come to see themselves as being controlled by a reward."

A second group of merit-pay critics argue that, although financial incentive schemes improve productivity in principle, in practice they induce significant adverse side effects that are costly to employee morale and productivity. The costs of dealing with many of the problems induced by merit systems simply outweigh the limited organizational benefits they offer.[3] Among the side effects often mentioned are horizontal equity concerns and problems associated with imperfect performance measurement. Hamner (1975) in his article "How to Ruin Motivation with Pay" argues that merit systems decrease motivation because managers systematically mismanage pay-for-performance programs.

Personnel executives often espouse the virtues of *horizontal equity* systems, which treat employees at the same level in an organization "fairly" and "equally."[4] Aggressive pay-for-performance systems ultimately involve distinguishing workers on the basis of their performance, and there is a large behavioral literature arguing that treating employees differently from each other is detrimental to employee morale. The notion is that a worker will "feel bad" if a co-worker gets a bigger bonus, and the net effect of this inequity is to reduce morale and ultimately productivity. It is difficult to provide an economic explanation for why horizontal equity is desirable, and yet it seems to be a powerful force that drives firms toward consistency of pay within job type, and even across job type when employees are viewed as being of "comparable worth." Pay scales throughout much of corporate America are determined by "job evaluation systems," which "stem from the need to establish internal pay equity" (Risher 1978, p. 24). Such plans set wage levels by conducting surveys within and across organizations to assess the "value of a job" according to a set of criteria such as the amount of training and education required, the total budget involved, the number of people supervised, and the amount of "independent decision making" the job entails. Traditional economic analysis, however, would indicate these variables are important only to the extent that they affect the opportunity cost of the relevant-quality worker and the salary level that determines the optimal turnover rate.

We believe that careful examination of the criticisms of monetary pay-for-performance systems indicates not that they are ineffective but rather that they are *too* effective: strong pay-for-performance motivates people to do exactly what they are told to do. Large monetary incentives generate unintended and sometimes counterproductive results because it is difficult to specify adequately exactly what people should do and therefore how their performance should be measured. Moreover, merit-pay systems encourage employees to spend effort lobbying about both the specification and application of the system to measure and evaluate output. Viewing the dispute between economists and others as centered on the counterproductive effects of strong monetary rewards is useful: it focuses attention on how these unintended effects are generated and on their importance, rather than on arguments about whether people are motivated by money or whether they "should be" motivated by money.

Objective versus Subjective Performance Measurement

Pay-for-performance systems can be based on objective measures (such as sales, divisional profits, or the number of relay switches produced) or subjective measures (such as the estimated "value" of the employee to the organization). While some jobs, such as sales, lend themselves to objective measurement, performance in most jobs cannot be measured objectively because joint production and unobservability mean that individual output is not readily quantifiable.

Objective merit systems appear to have several disadvantages over systems where performance is evaluated subjectively. One disadvantage is that misspecifying the performance measure in an objective system results in resourceful employees "gaming the system" by optimizing with respect to actual instead of intended measures. Piece-rate workers, for example, will sacrifice quality for quantity, while managers paid on the basis of annual accounting profits will sacrifice long-run profitability for short-run earnings.

Objective performance measurement and evaluation systems are hard to change because altering the measurement scheme inevitably harms some employees. Changing the rules of the game is thus costly, even when change is economically desirable. Such problems are particularly costly with piece-rate pay systems in an environment undergoing substantial technical change. Changing the standards is always contentious, and the fear of such changes generates incentives to withhold details of the production process from the performance evaluator. The threat of increased standards and reduced bonuses when production is greater than anticipated generates incentives for employees to restrict output.[5] Eliminating these incentives to restrict output requires that the compensation contract make changes in standards or piece rates difficult—except for productivity increases due to technological change and/or capital investments. Contracts preventing confiscatory standard or rate changes are, however, extremely difficult to write, and they will tend to reduce the rates at which new technologies or new capital equipment is introduced. Lincoln Electric, one of the best known pay-for-performance success stories, is known to have old equipment.[6]

Specifying the correct objective measure of employee performance is often impossible. Indeed, the primary reason decision-making authority is granted to subordinates is that they have superior specific knowledge about the job they are doing. The principal knows, in general terms, what he wants the agent to do, but the range of possible actions that the agent can take, and the range of possible outcomes, is enormous. It would be very costly for the principal to assign, *ex ante,* explicit rewards and punishments to all of the possible outcomes that might be induced by the agent's actions. Yet, *ex post,* the value of a particular outcome is much clearer.

Consider the performance-measurement process used to evaluate junior faculty at research universities. The exact nature of the evaluation scheme is not specified explicitly, although many components of what makes a good scholar can be described. Even if substantial effort were made to specify *ex ante* the correct performance-measurement formula, it is hard to imagine it would be complete. The problems arising from making such an evaluation formula explicit are obvious: assistant professors would devote time and effort to maximizing the explicit performance measure. *Ex post,* it would be painfully obvious, at least in a few cases, that good performers as measured by the formula were not the best scholars.

The problems associated with basing pay on objective measures suggest that subjective performance measures should be utilized, but subjective appraisal systems are unpopular with both employees and supervisors. Milkovich and Newman (1987, p. 334) summarize survey results indicating that 30% of employees believe their performance appraisals are ineffective. Supervisors tend to prefer objective measurement systems because they generate fewer conflicts with disgruntled employees than subjective systems do; supervisors do not have to justify their personal assessment of performance in an objective performance-measurement system.

Psychologists and behaviorists have provided an explanation for the lack of subjective performance-evaluation systems in practice. Lawler (1971, p. 171) concludes that "pay plans based on subjective criteria have little chance of success" because employees don't *trust* superiors to evaluate their performance accurately. He argues that "the more subjective the measure, the higher the degree of trust needed, because without high trust there is little chance that the subordinate will believe that his pay is really fairly based on performance." Similarly, Hamner (1975, p. 19) argues that employees are often dissatisfied with performance evaluations by their immediate superior and recommends that merit pay "should, whenever possible, be based on objective . . . rather than subjective measures."

Economic theory is founded on the assumption that individuals are self-interested; therefore an employee will trust her superior to take particular action (e.g., perform a careful evaluation) if she knows it is in her superior's self-interest to take the action. We do not have a well-developed economic theory of trust, but at its core trust is a set of beliefs about the veracity, honesty, and length of horizon of an individual, and the predictability and reliability of his future actions. Research on reputation promises to yield insights into the role of trust in employee-employer relationships. Further empirical work is required to understand better the popularity of objective performance-measurement systems and other problems associated with "trust."

Pay-for-performance systems are powerful motivators of human action, apparently so powerful that they induce counterproductive effects and the substitution of less effective motivational devices in organizations. Although not well understood, the forces leading organizations to avoid strong monetary incentives fall into two categories. The lack of trust between employees and supervisors and their distaste for conflict lead organizations to avoid pay-for-performance systems based on *subjective* performance evaluation. Similarly, problems associated with determining and modifying objective performance measures, and the dysfunctional behavior induced by resourceful employees faced with such measures, lead organizations to avoid pay-for-performance systems based on *objective* performance evaluation. The compensation system that results from this set of forces appears to be one with little or no pay for performance.

8.2 Promotion-Based Incentive Systems

Wage levels in a hierarchical organization are often tied to job levels in the firm and not to individuals; most of the average increases in an employee's compensation can be traced to promotions and not to continued service in a particular position. Medoff and Abraham (1980), for example, find that between-job-level earnings differentials are more important than within-job-level differentials.[7] In addition, Murphy (1985) finds that corporate vice presidents receive average pay increases of

18.8% upon promotion to another vice-presidential or higher position, compared to average pay increases of only 3.3% in years when they remain in the same position.

Promotions in organizations serve two important and distinct purposes. First, individuals differ in their skills and abilities, jobs differ in the demands they place on individuals, and promotions are a way to match individuals to the jobs for which they are best suited. This matching process occurs over time through promotions as employees accumulate human capital and as more information is generated and collected about the employee's talents and capabilities. A second role of promotions is to provide incentives for lower-level employees who value the pay and prestige associated with a higher rank in the organization.

Promotion-Based Incentives versus Bonus-Based Incentives

Promotions are used as the primary incentive device in most organizations, including corporations, partnerships, and universities. The empirical importance of promotion-based incentives, combined with the virtual absence of pay-for-performance compensation policies, suggests that providing incentives through promotion opportunities must be less costly or more effective than providing incentives through transitory financial bonuses. This prediction is puzzling to us because promotion-based incentive schemes appear to have many disadvantages and few advantages relative to bonus-based incentive schemes.

Lazear and Rosen (1981) model promotions as single-period tournaments and argue that, under some conditions, risk-averse workers prefer tournaments to linear piece rates. However, their one-period framework masks many of the complexities and inherent disadvantages of actual promotion systems. The incentives generated by promotion opportunities, for example, depend on the probability of promotion, which in turn depends on the identity and expected horizon of the incumbent superior. Promoting a young employee with a long expected horizon in the job commonly diminishes the incentives of the employee's former co-workers, who now expect to wait a long time until their next promotion opportunity. Promotion incentives are reduced for employees who have been passed up for promotion previously and whose future promotion potential is doubtful, and incentives will be absent for employees who clearly fall short of the promotion standard or who cannot conceivably win a promotion tournament. In addition, promotion possibilities provide no incentives for anyone to exceed the standard or to substantially outperform his or her co-workers.

Another important problem with promotion-based reward systems is that they require organizational growth to feed the reward system. This means that such systems can work well in rapidly growing firms, but are likely to generate problems in slowly growing or shrinking firms. Jensen (1986a, 1986b, 1988) has argued that, in slowly growing firms with free cash flow, promotion-based reward systems encourage managers to spend resources on unprofitable growth rather than paying out excess cash to shareholders. The reduction in profitable growth opportunities in many industries such as oil, chemicals, manufacturing, communications, forest products, tobacco, and food in the mid-1970s, coupled with the tendency for organizations with promotion-based reward systems to engage in unprofitable growth, provides a potential explanation for much of the hostile-takeover activity that has created major controversy in the political and regulatory sectors since the early 1980s.

Bonus-based incentives, transitory in the sense that this year's bonus depends on this year's performance, do not have the problems associated with promotion-based incentives. Bonus schemes can, in principle, provide incentives for all individuals in the organization, regardless of their ability, position, and promotion opportunities. For example, properly structured compensation policies at all levels in the organization can punish top executives for unprofitable expansion without degrading incentives for lower-level managers. Finally, it is often argued that promotion contests are desirable since they need only be based on rank order and thus can reduce risk or random noise common to all contestants—but bonus systems based on ranked or relative performance can easily achieve these same objectives.

We do not understand why firms systematically choose promotion-based incentive systems instead of bonus-based systems, and solving this mystery is an exciting direction for future research. Laying aside our ignorance of the benefits of promotion-based incentive systems, we can assume that such benefits do indeed exist and can analyze the characteristics of these systems.[8] Bonus-based incentives will be more important at higher levels in the organization since the probability of future promotion is lower; the CEO is not promotable, and therefore his or her financial incentives must come from bonuses. Promotion-based schemes will be used more in large organizations with many hierarchical levels than in smaller organizations with fewer levels. In addition, promotion-based reward systems will be more prevalent in growing industries (because there are more new jobs to feed the reward system), while bonus-based systems will be more prevalent in declining industries.

There is some evidence that, in the face of low growth in the last decade, there has been a gradual movement toward more use of annual transitory bonuses as rewards for exceptional performance, but we do not know whether this trend is more pronounced in declining industries than in stable or growing industries. Firms that shut down plants and eliminate layers of the managerial hierarchy should switch toward bonus-based reward systems. Recent field evidence on firms that have downsized through restructuring is consistent with a move to greater emphasis on pay for performance. FMC, Colt Industries, and Holiday Corporation (which all restructured in 1986–1987) have emphasized aligning managers' rewards more closely with the interests of shareholders. These changes include emphasis on equity ownership, stock options, and annual bonus systems to avoid the potential loss of valuable younger managers.

The increase in the number and size of leveraged buyouts (from $1.2 billion per year in 1979 to $77 billion in 1987)[9] is also consistent with the theory that argues that slow-growing firms must find ways to provide new and powerful incentives to management. Making LBO managers the owners of highly levered equity in their own firm has the effect of replacing the promotion-based reward system with an important financial stake that carries large payoffs for good performance.[10]

The sharp reduction in growth for much of the American economy in the 1980s implies that promotion-based incentives will be replaced by other forms of rewards, and the available evidence on trends in bonuses, restructurings, and LBOs is consistent with the economic predictions. Nevertheless, most organizations continue to rely on promotions to provide incentives, and the dominance of promotion-based incentive systems remains a major puzzle.

Can Promotion Systems Provide Both Incentives and Matching?

Given the virtual absence of incentive compensation, an organization's promotion policies must simultaneously provide incentives for lower-level employees and also provide a channel through which individuals can end up in the jobs for which they are best suited. Unfortunately, a serious but generally unrecognized limitation of using promotions as the primary incentive device is that promotion-based incentive systems cannot provide optimal effort incentives while simultaneously achieving the best match between employees and positions.

Tournament promotion systems, in which the best performer at each level is promoted to the next higher level, provide performance incentives for employees. In many cases, however, the best performer at one level in the hierarchy is not the best candidate for the job one level up—the best salesman is rarely the best manager, for example, and the best scholar is rarely the best dean. Firms that use promotion-based incentive systems commonly face problems with the loss of talented engineers, scientists, and salespeople who insist on moving into management to realize promotion possibilities when none are available in their area of expertise. Two-track systems attempt to resolve this problem,[11] but they often fail when the technical promotions are to jobs with higher rank but no real purpose. The Peter Principle (people are promoted to their level of incompetence) reflects problems generated when talents for the next level in the hierarchy are not perfectly correlated with talents required to be the best performer in the current job.

Tournament promotion systems cannot simultaneously provide optimal incentives and matching. For matching to matter, employees must differ. For tournaments to provide optimal incentives, employees must be alike, since differences in ability lead to reduced incentives if participants know that those of high ability will win. Lazear and Rosen (1981) suggest the use of handicapping to reintroduce incentives in promotional contests when employees have different abilities; O'Keeffe, Viscusi, and Zeckhauser (1984) suggest increasing the importance of random factors in the contest. Their solutions are technically elegant, but adding randomness and imposing handicaps are clearly in conflict with both casual empiricism and the objective of selecting the employee whose talents best match the demands of the new job.

Tournament Promotion Systems Cannot Provide Matching

Tournament promotion systems cannot in general match employees to the jobs for which they are best suited. This is demonstrated in Figure 8.1, which provides a plot of the output (net of wages) of two types of employees in jobs at three representative levels in the hierarchy—entry-level management, middle management, and top management. As

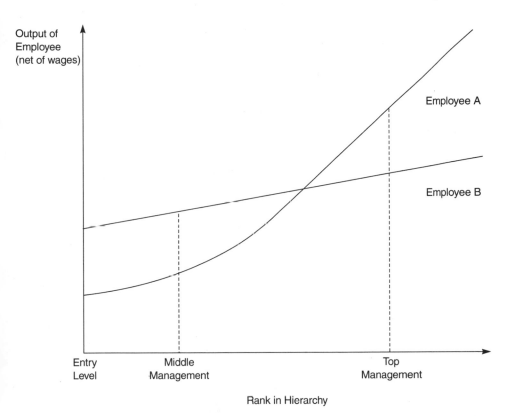

Figure 8.1 Relation between output (net of wages) in jobs at different levels in the hierarchy for employees of type A and B. Type-A employees, who are best suited for top management jobs, will lose promotion tournaments at lower management levels.

drawn in the figure, employees of type A are the best top managers, while type-B employees excel in lower-level management positions. A promotion tournament at the middle-management level, in which the best performing middle manager moves to the executive suite, will result in type-B employees being promoted to top management, which is clearly inconsistent with optimal matching.

Both types of employees in Figure 8.1 are assumed to be increasingly productive at higher levels, but the inability of tournament promotion systems to match employees with jobs is general and does not depend on these particular relations between output and hierarchical rank. In fact, matching problems in tournaments are even worse if output does not continuously increase as employees climb the hierarchy.

Each type of employee in Figure 8.1 is assumed to have an advantage over the other type in some jobs within the hierarchy. There are two other situations that should be considered—the case where the relation between output and rank is the same for both employee types, and the case where one type "outproduces" the other type at all levels.[12] Matching is important only when employees differ in their abilities to perform different jobs. Therefore, matching is trivial in the first case where the employee types are identical. Matching is also trivial in the second case where one type dominates the other in all jobs, as long as employee skills are observable, since the firm will never hire any of the inferior type. When skills are unobservable directly, employees can be matched to jobs as information about the employee's talents and capabilities is revealed by experience. Tournament promotion systems, in which the highest performing employee is promoted to the next level, can effectively match employees to jobs when talents are unobservable so long as the required talents for the next level in the hierarchy are the same as the talents required to win the tournament in the current job. Tournament systems provide optimal incentives as long as employees believe all workers in the competition are equally talented, but handicaps are required to maintain incentives after information is revealed about unequal talents.

Instead of promoting the best performing middle manager, an alternative promotion rule that seems to solve the matching problem in Figure 8.1 is to promote the middle manager with the best top-management potential. This promotion rule—in which the level n employee promoted to level $n + 1$ is the one with the highest expected output at level $n + 1$—does not guarantee matching with more than two hierarchical levels. Suppose, for example, that firms follow this alternative promotion rule and that type A and B entry-level managers compete for middle-management positions. Only type-B employees will be promoted to middle management because their expected middle-management output is higher than type A's. Thus, there are no type-A middle managers to promote to top management positions since they are selected out at lower levels. Type-A employees can, of course, be hired for top-management positions from the outside, but external hires lack the experience and firm-specific capital often required to succeed in an organization.

Although promotion decisions based on expected performance in the next-highest position solve the matching problem in a two-level hierarchy, these systems will not provide optimal effort incentives. Law firms, for example, will promote the associates who are likely to make the best partners, and not the highest performing associates. This induces incentive problems for associates, who will compete to demonstrate that they will make the best partners instead of striving to be the best associates. This is likely to result in nonoptimal associate behavior.

Tenure and Up-or-Out Promotion Systems

In tenure systems, after working for five to ten years with virtually no performance bonuses, the "best" employees are promoted and receive a grant of partnership or lifetime employment. The special characteristics of tenure systems, their effects on productivity, and why they are used in certain industries and not in others have not been thoroughly studied. These systems must be primarily used for matching rather than incentive purposes, since it is difficult to argue that the desire for tenure provides incentives for law associates and junior faculty and simultaneously to argue that no further incentives are required once tenure is achieved.[13] Tenure systems appear to prevail in situations where human capital, creativity, and an unstructured environment are particularly important in the production process, and where long lags between actions and the observation of outcomes make performance measurement and evaluation difficult. It can take years, for example, to discern whether a controversial paper is an intellectual breakthrough or an unproductive diversion of the profession's attention.

Tenure and partnership systems are often associated with up-or-out promotion policies, in which organizations force the unsuccessful candidate for tenure or partnership to leave the organization. This avoids the difficult problem of providing incentives for unpromotable employees in an organization using promotion-based incentives. But up-or-out policies seem to us to be a particularly harsh way of dealing with these employees. Such employees are often highly productive to the organization, and the inability to provide an alternative internal career path imposes costs through the loss of organization-specific human capital that is destroyed by the up-or-out policy.

Up-or-out systems work better in situations where the required human capital is general rather than organization-specific, and where turnover is important to provide the new energy, ideas, enthusiasm, and change that younger people generate. These factors seem to be important in research universities and in many professional partnerships.[14] In addition, up-or-out systems increase the size of the sample from which the best performers can be chosen, and this can lead to a large increase in quality of the promoted group so long as the policy does not reduce the quality of the applicant pool. Maintenance of the applicant-pool quality is undoubtedly why high-turnover up-or-out employers such as public accounting and law firms spend considerable effort on outplacement services for those not awarded partnership. Such outplacements can also have a positive effect on the demand for the firm's services—for example, when the individual becomes controller or general counsel of potential clients.

Tenure, partnership, and up-or-out systems tend to be associated with relatively small organizations with few hierarchical levels. With the exception of the military, up-or-out promotion systems are almost never observed in large multilevel hierarchical organizations. These firms, large hierarchies accounting for a substantial portion of corporate America, are characterized by strong promotion-based reward systems and little use of bonuses. The fact that these firms use "up-or-stay" policies, stressing low firing rates and long-term employment relations, is puzzling since the incentive problems associated with nonpromotable employees seem particularly pronounced in these organizations.

8.3   Profit-Sharing Plans

Profit-sharing, in which an individual's compensation is tied to the overall performance of the firm, has become increasingly popular in U.S. corporations. Kruse (1987) reports that 20% of the U.S. labor force (22 million employees) participate in more than 400,000 workplace profit-sharing plans, and that the number of profit-sharing pension plans has increased by 19,000 per year since 1970. Ehrenberg and Milkovich (1987) summarize studies in the personnel literature that show that merit pay and bonuses based on individual performance are less effective than profit-sharing, stock ownership, and team-based bonuses. A recent New York Stock Exchange survey indicates that 70% of firms with profit-sharing plans report that they lead to improved productivity. The NYSE Office of Economic Research study, summarized by Ehrenberg and Milkovich (1987, p. 31), concludes that "gain sharing can play an important role in motivating people to be more productive."

The productive effects and popularity of profit-sharing plans are poorly understood by economists. The free-rider problem associated with these plans seems insurmountable in large organizations; employees bear the full cost of working harder and yet receive only a fraction on the order of $1/n$ of the increased profits (where n is the number of participants in the plan). When measures of individual performance are available, it always seems better to tie pay to individual performance rather than to overall firm performance. Joint-production situations where only group, and not individual, output is observable lend themselves to team-based incentive plans, but this cannot possibly explain tying the janitor's wage to the stock price. Weitzman (1984) argues that profit-sharing plans have desirable macroeconomic properties but cannot explain why individual firms or employees would choose such a plan.

A common economic argument for team-based incentives is that these policies encourage mutual monitoring. Worker A has incentives to monitor co-workers if the co-workers' performance affects worker A's compensation, and vice versa. This type of mutual-monitoring system also suffers from the free-rider problem. An *over-monitoring problem* can also arise if workers prefer monitoring others to working themselves; shirking behavior by one worker may be observed and reported by dozens of co-workers even when it is more efficient to appoint a single monitor. More important, this system can only work when rewards and punishments are based on *individual performance* and not strictly on team performance—that is, mutual-monitoring systems only work if the shirkers are punished. Team-based compensation can sometimes create incentives for workers to reward and punish the performance of their colleagues with social courtesy, honors, and sanctions such as withholding of cooperation and exchanges. This makes sense when the workers have information about the performance of their peers that is not available to their superiors. Economists have little understanding of the dynamics of this phenomenon.

Compensation practitioners argue that fundamental changes in the "corporate culture" occur when employees are made partial owners of the firm. The effects of these plans include "rooting for the home team" and a growing awareness of and interest in the corporate bottom line. We do not understand how these effects translate into increased productivity, nor do we have a well-developed economic theory of the creation and effects of corporate culture.

8.4 Biased and Inaccurate Performance Evaluations

The lack of financial incentives reported by Medoff and Abraham (1980) and summarized in Table 8.1 is surprising, but even more surprising is the result that supervisors tend to assign uniform performance ratings and tend not to assign poor performance ratings. Only .2% of the 4,788 employees in Company A received the lowest rating; 94.5% were rated "Good" or "Outstanding." None of the 2,841 Company B employees received an "Unacceptable" or "Minimum Acceptable" rating, and only 1.2% received a rating of "Satisfactory"; 95% of the Company B employees were rated "Good" or "Superior."[15]

The general reluctance of managers to give poor performance evaluations to employees is puzzling but is consistent with well-documented evidence that most people believe their performance is better than average. Of several studies cited in Meyer (1975), one indicates that 58% of a sample of white-collar clerical and technical workers rated their own performance as falling within the top 10% of their peers in similar jobs, and 81% rated themselves in the top 20%. Only about 1% rated themselves below the median. Another study of 1,088 managerial and professional employees found an even stronger bias: 47% rated their own performance in the top 5%; 83% rated their performance in the top 10%; no one rated their performance below the 75th percentile.

The biased perceptions of individuals regarding their own performance may explain why supervisors appear to have a strong aversion to giving subordinates poor evaluations. There will be more dissatisfaction induced by telling someone that he or she is in the bottom 20% than there will be satisfaction induced by giving a top-20% rating. Telling all employees that they are average will make almost everyone unhappy. Forced-ranking systems will therefore generate considerable conflict in organizations. Similarly, pay-for-performance systems that provide large rewards for good performance and small rewards for mediocre performance will be avoided, since these schemes force managers to give poor evaluations to a large number of employees. Visible rewards will not be granted for superior performance unless there is significant incentive for superiors to undertake the unpleasant task of telling subordinates that they are poor or even average performers.

Understanding the causes and effects of biased and inaccurate performance ratings may help explain another recurring puzzle: the apparent asymmetry between rewards and punishments. Every economist understands that a compensation scheme paying a salary of $80 plus a bonus of $20 if a quota is met is equivalent to a compensation scheme paying a salary of $100 with a $20 penalty if the quota is not met. What economists don't understand is why compensation plans almost always are of the former type instead of the latter. Understanding this asymmetry may also shed some light on the prevalence of compensation systems that reward "winners" without explicitly identifying "losers." Promotion-based reward systems fit this category: the vast majority of employees who incorrectly rank themselves near the top of their peer group can still believe, when they are passed over for promotion, that they may not be the best but are nonetheless somewhere near the top.

It is difficult to motivate managers to devote the large amounts of resources necessary for performance measurement, and performance evaluations will tend to be more careful and less biased as the costs of making inaccurate appraisals increase. Managers spend more time agonizing over promotion decisions, for example, than they spend on dividing up the bonus pool because the costs of mistakes in promotion (where employees are given more decision rights in addition to higher salaries) are much higher than the costs of mistakes in awarding annual bonuses (Baker 1989). Similarly, in universities, more resources are devoted to evaluating performance for tenure decisions than for nontenure promotions and annual salary decisions.

Additional evidence consistent with the proposition that evaluations are more careful when the stakes are higher is available from an experiment in which University of Rochester business school faculty members (including two of the authors of this chapter) were given the right to award quarterly performance bonuses to their secretaries. Money not awarded as bonuses was available to the faculty member for purchase of a wide range of professional goods and services. In the first year, when the maximum award was $150/quarter, 90% of the secretaries were awarded the maximum bonus; no bonuses were less than $100. During the second year, when the maximum award was increased to $250/quarter, only 59% received the maximum bonus, and the variance in bonuses awarded was substantially higher. Over the two-year period the maximum bonus was awarded 76% of the time, suggesting that faculty members were generally reluctant to give poor evaluations. The decrease in maximum bonuses awarded and the increased variance of awards are consistent with the proposition that better evaluations result from higher stakes. The amounts were too small to motivate a professor to devote the necessary time and effort to the evaluation task, and to bear the personal non-pecuniary costs of explaining to his or her secretary why the award was less than the maximum.

Biased and inaccurate performance evaluation reduces productivity by reducing the effectiveness of incentives in the organization. If supervisors systematically make incorrect marginal decisions regarding performance evaluation, it may be optimal to induce more careful evaluations by raising the costs of inaccurate appraisals.[16] Tenure and up-or-out systems increase the costs imposed on the organization from granting lifetime employment to those mistakenly promoted and impose costs on those who are denied promotion and therefore must leave the organization. These systems, therefore, provide particularly strong incentives for monitors (faculty, colleagues, administrators, and partners) to invest large amounts of resources in performance measurement and evaluation. The analysis suggests that systems such as tenure and up-or-out provide incentives for the monitors as well as the employees; we do not, however, understand why organizations choose to motivate monitors in this particular way.

8.5 Compensation Surveys and the Relation Between CEO Pay and Firm Size

The best-documented empirical regularity regarding levels of executive compensation is an elasticity of compensation with respect to firm sales of about .3—a 10% larger firm will pay its executives an average of 3% more. The compensation/sales elasticities estimated by the Conference Board, reported in Table 8.2 for five years and for five industry groups, have been remarkably stable across time and industries; the mean and median elasticity equal .31, and two-thirds of the estimates fall in the range .275 to .35. Moreover, the correlation between size and compensation is very high; R-squares for the 1983 regressions, for example, are .60 (manufacturing), .53 (retail trade), .67 (utilities), .68 (banking), and .69 (insurance).

It is not surprising to economists that compensation increases with firm size; larger firms, for example, may employ better-qualified and better-paid CEOs. Economic theory cannot, however, explain why pay increases *at a decreasing rate,* and why the relation is constant across both time and industries. Even more perplexing is that the .3 elasticity continues to hold when analyzing individual wages over time. Murphy (1985) shows that, holding the value of the firm constant, a firm whose sales *grow* by 10% will *increase* the salary and bonus of its CEO by between 2 and 3%. This finding suggests that the size/pay relation is causal and therefore reflects more than a matching of CEOs to firms on

Table 8.2 Estimated Elasticity of CEO Salary and Bonus with Respect to Firm Sales, 1973–1983

	Year				
Industry	1973	1975	1979	1981	1983
Manufacturing	.313	.296	.297	.287	.285
Retail Trade	.253	.271	.230	.306	.298
Gas and Electric Utilities	.331	.236	.347	.313	.314
Commercial Banking	.317	.329	.367	.372	.404
Insurance	.313	.277	.299	.372	.345

Source: Top Executive Compensation, The Conference Board, various editions. Elasticities correspond to the estimated coefficient from a regression of Log (Salary + Bonus) on Log (Sales). Sales are defined as operating revenues for utilities, deposits for banks, and total premium income for insurance companies.

the basis of their abilities. It also suggests that CEOs can increase their pay by increasing firm size, even when the increase in size reduces the firm's market value. This could explain some of the vast amount of inefficient expenditures of corporate resources on diversification programs that have created large conglomerate organizations over the last twenty years.

Table 8.2 and Murphy's time-series evidence are consistent with widespread acceptance of the consultant's primary analytical tool: *the compensation survey.* Compensation surveys, which compare compensation levels for CEOs in different organizations, play a very important role in determining CEO compensation.

The use of surveys relating pay to firm size is widespread. A recent Conference Board report on compensation, for example, reports more than 250 separate regressions relating compensation to sales by industry and hierarchical rank.[17] The Conference Board, which is supported by member firms, does not report these regressions to document interesting empirical regularities, but rather to help compensation committees set and compare compensation levels across firms and industries.

Compensation consultant Howard Risher (1978, p. 34) defends regression-based pay determination, arguing that consistency "is one of the purposes of a formal salary administration program, [and] the regression equation will simulate the decision process and will produce results compatible with the prevailing value system." Risher contends that "regression techniques can provide a substitute for job evaluation plans and a means for integrating internal and external factors in compensation decisions." Moreover, "the regression approach all but eliminates any undue time commitment by line managers." This substitution of a mechanical pay/sales relationship means that job performance is no longer being evaluated, and it provides managers with incentives to behave according to Baumol's (1959) sales-maximization hypothesis.

Results from widely accepted compensation surveys are ultimately self-perpetuating—the uniformity of the elasticities in Table 8.2 is consistent with the hypothesis that the surveyed firms use the survey results to structure their own pay levels. The pay/sales elasticities of roughly .3 documented in Table 8.2 suggest that the decision rules used by boards of directors in setting CEO compensation relate pay directly to firm size as measured by sales. Consistent with this, Davidson Consultants' *Wage and Salary Administration in a Changing Economy* (1984, p. 175), explains how to set CEO compensation: "The general rule is that as sales volume doubles, executive pay increases by one-third."

Survey-based compensation systems seem inherently counterproductive. Surveys that report only pay levels encourage the establishment of compensation schemes that are independent of performance. In principle, surveys can be structured to describe the pay/performance relation across firms. That is, instead of focusing on "How much should a CEO in a firm with $1 billion sales be paid?" the survey could focus on "How much should pay *increase* for a CEO whose firm increased in value by $100 million?" To our knowledge, these surveys are never taken. Moreover, basing an employee's pay on external surveys leads naturally to pay decisions being made by centralized personnel departments rather than by managers who have better knowledge about an employee's performance. Economists must have a better understanding of the importance of these surveys in determining pay for CEOs and other employees.

8.6   Incentive Contracts for Top-Level Managers

Top management is an occupation where incentive pay is expected to play an important role, but Jensen and Murphy (Chapter 9 of this volume) have found that actual executive-compensation contracts look very different from those predicted by economic theory. The empiri-

cal relation between the pay of top-level executives and firm performance, while positive and statistically significant, is tiny. On average,
each $1,000 change in shareholder wealth corresponds to an increase in
this year's and next year's salary and bonus of only two cents. Jensen
and Murphy argue that this estimate is too small to be consistent with
the economic theory of compensation. A common criticism of this conclusion is that the theory says nothing about the *magnitude* of the pay/
performance relation. Two cents per $1,000 may be just about right, for
example, given risk aversion and the difficulty of writing binding contracts, or maybe it should be $2 or $200 per $1,000—economic theory
alone gives us little guidance because it is incomplete.

Contracting theory predicts that pay should not be based on factors beyond the control of the executive (Holmström 1979), and that
management compensation should therefore be based on performance
measured relative to the performance of all firms or firms in the same
industry, rather than on absolute measures of firm performance. The
theory is compelling but imprecise; managers should not be insulated
from outside factors if they can take actions that reduce the firm's expo-
sure to losses from such sources. This caveat aside, it seems desirable
and feasible to base pay on relative performance instead of absolute
performance. However, boards of directors do not use relative performance measures; Jensen and Murphy show that absolute firm-value
changes are a better predictor of changes in salary and bonus than value
changes measured relative to the industry and the market. Moreover,
incentives generated by cash compensation are trivial compared to incentives generated by stock options and stock ownership, and stock-related compensation is directly related to absolute returns and not relative returns.

Another anomalous result from Jensen and Murphy (see Chapter 9)
is that the pay/performance relation is independent of stock ownership.
It would make sense, for example, that CEOs with small stockholdings should have a stronger pay-for-performance compensation package than CEOs with large stockholdings. In fact, for this latter group it
might even make sense to have pay go up in bad years to compensate
for some of the loss the CEO is taking in the stock market. As an
empirical issue, however, this turns out not to be the case. The estimated
pay/performance relation is independent of stock ownership—boards
of directors systematically ignore CEO stock ownership when structuring incentive compensation plans.

Jensen and Murphy argue that the apparent anomalies in executive-compensation contracts may be explained by the strong political forces operating in both the organization and the public sector that effectively constrain the type of contracts written between managers and shareholders. This "implicit regulation argument" is currently unsatisfactory because we do not understand why boards of directors are so easily, and unprofitably, influenced by implicit political pressures.

8.7   Efficiency Wages and the Absence of Bonding Contracts

"Efficiency wage theory" is a term coined to explain persistent empirical regularities in inter-industry wage differentials that are inconsistent with the perfectly competitive model of labor markets. According to the competitive model, wages depend only on workers' abilities and on characteristics of their employers that influence non-pecuniary benefits of employment. In competitive equilibrium, equally productive workers receive compensation that provides equal utility. According to Krueger and Summers (1988), violation of this implies that "at least some employers are paying more than the going rate for workers of the type they attract. This behavior can be rationalized only by assuming that some firms do not profit maximize, or that some firms find that increasing wages above the going rate is profitable. The latter possibility is the defining characteristic of efficiency wage theories." Krueger and Summers argue that if firms maximize profits, the efficiency of such wages must be explained by one or more of the following four phenomena: reductions in total turnover costs, increases in the quality of workers the firm can attract, increases in productivity caused by increases in loyalty, and increases in worker effort.

To the extent that high wages are explainable by reductions in turnover costs or in higher-quality workers, they are, of course, not an anomaly but merely an indication of the incomplete notion of competitive wages in the simple model. To the extent that wage differentials are due to increased effort levels by employees that arise because the structure of pay provides superior productivity incentives, the notion of efficiency wages reflects a confusion induced by the incomplete characterization of compensation by the simple competitive model. It is useful to consider some elemental aspects of compensation policies as a basis for discussion of these issues.

A firm's compensation policy can be broken into three independent dimensions for purposes of analysis: the *level*, the *functional form*, and the *composition*. The *level* of compensation is the expected total cost of the pay package to the employer, or the expected total value of the pay package to the employee.[18] The level of compensation determines the quality and quantity of workers an organization can attract; in order to hire a worker, a firm must offer at least the worker's opportunity cost or reservation utility. The *functional form* of compensation provides the definition of the relation between pay and performance and the definition of performance. In general, while the level of compensation determines *whom* the firm can attract, the functional form determines *how the employees perform* once they are hired. The functional form provides the performance incentive for employees; simple increases in the level of compensation will have no effects on effort or performance except the usual income effects in the labor-supply decision. Finally, the *composition* of the pay package defines the relative amounts of the components of the package, such as cash compensation, fringe benefits, quality of the working environment, relationships with co-workers, leisure, and so on.

On the surface, the "incentive version" of the efficiency wage hypothesis would seem to relate to compensation *levels*—employees work harder and are more productive because they are paid a high wage. Formally, however, the theory cannot be about levels but rather about the *functional form*. In this view, the contracts are structured so that at any point in time the present value of continued employment exceeds the present value of the best alternative employment, that is, employees earn rents. It is not a high current wage, therefore, that provides the incentive not to shirk, but rather the possibility of suffering a penalty—the lost rents—if the worker shirks and gets caught. Becker and Stigler (1974) show that this theory of wage dynamics is consistent with a competitive equilibrium with zero rents to employees; for example, the rents implied by paying the employee a premium throughout his or her career can be recaptured by charging an entry fee for the job. Note that varying the entry fee affects the level of compensation and thus whether or not workers will apply for a given job. But varying the entry fee does not affect the functional form and thus does not affect the performance of employees on the job.

Thus, the puzzle of efficiency wages is not why wage levels differ across firms and industries but rather why the implicit rents are not dissipated in the form of bonds and up-front entry fees. In practice, with a few notable exceptions such as franchise contracts (see Rubin 1978), substantial entry fees and bonds are virtually never observed. Dickens, Katz, Lang, and Summers (1987, p. 18) argue that liquidity constraints and the possibility that the firm will renege on a bonding contract are insufficient to explain the lack of bonding in employment contracts. They conclude that implicit limits on bonding and up-front payments reflect the "society's unwillingness to enforce" bonding contracts, and also the "potential negative impact of bonds on employee morale." Some of these enforcement constraints and social pressures are explicit, they argue, such as the required vesting of pension plans, but most are implicit and "are connected to notions of fairness that lie outside of conventional treatments of the economics of agency and incentives." But this argument is inconsistent with commonly observed franchise fees that can run into the hundreds of thousands of dollars for jobs such as managing a hamburger stand. We do not understand why these up-front fees are feasible while others in the workplace are not.

8.8   What Happens When the Principal Isn't a Principal?

Many common features of compensation systems are not easily explained by traditional economic theory. Some researchers, like Jensen and Murphy (Chapter 9 of this volume) and Dickens, Katz, Lang, and Summers (1987), argue that economic analysis can only go so far; at some point we must defer to political pressure or to behavioral notions of fairness, social responsibility, trust, or culture. We are not yet willing to throw in the proverbial towel, but we admit that our economic understanding of internal incentive structures is far from complete. The first step on the road to a successful theory of organizational incentives is recognition of a variety of phenomena that economists have ignored either because they do not fit the extant theory or because they do not conform to familiar forms or standards of evidence.

One promising direction for research begins with the realization that managers in hierarchical organizations, from supervisors to CEOs and boards of directors, are not principals in the sense usually modeled in the principal-agent literature. Principals in this literature are 100% owners of the alienable residual claims to the cash flows, and it is this characteristic that provides incentives to structure contracts that maximize the joint welfare of the manager and the employee (subject, of course, to the inevitable agency costs). In hierarchies, substitutes for residual claims are allocated to managers in the form of incentive contracts and various direct-monitoring provisions. The absence of pay-for-performance compensation systems for managers implies that managers have few incentives to structure and enforce value-maximizing contracts with subordinates.

Consider, for example, a division manager deciding whether or not to terminate a popular but nonproductive employee. The personal costs borne by a manager making an unpopular termination decision are high and include personal discomfort with the task, chastisement by other employees and peers, the loss of important friendships, and the possibility of being sued for illegal discharge. Firing the unproductive employee will increase divisional profits, but this increased profitability will only benefit the manager to the extent that his or her compensation is tied to divisional performance. The smaller the relation between the manager's pay and divisional profits, the greater is the likelihood that the employee will be retained. The manager will likely argue that retention is "fair" and increases "employee morale," but in fact the uneconomic retention occurs because the manager lacks incentives to do anything else.

Similarly, it is rational for employees not to "trust" the performance appraisals they receive from superiors, since their superiors bear all of the monitoring costs but receive little of the benefit from conducting more accurate evaluations. Supervisors who are also residual claimants will have incentives to make correct marginal decisions regarding performance evaluation.

Horizontal equity systems are easy to administer, and managers have few incentives to switch to a more profitable system when their own compensation is determined not by performance, but rather by managers in the horizontal equity system one layer up. Profit-sharing plans are popular with employees and supervisors because they increase the level of compensation and do not require difficult individual-performance measurement. There may be more efficient ways to increase the level of pay, such as introducing bonuses based on individual performance, but managers and personnel executives have little incentive to adopt these economically efficient alternatives.

The absence of incentives to structure efficient compensation contracts permeates the corporate hierarchy—up to and including the compensation committee of the board of directors whose task is to design executive-compensation contracts. Boards of directors, who often own only a trivial fraction of their firm's common stock, are in no sense perfect agents for the shareholders who elected them. Board members are reluctant to terminate or financially punish poor-performing CEOs for the same reason supervisors are reluctant to punish subordinates—they personally bear a disproportionately large share of the non-pecuniary costs, but receive essentially none of the pecuniary benefits. The effect of structuring CEO contracts that are independent of performance is likely to cascade down the hierarchy—each successive layer has fewer incentives to structure effective contracts than the prior layer. The absence of incentives is pervasive, and it is not surprising that large organizations typically evolve into bureaucracies.

Managers respond to their lack of incentives by taking uneconomic actions that could be interpreted as being equitable and socially responsible. This lack-of-incentives hypothesis potentially explains the prevalence of horizontal equity systems, the asymmetric use of rewards and punishments, and the general reluctance of employers to penalize poor performance. The hypothesis does not, however, explain why competitive forces in the product, labor, and control markets are not sufficient to induce economically efficient compensation policies.

Ultimately, it may be that psychologists, behaviorists, human resource consultants, and personnel executives understand something about human behavior and motivation that is not yet captured in our economic models. Alternatively, it could be that practitioners are adopting policies that sacrifice organizational efficiency for egalitarian pay systems. If one of these reasons explains the gap between economic theory and compensation practices, then there are either intellectual profits or organizational efficiencies to be gained by focusing attention on the compensation puzzles we have outlined. We believe that both kinds of profit opportunities will materialize.

9 | Performance Pay and Top-Management Incentives

The conflict of interest between shareholders of a publicly owned corporation and the corporation's chief executive officer (CEO) is a classic example of a principal-agent problem. If shareholders had complete information regarding the CEO's activities and the firm's investment opportunities, they could design a contract specifying and enforcing the managerial action to be taken in each state of the world. Managerial actions and investment opportunities are not, however, perfectly observable by shareholders; indeed, shareholders often do not know what actions the CEO *can* take or which of these actions will increase shareholder wealth. In these situations, agency theory predicts that compensation policy will be designed to give the manager incentives to select and implement actions that increase shareholder wealth.

Shareholders want CEOs to take particular actions—for example, deciding which issue to work on, which project to pursue, and which to drop—whenever the expected return on the action exceeds the expected costs. But the CEO compares only his *private* gain and cost from pursuing a particular activity. If one abstracts from the effects of CEO risk aversion, compensation policy that ties the CEO's welfare to shareholder wealth helps align the private and social costs and benefits of alternative actions and thus provides incentives for CEOs to take appropriate actions. Shareholder wealth is affected by many factors in addition to the CEO, including actions of other executives and employees, demand and supply conditions, and public policy. It is appropriate, however, to pay CEOs on the basis of shareholder wealth since that is the objective of shareholders.

There are many mechanisms through which compensation policy can provide value-increasing incentives, including performance-based

By Michael C. Jensen and Kevin J. Murphy; originally published in *Journal of Political Economy* 98, no. 2 (April 1990), pp. 225–284.

bonuses and salary revisions, stock options, and performance-based dismissal decisions. The purpose of this chapter is to estimate the magnitude of the incentives provided by each of these mechanisms. Our estimates imply that each $1,000 change in shareholder wealth corresponds to an average increase in this year's and next year's salary and bonus of about two cents. We also estimate the CEO wealth consequences associated with salary revisions, outstanding stock options, and performance-related dismissals; our upper-bound estimate of the total change in the CEO's wealth from these sources that are under direct control of the board of directors is about 75¢ per $1,000 change in shareholder wealth.

Stock ownership is another way an executive's wealth varies with the value of the firm. In our sample CEOs hold a median of about 0.25 percent of their firms' common stock, including exercisable stock options and shares held by family members or connected trusts. Thus the value of the stock owned by the median CEO changes by $2.50 whenever the value of the firm changes by $1,000. Therefore, our final all-inclusive estimate of the pay-performance sensitivity—including compensation, dismissal, and stockholdings—is about $3.25 per $1,000 change in shareholder wealth.

In large firms CEOs tend to own less stock and have fewer compensation-based incentives than CEOs in smaller firms. In particular, our all-inclusive estimate of the pay-performance sensitivity for CEOs in firms in the top half of our sample (ranked by market value) is $1.85 per $1,000, compared to $8.05 per $1,000 for CEOs in firms in the bottom half of our sample.

We believe that our results are inconsistent with the implications of formal agency models of optimal contracting. The empirical relation between the pay of top-level executives and firm performance, while positive and statistically significant, is small for an occupation in which incentive pay is expected to play an important role. In addition, our estimates suggest that dismissals are not an important source of managerial incentives because the increases in dismissal probability due to poor performance and the penalties associated with dismissal are both small. Executive inside stock ownership can provide incentives, but these holdings are not generally controlled by the corporate board, and the majority of top executives have small personal stockholdings.

Our results are consistent with several alternative hypotheses: CEOs may be unimportant inputs in the production process, for example, or their actions may be easily monitored and evaluated by corporate boards. We offer an additional hypothesis relating to the role of political forces in the contracting process that implicitly regulate executive compensation by constraining the type of contracts that can be written between management and shareholders. These political forces, operating both in the political sector and within organizations, appear to be important but are difficult to document because they operate in informal and indirect ways. Public disapproval of high rewards seems to have truncated the upper tail of the earnings distribution of corporate executives. Equilibrium in the managerial labor market then prohibits large penalties for poor performance, and as a result the dependence of pay on performance is decreased. Our findings that the pay-performance relation, the raw variability of pay changes, and inflation-adjusted pay levels have declined substantially since the 1930s are consistent with such implicit regulation.

9.1   Estimates of the Pay-Performance Sensitivity

We define the pay-performance sensitivity, b, as the dollar change in the CEO's wealth associated with a dollar change in the wealth of shareholders. We interpret higher b's as indicating a closer alignment of interests between the CEO and his shareholders. Suppose, for example, that a CEO is considering a nonproductive but costly "pet project" which he values at $100,000 but which will diminish the value of his firm's equity by $10 million. The CEO will avoid this project if his pay-performance sensitivity exceeds $b = .01$ (through some combination of incentive compensation, options, stock ownership, or probability of being fired for poor stock price performance) but will adopt the project if $b < .01$.

Incentives Generated by Cash Compensation

The pay-performance sensitivity is estimated by following all 2,213 CEOs listed in the Executive Compensation Surveys published in *Forbes* from 1974 to 1986. These surveys include executives serving in 1,295 corporations, for a total of 10,400 CEO-years of data. We match these compensation data to fiscal year corporate performance data obtained from the data files of the Compustat and the Center for Research in Security Prices (CRSP). After observations with missing data are eliminated, the final sample contains 7,750 yearly "first differences" in compensation and includes 1,688 executives from 1,049 corporations. Fiscal year stock returns are unavailable for 219 of the 7,750 observations; calendar-year returns are used in these cases. (Deleting these 219 observations does not affect the results.) All monetary variables are adjusted for inflation (using the consumer price index for the closing month of the fiscal year) and represent thousands of 1986 constant dollars.

Table 9.1 summarizes estimates of the relation between CEO cash compensation and firm performance as measured by the change in shareholder wealth. Column 1 of the table reports estimated coefficients from the following least-squares regression:

$$\Delta(\text{CEO salary} + \text{bonus})_t = a + b\Delta(\text{shareholder wealth})_t. \qquad (1)$$

The change in shareholder wealth variable is defined as $r_t V_{t-1}$, where r_t is the inflation-adjusted rate of return on common stock realized in fiscal year t, and V_{t-1} is the firm value at the end of the previous year.

Our measure of firm performance is subject to two qualifications. First, performance should be evaluated *before* compensation expense, and yet $r_t V_{t-1}$ is the change in firm value *after* compensation expense; the associated bias in our estimates is small, however, because CEO pay changes are tiny relative to changes in firm value. Second, our measure of performance ignores payments to capital. When capital is an important input, a better performance measure is $r_t V_{t-1} - f_t K_{t-1}$, where f_t and K_{t-1} are the risk-free interest rate for period t and the opportunity cost of the capital stock at the beginning of period t. Since f and shareholder return r tend to be uncorrelated, this adjustment will not substantially affect our estimates. Fama and Schwert (1977) find an R^2 of .03 between nominal riskless rates and 1-month returns on a value-weighted portfolio of New York Stock Exchange (NYSE) firms.

The coefficient on the shareholder wealth variable of $b = .0000135$ in column 1 is statistically significant ($t = 8.0$), indicating a positive relation between cash compensation and firm performance. The economic significance of the estimated coefficient is low, however. The coefficients in column 1 imply, for example, that a CEO receives an average pay increase of $31,700 in years in which shareholders earn a zero return and receives on average an additional 1.35¢ for each $1,000 increase in shareholder wealth. These estimates are comparable with those of Murphy (1985, 1986), Coughlan and Schmidt (1985), and Gibbons and Murphy (1990), who find a pay-performance elasticity of

Table 9.1 Estimates of Pay-Performance Sensitivity: Coefficients of Ordinary Least Squares Regressions of Δ(Salary + Bonus), Δ(Total Pay), and Δ(Pay-Related Wealth) on Current and Lagged Δ(Shareholder Wealth)

	Dependent Variable (in Thousands of 1986 Constant Dollars)			
	Δ(Salary + Bonus)		Δ(Total Pay)[b]	Total Pay + PV[Δ(Salary + Bonus)][c]
Independent Variable	(1)	(2)	(3)	(4)
Intercept	31.7	30.8	36.6	918.0
Change in shareholder wealth (thousands of 1986 dollars)	.0000135 (8.0)	.0000139 (8.4)	.0000235 (5.2)	.000197 (9.7)
Change in shareholder wealth in year $t - 1$	—	.0000080 (5.5)	.0000094 (2.4)	.000103 (5.8)
R^2	.0082	.0123	.0041	.0157
Estimated pay-performance sensitivity, b[d]	.0000135	.0000219	.0000329	.000300
t-statistic for b	64.0[a]	93.0[a]	28.5[a]	117.7[a]
Sample size	7,750	7,688	7,688	7,688

Note: The sample is constructed from longitudinal data reported in Forbes on 1,668 CEOs serving in 1,049 firms for the years 1974–1986. Δ(shareholder wealth) is defined as the beginning-of-period market value multiplied by the inflation-adjusted rate of return on common stock; t-statistics are in parentheses.
a. Significant at the 0.01 percent level.
b. The Forbes definition of total compensation typically includes salary, bonus, value of restricted stock, savings and thrift plans, and other benefits but does not include the value of stock options granted or the gains from exercising stock options.
c. Present value based on the assumption that the CEO receives salary and bonus increment until age 70 at a discount rate of 3 percent.
d. Estimated b is the sum of the coefficients on the contemporaneous and lagged shareholder wealth change.

approximately .1: salaries and bonuses increase by about 1 percent for every 10 percent rise in the value of the firm. Converting this estimate of the pay-performance elasticity to absolute dollars by multiplying by the median pay to value ratio of 0.057 percent (calculated for the 9,976 CEO-years in the Forbes sample for 1974–1986) yields an estimated coefficient $b = .000057$, which is larger than, but consistent with, the estimate in column 1 of Table 9.1.

The median annual standard deviation of shareholder wealth changes for firms in our sample is about $200 million, so the average pay change associated with a stockholder wealth change two standard deviations above or below normal (a gain or loss of $400 million) is $5,400. Thus the average pay increase for a CEO whose shareholders gain $400 million is $37,100, compared to an average pay increase of $26,300 for a CEO whose shareholders lose $400 million.

Equation (1) assumes that current stock price performance affects current compensation, and yet the timing of performance payments is often ambiguous. At the simplest level, bonus decisions may be made before final fiscal year earnings data are available. In other cases boards may know this year's earnings, but the earnings and stock price changes available at the end of the fiscal year may not correctly incorporate the effects of managerial actions during the year. In addition, bonuses reported in proxy statements sometimes represent bonuses paid for performance in the previous year, and the proxies do not always clearly specify when the bonus payment year differs from the bonus measurement year.

Column 2 of Table 9.1 reports coefficients from the following regression, which allows current pay revisions to be based on past as well as current performance:

$$\Delta(\text{CEO salary} + \text{bonus})_t = a + b_1\Delta(\text{shareholder wealth})_t$$
$$+ b_2\Delta(\text{shareholder wealth})_{t-1}. \qquad (2)$$

The coefficient for year $t - 1$ is positive and statistically significant, indicating that last year's performance does matter in the determination of this year's pay revision. The sum of the coefficients, $b \equiv b_1 + b_2 = .0000219$, is statistically significant ($F = 93.0$), suggesting that the CEO receives a total pay revision of 2.2¢ for each $1,000 change in shareholder wealth. We cannot tell how much of this effect represents a real lag of rewards on performance and how much represents simple measurement errors caused by lags in reporting. We also estimate the relation with three years of lagged shareholder wealth changes with little difference from the results reported in column 2 of Table 9.1; the coefficients on the contemporaneous and first lagged performance variables are essentially unchanged, and those on the second and third lags are small in magnitude and statistically insignificant.

We reestimate the regression in column 1 of Table 9.1 using 2- and 3-year differences; the results are quantitatively unchanged from those in the table. We also reestimate the regression in column 2 of Table 9.1 after including year dummy variables and separate intercepts for each sample CEO, and the estimated coefficients and their sum are virtually identical to those reported in the table. To allow the pay-performance sensitivity to vary across CEOs, we also estimate separate regressions for each of 717 sample CEOs with five or more observations. The median estimated 2-year pay-performance relation for the sample of individually estimated coefficients is $b = .000073$, or a median pay raise of 7.3¢ per $1,000 increase in shareholder wealth.

The regressions in columns 1 and 2 of Table 9.1 are based only on the CEO's salary and bonus, but CEOs receive compensation in many additional forms, including deferred compensation, stock options, profit-sharing arrangements, stock grants, savings plans, long-term performance plans, and other fringe benefits. The *Forbes* surveys include data on many of these other components of compensation. The surveys do not, however, include stock option data prior to 1978, and after 1978 the surveys report gains from exercising options but do not report the value of outstanding options or the value of stock options granted during the year.

Column 3 of Table 9.1 reports the relation between total compensation and firm performance based on the *Forbes* total compensation data, excluding both stock option grants and the gains from exercising stock options. The *Forbes* definition of total compensation varies somewhat from year to year but in general includes salary, bonus, value of restricted stock, savings and thrift plans, and other benefits. The sum of the estimated coefficients of current and lagged change in shareholder wealth is $b = .0000329$, indicating that total compensation changes by 3.3¢ for each $1,000 change in firm value.

The dependent variable in column 3 of Table 9.1 represents the change in the current cash flows accruing to the CEO, while the independent variables represent the discounted present value of the change in all future cash flows accruing to the shareholders. A measure of the change in CEO wealth that is more consistent with the measure of the change in shareholder wealth is current compensation plus the discounted present value of the permanent component of the change in current compensation. Suppose, for example, that CEOs receive only a base salary and that firm performance is rewarded by a permanent shift in the base salary. Then the appropriate measure of the change in CEO wealth is salary + PV(Δsalary), where PV(Δsalary) is the present value of the salary change from next year through the year in which the CEO leaves the firm.

Measuring the discounted present value of a change in current compensation is difficult for several reasons. First, *Forbes* reports only the sum of salaries and bonuses, and while it may be appropriate to include PV(Δsalary) in the measure of Δ(CEO wealth), it is less clear that PV(Δbonus) should be included since bonuses may be transitory and not permanent components of income. In addition, assumptions must be made regarding the number of periods remaining over which Δsalary will be realized. Even when the firm has a 65-year mandatory retirement age, there is some probability that the CEO will leave the firm before age 65. At the other extreme, pension benefits are generally based on average salaries received during some period shortly before retirement; consequently an increase in salary may increase pension payments to the CEO long after the CEO leaves the firm.

The dependent variable in column 4 of Table 9.1 is Δ(CEO wealth), measured as:

$$\Delta(\text{CEO wealth}) = \text{total pay} + \text{PV}[\Delta(\text{salary} + \text{bonus})].$$

The present value of the salary and bonus increment is calculated assuming a real interest rate of 3% per year. In order to get an upper bound on the estimate of the pay-performance sensitivity, we assume that all changes in salary and bonus are permanent. We assume that the CEO receives the increment until age 70. If the CEO is younger than 70, we take the present value of his wage change until he reaches 70, but if he is older than 70, we assume that he is in his last year with the firm.

The coefficients in column 4 imply that, on average, CEO wealth increases by $918,000 in years in which shareholders earn a zero return (the average CEO total pay excluding stock options for the sample is $575,000). In addition, the estimate for b in column 4 implies that the CEO's pay-related wealth (exclusive of stock options) increases by 30¢ for each $1,000 increase in shareholder wealth. Thus the average pay-related wealth increase for a CEO whose shareholders gain $400 million is $1.04 million, compared to an average annual wealth increase of $800,000 for a CEO whose shareholders lose $400 million.

Incentives Generated by Stock Options

The *Forbes* definition of total pay excludes stock options, but stock options clearly provide value-increasing incentives for chief executives. Year-to-year stock option grants provide incentives if the size of the grant is based on performance. More important, the change in value of unexercised stock options granted in previous years also provides incentives.

To calculate a more complete measure of the CEO's wealth change, which includes options, we analyzed the proxy statements from Murphy's (1985) sample of 73 *Fortune* 500 manufacturing firms during the 15-year period 1969–1983. Data on stock options, salaries, bonuses, deferred compensation, and fringe benefits from these statements are used to construct a longitudinal sample of 154 CEOs. Total compensation is defined as the sum of salaries, bonuses, fringe benefits, the face value of deferred compensation unadjusted for the cost of restrictions on marketability and the time value of money, and restricted stock awarded during the year (valued at the end of year stock price).

At the end of each year, CEOs typically hold stock options granted in different years at different exercise prices and exercise dates. The value of all options held by the CEO is calculated by applying the Black-Scholes (1973) valuation formula, which allows for continuously paid dividends (Noreen and Wolfson 1981; Murphy 1985). The value of options held at the end of year τ is calculated as

$$\sum_{t=0}^{\tau} N_t \times [S_\tau e^{-dT} \Phi(Z_t) - P_t e^{-rT} \Phi(Z_t - \sigma\sqrt{T})],$$

where N_t is the number of options granted in year t at exercise price P_t, T is the number of months until expiration of these options, r is the average monthly market yield on 5-year government securities in year τ, d is the dividend yield in year $\tau - 1$ defined as $\ln[1 + (\text{dividends per share/closing stock price})]/12$, σ is the estimated standard deviation of stock returns over the previous 60-month period, S_τ is the stock price at the end of fiscal year τ, $Z \equiv \{\ln(S_\tau/P_t) + [r - d + (\sigma^2/2)]T\}/\sigma\sqrt{T}$, and $\Phi(\cdot)$ is the cumulative standard normal distribution function.

The change in the value of options held at the end of each year is calculated as the value of the options awarded during the year plus the change in the value of all outstanding options during the year plus the profits (price minus exercise price) from exercising options during the year. Data on actual exercise prices are not available; to get an upper bound on this measure, we assume that options are always exercised at the highest stock price observed during the year.

Column 1 of Table 9.2 reports least-squares regression results for the 73-firm sample in which the dependent variable is the change in the value of the CEO's stock options. The sum of the estimated coefficients implies that the value of CEO stock options increases an average of 14.5¢ for each $1,000 increase in shareholder wealth. Therefore, the

Table 9.2 Estimates of Pay-Performance Sensitivity Including Stockholdings and Options: Coefficients of Ordinary Least Squares Regressions of Δ(CEO Wealth) on Δ(Shareholder Wealth) for CEOs in 73 Manufacturing Firms for 1969–1983

| | Dependent Variable (in Thousands of 1986 Constant Dollars) | | | | |
| | Δ(Value of Stock Options) | Total Pay + PV[Δ(Salary + Bonus)] + Δ(Value of Stock Options) | | Δ (Value of Inside Stock)[b]+ Total Pay +PV[Δ(Salary + Bonus)] + Δ(Value of Stock Options) | |
Independent Variable	(1)	(2)	(3)	(4)	(5)
Intercept	79.4	815.9	816.1	818.4	892.9
Change in shareholder wealth ($ thousands)	.000105 (8.6)	.000176 (5.2)	.000174 (5.0)	.00118 (4.4)	.00019 (3.7)
Change in shareholder wealth in year $t-1$	.000040 (3.3)	.000131 (3.8)	.000130 (3.8)	.00031 (1.2)	.00016 (3.1)
CEO's fractional ownership $\times$ change in shareholder wealth	—	—	.00294 (.7)	—	1.020 (145.0
R^2	.0807	.0376	.0381	.0216	.9610
Estimated pay-performance sensitivity[b]	.000145	.000307	.000309[c]	.00149	.0020
F-statistic for b	58.3[a]	33.0[a]	33.2[a]	12.5[a]	565.2

Note: Sample size is 877 for all regressions. Δ(shareholder wealth) is defined as the beginning-of-period market value multiplied by the inflation-adjusted rate of return on common stock. Δ(value of stock options) includes profits from exercising options, value of options granted in current year, and the change in the value of previously granted options based on Black and Scholes (1973). Total pay includes salary, bonus, value of restricted stock, savings and thrift plans, and other benefits; PV[Δ(salary + bonus)] is based on the assumption that the CEO receives salary and bonus increment until age 70 at a discount rate of 3 percent. t-statistics are in parentheses.

a. Significant at the 0.01 percent level.

b. Inside stockholdings include shares held by family members and shares for which the CEO is a trustee or cotrustee without beneficial ownership. Δ(value of inside stock) is defined as the beginning-of-period value of inside stock multiplied by the inflation-adjusted rate of return on common stock. Stock ownership data are unavailable for 50 of the $(73 \times 15) = 1,095$ possible CEO-years.

c. Estimated b and related test statistic for a CEO with median fractional ownership for the sample, .0016.

incentives generated by stock options are large relative to the incentives generated by annual changes in cash compensation (3.3¢ per $1,000 from column 3 of Table 9.1) even though options valued at date of grant account for a relatively small share of the CEO's compensation (8.1% for CEOs in the 73-firm sample).

Column 2 of Table 9.2 reports regression coefficients for the 73-firm sample in which the dependent variable is the change in all pay-related wealth, defined as

$$\Delta(\text{CEO pay-related wealth}) = \text{total pay} + \text{PV}[\Delta(\text{salary} + \text{bonus})] \\ + \Delta(\text{value of stock options}).$$

The present value of the salary and bonus increment is again calculated assuming that the CEO receives the salary and bonus increment until age 70 at a real interest rate of 3% per year. The sum of the estimated coefficients on the current and lagged shareholder wealth change variables of $b - .000307$ ($F = 33.0$) implies that CEO wealth changes by over 30¢ for each $1,000 change in shareholder wealth.

To check on potential differences between the 73-firm sample and the *Forbes* sample, we reestimated the *Forbes* regression in column 2 of Table 9.1 for the 73 manufacturing firms and obtained $b = .0000196$ (compared to .0000219 for the *Forbes* sample). We also reestimated column 2 of Table 9.2 after excluding stock options and obtained $b = .0000163$ (compared to .000300 as reported in Table 9.1 for the *Forbes* sample).

Incentives Generated by Inside Stock Ownership

Stock ownership is another way in which an executive's welfare varies directly with the performance of his firm, independent of any link between compensation and performance. Although the process through which CEOs select their equilibrium stockholdings is not well understood, the incentives generated by these shareholdings clearly add to the incentives generated by the compensation package. Stock ownership data for the CEOs in the 73 firms in the manufacturing firm sample were obtained from the proxy statements; these executives held an *average* of $4.8 million (in 1986 constant dollars) of their firm's common stock in the period 1969–1983. When we include shares held by family members and shares for which the CEO serves as a trustee or cotrustee, the average increases to $8.8 million. Year-to-year changes in the value of these holdings often exceed levels of total compensation by orders of magnitude (Lewellen 1971; Benston 1985; Murphy 1985).

Column 4 of Table 9.2 reports regression coefficients in which the dependent variable is a measure of the change in the CEO's wealth that *includes* the change in the value of his inside stockholdings. Changes in the value of inside stockholdings are calculated as the value of the shares held at the beginning of the fiscal year multiplied by the realized rate of return on common stock. To get an upper bound on the estimate, inside stock ownership includes shares held by family members and shares for which the CEO is a nonbeneficial trustee or cotrustee, as well as shares held directly.

The sum of the shareholder wealth change coefficients in column 4 implies that the wealth of CEOs increases (or decreases) by about $1.50 whenever shareholder wealth increases (or decreases) by $1,000. The difference between the estimated b in columns 2 and 4 suggests that, on average, inside stock ownership plays an important role in providing managerial incentives.

Our regression specification in column 2 of Table 9.2 assumes that the pay-performance relation is the same for all executives, regardless of their stockholdings, but it is plausible that b is large and positive for executives with negligible stockholdings but small or even *negative* for executives with large holdings since their wealth may be tied "too closely" to the performance of their firms. We test for this potential heterogeneity by reestimating the regressions for the 15-year, 73-firm sample after including an interaction term, CEO's fractional ownership $\times$ Δ(shareholder wealth), to capture the effects of ownership on the sensitivity of pay to performance.

The dependent variable in the regression in column 3 of Table 9.2 is the change in all pay-related wealth (including stock options but excluding stock ownership). The small and insignificantly positive coefficient of the ownership interaction variable ($t = 0.7$) implies that the relation between compensation and performance is independent of an executive's stockholdings. The result that the pay-performance relation is not affected by stock ownership seems inconsistent with theory since optimal compensation contracts that provide incentives for managers to create shareholder wealth will not be independent of their shareholdings.

The dependent variable in the regression in column 5 of Table 9.2 is the change in CEO wealth, including all forms of compensation plus changes in the value of his individual shareholdings. The coefficient on the interaction term is highly significant ($t = 145.0$) and close to unity, suggesting that the pay-performance sensitivity for a CEO with nonnegligible stockholdings is closely approximated by his fractional ownership. Since the total pay-performance relation is given by $b = .000366 + 1.020 \times$ fractional ownership, the sensitivity for a CEO who owns no stock is equivalent, on average, to stockholdings of 0.0366 percent

Table 9.3 CEO Inside Stock Ownership: Summary Statistics and Quintile Boundaries for Percentage and Value of CEO Stock Ownership for 746 CEOs Listed in 1987 *Forbes* Executive Compensation Survey, by Firm Size

	CEO Stock Ownership as Percentage of Shares Outstanding			Value of CEO Stockholdings ($ millions)		
	All Firms (1)	Small Firms (2)	Large Firms (3)	All Firms (4)	Small Firms (5)	Large Firms (6)
Mean	2.42%	3.05%	1.79%	$41.0	$19.3	$62.6
Median	.25	.49	.14	3.5	2.6	4.7
Quintile Boundaries:						
Min	less than .01%			less than $0.1		
20%	.05	.11	.03	.7	.5	1.2
40%	.17	.33	.10	2.5	1.9	3.3
60%	.42	.73	.20	5.1	3.6	7.2
80%	1.38	1.95	.75	17.4	10.5	22.6
Max	83.00	83.00	53.50	2,304.2	1,041.0	2,304.2
Median value of equity ($ millions)				$1,200	$580	$2,590

Note: Stock ownership includes shares held by family members and also includes options that can be exercised within 60 days. Small firms have market value below the sample median ($1.2 billion); large firms have market value exceeding the median.

of the firm. The total pay-performance sensitivity for a CEO with shareholdings of 0.16 percent (the median shareholdings for CEOs in the 73-firm sample) is equivalent to $b = .0020$, or $2.00 per $1,000 change in shareholder wealth.

Table 9.3 summarizes fractional stock ownership data for a much larger sample of CEOs. The 746 CEOs included in the 1987 *Forbes* Executive Compensation Survey hold an average of 2.4% of their firms' common stock, including shares held by family members and options that can be exercised within 60 days. The distribution of inside stock ownership is skewed; the median CEO holds only 0.25% of his firm's stock. Twenty percent of the sample CEOs hold less than 0.05% of their firms' stock, and 60 percent hold less than 0.42%. Small fractional ownership is even more prevalent in the largest *Forbes* firms (ranked according to market value), where 80 percent of the CEOs hold less than 0.75% of their firms' common stock.

In dollar terms, Table 9.3 shows that CEOs in the *Forbes* survey firms hold an *average* of over $40 million of their firms' stock. Once again, the distribution is skewed: the median stock ownership is only $3.5 million (compared to median 1986 total compensation of $700,000). The CEOs in large firms, while owning a smaller fraction of their firms' common stock, tend to have a larger dollar investment in their firms' shares.

Incentives Generated by the Threat of Dismissal

The threat of management dismissal for poor performance also provides value-increasing incentives to the extent that managers are earning more than their opportunity cost. Recent studies by Coughlan and Schmidt (1985), Warner, Watts, and Wruck (1988), and Weisbach (1988) have documented an inverse relation between net-of-market firm performance and the probability of management turnover. These results suggest that managers are more likely to leave their firms after bad years than after good years and therefore are disciplined by the threat of termination.

Table 9.4 reports coefficients from logistic regressions predicting the probability of CEO turnover as a function of firm performance for the 13-year sample of 2,213 CEOs listed in the *Forbes* surveys. We estimate the following relation:

$$\ln\left[\frac{\text{prob(turnover)}}{1-\text{prob(turnover)}}\right] = a + b_1 \text{ (net-of-market return)} + b_2 \text{(lagged net-of-market return).}$$

The dependent variable equals one if the CEO is serving in his last full fiscal year and equals zero otherwise. The 1988 *Forbes* survey was examined to identify CEOs whose last fiscal year was 1986. The final CEO-year for firms leaving the *Forbes* survey is excluded since we cannot determine whether or not this is the last year for that CEO. A total of 582 firms were deleted from the *Forbes* surveys during the 1974–1986 sample period. Of these, 293 were still "going concerns" as of 1987, 214 were acquired by or merged with another firm (118 of these were acquired or merged within two years of the *Forbes* delisting), and 35 were liquidated, went bankrupt, or went private. Current status data are unavailable for 40 of the 582 firms.

Consistent with the previous studies, column 1 of Table 9.4 shows

Table 9.4 Relation between CEO Turnover and Firm Performance: Estimated Logistic Models Predicting CEO Turnover Using Current and Lagged Net-of-Market Shareholder Return for CEOs Grouped According to Age

Independent Variable	Coefficient Estimates, by Age Group					
	Full Sample (1)	Less Than 50 Years Old (2)	Between 50 and 55 (3)	Between 55 and 60 (4)	Between 60 and 64 (5)	64 Years or Older (6)
Intercept	−2.08	−3.30	−3.03	−2.66	−1.97	−.442
Current net-of-market return	−.6363 (−5.1)	−1.921 (−3.4)	−.3946 (−1.0)	−.5307 (−1.8)	−1.216 (−4.3)	−.2453 (−1.1)
Lagged net-of-market return	−.4181 (−3.5)	−.6219 (−1.3)	−.0651 (−.2)	−.2913 (−1.0)	−.5510 (−2.1)	−.5154 (−2.3)
Sample size	9,291	1,345	1,935	2,728	2,171	1,112
Number of CEO turnovers	992	47	87	174	258	426
Significance of model	.0001	.0021	.5683	.1046	.0001	.0298

Note: The sample is constructed from longitudinal data reported in *Forbes* on 1,896 CEOs serving in 1,092 firms for 1974–1986. Net-of-market return is defined as the fiscal year shareholder return minus the value-weighted return of all NYSE firms. The dependent variable is equal to one if the CEO is serving in his last full fiscal year and zero otherwise. Asymptotic *t*-statistics are in parentheses.

that the probability that a CEO is serving in his last full fiscal year is negatively related to current and past firm performance as measured by the return realized by shareholders in excess of the value-weighted return on the common stock of all NYSE firms. If we convert the regression coefficients into estimated dismissal probabilities, the regression in column 1 implies that a CEO in a firm realizing returns equal to the market return in each of the past 2 years has a .111 dismissal probability, calculated as $p = e^x/(1 + e^x)$, where $x = -2.08 - .6363$(net-of-market return) $-$ .4181(lagged net-of-market return). The same CEO has a .175 dismissal probability when the firm earns a −50% return relative to the market in each of the two previous years. Because it is usually impossible to tell whether the CEO was fired or simply quit or retired, the term "dismissal probability" is used only as shorthand for the more accurate "probability of CEO turnover."

The specification in column 1 of Table 9.4 assumes that the relation between performance and turnover likelihood is the same for all executives, but Vancil (1987) argues that CEOs are more likely to be fired when they are young than when they are closer to normal retirement. Columns 2–6 of Table 9.4 report results from logistic dismissal regressions for CEOs grouped according to age: younger than 50, between 50 and 55, between 55 and 60, between 60 and 64, and 64 years or older. The magnitudes of the coefficients are largest for the youngest CEOs, confirming Vancil's hypothesis that younger CEOs are more likely to be disciplined by turnover. The relation between turnover and performance is insignificant for 50- to 55-year-old CEOs and marginally significant for 55- to 60-year-old CEOs, suggesting that managers between the ages of 50 and 60 are unlikely to be dismissed subsequent to poor performance. The dismissal-performance relation is highly significant for CEOs approaching retirement (between ages 60 and 64) and marginally significant for CEOs at or past normal retirement age.

The authors of the earlier studies documenting the dismissal-performance relation generally interpret their results as being consistent with the hypothesis that management termination decisions are designed to align the interests of managers and shareholders. Each author stresses, however, that managers are rarely openly fired from their positions. Warner, Ross, and Wruck (1988), for example, analyzed 272 firms for the years 1963–1978 and found only a single case of an outright firing and only 10 cases in which poor performance was cited as one of the reasons for the separation. Weisbach (1988) examined 286 management changes for 1974–1983 and found only 9 cases in which boards mentioned performance as a reason why the CEO was replaced.

The data suggest that CEOs bear little risk of being dismissed by their boards of directors. The CEOs in our sample who leave their firms during the 13-year sample period hold their jobs an average of more than 10 years before leaving, and most leave their position only after reaching normal retirement age. Of the sample CEOs, 60% are between ages 60 and 66 when they leave their firm; 32% are aged 64 or 65. Moreover, CEOs seldom leave in disgrace. Vancil (1987) estimates that 80% of exiting (nondeceased) CEOs remain on their firms' board of directors, and 36% continue serving on the board as chairmen.

The infrequent termination of poorly performing CEOs does not, by itself, imply the absence of incentives since even a low probability of getting fired can provide incentives if the penalties associated with termination are sufficiently severe. Table 9.5 presents our estimates of the turnover-related penalties for poor performance for four hypothetical

CEOs of various ages. Column 1 of Table 9.5 shows the predicted turnover probability (based on the estimated coefficients in Table 9.4) for a CEO in a firm realizing exactly the market return in both the current and past fiscal years. Column 3 shows the predicted turnover probability for a CEO in a firm realizing a −50% net-of-market return in each of the past 2 years. A 46-year-old CEO, for example, has a .036 turnover probability after 2 years of 0% net-of-market returns but has a .116 turnover probability after 2 years in which his firm earns 50% below market.

Columns 2 and 4 of Table 9.5 report the expected wealth losses associated with dismissals for CEOs in firms realizing 0% and −50% net-of-market returns, respectively, in each of the two preceding fiscal years. In order to obtain an upper bound on our estimate of the turnover wealth loss, we assume that the CEO has no alternative employment opportunities and that his wealth loss on dismissal is the present value (at 3%) of $1 million per year starting the year after dismissal and lasting until the CEO is 66 years old. The expected wealth loss is calculated as this present value multiplied by the dismissal probabilities calculated from Table 9.4 and reported in columns 1 and 3 of Table 9.5. Column 5 reports the difference in the dismissal-related wealth loss associated with average performance (0%) and dismal performance (−50%), and column 6 compares the CEO's dismissal-related wealth loss with the wealth loss of shareholders of an average-size firm ($1.73 billion in our sample), realizing a sequence of two net-of-market returns of −50% (i.e., a 2-year cumulative return of 75%).

Table 9.5 predicts, for example, that the expected turnover-related wealth loss for a 62-year-old CEO in a firm realizing a 0% net-of-market return is $346,000, compared to an expected loss of $714,000 if his firm earns −50% below market in each of the two previous years. Although the difference in the expected wealth loss associated with dismal performance (compared to average performance) of $368,000 seems large, it is small compared to the CEO's losses on his own stockholdings and trivial compared to shareholder losses. The CEOs in the 1987 *Forbes* survey between 60 and 64 years old hold a median of $3.2 million worth of stock, and therefore the stock market losses on a −75% return for a median CEO are $2.4 million. Moreover, shareholders lose an average of almost $1.3 billion on a −75% return; the CEOs' expected dismissal-related losses of $368,000 imply that CEOs lose 28.4¢ for each $1,000 lost by shareholders.

Column 6 of Table 9.5 shows that our upper-bound estimate of the

Table 9.5 Pay-Performance Sensitivity from CEO Dismissals: Implied Turnover Probabilities and Upper-Bound Expected Wealth Losses from Turnover for 46-, 53-, 58-, and 62-Year-Old CEOs

CEO Age[a]	CEOs in Firms Earning 0% Returns Relative to the Market in Each of the Two Previous Years		CEOs in Firms Earning −50% Returns Relative to the Market in Each of the Two Previous Years		Difference in Expected Wealth Loss from Turnover for 0% and −50% Net-of-Market Returns (5)	Estimated Pay-Performance Sensitivity for CEO Dismissal with −50% Net-of-Market Return in Two Previous Years[d] (6)
	Turnover Probability[b] (1)	Expected Wealth Loss[c] (2)	Turnover Probability[b] (3)	Expected Wealth Loss[c] (4)		
46	.036	$510,000	.116	$1,665,000	$1,155,000	89.0¢ per $1,000
53	.046	459,000	.057	571,000	112,000	8.6¢ per $1,000
58	.065	407,000	.095	595,000	188,000	14.5¢ per $1,000
62	.122	346,000	.252	714,000	368,000	28.4¢ per $1,000

a. Ages 46, 53, 58, and 62 are sample average ages for CEOs less than 50, between 50 and 55, between 55 and 60, and between 60 and 64, respectively.

b. Turnover probabilities for each age are calculated from the associated age group logistic regressions in Table 9.4.

c. Expected wealth loss is calculated as the turnover probability multiplied by the present value of $1 million per year beginning next year and lasting until the CEO is 66 years old. All amounts are in 1986 constant dollars, and the real interest rate is assumed to be 3 percent.

d. Based on $1.3 billion shareholder loss, which is the shareholder loss on an average-size ($1.73 billion) firm realizing −50 percent returns in two consecutive years.

CEO's dismissal-performance sensitivity for an average-size firm with a −75% 2-year return is 8.6¢ and is 14.5¢ for a 53- and 58-year-old CEO, respectively. We find a much larger dismissal-performance sensitivity for a 46-year-old CEO—89.0¢ per $1,000—but this result is driven by our inappropriate assumption that the CEO will never work again if dismissed but will work for his firm until age 66 if not dismissed. The dismissal-performance sensitivity for the 46-year-old CEO falls to 44.5¢ per $1,000 if he accepts employment at half his current pay.

Our estimates of the dismissal-performance sensitivity in column 6 represent an upper bound for several reasons. First, we have assumed that CEOs leave the labor market after turnover; this assumption may be appropriate for older CEOs but is clearly inappropriate for very young CEOs. Second, Table 9.5 is based on extraordinarily poor performance—2 years at 50% per year—and the estimated dismissal-performance sensitivity increases with shareholder losses. For example, the difference in expected wealth loss for a 62-year-old CEO earning 10% less than the market in two consecutive years (compared to 0% net-of-market returns) is $58,000, or about 18¢ per $1,000 (based on cumulative shareholder losses of 19% or $330 million for an average-size firm), compared to 28¢ per $1,000 for the $1.3 billion loss in column 6 of Table 9.5. Finally, most CEOs are covered by employment contracts, severance agreements, or golden parachute arrangements that further reduce or eliminate the pecuniary punishment for failure; and pensions, outstanding stock options, and restricted stock typically become fully vested on an involuntary separation.

The dismissal-performance sensitivities in column 6 of Table 9.5 can be added to the 30¢ per $1,000 pay-performance sensitivity in column 2 of Table 9.1 and the 15¢ per $1,000 pay-performance sensitivity for outstanding stock options in column 2 of Table 9.2 to construct an estimate of the *total* pay-performance sensitivity under direct control of the board of directors. With an average dismissal-performance sensitivity (weighted by the number of observations in each age group) of 30¢ per $1,000, our estimate of the total pay-performance sensitivity—including both pay and dismissal—is about 75¢ per $1,000 ($b \approx .00075$). Stock ownership adds another $2.50 per $1,000 for a CEO with median holdings, for a total sensitivity of $3.25 per $1,000 ($b \approx .00325$) change in shareholder wealth.

9.2 Is the Small Pay-Performance Sensitivity Consistent with Agency Theory?

Agency theory predicts that compensation policy will tie the agent's expected utility to the principal's objective. The objective of shareholders is to maximize wealth; therefore, agency theory predicts that CEO compensation policies will depend on changes in shareholder wealth. The empirical evidence presented in Section 9.1 is consistent with this broad implication: changes in both the CEO's pay-related wealth and the value of his stockholdings are positively and statistically significantly related to changes in shareholder wealth, and CEO turnover probabilities are negatively and significantly related to changes in shareholder wealth.

Although the estimated pay-performance sensitivity (with respect to compensation, dismissal, and stock ownership) is statistically significant, the magnitude seems small in terms of the implied incentives. Consider again our example of the CEO contemplating a pet project that reduces the value of the firm by $10 million. A risk-neutral CEO with median holdings ($b \approx .00325$) will adopt the project if his private value exceeds $32,500, while a CEO with no stock ownership ($b \approx .00075$) will adopt the project if his private value exceeds $7,500. For comparison, the median *weekly* income of our sample CEOs is approximately $9,400.

The purpose of this section is to explore whether our results are consistent with formal agency models of optimal contracting. Our task is made difficult by the fact that the theory offers few sharp predictions regarding the form of the contract other than predicting that wages generally increase with observed output. The formal models do yield clear predictions regarding the pay-performance sensitivity when the CEO is risk-neutral. Given the impossibility of isolating the CEO's marginal contribution to firm value, a risk-neutral CEO has incentives to pursue appropriate activities only when he receives 100% of the marginal profits, or $b = 1$. The optimal contract, in effect, sells the firm to the CEO: he receives the entire output as compensation but pays the shareholders an up-front fee so that the CEO's expected utility just equals his reservation utility. Jensen and Murphy (1990a) show that the $b = 1$ contract that provides optimal incentives is also the contract that causes managers to optimally sort themselves among firms.

Chief executive officers are not risk-neutral; indeed, the major reason for the existence of the publicly held corporation is its ability to achieve efficiencies in risk bearing. By creating alienable common stock equity claims that can be placed in well-diversified portfolios of widely diffused investors, risk-bearing costs are reduced to a fraction of those borne by owner-managers of privately held organizations. Thus setting $b = 1$ in a risky venture subjects risk-averse executives to large risks, and setting $b < 1$ to transfer risk from executives to shareholders generates costs from poor executive incentives. Optimal compensation contracts must reflect the trade-off between the goals of providing efficient risk sharing and providing the CEO with incentives to take appropriate actions.

Executives are Risk-Averse

It is tempting to attribute the generally low pay-performance sensitivity to CEO risk aversion, but the amount of income "at risk" for poor performance is a trivial percentage of the CEO's total income. The total compensation pay-performance sensitivity of $b = .0000329$ in column 3 of Table 9.1 implies, for example, that the pay revision associated with a wealth change two standard deviations below normal (a shareholder loss of $400 million) is about $13,000. The median total compensation for CEOs in our sample is $490,000; therefore, the amount of compensation "at risk" for a $400 million corporate loss is only 2.7% of the CEO's total pay.

It is more difficult to compare the amount of the CEO's *wealth* at risk to his total wealth since we cannot calculate the CEO's total wealth. Column 5 of Table 9.2 implies, however, that a CEO's wealth increases an average of $893,000 in years in which both the CEO and his shareholders earn a zero return on their shareholdings. In years in which shareholders lose $400 million, however, the wealth of a non-stockholding CEO increases by about $746,000, while the wealth of a large-firm CEO with median inside stockholdings increases by only $93,000.[1] In addition, the expected wealth loss associated with dismissal is approximately 30¢ per $1,000, or $120,000. Therefore, although the wealth effects of dramatically poor performance are substantial, they are not large relative to the normal $893,000 annual change in the CEO's wealth, which is independent of performance.

High Pay-Performance Contracts Are Not Feasible

Highly sensitive pay-performance contracts may not be feasible even under risk neutrality since executives with limited resources cannot credibly commit to pay firms for large negative realizations of corporate performance, and shareholders cannot credibly commit to huge bonuses that amount to "giving away the firm" for large positive realizations. The numerical examples above, however, suggest that it would certainly be feasible to write binding contracts with a much larger share of income or wealth at risk.

Moreover, successful entrepreneurs regularly sell off large equity claims, thereby lowering b; avoiding such sales to maintain a high b is a feasible contracting strategy. Management buyouts (MBOs), in which top managers make the firm private by borrowing large sums to repurchase stock from public shareholders, are a feasible way to undo previous equity sales and are another way to accomplish high-b contracts. For example, Kaplan (1991) finds in a sample of 76 MBOs that the median CEO holdings increase from 1.4% to 6.4% ($b = .064$), and median holdings for the management team as a whole increase from 5.9% to 22.6% ($b = .226$). These high-b contracts not only are feasible but are growing in importance: MBOs of public corporations and divisions increased from $1.2 billion in 1979 to almost $77 billion in 1987 (Jensen 1989b).

Franchising, which accounted for 12% of gross national product in 1986, is another feasible way to accomplish high-b contracts (U.S. Department of Commerce 1987). These contracts are very similar to optimal contracts under risk neutrality which, in effect, sell the firm to the CEO. The franchisee pays a fixed entry fee for purchase of the franchise and receives all profits after payment of an annual fee to the franchisor that commonly amounts to between 5 and 10% of revenues. By granting the franchisee alienable rights in the franchise, these contracts resolve most of the horizon problem associated with motivating managers to make correct trade-offs among cash flows through time (Jensen and Meckling 1979). This means that the franchisee has a 100% claim on the capital value of the franchise on its sale, although the alienability is subject to various restrictions such as approval by the franchisor. Thus for these elements of changes in value the franchisee contract has $b = 1$. Franchise contracts have many other characteristics that reduce the conflicts of interest between the franchisee and franchisor and thereby reduce the agency costs that result therefrom (Rubin 1978; Brickley and Dark 1987), but these issues are beyond the scope of this chapter.

Firm Value Changes Are Imperfect Measures of the CEO's Choice of Actions

The change in shareholder wealth is the appropriate measure of the principal's objective in the CEO-shareholder agency relationship, but it is an imperfect measure of the CEO's individual performance. Holmström (1979) argues that optimal compensation contracts for risk-averse CEOs should be based not only on the principal's objective (i.e., change in shareholder wealth) but also on any variables that provide incremental information valuable in assessing the CEO's unobservable choice of action. Examples of potentially informative determinants of incentive compensation include direct measures of CEO activity, accounting measures of firm performance, and measures of "relative performance" based on other executives in the same industry or market. Unfortunately, the structure of the Holmström model makes its conclusions irrelevant to most compensation contracts, including those of CEOs. His model assumes that the principal knows the utility function of the manager as well as the production function relating actions to expected outcomes. For CEOs this means that shareholders know with certainty all possible actions of the CEO and the distribution of outcomes of each action. In addition, shareholders must know the set of *optimal* CEO actions. It is unlikely that these conditions are often satisfied.

More important, Gibbons and Murphy (1989) argue that basing compensation on potentially informative additional variables can be counterproductive because their use provides incentives for CEOs to devote effort to actions that do not increase shareholder wealth—a phenomenon that is not modeled in Holmström's analysis. Accounting profits, for example, may yield information that is valuable in assessing an executive's unobservable actions. But paying executives on the basis of accounting profits rather than changes in shareholder wealth not only generates incentives to directly manipulate the accounting system but also generates incentives to ignore projects with large net present values in favor of less valuable projects with larger immediate accounting profits.

Table 9.6 reports coefficients of regressions of the change in salary plus bonus on changes in shareholder wealth, changes in shareholder wealth in the industry and market, and two accounting measures of performance: changes in accounting profits and changes in sales. We focus on the CEO's compensation and ignore changes in the value of his options or stockholdings because these latter components are determined exclusively by firm performance, independent of other variables such as relative performance and accounting profits. Thus if other variables are more important than shareholder wealth changes in providing CEO incentives, their importance should show up in a strong relation with CEO compensation.

Relative Performance

Basing CEO compensation on performance measured relative to aggregate performance in the industry or market provides CEOs with incentives to increase shareholder wealth while filtering out the risk-increas-

Table 9.6 Pay-Performance Sensitivity of CEO Pay Using Additional Performance Measures: Coefficients of Ordinary Least Squares Regressions of Δ(Salary + Bonus) on Various Stock Market and Accounting Measures of Performance

Independent Variable[a]	Regression Coefficients[b]				
	(1)	(2)	(3)	(4)	(5)
Intercept	31.5	31.9	32.5	31.0	32.8
Δ(shareholder wealth)	.0000140	.0000126	.0000074	.0000120	.0000074
	(7.5)	(4.8)	(4.3)	(7.1)	(4.4)
Δ(wealth net-of-industry)[c]	−.0000012	—	—	—	—
	(−.7)				
Δ(wealth net-of-market)[c]	—	.0000013	—	—	—
		(.4)			
Δ(accounting profits)	—	—	.000177	—	.000187
	—	—	(17.2)		(15.7)
Δ(sales)	—	—	—	.0000122	−.000003
				(7.2)	(−1.7)
R^2	.0083	.0082	.0449	.0148	.0453
Sample size	7,747	7,747	7,721	7,721	7,721

Note: The sample is constructed from longitudinal data reported in *Forbes* on 1,668 CEOs serving in 1,049 firms, 1974–1986; *t*-statistics are in parentheses.

a. The variables are all measured in thousands of 1986 dollars.

b. The dependent variable is Δ(salary + bonus), measured in thousands of 1986 constant dollars. The qualitative results are unchanged when Δ(total pay) is used as the dependent variable.

c. Δ(wealth net-of-industry) is defined as $(r_t - i_t)V_{t-1}$, where r_t is shareholder return, V_{t-1} is beginning-of-period market value, and i_t is the value-weighted return for all other firms in the same two-digit industry. Similarly, Δ(wealth net-of-market) is defined as $(r_t - m_i)V_{t-1}$, where m_t is the value-weighted return for all NYSE stocks.

ing effects of industrywide and marketwide factors beyond the control of executives (Holmström 1982). Column 1 of Table 9.6 reports coefficients from a regression that includes firm performance measured relative to the performance of other firms in the same industry as an additional explanatory variable. In particular, the net-of-industry shareholder wealth change variable is defined as $V_{t-1}(r_t-i_t)$, where r_t and V_{t-1} are inflation-adjusted shareholder return and beginning-of-period market value of the sample firm, respectively, and i_t is the value-weighted inflation-adjusted rate of return in year t for all other Compustat firms in the same two-digit Standard Industrial Classification industry. Thus the industry variable measures the difference between the wealth change shareholders received and what they *would have received* had they invested in other firms in the industry instead of investing in the sample firm. Column 2 repeats the analysis using wealth changes measured net of market instead of net of industry, where the market return is the value-weighted return of all NYSE stocks.

The shareholder wealth change coefficients in columns 1 and 2 of Table 9.6 are positive and significant, indicating that firm performance continues to be an important determinant of compensation even after net-of-industry and net-of-market performance is controlled for. The net-of-industry and net-of-market variables are insignificant; therefore it does not appear that *relative performance* is an important source of managerial incentives. While we find that pay changes are unrelated to relative *value* changes, $V_{t-1}(r_t-i_t)$, Gibbons and Murphy (1990) find that pay changes are significantly related to relative *rates of return*, r_t-i_t.

Accounting Measures of Performance

Column 3 of Table 9.6 reports estimated coefficients from a regression of change in CEO salary and bonus on change in net accounting income measured before extraordinary items. The estimated coefficient of .000177 indicates that CEOs receive 17.7¢ for each $1,000 change in annual income. The increased explanatory power (compared to column 2 of Table 9.1) indicates that changes in accounting income are an additional important determinant of pay changes. Since income is a flow rather than a stock, however, the implied pay-performance sensitivity for accounting profits is roughly comparable to the pay-performance sensitivity for firm value changes of 0.74¢ per $1,000 in column 3. Suppose, for example, that the market value of the firm is the capitalized value of future earnings and that earnings follow a random walk. Then, with a real discount rate of 5%, each $1,000 change in earnings corresponds to a pay change of 17.7¢ and a firm value change of $20,000, or just under a penny per $1,000.

Column 4 of Table 9.6 reports estimated pay-performance coefficients from a regression that includes the change in firm sales as an additional determinant of incentive compensation. The estimated coefficient of .0000122 suggests that CEOs receive 1.2¢ for every $1,000 of increased firm revenues, implying a pay revision of $1,900 for each standard deviation change in sales (based on the median standard deviation for sales changes of $160 million), compared to pay revisions of $2,400 for each standard deviation change in shareholder wealth (based on an estimated pay-performance sensitivity of .000012 and a standard deviation for wealth changes of $200 million). The explanatory variables in column 5 include both accounting measures of performance—changes in sales and earnings—and also the change in shareholder wealth. The earnings change coefficient remains large and positive, indicating that CEOs receive pay raises of about 19¢ for each $1,000 change in income. The sales change coefficient in column 5 is *negative* and marginally significant, suggesting that, with income and firm value held constant, CEOs receive pay cuts of about one-third of a penny for each $1,000 increase in firm revenues. Finally, the shareholder wealth change coefficients suggest that, with earnings and sales held constant, each $1,000 change in shareholder wealth corresponds to a CEO pay change of three-fourths of a penny.

The purpose of including additional variables in the regression in Table 9.6 is to analyze whether compensation is highly sensitive to variables other than the change in shareholder wealth. The results in Table 9.6 indicate that CEO compensation is related to changes in accounting profits and sales but is unrelated to market and industry performance. While CEO pay appears to be about equally sensitive to accounting profits and shareholder wealth, the estimated magnitude of both effects is still small: the amount of CEO pay "at risk" for a $48 million change in accounting profits (which is twice the median standard deviation) is $9,000, or less than 2% of compensation for a CEO with median earnings of $490,000.

Unobservable Measures of Performance

The small relation between CEO pay and measures of market or accounting performance seems inconsistent with the fact that CEOs receive a large share of their total compensation in the form of explicit incentive bonuses. The Conference Board (1984) reports that over 90% of all large manufacturing firms had bonus plans in 1983, and 87% of firms with bonus plans paid bonuses for 1983 performance. The median bonus award for CEOs in the Conference Board's survey is 50% of base salary; more than 20% of the surveyed firms report CEO bonuses exceeding 70% of salary.

It is possible that CEO bonuses are strongly tied to an unexamined or unobservable measure of performance. If bonuses depend on performance measures observable only to the board of directors and are highly variable, they could provide significant incentives. One way to detect the existence of such "phantom" performance measures is to examine the magnitude of year-to-year fluctuations in CEO compensation. Large swings in CEO pay from year to year are consistent with the existence of an overlooked but important performance measure; small annual changes in CEO pay suggest that it is essentially unrelated to all relevant performance measures. To test for the existence of such unobserved but important pay-performance sensitivity, we compare the variability of CEO pay to that of a sample of randomly selected workers.

The data indicate that year-to-year fluctuations in CEO income are not much different from income fluctuations for conventional labor groups. Column 1 in Table 9.7 presents the frequency distribution of inflation-adjusted annual percentage changes in CEO salary plus bonus for all CEOs listed in the *Forbes* surveys from 1974 to 1986. A third of the sample observations correspond to inflation-adjusted pay changes between 0% and 10%, and three-fourths of the observations reflect pay changes between −10% and 25%. Raises in salaries and bonus exceeding 50% account for only 4.4% of the sample, and pay cuts of more than 25% account for only 3.2% of the sample. Column 2 in Table 9.7 summarizes the frequency distribution of the inflation-adjusted total pay (excluding stock options). Changes in CEO compensation exceeding ±25% account for only 21.8% of the sample observations.

Column 3 of Table 9.7 presents the frequency distribution of annual inflation-adjusted percentage wage changes for managerial and non-managerial workers in the Michigan Panel Study of Income Dynamics (PSID). These distributions were made available to us by Ken McLaughlin, who reports similar distributions for logarithmic wage changes (McLaughlin 1987). The subset of the PSID sample analyzed by him covers the years 1975–1980 and includes 10,247 annual wage changes for male workers aged 18–59. The wage change distributions for the random sample in column 3 are remarkably similar to the wage change distribution for CEOs in columns 1 and 2. The standard deviation of percentage wage changes for the PSID sample is 41.7, compared to 30.5 and 49.3 for CEO salary plus bonus and CEO total compensation, respectively. There are a few minor differences that are interesting. Executives are less likely to receive real pay cuts than workers selected

Table 9.7   Comparison of Pay Variability of CEOs and Randomly Selected
Workers: Frequency Distribution of Annual Percentage Changes in
Real Salary and Bonus and Total Pay for CEOs Listed in *Forbes*
Compensation Surveys, 1974–1986, and Changes in Real Wages for
Workers in the 1975–1980 Michigan PSID

Inflation-Adjusted Annual Percentages	CEOs in *Forbes* Surveys, 1974–1986		Workers in Michigan PSID Sample, 1975–1980[b]
	Salary + Bonus (1)	Total Pay[a] (2)	(3)
More than 50%	4.4	6.3	4.6
25% to 50%	9.4	10.5	6.8
10% to 25%	21.1	21.3	14.0
0% to 10%	32.3	29.1	34.0
−10% to 0%	21.9	18.9	28.6
−25% to −10%	7.7	8.9	7.8
Less than −25%	3.2	5.0	4.2
Sample size	8,027	8,027	10,247
Standard deviation	30.5	49.3	41.7

a. Total pay typically includes salary, bonus, value of restricted stock, savings and thrift plans, and other benefits but does *not* include the value of stock options granted or the gains from exercising stock options.

b. The wage change distributions for the PSID were made available to us by Ken McLaughlin and include 10,247 male workers aged 18–59 reporting wages earned in consecutive periods.

at random; CEOs receive cuts in both salary plus bonus and total pay 32.8% of the time, while the workers in the PSID sample received pay cuts 40.6% of the time. Executives are more likely to receive raises exceeding 10% than random workers: 34.8% and 38% for salary plus bonus and total pay, respectively, for CEOs compared to 25.4% for all workers.

Corporate management is an occupation in which, a priori, we would expect incentive compensation to be especially important. It is therefore surprising that the distribution of wage changes for CEOs is so similar to the distribution for randomly selected workers. It appears that annual executive bonuses are not highly variable. These data seem inconsistent with economic theories of compensation: in spite of the fact that bonuses nominally amount to 50% of salary, there seem to be too few major year-to-year percentage changes in CEO compensation to provide the incentives that are likely to make a substantial difference in executive behavior.

Direct Measures of Performance

Incentive contracts are unnecessary when CEO activities are perfectly observable and when shareholders (or boards of directors) can tell the CEO precisely which actions to take in each state of the world. When their activities are imperfectly observable, CEOs will be evaluated in part by observing output (change in shareholder wealth) and in part by observing input (CEO activities). One explanation for the small pay-performance sensitivity is that boards have fairly good information regarding managerial activity, and therefore the weight on output is small relative to the weight on input.

The hypothesis that corporate boards directly monitor managerial input is consistent with the data but inconsistent with generally held beliefs in the business and financial community. Outside members of corporate boards have only limited contact with the CEO—at most 1 or 2 days a month—and the meetings that do occur are typically held in the CEO's office with agendas and information controlled by him. More important, the hypothesis that "forcing contracts" can be written when managerial actions are observable hinges crucially on the assumption that shareholders or boards know what actions *should* be taken. Managers often have better information than shareholders and boards in identifying investment opportunities and assessing the profitability of potential projects; indeed, the expectation that managers will make superior investment decisions explains why shareholders relinquish decision rights over their assets by purchasing common stock. Basing compensation on observed managerial actions cannot provide CEOs with incentives to engage in value-increasing activities when the expected wealth consequences of alternative actions are unknown to shareholders and board members. Appropriate incentives can be generated in these cases, however, by basing compensation on changes in shareholder wealth.

Non-pecuniary Rewards Provide Adequate Incentives

Our estimates of the pay-performance sensitivity (with respect to compensation, stock ownership, and dismissal) include only *monetary* rewards for performance and ignore potentially important non-pecuniary rewards associated with managing a firm. These non-pecuniary rewards could provide incentives for CEOs to take appropriate actions even when direct monetary incentives are absent.

Non-monetary rewards such as power, prestige, and honor will definitely affect the level of monetary compensation necessary to attract properly qualified people to the firm, but unless non-monetary rewards vary positively with the value of the firm they will not increase the CEO's incentives to take appropriate actions (except through the threat of performance-related dismissal). Moreover, because non-pecuniary benefits tend to be a function of position or rank, it is difficult to vary the amount of non-pecuniary benefits received by an executive from period to period to correspond with increases or decreases in productivity. It is therefore unlikely that non-pecuniary factors are an important source of incentives pushing managers to maximize value.

Non-pecuniary rewards associated with success and accomplishment and non-pecuniary punishments associated with failure do provide incentives for managers. However, these non-pecuniary incentives, generally associated with reputation in the firm and standing in the community, will motivate managers to act in shareholders' interest only if the non-pecuniary rewards and punishments are directly associated with firm value changes. This is a serious problem because there are strong political and organizational forces that tend to define success in dimensions other than shareholder wealth and exert pressures for actions that reduce firm value. Managerial conformance to pressures to maintain employment, peace with unions, or major contributions to communities by keeping unprofitable plants open can easily become synonymous with "success." In such situations, the non-pecuniary rewards come at the expense of shareholder value and economic efficiency.

External Forces Provide Adequate Incentives

Compensation and termination policies are *internal* tools utilized by boards of directors to provide managerial incentives. There are also competitive forces *external* to the corporation that provide incentives, including competition in the product market (Hart 1983), the managerial labor market (Fama 1980), and the market for corporate control (Manne 1965). Product market competition disciplines managers since firms that are inefficiently managed will be unprofitable and will not survive. Competition in the managerial labor market, especially the labor market internal to the organization, includes the incentives of subordinates to replace inferior superiors. The threat of takeovers also provides incentives since managers are often replaced following a successful takeover. Martin and McConnell (1988) report, for example, that 61% of target firm managers depart within 3 years after a successful takeover compared with 21% for a nonmerged control sample, and Walsh (1988) reports that 37% of the entire top-management team leaves the target firm within 2 years of a takeover compared with 13% of a nonmerged control sample.

Although these external forces provide incentives for existing management, we focus on internal incentive mechanisms because these are under the direct control of boards of directors. Moreover, external forces such as takeovers may be a response to, instead of an efficient substitute for, ineffective internal incentives.

9.3 Alternative Hypotheses

The conflict of interest between managers and shareholders is a classical agency problem, but the small observed pay-performance sensitivity seems inconsistent with the implications of formal principal-agent models. Two alternative hypotheses consistent with the observed relation between pay and performance are (1) that CEOs are not, in fact, important agents of shareholders, and (2) that CEO incentives are unimportant because their actions depend only on innate ability or competence. There has not yet been careful empirical documentation of the ways in which CEOs affect the performance of their firms, but there is considerable evidence that the competence and actions of a CEO are important to the productivity of the firm. The fact that stock prices react significantly to the death (Johnson et al. 1985) or replacement (Warner et al. 1988) of CEOs, for example, is inconsistent with the hypothesis that CEOs do not matter.

The wave of management buyouts (MBOs) and the improved productivity they generate are consistent with the hypothesis that CEOs and the incentives they face are important to firm performance. There is strong evidence that the 96% average net-of-market increase in value associated with these buyouts is caused by new top-management incentives (Jensen 1989; Kaplan 1991). The experience with MBOs is inconsistent with the hypothesis that managerial incentives are unimportant because in these transactions the same top managers manage the same assets after the company goes private. Data from takeovers, which are associated with high management turnover and produce average increases in firm value of 50%, are also consistent with the hypothesis that top-level managers can have a large effect on firm performance.

Another hypothesis that we believe helps to reconcile our empirical results concerns the important role of third parties in the contracting process. Managerial labor contracts are not, in fact, a private matter between employers and employees. Strong political forces operate in both the private sector (board meetings, annual stockholder meetings, and internal corporate processes) and the public sector that affect executive pay. Managerial contracts are not private because by law the details of the pay package are public information open to public scrutiny and criticism. Moreover, authority over compensation decisions rests not with shareholder-employers but rather with compensation committees composed of outside members of the boards of directors who are elected by, but are not perfect agents for, shareholders. Fueled by the public disclosure of executive pay required by the Securities and Exchange Commission, parties such as employees, labor unions, consumer groups, Congress, and the media create forces in the political milieu that constrain the type of contracts written between management and shareholders.

The benefits of the public disclosure of top-management compensation are obvious since this disclosure can help provide a safeguard against "looting" by management (in collusion with "captive" boards of directors). The costs of disclosure are less well appreciated. Public information on "what the boss makes" affects contracts with other employees and provides emotional justification for increased union demands in labor negotiations. Media criticism and ridicule and the threat of potential legislation motivated by high payoffs to managers reduce the effectiveness of executives and boards in managing the company. The media are filled with sensational stories about executive compensation each spring at the height of the proxy season. Board members are subject to lawsuits if top-management pay is "too high" relative to pay observed in similar firms (but never if it is "too low"). Since the subjective "reasonableness" of a compensation package is strongly influenced by the political process, it is natural that well-intentioned but risk-averse board members will resist innovative incentive contracts.

Strong public antagonism toward large pay changes is illustrated by the defeat of congressional pay increases in 1989. National polls indicate that 85% of voters opposed the 50% increase in congressional salaries (from $89,500 to $135,000) even though this increase would have left salaries lower in real terms than 1969 levels (Rogers 1989).

The Implicit Regulation Hypothesis: Evidence from the 1930s

It is difficult to document the influence of the political process on compensation because the constraints are implicit rather than explicit and the public disclosure of top-management compensation has existed for half a century. One possible way to test this implicit regulation hypothesis is to compare our pay-performance results for 1974–1986 to the pay-performance relation when regulatory pressures were less evident. We have constructed a longitudinal sample of executives from the 1930s using data collected by the U.S. Work Projects Administration (WPA) in a 1940 project sponsored by the Securities and Exchange Commission (1940–1941). The WPA data, covering fiscal years 1934–1938, include salary and bonus paid to the highest-paid executive in 748 large U.S. corporations in a wide range of manufacturing and nonmanufacturing industries. Of the WPA sample firms, 394 are listed on the NYSE; market value data for these firms are available on the CRSP Monthly Stock Returns Tape.

Comparing corporate data from the 1934–1938 WPA sample to corresponding data from the 1974–1986 *Forbes* sample is difficult because of reporting differences and because of major secular changes in the number and the size distribution of corporations over the past five decades. The "CEO" designation was rarely used in the 1930s, and therefore for comparison purposes we define CEO as the highest-paid executive. In addition, the WPA data do not reveal the name of the highest-paid executive, and therefore some salary and bonus changes reflect management changes rather than pay revisions for a given manager. For comparison purposes, the 1974–1986 pay change data utilized in Tables 9.8 and 9.9 were constructed ignoring management changes. Finally, in order to compare similar firms in the two time periods, we restricted our analysis to firms that are in the top quartile of firms listed on the NYSE (ranked by market value). The WPA compensation data are available for 60% of the top-quartile NYSE firms for 1934–1938 (averaging 114 firms per year), and *Forbes* compensation data are available for 90% of the top-quartile NYSE firms for 1974–1986 (averaging 335 firms per year).

Table 9.8 presents sample compensation statistics for CEOs in the top quartile of NYSE corporations ranked by market value for 1934–1938 and compares these results to similarly constructed data for 1974–1986. The CEOs in the largest-quartile firms earned an average of $813,000 measured in 1986 constant dollars in the 1930s, signifi-

Table 9.8 CEO Compensation in 1934–1938 versus 1974–1986 Sample Compensation Statistics for CEOs in the Top Quartile of NYSE Corporations Ranked by Market Value

Variable (in 1986 Dollars)	1934–1938	1974–1986	Test Statistic for Difference
CEO salary + bonus:			
Mean	$813,000	$645,000	$t = 9.1$
Median	$639,000	$607,000	
Mean market value of firm	$1.6 billion	$3.4 billion	$t = -6.1$
Mean CEO salary + bonus as a percentage of firm market value	.110%	.034%	$t = 29.6$
Change in CEO salary + bonus:			
Mean	$31,900	$27,800	$t = .4$
Median	$200	$21,600	
Average standard deviation[a]	$205,000	$127,000	$t = 2.7$

Note: For the 1934–1938 data, CEOs are defined as the highest-paid executive. Sample sizes are 456 and 3,988 CEO-years for the 1934–1938 and 1974–1986 samples, respectively.

a. The standard deviation for Δ(salary + bonus) was calculated for each firm with at least three years of data; sample sizes are 108 firms and 436 firms for the earlier and later time periods, respectively. The *t*-statistic tests the equality of the average standard deviations in the two samples. The samplewide (pooled) standard deviation of pay changes was $167,500 for 3,928 CEO-years for 1974–1986, compared to $463,500 for 448 CEO-years for 1934–1938.

cantly more than the average pay of $645,000 earned by CEOs in the NYSE top quartile from 1974 to 1986. Over this same period, median pay fell from $639,000 to $607,000. The current popular belief that CEO pay in the largest corporations has increased dramatically over the past several decades is therefore not supported by these sample averages. Over this same time period, there has been a doubling (after inflation) of the average market value of a top-quartile firm—from $1.6 billion in the 1930s to $3.4 billion for 1974–1986. Along with the decline in salaries, this means that the ratio of CEO pay to total firm value has fallen significantly in 50 years—from 0.11% in the early period to 0.03% in the later period. The mean annual change in compensation in the earlier period was $31,900 as compared to $27,800 in the 1974–1986 period. More important, the variability of annual changes in CEO pay fell considerably over this period; the average standard deviation of the annual pay changes was $127,000 in the 1970s and 1980s, significantly lower than the $205,000 average in the 1930s.

Table 9.9 CEO Pay-Performance Sensitivity in 1934–1938 versus 1974–1986: Regressions of Change in CEO Salary + Bonus on Change in Shareholder Wealth for CEOs in the Top Quartile of NYSE Corporations Ranked by Market Value

Independent Variable	Regression Coefficients[a]	
	1934–1938	1974–1986
Intercept	6.3	22.3
Δ(shareholder wealth) (thousands of 1986 dollars)	.000114 (5.6)	.000012 (7.0)
Δ(shareholder wealth) in year $t - 1$	.000061 (2.8)	.000007 (4.4)
R^2	.0702	.0165
Estimated pay-performance sensitivity, b	.000175	.000019
Estimated cents per $1,000	17.5¢	1.9¢

Note: For the 1934–1938 data, CEOs are defined as the highest-paid executive. Sample sizes are 427 and 3,826 CEO-years for the 1934–1938 and the 1974–1986 samples, respectively; t-statistics are in parentheses.

a. Dependent variable is Δ(salary + bonus), measured in thousands of 1986 constant dollars.

The pronounced decline in the raw variability of salary changes evident in Table 9.8 suggests the possibility of a decreased sensitivity in the pay-performance relation. Table 9.9 reports estimated coefficients from regressions of change in CEO salary and bonus on this year's and last year's change in shareholder wealth. The 1930s regression indicates that each $1,000 increase in shareholder wealth corresponds to an 11.4¢ increase in this year's pay and a 6.1¢ increase in next year's pay; thus the total effect of a $1,000 increase in shareholder wealth is 17.5¢. In contrast, the regression using the 1974–1986 data implies only a 1.9¢ pay change for each $1,000 change in shareholder wealth. Thus the pay-performance relation for CEOs in the top quartile of NYSE firms has fallen by a factor of 10 over the past 50 years. These results, although not conclusive, are consistent with the implicit regulation hypothesis because political constraints and pressures, disclosure requirements, and the overall regulation of corporate America have increased substantially over the same period.

The incentives generated by CEO stock ownership have also declined substantially over the past 50 years. Table 9.10 shows time trends in the

Table 9.10   Time Trends in CEO Inside Stock Ownership: Median CEO Stock Ownership for Two Samples of Firms

Sample and Year	Median Value of Stock Owned (1986 Dollars)	Median Percentage of Firm Owned
A. 120 largest firms ranked by market value:		
1938	$2,250,000	.30%
1974	2,061,000	.05
1984	1,801,000	.03
B. 73 manufacturing firms:		
1969–1973	3,531,000	.21
1974–1978	1,397,000	.14
1979–1983	1,178,000	.11
15-year sample	1,697,000	.16

Note: Stock ownership obtained from proxy statements includes not only shares held directly but also shares held by family members or related trusts.

stock ownership of CEOs for two different samples of firms. The first sample consists of all CEOs in the 120 largest firms (ranked by stock market value) in 1938, 1974, and 1984; we collected stock ownership data for these CEOs from proxy statements. Proxy statements for 1938 were available for only 53 of the largest 120 firms in 1938; stock ownership data for CEOs in 16 additional firms were obtained using 1939 and 1940 proxy statements.

Part A of Table 9.10 shows that CEO percentage of ownership (including shares held by family members and trusts) in the largest 120 firms fell from a median of 0.30% in 1938 to 0.05% in 1974 and fell further to 0.03% in 1984 (average percentage of ownership fell from 1.7% in 1938 to 1.5% and 1.0% in 1974 and 1984, respectively). In addition, the median dollar value of shares held (in 1986 constant dollars) fell from $2,250,000 in 1938 to $2,061,000 in 1974 and to $1,801,000 in 1984. The decline in the value of shares held between 1974 and 1984 is especially significant because 1974 was a "bust" year in the stock market, while 1984 was a "boom" year. The value-weighted portfolio of all NYSE stocks increased by 112.4% (after inflation) over this interval, so if the median executive had maintained his stockholdings and if these had increased by the same percentage as that of the market portfolio, the value of his holdings would have increased from $2,061,000 in 1974 to $4,400,000 in 1984 instead of falling to $1,801,000.

Part B of Table 9.10, based on the 73 manufacturing firm sample, shows the median value of stock owned by CEOs and their percentage of ownership for the full 15-year sample and for 5-year intervals. For 1969–1973, the median CEO in the 73 sample firms held $3,531,000 in common stock (1986 dollars), which accounted for 0.21% of the shares outstanding. By 1979–1983, the median ownership had fallen 67% to $1,178,000, accounting for only 0.11% of the shares outstanding. Over the same time period, the *average* stock ownership, which is strongly influenced by a few CEOs with extraordinarily large holdings, fell from $14,100,000 to $8,500,000.

The political pressures associated with high pay-performance contracts do not appear to extend to gains from stock ownership. We therefore expect increases in political pressure to correspond to decreases in pay-performance sensitivity and *increases* in incentives associated with stock ownership. The dramatic decline in CEO stock ownership over the past 50 years is contrary to the implicit regulation hypothesis and suggests a significant downward trend in managerial incentives that is not explained by existing theories.

Political Influence and the Effect of Firm Size on the Pay-Performance Sensitivity

Political influence is likely to be more pronounced in large firms since larger firms tend to be more visible and more closely scrutinized than smaller firms (Watts and Zimmerman 1986, chap. 10). The implicit regulation hypothesis thus predicts that the pay-performance sensitivity declines with firm size, but our all-inclusive estimate of $3.25 per $1,000 is based on a constant pay-performance sensitivity across firms. Although the *Forbes* sample analyzed in this chapter includes the nation's largest firms, the size distribution of firms *within* the sample is highly skewed. The average and median market values of firms in our sample are $1.73 billion and $810 million (1986 dollars), respectively. The average and median market values for firms larger than the sample median are $3.1 billion and $1.6 billion, respectively, while the average and median market values for firms smaller than the sample median are $400 million and $360 million, respectively.

We test for the effect of firm size on the pay-performance sensitivity by reestimating the results in Tables 9.1, 9.3, 9.4, 9.5, and 9.6 for firms with market value in a given year above or below the sample median market value for that year. Of the 73 manufacturing firm sample (Table 9.2), 80% fall into the "above-median" category (on the basis of the *Forbes* sample); thus we did not reestimate the results in Table 9.2 by firm size. Our overall results are summarized in Columns 2 and 3 of Table 9.11; to save space, details of the estimates are not provided but are available upon request. We have previously noted substantial differences in CEO stockholdings in small and large firms (Table 9.3); Table 9.11 suggests other interesting differences between the two samples. Row 1 shows that each $1,000 change in shareholder wealth corresponds to a 4.1¢ pay raise for CEOs in small firms, but only 2.0¢ for CEOs in large firms. Also, current and past net-of-market performance is a strong predictor of CEO turnover in below-median-size firms, but performance and turnover are both economically and statistically insignificantly related for large firms. As reported in row 5, the average dismissal-performance sensitivity (weighted by the number of observations in each age group) is $2.25 per $1,000 change in shareholder wealth for CEOs in small firms, but only 5¢ per $1,000 for CEOs in large firms. Our all-inclusive estimated pay-performance sensitivity (row 8) for small firms is $8.05 per $1,000, four times greater than our large-firm estimate of $1.85 per $1,000.

Varying degrees of political pressure across firms or decades are not of course the only potential explanations for the size effect or secular decline in pay-performance sensitivities; thus the evidence presented is supportive of the implicit regulation hypothesis but not conclusive. For example, higher pay-performance sensitivities for smaller firms could reflect that CEOs are more influential in smaller companies. A thorough empirical investigation of the implicit regulation of executive compensation would be useful, but such an investigation requires detailed data on the compensation practices of partnerships, closely held corporations, and other nonpublic organizations. These data are inherently difficult to obtain. In fact, it is precisely this asymmetry in data availability that forms the basis for the implicit regulation of executive compensation in publicly held corporations.

9.4 Conclusions

Our analysis of performance pay and top-management incentives for more than 2,000 CEOs in three samples spanning five decades indicates that the relation between CEO wealth and shareholder wealth is small

Table 9.11 Estimated Pay-Performance Sensitivity: Total Effects (over 2 years) on CEO Compensation-Related Wealth Corresponding to Each $1,000 Change in Shareholder Wealth for CEOs in *Forbes* Sample, 1974–1986, by Firm Size

	Predicted CEO Wealth Change per $1,000 Change in Shareholder Wealth		
	All Firms (1)	Large Firms (2)	Small Firms (3)
Change in this year's and next year's salary + bonus	$.022	$.020	$.041
Total compensation + present value of the change in salary + bonus	.30	.25	.75
Change in the value of stock options	.15	.15	.15
Change in direct pay-related wealth (row 2 + row 3)[a]	.45	.40	.90
Change in wealth due to dismissal from poor performance	.30	.05	2.25
Change in total pay-related wealth (row 4 + row 5)	.75	.45	3.15
Change in wealth related to stock ownership for CEO with median stockholdings	2.50	1.40	4.90
Change in all pay- and stock-related wealth[b]	$3.25	$1.85	$8.05

Source: Row 1: Table 9.1, col. 2. Row 2: Table 9.1, col. 4. Row 3: Table 9.2, col. 1, estimated for the -firm sample. We assume that the option-performance sensitivity is the same for both size groups. Row Table 9.5, col. 6. This is the weighted average of estimates for each age group. Row 7: Table 9.3, cols. 2, and 3. Stock ownership includes shares held by family members and connected trusts. Ownership o includes options that can be exercised within 60 days; thus there is some "double counting" in rows and 7.

Note: Estimates are rounded to the nearest nickel (except for row 1). Large firms have market value in given year above the *Forbes* sample median for that year, while small firms have market value below the dian. Details of the estimates by firm size are not provided in the text but are available on request.

a. The direct estimate from the 73 manufacturing firms is only 31¢ (table 9.2, col. 2); we have reported larger estimate as an upper bound.

b. Cols. 3 and 5 of Table 9.2 show that fractional stockholdings can be added to other sources of entives to construct an overall pay-performance sensitivity.

and has fallen by an order of magnitude in the last 50 years. Table 9.11, based primarily on the *Forbes* sample of 1,295 firms, provides an overview of our final results for the full sample and for firms with market value in a given year above or below the sample median market value for that year. In sum, our evidence yields the following conclusions:

1. On average, each $1,000 change in shareholder wealth corresponds to an increase in this year's and next year's salary and bonus of about two cents. The CEO's *wealth* due to his cash compensation—defined as his total compensation plus the discounted present value of the change in his salary and bonus—changes by about 30¢ per $1,000 change in shareholder wealth. In addition, the value of the CEO's stock options—defined as the value of the outstanding stock options plus the gains from exercising options—changes by 15¢ per $1,000. Our final upper-bound estimate of the average compensation-related wealth consequences of a $1,000 change in shareholder value is 45¢ for the full sample, 40¢ for large firms, and 90¢ for small firms.

2. Our weighted-average estimate of the CEO's dismissal-related wealth consequences of each $1,000 shareholder loss for an average-size firm with −50% net-of-market returns for two consecutive years is 30¢ for the full sample, 5¢ for large firms, and $2.25 for small firms. Therefore, the total pay-performance sensitivity—including both pay and dismissal—is about 75¢ per $1,000 change in shareholder wealth for the full sample (45¢ and $3.15 per $1,000 for large and small firms, respectively).

3. The largest CEO performance incentives come from ownership of their firms' stock, but such holdings are small and declining. Median 1986 inside stockholdings for 746 CEOs in the *Forbes* compensation survey are 0.25%, and 80% of these CEOs hold less than 1.4% of their firms' shares. Median ownership for CEOs of large firms is 0.14% and for small firms is 0.49%. Adding the incentives generated by median CEO stockholdings to our previous estimates gives a total change in all CEO pay- and stock-related wealth of $3.25 per $1,000 change in shareholder wealth for the full sample, $1.85 per $1,000 for large firms, and $8.05 for small firms.

4. Boards of directors do not vary the pay-performance sensitivity for CEOs with widely different inside stockholdings.

5. Although bonuses represent 50% of CEO salary, such bonuses are awarded in ways that are not highly sensitive to performance as measured by changes in market value of equity, accounting earnings, or sales.

6. The low variability of changes in CEO compensation reflects the fact that in spite of the apparent importance of bonuses in CEO compensation, they are not very variable from year to year. The frequency distributions of annual percentage changes in CEO salary plus bonus and total pay are comparable to that of a sample of 10,000 randomly selected workers. Thus our results indicating a weak relation between pay and performance are not due to boards of directors using measures of managerial performance that are unobservable to us.

7. Median CEO inside stockholdings for the 120 largest NYSE firms fell by an order of magnitude from 0.3% in 1938 to 0.03% in 1984.

8. The average standard deviation of pay changes for CEOs in the top quartile (by value) of all NYSE firms fell from $205,000 in 1934–1938 to $127,000 in 1974–1986.

9. The pay-performance sensitivity for top-quartile CEOs fell by an order of magnitude from 17.5¢ per $1,000 in 1934–1938 to 1.9¢ per $1,000 in 1974–1986.

10. The average salary plus bonus for top-quartile CEOs (in 1986 dollars) fell from $813,000 in 1934–1938 to $645,000 in 1974–1986, while the average market value of the sample firms doubled.

The lack of strong pay-for-performance incentives for CEOs indicated by our evidence is puzzling. We hypothesize that political forces operating both in the public sector and inside organizations limit large payoffs for exceptional performance. Truncating the upper tail of the payoff distribution requires that the lower tail of the distribution also be truncated in order to maintain levels of compensation consistent with equilibrium in the managerial labor market. The resulting general absence of management incentives in public corporations presents a challenge for social scientists and compensation practitioners.

10 | CEO Incentives: It's Not How Much You Pay, But How

Every spring brings yet another round in the national debate over executive compensation. Each year the business press trumpets answers to the same questions: Who were the highest paid CEOs? How many executives made more than a million dollars? Who received the biggest raises? Political figures, union leaders, and consumer activists issue now-familiar denunciations of executive salaries and urge that directors curb top-level pay in the interests of social equity and statesmanship.

The critics have it wrong. There are serious problems with CEO compensation, but "excessive" pay is not the biggest issue. The relentless focus on *how much* CEOs are paid diverts public attention from the real problem—*how* CEOs are paid. In most publicly held companies, the compensation of top executives is virtually independent of performance. On average, corporate America pays its most important leaders like bureaucrats. Is it any wonder then that so many CEOs act like bureaucrats rather than the value-maximizing entrepreneurs companies need to enhance their standing in world markets?

We recently completed an in-depth statistical analysis of executive compensation. Our study incorporates data on thousands of CEOs spanning five decades. The base sample consists of information on salaries and bonuses for 2,505 CEOs in 1,400 publicly held companies from 1974 through 1988. We also collected data on stock options and stock ownership for CEOs of the 430 largest publicly held companies in 1988. In addition, we drew on compensation data for executives at more than 700 public companies for the period 1934 through 1938.

Our analysis leads us to conclusions that are at odds with the prevailing wisdom on CEO compensation:

Despite the headlines, top executives are not receiving record salaries

By Michael C. Jensen and Kevin J. Murphy; originally published in *Harvard Business Review,* no. 3 (May–June 1990), pp. 138–153.

and bonuses. Salaries and bonuses have increased over the last 15 years, but CEO pay levels are just now catching up to where they were 50 years ago. During the period 1934 through 1938, for example, the average salary and bonus for CEOs of leading companies on the New York Stock Exchange was $882,000 (in 1988 dollars). For the period 1982 through 1988, the average salary and bonus for CEOs of comparable companies was $843,000.

Annual changes in executive compensation do not reflect changes in corporate performance. Our statistical analysis posed a simple but important question: For every $1,000 change in the market value of a company, how much does the wealth of that company's CEO change? The answer varied widely across our 1,400-company sample. But for the median CEO in the 250 largest companies, a $1,000 change in corporate value corresponds to a change of just 6.7 cents in salary and bonus over two years. Accounting for all monetary sources of CEO incentives—salary and bonus, stock options, shares owned, and the changing likelihood of dismissal—a $1,000 change in corporate value corresponds to a change in CEO compensation of just $2.59.

Compensation for CEOs is no more variable than compensation for hourly and salaried employees. On average, CEOs receive about 50% of their base pay in the form of bonuses. Yet these "bonuses" do not generate big fluctuations in CEO compensation. A comparison of annual inflation-adjusted pay changes for CEOs from 1975 through 1988 and pay changes for 20,000 randomly selected hourly and salaried workers shows remarkably similar distributions. Moreover, a much lower percentage of CEOs took real pay cuts over this period than did production workers.

With respect to pay for performance, CEO compensation is getting worse rather than better. The most powerful link between shareholder wealth and executive wealth is direct stock ownership by the CEO. Yet CEO stock ownership for large public companies (measured as a percentage of total shares outstanding) was *ten times* greater in the 1930s than in the 1980s. Even over the last 15 years, CEO holdings as a percentage of corporate value have declined.

Compensation policy is one of the most important factors in an organization's success. Not only does it shape how top executives behave, but it also helps determine what kinds of executives an organization attracts. This is what makes the vocal protests over CEO pay so damaging. By aiming their protests at compensation *levels,* uninvited but influential guests at the managerial bargaining table (the business press, labor unions, political figures) intimidate board members and constrain the types of contracts that are written between managers and shareholders. As a result of public pressure, directors become reluctant to reward CEOs with substantial (and therefore highly visible) financial gains for superior performance. Naturally, they also become reluctant to impose meaningful financial penalties for poor performance. The long-term effect of this risk-averse orientation is to erode the relation between pay and performance and entrench bureaucratic compensation systems.

Are we arguing that CEOs are underpaid? If by this we mean "Would average levels of CEO pay be higher if the relation between pay and performance were stronger?" the answer is yes. More aggressive pay-for-performance systems (and a higher probability of dismissal for poor performance) would produce sharply lower compensation for less talented managers. Over time, these managers would be replaced by more able and more highly motivated executives who would, on average, perform better and earn higher levels of pay. Existing managers would have greater incentives to find creative ways to enhance corporate performance, and their pay would rise as well.

These increases in compensation—driven by improved business performance—would not represent a transfer of wealth from shareholders to executives. Rather, shareholders would reward managers for the increased success fostered by greater risk taking, effort, and ability. Paying CEOs "better" would eventually mean paying the average CEO more. Because the stakes are so high, the potential increase in corporate performance and the potential gains to shareholders are great.

10.1   How Compensation Measures Up

Shareholders rely on CEOs to adopt policies that maximize the value of their shares. Like other human beings, however, CEOs tend to engage in activities that increase their own well-being. One of the most critical roles of the board of directors is to create incentives that make it in the CEO's best interest to do what is in the shareholders' best interests. Conceptually this is not a difficult challenge. Some combination of three basic policies will create the right monetary incentives for CEOs to maximize the value of their companies:

1. Boards can require that CEOs become substantial owners of company stock.
2. Salaries, bonuses, and stock options can be structured so as to provide big rewards for superior performance and big penalties for poor performance.
3. The threat of dismissal for poor performance can be made real.

Unfortunately, as our study documents, the realities of executive compensation are at odds with these principles. Our statistical analysis departs from most studies of executive compensation. Unlike the annual surveys in the business press, for example, we do not focus on this year's levels of cash compensation or cash compensation plus stock options exercised. Instead, we apply regression analysis to 15 years' worth of data and estimate how changes in corporate performance affect CEO compensation and wealth over all relevant dimensions.

We ask the following questions: How does a change in performance affect current cash compensation, defined as changes in salary and bonus over two years? What is the "wealth effect" (the present value) of those changes in salary and bonus? How does a change in corporate performance affect the likelihood of the CEO being dismissed, and what is the financial impact of this new dismissal probability? Finally, how does a change in corporate performance affect the value of CEO stock options and shares, whether or not the CEO exercised the options or sold the shares? (For a discussion of our methodology, see Section 10.2, "How We Estimate Pay for Performance.")

Table 10.1 provides a detailed review of our main findings for a subsample of CEOs in the 250 largest publicly held companies. Together, these CEOs run enterprises that generate revenues in excess of $2.2 trillion and employ more than 14 million people. The results are both striking and troubling. A $1,000 change in corporate market value (defined as share price appreciation plus dividends) corresponds to a two-year change in CEO salary and bonus of less than a dime; the long-term effects of that change add less than 45 cents to the CEO's wealth. A $1,000 change in corporate value translates into an estimated median change of a nickel in CEO wealth by affecting dismissal prospects. At the median, stock options add another 58 cents' worth of incentives. Finally, the value of shares owned by the median CEO changes by 66 cents for every $1,000 increase in corporate value. All told, for

Table 10.1   The Weak State of Pay for Performance

A $1,000 Change in Shareholder Wealth Corresponds to:	Estimates for CEOs in the 250 Largest Companies	
	Median	Middle 50%
Change in this year's and next year's salary and bonus	$0.067	$0.01 to $0.18
Present value of the two-year change in salary and bonus	0.44	0.05 to 1.19
Change in the value of stock options	0.58	0.16 to 1.19
Wealth effect for change in likelihood of dismissal	0.05	0.02 to 0.14
Total change in all pay-related wealth	$1.29	$0.43 to $2.66
Change in value of direct stockholdings	0.66	0.25 to 1.98
Total change in CEO wealth	$2.59	$0.99 to $5.87

Note: The median individual components do not add to the median total change in CEO wealth since sums of medians do not in general equal the median of sums.

the median executive in this subsample, a $1,000 change in corporate performance translates into a $2.59 change in CEO wealth. The table also reports estimates for CEOs at the lower and upper bounds of the middle two quartiles of the sample. (For an extensive review and comparison of the pay-for-performance relation for individual CEOs, see Section 10.3, "A New Survey of Executive Compensation.")

This degree of pay-for-performance sensitivity for cash compensation does not create adequate incentives for executives to maximize corporate value. Consider a corporate leader whose creative strategic plan increases a company's market value by $100 million. On the basis of our study, the median CEO can expect a two-year increase in salary and bonus of $6,700—hardly a meaningful reward for such outstanding performance. His lifetime wealth would increase by $260,000—less than 4% of the present value of the median CEO's shareholdings and remaining lifetime salary and bonus payments.[1]

Or consider instead a CEO who makes a wasteful investment—new aircraft for the executive fleet, say, or an elaborate addition to the headquarters building—that benefits him but diminishes the market value of the company by $10 million. The total wealth of this CEO, if he is representative of our sample, will decline by only $25,900 as a result of this misguided investment—not much of a disincentive for someone who earns on average $20,000 a week.

One way to explore the realities of CEO compensation is to compare current practices with the three principles that we outlined earlier. We will address them one at a time.

CEOs should own substantial amounts of company stock. The most powerful link between shareholder wealth and executive wealth is direct ownership of shares by the CEO. Most commentators look at CEO stock ownership from one of two perspectives—the dollar value of the CEO's holdings or the value of his shares as a percentage of his annual cash compensation. But when trying to understand the incentive consequences of stock ownership, neither of these measures counts for much. What really matters is *the percentage of the company's outstanding shares the CEO owns.* By controlling a meaningful percentage of total corporate equity, senior managers experience a direct and powerful "feedback effect" from changes in market value.

Think again about the CEO adding jets to the corporate fleet. The stock-related "feedback effect" of this value-destroying investment—about $6,600—is small because this executive is typical of our sample, in which the median CEO controls only .066% of the company's outstanding shares. Moreover, this wealth loss (about two days' pay for the average CEO in a top-250 company) is the same whether the stockholdings represent a big or small fraction of the CEO's total wealth.

But what if this CEO held shares in the company comparable to say, Warren Buffett's stake in the Berkshire Hathaway conglomerate? Buffett controls, directly and indirectly, about 45% of Berkshire Hathaway's equity. Under these circumstances, the stock-related feedback effect of a $10 million decline in market value is nearly $4.5 million—a much more powerful incentive to resist wasteful spending.

Moreover, these differences in CEO compensation are associated with substantial differences in corporate performance. From 1970 through 1988, the average annual compound stock return on the 25 companies with the best CEO incentives (out of the largest 250 companies examined in our survey) was 14.5%, more than one-third higher than the average return on the 25 companies with the worst CEO incentives. A $100 investment in the top 25 companies in 1970 would have grown to $1,310 by 1988, as compared with $702 for a similar investment in the bottom 25 companies.

As a percentage of total corporate value, CEO share ownership has never been very high. The median CEO of one of the nation's 250 largest public companies owns shares worth just over $2.4 million— again, less than 0.07% of the company's market value. Also, 9 out of 10 CEOs own less than 1% of their company's stock, while fewer than 1 in 20 owns more than 5% of the company's outstanding shares.

It is unreasonable to expect all public-company CEOs to own as large a percentage of their company's equity as Warren Buffett's share of Berkshire Hathaway. Still, the basic lesson holds. The larger the share of company stock controlled by the CEO and senior management, the more substantial is the linkage between shareholder wealth and executive wealth. A few companies have taken steps to increase the share of corporate equity owned by senior management. Employees of Morgan Stanley now own 55% of the firm's outstanding equity. Companies such as FMC and Holiday have used leveraged recapitalizations to reduce the amount of outstanding equity by repurchasing public shares, and thus allow their managers to control a bigger percentage of the company. After FMC adopted its recapitalization plan, for example, employee ownership increased from 12% to 40% of outstanding equity. These recapitalizations allow managers to own a bigger share of their company's equity without necessarily increasing their dollar investment.

Truly giant companies like IBM, General Motors, or General Electric will never be able to grant their senior executives a meaningful share of outstanding equity. These and other giant companies should understand that this limitation on executive incentives is a real cost associated with bigness.

Cash compensation should be structured to provide big rewards for outstanding performance and meaningful penalties for poor performance. A two-year cash reward of less than 7 cents for each $1,000 increase in corporate value (or, conversely, a two-year penalty of less than 7 cents for each $1,000 decline in corporate value) does not create effective managerial incentives to maximize value. In most large companies, cash compensation for CEOs is treated like an entitlement program.

There are some notable exceptions to this entitlement pattern, however. The cash compensation of Walt Disney CEO Michael Eisner, whose pay has generated such attention in recent years, is more than ten times more sensitive to corporate performance than the median CEO in our sample. Yet the small number of CEOs for whom cash compensa-

tion changes in any meaningful way in response to corporate performance shows how far corporate America must travel if pay is to become
an effective incentive.

Creating better incentives for CEOs almost necessarily means increasing the financial risk CEOs face. In this respect, cash compensation
has certain advantages over stock and stock options. Stock-based incentives subject CEOs to vagaries of the stock market that are clearly
beyond their control. Compensation contracts based on company performance relative to comparable companies could provide sound incentives while insulating the CEO from factors such as the October 1987
crash. Although there is some evidence that directors make implicit
adjustments for market trends when they set CEO pay, we are surprised
that compensation plans based explicitly on relative performance are so
rare.[2]

The generally weak link between cash compensation and corporate
performance would be less troubling if CEOs owned a large percentage
of corporate equity. In fact, it would make sense for CEOs with big
chunks of equity to have their cash compensation less sensitive to performance than CEOs with small stockholdings. (For example, Warren
Buffett's two-year cash compensation changes by only a penny for every
$1,000 increase in market value.) In some cases, it might even make
sense for pay to go up in bad years to serve as a financial "shock ab-
sorber" for losses the CEO is taking in the stock market. Yet our statistical analysis found no correlation between CEO stock ownership and
pay-for-performance sensitivity in cash compensation. In other words,
boards of directors ignore CEO stock ownership when structuring incentive compensation plans. We find this result surprising—and symp-
tomatic of the ills afflicting compensation policy.

Make real the threat of dismissal. The prospect of being fired as a
result of poor performance can provide powerful monetary and nonmonetary incentives for CEOs to maximize company value. Because
much of an executive's "human capital" (and thus his or her value in
the job market) is specific to the company, CEOs who are fired from
their jobs are unlikely to find new jobs that pay as well. In addition,
the public humiliation associated with a high-visibility dismissal should
cause managers to weigh carefully the consequences of taking actions
that increase the probability of being dismissed.

Here too, however, the evidence is clear: the CEO position is not a
very risky job. Sports fans are accustomed to baseball managers being

fired after one losing season. Few CEOs experience a similar fate after years of underperformance. There are many reasons why we would expect CEOs to be treated differently from baseball managers. CEOs have greater organization-specific capital; it is harder for an outsider to come in and run a giant company than it is for a new manager to take over a ball club. There are differences in the lag between input and output. The measure of a baseball manager's success is the team's won-lost record this year; the measure of a corporate manager is the company's long-term competitiveness and value. For these and other reasons, it is not surprising that turnover rates are lower for CEOs than for baseball managers. It *is* surprising that the magnitude of the discrepancy is so large.

On average, CEOs in our base sample (2,505 executives) hold their jobs for more than ten years before stepping down, and most give up their title (but not their seat on the board) only after reaching normal retirement age. Two recent studies, spanning 20 years and more than 500 management changes, found only 20 cases where CEOs left their jobs because of poor performance.[3] To be sure, directors have little to gain from publicly announcing that a CEO is leaving because of failure—many underperforming CEOs leave amidst face-saving explanations and even public congratulations. But this culture of politeness does not explain why so few underperforming CEOs leave in the first place. Michael Weisbach at the University of Rochester found that CEOs of companies that rank in the bottom 10% of the performance distribution (measured by stock returns) are roughly twice as likely to leave their jobs as CEOs whose companies rank in the top 10% of the performance distribution. Yet the differences that Weisbach quantifies—a 3% chance of getting fired for top performers versus a 6% chance of getting fired for laggards—are unlikely to have meaningful motivational consequences for CEOs.

Our own research confirms these and other findings. CEOs of large public companies are only slightly more likely to step down after very poor performance (which we define as company earnings 50% below market averages for two consecutive years) than after average performance. For the entire 1,400-company sample, our analysis estimates that the poor-performing CEOs are roughly 6% more likely to leave their jobs than CEOs of companies with average returns. Even assuming that a dismissed CEO never works again, the personal wealth consequences of this increased likelihood of dismissal amount to just 5 cents for every $1,000 loss of shareholder value.

With respect to pay for performance, there is no denying that the results of our study tell a bleak story. Then again, perhaps corporate directors are providing CEOs with substantial rewards and penalties based on performance, but they are measuring performance with metrics other than long-run market value. We tested this possibility and reached the same conclusion as in our original analysis. Whatever the metric, CEO compensation is independent of business performance.

For example, we tested whether companies rewarded CEOs on the basis of sales growth or accounting profits rather than direct changes in shareholder wealth. We found that while more of the variation in CEO pay could be explained by changes in accounting profits than stock market value, the pay-for-performance sensitivity was economically just as insignificant as in our original model. Sales growth had little explanatory power once we controlled for accounting profits.[4]

Of course, incentives based on other measures will be captured by our methodology only to the extent that they ultimately correlate with changes in shareholder wealth. But if they do not—that is, if directors are rewarding CEOs on the basis of variables other than those that affect corporate market value—why use such measures in the first place?

Moreover, if directors varied CEO compensation substantially from year to year on the basis of performance measures not observable to us, this policy would show up as high raw variability in CEO compensation. But over the past 15 years, compensation for CEOs has been about as variable as cash compensation for a random sample of hourly and salaried workers dramatic evidence of compensation's modest role in generating executive incentives.[5] Figure 10.1 compares the distribution of annual raises and pay cuts of our CEO sample with national data on hourly and salaried workers from 1975 through 1986. A larger percentage of workers took real pay cuts at some time over this period than did CEOs. Overall, the standard deviation of annual changes in CEO pay was only slightly greater than for hourly and salaried employees (32.7% versus 29.7%).

Looking Backward: Pay for Performance in the 1930s

CEO compensation policies look especially unsatisfactory when compared with the situation 50 years ago. All told, CEO compensation in the 1980s was lower, less variable, and less sensitive to corporate performance than in the 1930s. To compare the current situation with the past, we constructed a longitudinal sample of executives from the 1930s using data collected by the Work Projects Administration. The WPA data, covering fiscal years 1934 through 1938, include salary and bonus for the highest paid executive (whom we designate as the CEO) in 748 large U.S. corporations in a wide range of industries. Nearly 400 of the WPA sample companies were listed on the New York Stock Exchange, and market values for these companies are available on the CRSP Monthly Stock Returns Tape. In order to compare similar companies over the two time periods, we restricted our analysis to companies in the top 25% of the NYSE, ranked by market value. WPA compensation data are available for 60% of this top quartile group (averaging 112 companies per year), while data for more recent times are available for 90% of the top quartile companies (averaging 345 companies per year).

The results are striking. Measured in 1988 constant dollars, CEOs in top quartile public companies earned an average salary and bonus of $882,000 in the 1930s—more than the 1982 through 1988 average of $843,000 and significantly more than the 1974 through 1981 average of $642,000. Over this same time period, there has been a tripling (after inflation) of the market value of top quartile companies—from $1.7

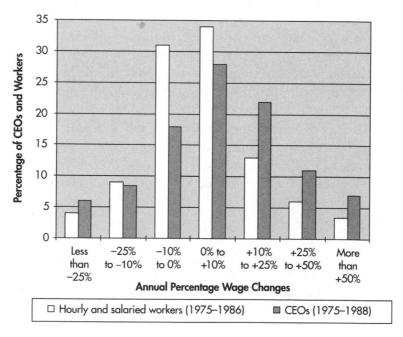

Figure 10.1 Common variability: CEO and worker wages.

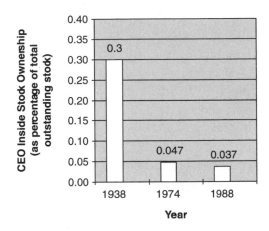

Figure 10.2 Whatever happened to CEO stock ownership?

billion in the 1930s to $5.9 billion in 1982 through 1988. Coupled with the decline in salaries, the ratio of CEO pay to total company value has fallen significantly—from 0.11% in the 1930s to 0.03% in the 1980s. Compensation was more variable in the 1930s as well. The average standard deviation of the annual pay changes—the best statistical measure of the year-to-year variability of compensation—was $504,000 in the 1930s compared with $263,500 in the 1980s.

The incentives generated by CEO stock ownership have also declined substantially over the past 50 years. To test this trend, we reviewed stock ownership data for CEOs in the 120 largest companies (ranked by market value) in 1938, 1974, and 1988. Figure 10.2 reports our findings. The percentage of outstanding shares owned by CEOs (including shares held by family members) in the top 120 companies fell by a factor of nearly ten from 1938 to 1988. The trend is unmistakable: as a percentage of total market value, CEO stock ownership has declined substantially over the last 50 years and is continuing to fall.

The Costs of Disclosure

Why don't boards of directors link pay more closely to performance? Commentators offer many explanations, but nearly every analysis we have seen overlooks one powerful ingredient—the costs imposed by making executive salaries public. Government disclosure rules ensure that executive pay remains a visible and controversial topic. The benefits of disclosure are obvious; it provides safeguards against "looting" by managers in collusion with "captive" directors. The costs of disclosure are less well appreciated but may well exceed the benefits.

Managerial labor contracts are not a private matter between employers and employees. Third parties play an important role in the contracting process, and strong political forces operate inside and outside companies to shape executive pay. Moreover, authority over compensation decisions rests not with the shareholders but with compensation committees generally composed of outside directors. These committees are elected by shareholders but are not perfect agents for them. Public disclosure of "what the boss makes" gives ammunition to outside constituencies with their own special-interest agendas. Compensation committees typically react to the agitation over pay levels by capping—explicitly or implicitly—the amount of money the CEO earns.

How often do shareholder activists or union leaders denounce a corporate board for *under*paying the CEO? Not very often—and that is precisely the problem. Most critics of executive pay want it both ways. They want companies to link pay to performance, yet they also want to limit compensation to arbitrary amounts or some fuzzy sense of "what's fair." That will not work. Imposing a ceiling on salaries for outstanding performers inevitably means creating a floor for poor performers. Over time, by cutting off the upper and lower tails of the distribution, the entire pay-for-performance relation erodes. When mediocre outfielders earn a million dollars a year, and New York law partners earn about the same, influential critics who begrudge comparable salaries to the men and women running billion-dollar enterprises help guarantee that these companies will attract mediocre leaders who turn in mediocre performances.

Admittedly, it is difficult to document the effect of public disclosure on executive pay. Yet there have been a few prominent examples. Bear, Stearns, the successful investment bank, went public in 1985 and had to submit to disclosure requirements for the first time. CEO Alan Greenberg's $2.9 million salary and bonus was the nation's fourth highest that year, and his ranking drew attention to the firm's compensation system. Under private ownership, compensation of the firm's managing directors was set at a modest $150,000 base plus a bonus pool tied to earnings—a tight link between pay and performance. Because the firm was so profitable in 1986, the bonus pool swelled to $80 million, an average of $842,000 for each of the firm's 95 managing directors. A public outcry ensued. Six months after going public, Bear, Stearns announced that it was lowering the bonus pool from 40% to 25% of the firm's adjusted pretax earnings in excess of $200 million. According to one account, the firm's business success had "yielded an embarrassment of riches for top executives."[6]

More recently, we interviewed the president of a subsidiary of a thriving publicly traded conglomerate. This president is compensated with a straight fraction of his subsidiary's earnings above a minimum threshold, with no upper bound. Today he makes roughly five times what he made before his operation was acquired by the conglomerate, and corporate headquarters recognizes him as one of the company's outstanding executives. Why doesn't he want to be an officer of the conglomerate? For one, because his salary would have to be made public—a disclosure both he and the CEO consider a needless invitation to internal and external criticism.

We are not arguing for the elimination of salary disclosure. (Indeed, without disclosure we could not have conducted this study.) But it is time that compensation committees stood up to outside criticism and stopped adopting policies that make their companies' incentive problem worse. The costs of negative publicity and political criticism are less severe than the costs to shareholder wealth created by misguided compensation systems.

Corporate Brain Drain

The level of pay has very little to do with whether or not CEOs have incentives to run companies in the shareholders' interests—incentives are a function of how pay, whatever the level, changes in response to corporate performance. But the level of pay does affect the quality of managers an organization can attract. Companies that are willing to pay more will, in general, attract more highly talented individuals. So if the critics insist on focusing on levels of executive pay, they should at least ask the right question: Are current levels of CEO compensation high enough to attract the best and brightest individuals to careers in corporate management? The answer is, probably not.

Who can disagree with these propositions?

- It is good when our most talented men and women are attracted to the organizations that produce the goods and deliver the services at the heart of the economy.
- People evaluate alternative careers at least in part on the basis of lifetime monetary rewards.
- People prefer to make more money than less, and talented, self-confident people prefer to be rewarded on the basis of performance rather than independent of it.
- If some organizations pay more on average and offer stronger pay-for-performance systems than other organizations, talent will migrate to the higher-paying organizations.

These simple propositions are at the heart of a phenomenon that has inspired much hand-wringing and despair over the last decade—the stream of talented, energetic, articulate young professionals going into business law, investment banking, and consulting. Data on career choices of Harvard Business School graduates document the trend that troubles so many pundits. In 1980, nearly 55% of newly graduated HBS students chose careers in the corporate sector, while fewer than 30% chose investment banking or consulting. By 1987, more than half of all HBS graduates entered investment banking or consulting, while under 30% chose careers in the corporate sector. In 1989, just over one-third of all graduating HBS students chose corporate careers, while nearly 40% chose careers in investment banking or consulting. And Harvard Business School is not alone; we gathered data on other highly rated MBA programs and found similar trends.

We don't understand why commentators find this trend so mysterious. A highly sensitive pay-for-performance system will cause high-quality people to self-select into a company. Creative risk takers who perceive they will be in the upper tail of the performance and pay distribution are more likely to join companies who pay for performance. Low-ability and risk-averse candidates will be attracted to companies with bureaucratic compensation systems that ignore performance.

Compensation systems in professions like investment banking and consulting are heavily weighted toward the contributions made by individuals and the performance of their work groups and companies. Compensation systems in the corporate world are often independent of individual, group, or overall corporate performance. Moreover, average levels of top-executive compensation on Wall Street or in corporate law are considerably higher than in corporate America. Financially speaking, if you are a bright, eager 26-year-old with enough confidence to want to be paid on the basis of your contribution, why would you choose a career at General Motors or Procter & Gamble over Morgan Stanley or McKinsey & Company?

Most careers, including corporate management, require lifetime investments. Individuals must choose their occupation long before their ultimate success or failure becomes a reality. For potential CEOs, this means that individuals seeking careers in corporate management must join their companies at an early age in entry-level jobs. The CEOs in our sample spent an average of 16 years in their companies before assuming the top job. Of course, many people who reach the highest ranks of the corporate hierarchy could also expect to be successful in professional partnerships such as law or investment banking, as proprietors of their own businesses, or as CEOs of privately held companies. It is instructive, therefore, to compare levels of CEO compensation with the compensation of similarly skilled individuals who have reached leadership positions in other occupations.

The compensation of top-level partners in law firms is one relevant comparison. These numbers are closely guarded secrets, but some idea of the rewards to top partners can be gleaned from data on average partner income reported each year in a widely read industry survey. The top portion of Table 10.2 reports 1988 estimated average incomes earned by partners in the highest paying corporate law firms. These five firms paid their 438 partners *average* incomes ranging from $1.35 million to nearly $1.6 million. Partners at the very top of these firms earned substantially more. When comparing these results with corporate compensation, the appropriate question to ask is: "How many public companies paid their top 67 or 177 executives average salaries of $1.6 million or $1.2 million in 1989?" The answer is, few or none. How surprising is it, then, that law school classes are bulging with some of the country's brightest students?

Compensation for the most successful corporate managers is also modest in comparison with compensation for the most successful Wall Street players. Here too it is difficult to get definitive numbers for a large sample of top executives. But a recent annual survey, as reported in the bottom part of Table 10.2, documents the kinds of rewards available to top investment bankers. At Goldman, Sachs, for example, 18 partners earned more than $3 million in 1988, and the average income for those

Table 10.2 Salaries for Top Lawyers Are High

Rank	Firm	Average Income per Partner	Number of Partners
1	Cravath, Swaine, & Moore	$1,595,000	67
2	Cahill Gordon & Reindel	$1,420,000	57
3	Sullivan & Cromwell	$1,375,000	91
4	Wachtell Lipton, Rosen & Katz	$1,350,000	46
5	Skadden, Arps, Slate, Meagher & Flom	$1,155,000	177

. . . So Are Salaries on Wall Street

Firm	Number of Partners Earning More Than $3 Million in 1988	Average Earnings for Partners Earning More Than $3 Million in 1988
Drexel Burnham Lambert	20	$18,000,000
Goldman, Sachs	18	$ 9,100,000
Morgan Stanley	11	$ 4,300,000
Sterling Group	6	$36,700,000
Kohlberg Kravis Roberts	5	$59,000,000
Lazard Freres	5	$17,200,000
Salomon Brothers	5	$ 4,700,000
Neuberger & Berman	5	$ 4,700,000

Source: Top half: *The American Lawyer,* July-August 1989, p. 34. Bottom half: *Financial World,* July 11, 1989. Average earnings are based on *Financial World's* lower bound earnings estimate, p. 32.

partners was more than $9 million. Only nine public-company CEOs had incomes in excess of $9 million in 1988 (mostly through exercising stock options), and no public company paid its top 18 executives more than $3 million each.

The compensation figures for law and investment banking look high because they reflect only the most highly paid individuals in each occupation. Average levels of compensation for lawyers or investment bankers may not be any higher than average pay levels for executives. But that is not the relevant comparison. The very best lawyers or investment bankers can earn substantially more than the very best corporate executives. Highly talented people who would succeed in any field are likely to shun the corporate sector, where pay and performance are weakly related, in favor of organizations where pay is more strongly related to performance—and the prospect of big financial rewards more favorable.

Money Isn't Everything

Some may object to our focus on monetary incentives as the central motivator of CEO behavior. Are there not important nonmonetary rewards associated with running a large organization? Benefits such as power, prestige, and public visibility certainly do affect the level of monetary compensation necessary to attract highly qualified people to the corporate sector. But unless nonmonetary rewards vary positively with company value, they are no more effective than cash compensation in motivating CEOs to act in the shareholders' interests. Moreover, because nonmonetary benefits tend to be a function of position or rank, it is difficult to vary them from period to period on the basis of performance.

Indeed, nonmonetary rewards typically motivate top managers to take actions that *reduce* productivity and harm shareholders. Executives are invariably tempted to acquire other companies and expand the diversity of the empire, even though acquisitions often reduce shareholder wealth. As prominent members of their community, CEOs face pressures to keep open uneconomic factories, to keep the peace with labor unions despite the impact on competitiveness, and to satisfy intense special-interest pressures.

Monetary compensation and stock ownership remain the most effective tools for aligning executive and shareholder interests. Until directors recognize the importance of incentives—and adopt compensation systems that truly link pay and performance—large companies and their shareholders will continue to suffer from poor performance.

10.2   How We Estimate Pay for Performance

Our analysis draws primarily on two sources of data: annual executive compensation surveys published in *Forbes* magazine from 1975 through 1988 and Standard & Poor's Compustat file. The base sample includes information on 2,505 CEOs from 1,400 companies. We estimated pay-for-performance sensitivities for each CEO using a variety of statistical techniques. The findings reported in Table 10.1 represent the median and "middle 50%" CEOs in a sample of the 250 largest companies.

Perhaps the best way to illustrate our methodology is to review pay-for-performance calculations for a single CEO—for example, David H.

Murdock of Castle & Cooke, Inc., who tops our list of large-company CEOs with the best incentives. For each element of Mr. Murdock's compensation, we estimated answers to the same question: How does that compensation element change in response to a $1,000 change in corporate value, as measured by annual share price appreciation and dividends?

Two-Year Change in Salary and Bonus. We used least squares regression to calculate the relation between the dollar change in salary and bonus and the dollar change in shareholder wealth for all companies with at least seven years of pay-change data from 1975 through 1988. We estimate a single pay-for-performance sensitivity for each company; therefore our estimates for Castle & Cooke use data on both Murdock and his predecessor, Donald Kirchhoff. We did not use data on three other former CEOs—Robert Cook, Ian Wilson, and Henry Clark, Jr.— because they each served as CEO for less than two years and we therefore could not calculate pay changes. The regression equation uses last year's performance in addition to this year's performance as explanatory variables. The result is as follows:

> (change in salary and bonus) = $32,300
> + .000986 (change in this year's shareholder wealth)
> − .000219 (change in last year's shareholder wealth)

The pay-for-performance sensitivity is defined as the estimated slope coefficient in the regression equation. For this regression, the sum of the estimated coefficients implies that each $1,000 increase in the wealth of Castle & Cooke shareholders corresponds to an increase of 98.6 cents in this year's salary and bonus for Murdock, and a decrease of 21.9 cents in next year's salary and bonus. Thus the total expected increase in salary and bonus over two years is 77 cents per $1,000 change in value.

We estimated 430 separate regressions like the one for Murdock, having eliminated 740 companies as a result of incomplete information and 230 companies that were no longer in the sample in 1988. The pattern of t-statistics for the individual regressions implies that the average pay-performance coefficients are positive and statistically different from zero at confidence levels exceeding 99%.

Pay-Related Wealth. The estimate of 77 cents is an accurate measure of how David Murdock's and Donald Kirchhoff's salary and bonus change as a result of a $1,000 change in shareholder value. But it underestimates the change in their wealth. Since part of the change is permanent, they will earn it for the rest of their careers. In addition, Murdock and Kirchhoff received "other" income as fringe benefits and payoffs from long-term performance plans. We measure the change in their total wealth as the discounted present value of the permanent component of the change in compensation plus other income for the year.

To estimate the wealth change, we make three assumptions: (1) all changes in salary and bonus are permanent, while other forms of pay are transitory; (2) the CEO receives the change in salary and bonus until age 66; and (3) the wage increase to age 66 is discounted at the real interest rate of 3%. The resulting regression equation for Castle & Cooke, based on these assumptions, is:

(other income + present value of change in salary and bonus) = $150,000
+ .00310 (change in this year's shareholder wealth)
+ .00060 (change in last year's shareholder wealth)

The sum of the estimated coefficients in this regression implies that Murdock's and Kirchhoff's wealth (as a result of changes in salary and bonus) changes an average of $3.70 for every $1,000 change in the market value of Castle & Cooke.

Stock Options. Stock options are an increasingly important component of executive compensation packages, and their value relates directly to changes in share price. However, holding a stock option does not provide the same incentives as owning a share of stock—a distinction sometimes overlooked by compensation practitioners. For example, stock ownership rewards both price appreciation and dividends, while options reward only appreciation.

Moreover, the value of an option changes by less than $1 when the stock price changes by $1. How much less depends on factors such as interest rates, dividend yields, and whether the option is in or out of the money. Our simulation results show that 60 cents is a good approximation for the value change of at-the-money options for a company with a (sample average) dividend yield of 5%. This holds for a reasonable range of maturities, variance of stock returns, and interest rates.

We collected data on total stock options held by each of the sample CEOs from the proxy statements issued in advance of the company's 1989 annual meeting. Unfortunately, outstanding options are not always reported on proxy statements. So we estimated Murdock's outstanding options as options granted in 1988 (50,000 shares) plus options exercisable within 60 days (300,000 shares). Castle & Cooke had 59.3 million shares outstanding. A $1,000 change in shareholder wealth corresponds to the following change in the value of Murdock's options:

$$\left(\frac{\$.60 \text{ change in value of option}}{\$1 \text{ change in stock price}} \right) \times \left(\frac{350,000 \text{ Options}}{59,250,000 \text{ Total Shares}} \right) \times \$1,000 = \$3.54$$

Thus Murdock's option-related wealth changes by $3.54 for every $1,000 change in shareholder wealth. This estimate understates the change in the value of his options to the extent that he holds options granted prior to 1988 that are not exercisable within 60 days. We also underestimate the option-value change if his outstanding options are in the money, while we overstate the value change of out-of-the-money options.

Dismissal Incentives. The threat of being fired for poor performance provides monetary as well as nonmonetary incentives for CEOs to maximize value. We estimate the financial incentives associated with dismissal through a four-stage process. First, using nonlinear "logistic" regression techniques on our 1974 through 1988 sample of 2,505 CEOs, we estimate the probability that a CEO will leave the job as a function of industry, company size, CEO age, market-relative performance, and lagged market-relative performance. Second, we compute point estimates of the departure probabilities when the company earns the market rate of return for two years versus when the company realizes share-price returns 50% below the market in two consecutive years. Third, we multiply the difference in these two "dismissal probabilities" by the discounted value of the CEO's potential lost wages, assuming that the CEO would have received the current salary until age 66, and, if dismissed, never works again. Fourth, we calculate the dismissal performance sensitivity by dividing the CEO's potential wealth loss by the shareholder loss associated with earning 50% below-market returns for two years.

In Murdock's case, the probability that a 65-year-old CEO in a smaller-than-median-size company leaves his job is 20.7% in years when the company earns the market return and 23.9% when his company earns 50% below the market return for two straight years. The probability that Murdock will be fired (or encouraged to leave) for poor performance is 3.2%. Murdock's dismissal-related loss is his $1.5 million 1988 pay multiplied by the turnover-probability difference, or about $48,000. (If Murdock had been younger than 65, we would have calculated the present value of his 1988 pay until he reached 66.) Castle & Cooke shareholders, on the other hand, would lose about $1.25 billion of their $1.67 billion equity from two straight years of 50% below-market performance. Thus Murdock's potential wealth loss is about 3.8 cents per $1,000 lost by shareholders.

It is important to note that although our estimates of other CEO incentive sources use data for the individual CEO's company, our estimates of CEO-dismissal performance sensitivities are based on the entire sample. It is generally impossible to make company-specific estimates of the wealth effects of dismissal threats.

Stock Ownership. The most important component of CEO incentives is also the easiest to measure. As of March 1989, Murdock held directly 13,203,932 shares of Castle & Cooke. In addition, his children hold 80,870 shares in trusts. All told, his family holds 13,284,802 shares, or 22.42% of Castle & Cooke's outstanding stock. His total stock-related incentives are roughly $224.24 per $1,000 change in market value.

Putting It All Together. David Murdock's total pay-for-performance sensitivity is simply the sum of the sensitivities of each compensation element, of $231.53 per $1,000 change in shareholder value. This makes Murdock the CEO with the best incentives in the 250 largest companies in the period 1975–1988.

10.3 A New Survey of Executive Compensation

Routinely misused and abused, surveys contribute to the common ills of corporate compensation policy. Surveys that report average compensation across industries help inflate salaries, as everyone tries to be above average (but not in front of the pack). Surveys that relate pay to company sales encourage systems that tie compensation to size and growth, not performance and value. Surveys that rank the country's highest paid executives stir public outrage, raise legislative eyebrows, and provide emotional justification for increased demands in labor negotiations.

The basic problem with existing compensation surveys is that they focus exclusively on *how much* CEOs are paid instead of *how* they are paid. Our focus on incentives rather than levels leads naturally to a new and different kind of survey. Instead of reporting who is paid the most, our survey reports who is paid the best—that is, whose incentives are most closely aligned with the interests of their shareholders.

Our survey considers incentives from a variety of sources—including salary and bonus, stock options, stock ownership, and the threat of getting fired for poor performance. It includes only companies listed in the *Forbes* executive compensation surveys for at least eight years from 1975 through 1989, since we require at least seven years of pay change to estimate the relation between pay and performance. Our methodology has been described in Section 10.2, "How We Estimate Pay for Performance."

Compensation surveys in the business press, such as those published by *Fortune* and *Business Week,* are really about levels of pay and not about pay for performance. Yet they often include an analysis or ranking of the appropriateness of a particular CEO's pay by relating it to company performance in some fashion. The methods adopted by *Fortune* and *Business Week* share a common flaw. CEOs earning low fixed salaries while delivering mediocre performance look like stars; on the flip side, CEOs with genuinely strong pay-for-performance practices rank poorly. For example, *Business Week*'s 1989 survey calculates the ratio of the change in shareholder wealth to the CEO's total compensation, both measured over three years. Executives with the highest ratios are labeled the "CEOs Who Gave the Most for Their Pay." Low-ratio CEOs purportedly gave shareholders the least. *Fortune*'s 1989 compensation issue uses a regression model to estimate how compensation varies with factors such as the CEO's age and tenure, company size, location, industry, and performance. Although the author cautions against taking the results too literally, CEOs earning more than predicted are implicitly designated as "overpaid," while those earning less than predicted are "underpaid."

Consider the case of Disney's Michael Eisner. By all accounts, Mr. Eisner's pay is wedded to company performance—in addition to loads of stock options, he gets 2% of all profits above an annually increasing threshold. Shareholders have prospered under Eisner, and few have complained that his compensation is unreasonable in light of the $7 billion in shareholder wealth he has helped to create since joining the company in 1984. But *Business Week* ranks Eisner second on the list of CEOs who gave their shareholders the least (right behind option-laden Lee Iacocca, who over the past decade helped created $6 billion in wealth for the Chrysler shareholders), while *Fortune* flags Eisner as the nation's third most overpaid CEO. Surveys that rank Eisner and Iacocca low are clearly not measuring incentives. In contrast, our survey ranks

Eisner and Iacocca as the nation's fourth and ninth respectively "best paid" CEOs measured on the basis of pay-related wealth alone.

We estimated the pay-for-performance relation for each of the 430 companies for which we have sufficient data.[7] The results are summarized in Tables 10.3 through 10.6. Three of the tables include results for the 250 largest companies ranked by 1988 sales. The 25 CEOs with the best and worst overall incentives, as reflected by the relation between their total compensation (composed of all pay-related wealth changes and the change in the value of stock owned), are summarized in Tables 10.3 and 10.4. Castle & Cooke, whose current CEO is David Murdock, ranks first with a total change in CEO wealth of $231.53 for every $1,000 change in shareholder wealth. His stockholdings contribute $224.24 of this amount, while the change in all pay-related wealth adds another $7.29.

With a few exceptions, it is clear that the best incentives are determined primarily by large CEO stockholdings. Donald Marron of Paine Webber is such an exception, with more than $55 of his total of $67 coming from changes in pay-related wealth. So too are Philip Hawley of Carter Hawley Hale, Henry Schacht of Cummins Engine, and Disney's Eisner.

The 25 companies providing their CEOs with the worst total incentives are led by Navistar International, whose CEO, James Cotting, on average receives a $1.41 *increase* in wealth for every $1,000 *decrease* in shareholder value. Carolina Power & Light's Sherwood Smith, Jr. receives a 16-cent increase for every $1,000 decrease in shareholder wealth. Other well-known corporations whose CEOs appear on the worst-incentives list include Chevron, Johnson & Johnson, Eastman Kodak, and IBM.

Although one has to recognize that there is statistical uncertainty surrounding our estimates of pay-related wealth sensitivity, no CEO with substantial equity holdings (measured as a fraction of the total outstanding equity) makes our list of low-incentive CEOs. As we point out, an important disadvantage of corporate size is that it is extremely difficult for the CEO to hold a substantial fraction of corporate equity.

The inverse relation between size and stockholdings (and therefore the negative effect of size on incentives) is readily visible in the much higher sensitivities shown for the top 25 CEOs in smaller companies, those ranking from 251 to 430 in 1988 sales (see Table 10.5). Warren Buffett of Berkshire Hathaway leads this list with $446 per $1,000,

Table 10.3 The 25 CEOs of Large Companies with the Best Incentives

Rank	Company	CEO	Total Effects (Over Two Years) on CEO Wealth Corresponding to Each $1,000 Change in Shareholder Wealth		
			Change in All Pay-Related Wealth	Change in the Value of Stock Owned	Change in Total CEO Wealth
1	Castle & Cooke	David H. Murdock	$7.29	$224.24	$231.53
2	Amerada Hess	Leon Hess*	0.02	152.71	152.73
3	Wang Laboratories	An Wang*	0.84	137.83	138.68
4	Aon Corp.	Patrick G. Ryan	0.76	137.46	138.22
5	Loews	Laurence A. Tisch	0.00	126.40	126.40
6	Ethyl	Floyd D. Gottwald, Jr.	−0.25	90.73	90.48
7	Marriott	J. Willard Marriott, Jr.*	1.55	72.58	74.14
8	MCA	Lew R. Wasserman	0.05	70.10	70.15
9	Paine Webber Group	Donald B. Marron	55.59	11.44	67.03
10	Paccar	Charles M. Pigott	2.25	50.86	53.12
11	Times Mirror	Robert F. Erburu	3.29	45.39	48.67
12	Coastal Corp.	Oscar S. Wyatt, Jr.*	0.43	44.33	44.75
13	Archer-Daniels-Midland	Dwayne O. Andreas	−0.15	41.23	41.07
14	Carter Hawley Hale	Philip M. Hawley*	23.36	16.25	39.60
15	McDonnell Douglas	John F. McDonnell*	0.09	33.79	33.88
16	CBS	Laurence A. Tisch	1.79	31.58	33.37
17	Humana	David A. Jones*	1.34	25.88	27.22
18	Winn-Dixie Stores	A. Dano Davis	2.72	23.22	25.95
19	Masco	Richard A. Manoogian	8.78	14.08	22.86
20	American Int'l Group	Maurice R. Greenberg	0.50	21.72	22.22
21	Digital Equipment	Kenneth H. Olsen*	1.00	19.06	20.07
22	MCI Communications	William G. McGowan*	1.77	17.95	19.73
23	Cummins Engine	Henry B. Schacht	18.46	0.87	19.33
24	Walt Disney	Michael D. Eisner	15.62	2.88	18.50
25	FMC	Robert H. Malott	8.43	7.04	15.47

Note: Sample consists of CEOs in the 250 largest companies, ranked by 1988 sales.
*Denotes founder or founding-family CEO.

Table 10.4 The 25 CEOs of Large Companies with the Worst Incentives

Rank	Company	CEO	Total Effects (Over Two Years) on CEO Wealth Corresponding to Each $1,000 Change in Shareholder Wealth		
			Change in All Pay-Related Wealth	Change in the Value of Stock Owned	Change in Total CEO Wealth
26	Central & South West	Merle L. Borchelt	$0.14	$0.32	$0.46
27	Campbell Soup	R. Gordon McGovern	$0.07	0.38	0.44
28	3M	Allen F. Jacobson	0.28	0.11	0.39
29	Sears Roebuck	Edward A. Brennan	0.17	0.20	0.37
30	AMP	Walter F. Raab	−0.03	0.39	0.36
31	Consolidated Edison	Arthur Hauspurg	0.22	0.12	0.34
32	Detroit Edison	Walter J. McCarthy, Jr.	0.24	0.07	0.31
33	Commonwealth Edison	James J. O'Connor	0.24	0.06	0.30
34	Texas Utilities	Jerry S. Farrington	0.23	0.07	0.29
35	Exxon	Lawrence G. Rawl	0.14	0.11	0.25
36	AT&T	Robert E. Allen	0.19	0.04	0.24
37	ARCO	Lodwrick M. Cook	−0.10	0.33	0.23
38	IBM	John F. Akers	0.13	0.06	0.19
39	Borden	Romeo J. Ventres	−0.20	0.38	0.18
40	Eastman Kodak	Colby H. Chandler	−0.09	0.08	0.17
41	R.R. Donnelley & Sons	John R. Walter	−0.18	0.34	0.16
42	Johnson & Johnson	Ralph S. Larsen	0.11	0.05	0.15
43	Chevron Corp.	Kenneth T. Derr	−0.04	0.15	0.11
44	GTE	James J. Johnson	0.04	0.07	0.11
45	Pacific Gas & Electric	Richard A. Clarke	0.06	0.04	0.10
46	Philadelphia Electric	Joseph F. Paquette, Jr.	0.07	0.01	0.08
47	PacifiCorp	Al M. Gleason	−0.04	0.08	0.04
48	Honeywell	James J. Renier	−0.51	0.40	−0.10
49	Carolina Power & Light	Sherwood H. Smith, Jr.	−0.61	0.45	−0.16
50	Navistar International	James C. Cotting	−1.61	0.20	−1.41

Note: Sample consists of CEOs in the 250 largest companies, ranked by 1988 sales.

Table 10.5 The Best of the Rest: CEO Incentives in Smaller Companies

Rank	Company	CEO	Total Effects (Over Two Years) on CEO Wealth Corresponding to Each $1,000 Change in Shareholder Wealth		
			Change in All Pay-Related Wealth	Change in the Value of Stock Owned	Change in Total CEO Wealth
1	Berkshire Hathaway	Warren E. Buffett	$0.06	$446.77	$446.83
2	Williamette Industries	William Swindells, Jr.	0.64	427.10	427.75
3	Riggs National	Joe L. Allbritton	1.22	358.19	359.40
4	Hilton Hotels	Barron Hilton*	0.85	245.90	246.75
5	Timken	William R. Timkin, Jr.*	5.20	142.46	147.66
6	United Missouri Bancshares	R. Crosby Kemper	1.08	118.65	119.73
7	Zions Bancorporation	Roy W. Simmons	2.76	89.17	91.93
8	First Empire State	Robert G. Wilmers	18.72	71.63	90.36
9	Florida National Banks	John D. Uible	1.85	87.66	89.51
10	Equimark	Alan S. Fellheimer	15.53	72.28	87.81
11	W.W. Grainger	David W. Grainger*	0.21	79.13	79.34
12	Fin'l Corp. of Santa Barbara	Philip R. Brinkerhoff	54.68	21.41	76.09
13	Golden West Financial	Herbert M. Sandler*	4.48	67.36	71.83
14	Merchants National	Otto N. Frenzel, III	9.59	60.19	69.79
15	First City Bancorp of Texas	A. Robert Abboud	−0.21	58.75	58.54
16	First Security	Spencer F. Eccles	2.63	44.84	47.47
17	Central Bancshares of the South	Harry B. Brock, Jr.*	4.89	38.25	43.15
18	Freuhauf	T. Neal Combs	16.20	21.14	37.34
19	Holiday	Michael D. Rose	14.01	20.94	34.94
20	Cullen/Frost Bankers	Thomas C. Frost*	8.90	25.95	34.85
21	Beneficial Corp.	Finn M.W. Caspersen	3.37	29.87	33.23
22	Yellow Freight System	George E. Powell, Jr.	0.86	30.90	31.76
23	Data General	Edison D. deCastro*	1.89	29.79	31.68
24	Equitable Bancorporation	H. Grant Hathaway	11.01	17.23	28.24
25	Imperial Corp. of America	Kenneth J. Thygerson	24.98	2.52	27.51

Note: Sample consists of CEOs in companies ranked 251 to 430 by 1988 sales.
*Denotes founder or founding-family CEO.

Table 10.6   Best-Paid CEOs of Large Companies

Rank	Company	CEO	Change in Salary + Bonus over Two Years	Change in Pay-Related Wealth Corresponding to Each $1,000 Change in Shareholder Wealth			
				Present Value of Pay Change	Change in Wealth due to Dismissal Likelihood	Change in Value of Stock Options	Change in All Pay-Related Wealth
	Paine Webber Group	Donald B. Marron	$4.11	$46.91	$1.18	$7.51	$55.59
	Carter Hawley Hale	Philip M. Hawley*	0.03	0.54	0.98	21.83	23.36
	Cummins Engine	Henry R. Schacht	1.11	18.29	0.03	0.14	18.46
	Walt Disney	Michael D. Eisner	0.72	11.35	0.00	4.27	15.62
	George A. Hormel	Richard L. Knowlton	0.76	7.47	0.19	4.70	11.36
	UAL	Stephen M. Wolf	0.01	0.45	0.02	11.57	12.05
	Fleet/Norstar	J. Terrence Murray	0.72	10.93	0.03	1.02	11.98
	Continental Bank	Thomas C. Theobald	0.26	2.01	0.04	9.40	11.46
	Chrysler Corp.	Lee A. Iacocca	0.43	5.38	0.02	4.74	10.14
	Zenith Electronics	Jerry K. Pearlman	0.77	7.44	0.05	2.27	9.76
	NCNB	Hugh L. McColl, Jr.	0.76	8.43	0.01	0.63	9.07
	Masco	Richard A. Manoogian	0.01	2.38	0.16	6.24	8.78
	FMC	Robert H. Malott	0.01	0.13	0.47	7.82	8.43
	Turner	Alfred T. McNeill	2.01	4.27	0.27	3.52	8.06
	B.F. Goodrich	John D. Ong	0.51	4.73	0.14	2.85	7.72
	Alco Standard	Ray B. Mundt	0.88	5.46	0.88	1.28	7.61
	Black & Decker	Nolan D. Archibald	0.25	3.89	0.34	3.30	7.53
	Castle & Cooke	David H. Murdock	0.77	3.70	0.04	3.54	7.29
	Brunswick Corp.	Jack F. Reichert	0.40	6.59	0.26	0.00	6.85
	Mellon Bank	Frank V. Cahouet	0.42	3.69	0.65	2.38	6.72
	Enron	Kenneth L. Lay	0.46	3.99	0.05	2.58	6.62
	Pan Am	Thomas G. Plaskett	0.25	0.77	0.13	5.55	6.46
	Toys "R" Us	Charles Lazarus*	−0.13	1.06	0.11	5.27	6.45
	Norwest	Lloyd P. Johnson	0.22	1.30	0.10	4.98	6.37
	First Union	Edward E. Crutchfield, Jr.	0.48	5.59	0.03	0.08	5.71

Note: Sample consists of CEOs in the 250 largest companies, ranked by 1988 sales.
*Denotes founder of founding-family CEO.

followed by William Swindells, Jr. of Williamette Industries, Joe Allbritton of Riggs National, and Barron Hilton of Hilton Hotels. Again, the importance of large stockholdings is clear.

Indeed, one problem with current compensation practices is that boards often reward CEOs with substantial equity through stock options but then stand by to watch CEOs undo the incentives by unloading their stockholdings. Boards seldom provide contractual constraints or moral suasion that discourages the CEO from selling such shares to invest in a diversified portfolio of assets. One of the ironies of the situation is that the corporation itself often funds executive financial counseling by consultants whose common mantra is "sell and diversify, sell and diversify." While this can be personally advantageous to executives, it is not optimal for shareholders or society because it significantly reduces CEOs' incentives to run their companies efficiently.

Pay-related incentives are under the direct control of the compensation committee and the board. Table 10.6 lists the 25 companies that reward their CEOs in a way that provides the best incentives from pay-related wealth alone—changes in salary and bonus, long-term incentive plans, dismissal likelihood, and stock options. Each of these estimates is given in the table, along with the sum of the effects in the last column. The table makes clear that the major contributors to pay-related incentives are stock options and the present value of the change in salary and bonus.

We are confident that increasing the sensitivity of pay-for-performance for the directors and managers of most corporations will improve substantially their productivity and competitiveness. Although designing and managing these systems is complex, we believe it can and will be done. We also look forward to the extension of these pay-for-performance systems to the rank-and-file employees.

PART IV   **Organizational Applications of the Theory**

11 | Science, Specific Knowledge, and Total Quality Management

11.1   Introduction

In this chapter we analyze Total Quality Management (TQM) programs from an economic and organizational perspective. The core of TQM's ability to create value lies in its power to bring about an efficient creation and utilization of valuable specific knowledge at all levels of the organization. By specific knowledge we mean knowledge valuable to decision making that is costly to transfer among agents (see Chapter 4 for a general analysis of the role of specific knowledge in decision making). TQM improves the creation of specific knowledge through the application of science and widespread teamwork. In addition, TQM establishes a process for reallocating decision rights that colocates them with the relevant specific knowledge. This results in a more effective utilization of specific knowledge in decision making, thereby increasing efficiency. The TQM process temporarily transfers decision rights from their location in the hierarchy to problem-solving teams, and often permanently reassigns them based on the outcome of the problem-solving process.

While our approach is new, the study of TQM certainly is not. The development, application, and assessment of TQM techniques by scholars in the production and operations research fields and by consultants and managers have been under way for more than a few decades.[1] Our purpose is neither to reiterate their findings nor to present formal large-sample tests of hypotheses about TQM. Instead, we focus on important organizational aspects of effective TQM programs that are often ignored or treated as incidental implementation issues. We have spent time in the field studying organizations, interviewing managers and employees, and directly observing the TQM process and its effects with the

By Karen Hopper Wruck and Michael C. Jensen; originally published in *Journal of Accounting and Economics* 18 (1994), pp. 247–287.

purpose of identifying the critical economic and organizational components that contribute to its success or failure. Our findings and conclusions provide a base from which to generate hypotheses for future research on TQM.

Considerable controversy surrounds TQM—including what defines it, whether it improves performance, and if it does, under what circumstances. Although it is grounded in a concern for product quality, TQM reaches beyond these issues to emphasize efficiency throughout the organization, from accounts receivable management to equipment maintenance and even the management of travel arrangements—issues that bear little or no direct relation to product quality. So while TQM programs use the "quality" rhetoric to accomplish change (who can be opposed to quality?), many, if not most, such programs are actually efficiency improvement initiatives that necessitate major reorganization and restructuring.[2] We find that effective implementation of TQM generally requires fundamental changes in what Jensen and Meckling (Chapter 4 of this volume) have identified as the critical organizational rules of the game that determine performance, namely an organization's systems for allocating decision rights, its performance measurement systems, and its reward and punishment systems.

We conclude that the management practices falling under the TQM umbrella constitute an innovation in organizational technology that enables firms to increase the productivity of both labor and capital.[3] Indeed, we define TQM as a science-based, non-hierarchical, and non-market-oriented organizing technology that increases efficiency and quality. We describe TQM as science-based because individuals at all levels of the organization are trained to use scientific method in everyday decision making. It is non-hierarchical because it provides a process for allocating decision rights in ways that do not correspond to the traditional corporate hierarchy. It is non-market-oriented because it does not use prices or formal exchange mechanisms, such as transfer pricing systems, to motivate cooperation or the transfer of decision rights.

Although our research has led us to become supporters of TQM, we recognize that it is but one element of a wide variety of efficiency-increasing organizing technologies. TQM cannot remedy all organizational shortcomings, and it does not generate value for all firms. Indeed, taken separately, few elements of a TQM program appear new, although our interpretation and characterization of them as changing the organizational rules of the game are new. For example, organizations have long restructured to decentralize decision making, or have assembled teams of individuals from different functional areas to address difficult problems. The ability of TQM to generate lasting change and create value lies in the effective combination of both new and old management practices.

Quantitative data on the effect of TQM are relatively scarce. This is somewhat surprising in light of its widespread implementation, and the obvious imperative for a TQM organization to apply the principles of quality management to measure the success or failure of TQM itself. Baldwin and Clark (1992) analyze field-based evidence on investments in organizational capabilities such as TQM and find that such investments substantially improve performance relative to the competition.[4] In addition, the financial and marketing success of many TQM firms (most notably the Japanese) provide evidence on the efficiency effects of TQM.

There is evidence that TQM is not easy to implement. For example, a study by Ernst & Young and the American Quality Foundation (1992), although presenting no formal evidence on TQM's effectiveness, argues that firms often adopt inappropriate, and therefore ineffective, quality practices (see also Fuchsberg 1992a, 1992b). Even preliminary consideration illustrates why implementing TQM is difficult; in addition to a large and continuing investment in employee training, it requires major changes in the organizational rules of the game. And because the components of TQM are interdependent, problems in implementing one or more components can cripple the effectiveness of the entire program. Moreover, while some quality experts discuss organizational issues relevant to the success of TQM (see, for example, Juran 1989, pp. 42–80), the development of a systematic approach to understanding and solving TQM's organizational problems lags behind the development of its statistical tools and techniques. One of our objectives is to clarify and emphasize the organizational changes required to implement TQM effectively.

Because quality management is process-oriented, it is difficult to gain a strong understanding of how it works without examples or case studies. An analogy can be made to the legal process. The memorization of laws, regulations, and judicial procedures does not provide a satisfactory understanding of the legal process; it is also necessary to study the details of their application to specific cases. For this reason, where relevant, we draw on examples from the firms we have studied, especially Sterling Chemicals, Inc. Sterling is a manufacturer of commodity chemicals which redesigned its organization to turn a floundering quality program into a successful one, and we use it as a vehicle to lay out our analysis of quality programs.

The rest of the chapter proceeds as follows. In Section 11.2, we present background information on Sterling Chemicals and discuss methodological issues relevant to our study of the company. In Section 11.3, we discuss the use of theory and science in decision making. We also discuss how TQM's simplification and systematization of science make it possible to effectively train all employees to use science in everyday decision making. In Sections 11.4 through 11.6, we analyze the rules of the game necessary for the effective functioning of TQM programs. Section 11.4 defines specific knowledge and explains the importance of its efficient utilization; Section 11.5 analyzes the process of allocating decision rights in TQM organizations; and Section 11.6 discusses changes in performance measurement and reward and punishment systems necessary for effective TQM. Section 11.7 presents conclusions and directions for future research. A brief appendix provides additional information about Sterling Chemicals' TQM efforts and financial performance.

11.2 A Brief History of Sterling Chemicals and Our Study

Sterling Chemicals, Inc. was founded in 1986 in a $213 million leveraged buyout of Monsanto Corporation's Texas City plant. The plant is located on Galveston Bay and manufactures seven commodity chemicals and their co-products. The plant has the world's largest styrene monomer unit, and is the only domestic producer of synthetic lactic acid and tertiary-butylamine.[5] In 1987, its first year of operation, Sterling employed 950 people and had sales of $413 million. (For a more complete discussion of Sterling's history, culture, and management practices, see Keating and Wruck 1993.)

Implementing TQM at Sterling Chemicals posed a formidable challenge because inflexibility and resistance to change were deeply embedded in the plant's culture. The factors contributing to this recalcitrance included a highly unionized work force with strict work rules, a long history of adversarial labor-management relations, and Monsanto's false start on a quality initiative at the plant in the early 1980s, which

Table 11.1   Sampling of Titles of over 40 Employees Interviewed as Part of the Data Collection Process (in Alphabetical Order)

Accounts Payable Clerk

Area Cost Accountant

Carpenter and President of Carpenter's Union

Chairman of the Board, Sterling Chemical, Inc., and Chairman of the Sterling Group

Chief Chemist

Controller

Director of Human Resources

Maintenance Supervisor

Manager of Maintenance and Engineering

Manufacturing Manager

Operator

President and Chief Executive Officer

Quality Facilitator

Systems and Control Accounting Manager

Vice President of Finance and Chief Financial Officer

Vice President of Operations and Texas City Plant Manager

made employees skeptical about another attempt to implement TQM. To allay employees' fears that a successful quality program would reduce employment, management promised that there would be no layoffs due to TQM. Any necessary reductions in labor would be made through attrition. The company also created three quality facilitator positions and formed a quality steering committee composed of the plant's top managers to oversee the quality program.

We began studying Sterling Chemicals in 1990 and visited the company's headquarters and the Texas City plant on three separate occasions. In addition, top managers have made three trips to the Harvard Business School, and we have communicated extensively by telephone and mail. Over the course of the project, we reviewed internal documents and interviewed over 40 Sterling employees, whose titles are summarized in Table 11.1. We use employees' words when possible to communicate their experiences with TQM. We do this because their statements not only present the facts, but also provide verifiable data on their views of whether and how TQM affected their actions and decision making. The individuals quoted here have reviewed and approved the accuracy of their quotations.

To ensure the integrity of the data collection process, management agreed at the beginning of the project that the company would review our work to correct inaccuracies, but would not dictate the substance of our analysis or conclusions. It was also understood that the company would retain the right to remove or disguise any internal data that would potentially damage the firm's competitive position. Little of this was required.

11.3   Using Science to Create Human Capital and Knowledge

Theory and Science in Management Decision Making

No purposeful action—that is, one meant to achieve an end or goal—can be taken without the implicit or explicit use of a theory. By theory (or hypothesis; we use the two interchangeably here) we mean a statement of the form "if A then B" that is refutable by data. Any time a manager takes an action to accomplish some end, he or she implicitly, if not explicitly, has in mind a theory predicting that the action taken is more likely to achieve the desired end than would another action. Behavioral evidence suggests that individuals often take actions on the basis of theories that are unrecognized, unstated, untested, and often wrong.[6] Actions based on poor theories lead to decisions that destroy value. One solution is to educate employees at all levels of the organization to make regular, effective use of science in decision making and problem solving in order to improve their ability to create and use better theories.[7] Effective TQM programs implement this solution.

Systematizing Science Through TQM

Superficially, it appears that the primary purpose of TQM is to encourage large numbers of employees to use simplified statistical methods. Indeed, a prerequisite for initiating TQM is training the work force in the use of statistical tools and problem-solving methods. As we have said, however, effective TQM moves beyond this to teach employees

Table 11.2   Two Problem-Solving Sequences by TQM Experts

Juran (1989, pp. 59–60)	Mizuno (1988, pp. 155–156)
. Analyze the symptoms	1. Seek out problem points
. Theorize as to causes	2. List possible causes
. Test the theories	3. Identify the primary causes of the problem
. Establish the cause(s)	4. Devise measures to correct the problem
. Simulate a remedy	5. Implement the corrective measures
. Test the remedy under operating conditions	6. Check the results
. Establish controls to hold the gain	7. Institutionalize the new measures

how to apply science to improve everyday decision making. Employees faced with a problem are taught to formulate hypotheses, collect and analyze data, test hypotheses, and then to formulate new hypotheses based on their findings.

Leading figures in the quality movement each present a sequence of problem-solving steps. While the wording of the steps differs, examination of them makes apparent that each is systematizing science in a simplified way. The problem-solving sequences of two quality movement leaders, Juran and Mizuno, shown in Table 11.2, illustrate this point.

The steps outlined in Table 11.2, which are similar to those provided in other quality writings, parallel the procedures followed by researchers in the hard sciences. Both Juran and Mizuno emphasize the benefits of fact-based decision making and their systematized decision processes, although they do not explicitly recognize their processes as scientific method (see, for example, Mizuno 1988, p. 18; Juran 1989, p. 170).

In addition to improving the quality of analysis underlying decision making, the application of science reduces the likelihood that politics, power, or fear will impede effective decision making. Both quality and organizational behavior experts view such forces as major impediments to performance improvement (see, for example, Suzaki 1987, pp. 219, 224; Mizuno 1988, p. 24). Argyris (1990), a leading behavioral researcher, finds that individuals routinely inhibit learning by making the theories underlying organizational practices undiscussable. This undiscussability arises from a fear that disclosure of inefficient or irrational practices will impose pain and embarrassment on everyone involved.[8] TQM's reliance on scientific analysis and its rejection of scapegoating behavior encourage and reward (rather than discouraging and punishing) the identification and discussion of problems.

TQM's systematization of science makes it easier for everyone, from hourly employees to the chief executive, to learn and apply scientific method without years of training in all its subtleties. We observed many TQM analyses conducted by hourly employees (often with no more than a high school education) that demonstrated extremely effective use of science. Indeed, it appears that TQM programs are better at teaching the use of science than colleges and universities. This is not to say that a few days of TQM training are sufficient to make employees experts. The short courses teaching TQM methods and analytical tools constitute only a small part of TQM training. Everyday work provides practice and further training. In addition, many organizations not only offer ongoing TQM education, but employ expert quality coaches or facilitators. These facilitators assist and teach employees engaged in TQM activities day-to-day.

TQM also systematizes and simplifies the set of analytical tools used to organize ideas and information, and to collect and analyze data. Once a problem has been identified, the first step is generally to create a flow-chart of the process or activity associated with the problem. Second, the team brainstorms—a process in which team members create hypotheses of possible causes without judging their validity (Juran 1989, p. 60, describes brainstorming as "a process for theorizing"). Causal hypotheses or theories generated in the brainstorming process are then sorted and categorized using a cause-and-effect diagram (also called a fishbone or Ishikawa diagram). Then data are collected and analyzed.

The tools used at the data analysis stage include scatter diagrams, histograms, statistical control charts, and Pareto diagrams, which graph the frequency distribution of factors causing the problem under study. This data-driven approach allows employees to prioritize alternative hypotheses, and to focus scarce organizational resources on eliminating important, correctable causes of a problem.

Another way in which TQM systematizes science is by implementing simple rules of thumb. Economists have long speculated that habits and rules of thumb improve efficiency by conserving scarce cognitive resources.[9] TQM's rules of thumb are no exception; they provide an efficient way to teach scientific inquiry and a simple vocabulary to reference a complex set of ideas. Take, for example, the popular "5-whys" or the "5-w's and 1-h" (who, what, where, when, why, and how). Following the "5-whys" requires a team that asks "what causes bottlenecks in this production process?" to push to find the root causes of a problem. An answer such as "because Joe's machine always breaks down" is not sufficient. The team must then ask, "what causes Joe's machine to break down so frequently?" and so forth until they have reached the answer to "5-whys." These rules of thumb encourage deeper inquiry as employees struggle to identify the fundamental theory of cause and effect that underlies a business problem. This, in turn, encourages the construction of complex theories that are useful in problem solving. Getting four levels below what seems to be the obvious cause of a problem increases the likelihood that employees will find an effective solution by treating the real causes rather than mere symptoms of a problem.

Example: Using Science—Sterling's Scaffolding Team

At Sterling's Texas City plant, setting up scaffolding is the first task in most repair and maintenance jobs. If the required scaffolding is not available, the job falls behind schedule and tradesmen end up waiting rather than working. Prior to the formation of the scaffolding team, scaffolding was available for only 43% of scheduled jobs. The scaffolding team's charter was to determine the reason for scaffolding shortages and recommend a solution.

Gilbert Bills, a carpenter with 14 years of experience at the plant and president of his union, led the scaffolding team. Below we excerpt his discussion with us about the scaffolding team's work. Recall Juran's and Mizuno's seven steps for applying the scientific method and note that they are virtually identical to the steps followed by the scaffolding team.

Carpenters always complained about not being able to find enough scaffolding. The shortages were so bad that we were spending more time trying to find scaffolding than we spent erecting it. The necessary scaffolding was never at the scaffolding storage racks near the project site, so we usually had to check storage racks throughout the plant. We calculated that $500,000 worth of labor was being spent each year looking for scaffolding. So we put together a quality team to see if we could correct the problem.

The first task of the team was to develop a detailed flow-chart of the process. Then we brainstormed, listing all our ideas about what might be causing the problem. We used a fishbone chart to refine and organize our brainstorming list. We found that in 57% of all maintenance projects there was not enough scaffolding available at the scaffolding storage area nearest the project site. In 19% of the cases we got the necessary scaffolding from other nearby racks, and in 24% of the cases we asked the truck department to search the plant for the scaffolding we needed.

We thought the problem was obvious—the plant didn't have enough scaffolding. Our team proposed buying $100,000 worth of additional scaffolding. We also proposed constructing a centralized scaffolding storage area where all the plant's scaffolding would be kept.

Management tries to avoid spending money on improvements unless it is absolutely necessary, so they asked us to confirm that the problem really was due to too little scaffolding. So we went back and set up a program to monitor scaffolding availability over time. We counted scaffolding units at each of the storage locations on a daily basis and plotted them on a statistical control chart.

What we found was that we had more than enough scaffolding on site, but that it was frequently in the wrong place at the wrong time. This made sense to a lot of guys. We all knew that there were guys out there who hoarded scaffolding. If you ever needed a cross brace, you knew that Charley would have some. And if you needed a ladder section, you knew that Bob was a specialist in those. They hoarded what they used frequently so that they wouldn't have to go scavenging. But this caused shortages at other storage racks. In fact, we found that, if the scaffolding was properly distributed, the plant had 133 extra units of scaffolding.

We showed these results to all of the carpenters. We explained that as long as people kept scavenging and hoarding, the problem would not go away. We got everybody to agree to stop. Then we determined how much scaffolding was required at each storage location to meet typical demands and stocked each location to that level. We also established a central surplus scaffolding storage area. If the necessary scaffolding was not available at the local storage area, carpenters were required to get additional parts from the central storage area rather than scavenging from other local storage locations.

The results have been significant. Scaffolding availability has risen to 97%. We haven't had to buy any more scaffolding, so already we've saved $100,000. In fact, in the course of restocking the locations we found lots of scaffolding equipment that we had rented from a local supplier but never returned. We'd been paying rent on this equipment for years. It has all been returned now. We've painted all our own scaffolding Sterling blue, so that if we ever have to rent extra scaffolding again, we'll be able to keep better track of it. And now we spend almost no time searching for scaffolding.

The decentralized, scientific process through which the scaffolding team came to its final recommendation is critical. A quality team identifies with the ideas that emerge from its work. And unlike ideas imposed on them by management, team members are more committed to the successful implementation of their own ideas. However, as the example makes clear, the quality process is not totally unmanaged. One of Sterling's three quality facilitators along with a quality committee provide guidance, but they do not conduct analysis or suggest solutions. Quality facilitator Harry Conrad described why the scaffolding team was encouraged to re-evaluate its findings:

The inclination of any team is to throw money or people at the problem. The sponsor and the quality facilitator working with the team will push team members for a harder look at the problem. If solving the problem really requires spending a lot of money or hiring additional people we want to know that, but we've found it is generally not an effective solution to most problems we've tackled.

The scaffolding team was persuaded to collect data and test their initial hypothesis that the firm should purchase $100,000 of additional scaffolding. On the basis of their own analysis, the team decided on a different solution. The scientific process revealed the previously undiscussable hoarding as a potential cause of scaffolding shortages. Because the idea to stop hoarding scaffolding came from peers who had studied the problem in depth, other employees accepted the solution more easily than if it had been discovered and dictated by upper-level management.

11.4 Utilizing Specific Knowledge Effectively

The Role of Specific Knowledge in Decision Making

Centralized decision-making systems in large, complex organizations run a risk of failure that turns on their inability to utilize knowledge effectively. As Hayek (1945) shows, centrally planned economic systems cannot access and utilize valuable bits of diffusely held knowledge that he calls "knowledge of particular circumstances of time and place." Extending Hayek's analysis, in Chapter 4, Jensen and Meckling focus on the cost of transferring knowledge, which includes both the cost of communicating and the cost of assuring that the receiving agent can use the knowledge effectively. Following Jensen and Meckling, we define "general knowledge" as knowledge that is inexpensive to transfer between agents, for example prices and quantities. We define "specific knowledge" as knowledge that is costly to transfer, for example idiosyncrasies of customers, machines, or processes.

As Jensen and Meckling have shown, a decentralized market economy is founded on a system of alienable decision rights. As people trade decision rights, they create a system that helps move decision rights to the individual(s) who value them most highly (at least partly because the individual(s) possess specific knowledge relevant to the exercise of the right). This process of exchange determines prices which themselves measure the performance of the decision maker who owns the right. Because the owner can capture the proceeds offered in exchange for his or her right, the system also capitalizes the costs and benefits of decision making on the owner. Such alienable decision rights, however, do not exist inside organizations. Indeed, as Jensen and Meckling point out, the refusal to delegate alienability along with the decision right to agents in an organization is the characteristic that distinguishes an organization from a market. The organizational rules of the game must, therefore, be structured to provide individuals with incentives to create and use specific knowledge effectively.

Valuable specific knowledge exists at all levels of the organization. For example, specific knowledge about corporate strategy or interdependencies across departments or divisions is likely to reside with upper management, while specific knowledge of a particular machine is likely to reside with employees on the factory floor. Because transfer costs are high, specific knowledge can best be utilized by colocating decision rights with the relevant specific knowledge. Partitioning out decision rights, however, leads to conflicts of interest and agency problems, which then require control systems. Because the three components of the rules of the game are interdependent, an organization that changes its allocation of decision rights will likely find it desirable to institute new performance measurement and reward and punishment systems. As we discuss later, TQM systems frequently ignore the importance of changing the reward and punishment systems.

Utilizing Specific Knowledge at Low Levels of the Organization

TQM experts deride managers' tendency to over-centralize, or equivalently their reluctance to relinquish control and decentralize decision making.[10] Our discussion of the importance of utilizing specific knowledge explains why some amount of decentralization is generally desirable. In addition to TQM, other common efforts to effectively utilize valuable specific knowledge at lower levels of the organization include movements to adopt employee empowerment, participative management, and suggestion systems. Using our terminology, the effective implementation of such policies encourages the colocation of decision rights with the relevant specific knowledge. It is very important to note that, in TQM organizations, when the relevant specific knowledge does not exist, application of science aids in its creation.

Two types of mistakes lead managers to over-centralize: systematic overestimates of the agency costs associated with delegation and systematic underestimates of the value of specific knowledge located at low levels of the organization. The writings of quality experts and our own observations are replete with examples illustrating the benefits of decentralizing decision rights to individuals with the relevant specific knowledge. For example, Wruck (1994) recounts a Sealed Air manager's observation of changes in employees' behavior following the adoption of a TQM program:

> I've found that it's important to have decisions made at the lowest possible level. The operator has to adjust constantly. We make billions of [units] per year on several machines. The operator needs to make the

right decision at the right moment. Only the operator knows if a bearing needs replacement, and can replace it before it breaks. After [TQM] we took 20 operators and had our first training seminar. They shared ideas and concepts. They were so interested that they stayed at the table talking through the break. We let our operators know that we wanted to improve one of our products. We had been making it largely by hand and we wanted ideas for how to make it on our automated equipment. Within two weeks we had three sample products from our plants. A third shift operator was coming in during his time off to run quality control on the samples. Our quality is up, productivity is up, and the level of excitement is up.

Keating and Wruck (1993) interviewed a manager at Sterling Chemicals, who provides other examples:

The quality process works, but you must be capable of understanding the data. People must be willing to work together, willing to break down barriers. We have to accept the fact that much of the expertise resides in the people who are doing the work. I can relate story after story in which higher levels of management could not solve the problem, but accounting clerks, storeroom clerks, maintenance craftsmen, lab analysts, and operators could. Previous management put together a group of chemical engineering PhDs to find a way to get the lactic acid concentrator to work better. They couldn't do it. Solutions identified by one of our quality teams saved us $2.5 million per year. The ideas came from hourly workers who spend every day of the week working with the process, not from engineers.

Assigning decision rights becomes more complex when the specific knowledge required to solve a problem and/or implement its solution is dispersed across individuals. In these situations TQM calls for the assembly of a team of individuals, each of whom possesses relevant bits of specific knowledge. Decision rights are then assigned to the team. This results in a closer colocation of decision rights with the relevant specific knowledge than would assignment of the decision rights to a particular individual.[11] Hackman (1986), an expert on teamwork, finds that the availability of expert coaches is critical to the success of self-managed teams. Consistent with this, we observe that quality coaches or facilitators, who possess specific knowledge about the TQM process itself, provide strong support in team efforts to create and utilize specific knowledge. The extensive use of group or team-based problem solving by successful TQM organizations provides indirect evidence that the benefits of assimilating diffusely held specific knowledge are often greater than the costs of training and time spent on such efforts.[12]

Example: Creating Specific Knowledge—Sterling's Pump Failure Team

Pump failures in the phthalic anhydride production process cost Sterling at least an average of $149,000 per year (an average of 14.9 failures per year at $10,000 in repair costs per failure). These costs do not include the opportunity cost of downtime or the cost of accidents potentially associated with the failures. The charter of the pump failure quality team was to identify the reason for frequent pump failures and implement solutions.

The impetus for solving the pump failure problem came from plant-level management. In their initial attempt to address the problem, they formed a team consisting solely of engineers. After almost a year, this team was unable to recommend any effective solutions. Then a second team was formed which had nine members, only two of whom were engineers. The remaining members were hourly employees who worked with the pumps regularly. Quality facilitator Harry Conrad described the history of both pump failure teams:

In 1988, a team of engineers and manufacturing supervisors [also engineers by training] was formed to address the pump failure problem. This team immediately concluded that each of the 22 pump failures that occurred over the last year was due to a special or one-of-a-kind cause. There was some finger pointing by team members trying to assign blame. Maintenance engineers claimed that production personnel didn't know how to operate the pumps, and production supervisors blamed maintenance people for poor repair work. Eventually they developed an action plan based on their findings.

During the first few months of 1989, the failure rate continued at about one per month. Although there appeared to be some improvement, the failure rate was still too high. In mid-1989 a quality facilitator was assigned to the pump failure problem. A second team was formed. This new team consisted primarily of hourly personnel: three operators from the production unit, four machinists, one mechanical engineer, and a technical services engineer.

The first action of the new team was to get pump failure data. They went all the way back to 1977. They found that 22 failures per year was not far out of the ordinary. The average failure rate since 1977 was 14.9 per year. The first team had been wrong in concluding that the failures were due to "special" causes. The failures were due to our established methods for installing, starting, and operating the pumps.

Once the team recognized that it was a systems problem, they moved to identify sources of "common cause" variation. They identified inconsistencies in both operating and maintenance procedures. Standardizing startup and repair procedures were "gimmies"—they took these inconsistencies out of the system. But it was apparent that this alone would not eliminate the failures.

Based on their knowledge and the data they had collected, the team brainstormed and listed 57 theories that potentially explained the high pump failure rates. The team reviewed and edited the brainstorming list, testing each theory against the data. Through this process, they reduced the brainstorming list to four potential causes of failure: (1) the pump seal installation procedure, (2) pump suction pressure, (3) excessive pump vibration, and (4) missing or broken equipment upstream from the pump.

They then experimented to determine which of these causes were important determinants of pump failure. Testing the pump suction theory rejected it as a cause of failure. The broken or missing equipment theory was eliminated through inspection. Since testing the two remaining theories required making changes and observing the results of those changes upstream from the pump over time, the team developed recommendations to address both the pump seal installation procedures and excessive pump vibration. The recommendations were implemented in early 1990. Since then we have had no pump failures.

Sterling's second pump failure team provides an example of the value of mobilizing specific knowledge from lower levels of the hierarchy and of creating new knowledge through TQM's problem-solving process. From the implementation of the second team's recommendations to date (almost four years), there have been no pump failures.

11.5 Solving the Decision Rights Assignment Problem

One of the more difficult problems in implementing TQM is how to change an organization's system for assigning decision rights. The writings of quality experts seem to encourage massive and largely indiscriminate decentralization. Such decentralization can easily destroy value. The optimal policy is far more subtle: decentralization is the efficient approach to creating value when individuals at lower levels both possess (or can create) the relevant specific knowledge at a low cost and can be motivated to use their decision rights to further the organization's objective; otherwise, more centralized decision making is efficient. Successful TQM firms must establish a system for assigning decision rights that curbs managers' tendency to over-centralize, but at the same time provides a structure to guard against excessive decentralization.

In the next subsection we present an example of the costs of excessive decentralization experienced by Sterling Chemicals shortly after it adopted TQM. The following subsection analyzes managers' tendency to over-centralize and TQM programs' tendencies to decentralize excessively with a specific discussion of how Sterling Chemicals resolved these problems.

A Failed Allocation of Decision Rights: Team Mania at Sterling

The first two years of Sterling's TQM program were less than successful, in spite of a commitment by top management, widespread training, the appointment of quality facilitators, and the formation of the quality steering committee. The problem was not that employees refused to participate (as one might have anticipated based on Sterling's culture). On the contrary, employee enthusiasm for TQM was so high that at one point a large fraction of the plant's 950 employees were involved in 77 quality teams, each composed of six to ten people.

Looking back, managers describe this time as a period of "team mania." Quality facilitator Harry Conrad described the situation this way:

> There are really two important components to any quality program: the technical part and the people part. We started with the technical part—this is what our consultants were really expert at—you have to have the technical tools intact or you can't get anywhere. Even with the best

intentions and advice of a consulting firm who had done it many times before, we made a lot of mistakes. I think our major error was that we didn't get people empowered fast enough.

There were so many teams there was no way we could provide each one with the direction and support required to implement their solutions. A team would develop a recommendation and then be told "there's no buy-in, you have no support." Also, there were a few people everyone wanted on their team and a lot of people no one wanted. We had some guys on 19 teams and 19 guys on no teams.

Not only were there too many teams for managers to direct, but many teams worked diligently on relatively unimportant or poorly defined problems. Moreover, teams that did manage to develop valuable ideas had no organizational support for their implementation. An example is Sterling's accounts payable team, which was formed to work on the problem of late invoice payments. At the time of that team's formation in 1988, 21% of Sterling's invoices were paid late. This compromised the company's ability to get the best prices from its suppliers.

An accounts payable clerk who served on the team described one aspect of its work:

> After collecting data and applying statistical control methods, we discovered that the main cause of late payment was late approval. Operations managers were slow in signing invoices for raw materials ordered, and this caused delay in processing payment. Frequently such signatures were redundant because the manager had signed the purchase order and receipt of the materials had already been confirmed. We designed a new policy which eliminated the need for the invoice signature when the manager had already authorized the purchase order.

Implementing this new policy required that operations managers adopt new procedures. When team members proposed their new policy, they found these managers were unwilling to cooperate—no team composed of clerks and accountants could make them change their behavior. Because the team had no support from higher-level managers, their project got stuck and they became disillusioned.

In spite of its severe problems in implementing TQM, Sterling won Ford's QI quality award during this period. Although the award was greeted with enthusiasm, managers later viewed it as certifying that employees understood and used certain technical tools, not that Sterling's TQM initiative was effective.

Solving Team Mania: Separating Decision Management from Decision Control

When resource allocation goes unchecked as it did during Sterling's period of team mania, value is destroyed because specific knowledge at higher levels of the organization is ignored, and because there are conflicts of interest that lead to agency problems. Particularly important is the allocation of employee time toward TQM efforts and away from other activities. If any person in an organization can allocate resources to work on any issue with whomever he or she pleases, it is obvious that TQM will fail. For example, individuals or teams will expend effort solving problems which they believe are important, interesting, and fun, but which are unimportant from an overall company perspective. As another example, individuals or teams will choose to work on a problem even though it is poorly defined and/or they have no comparative advantage in solving it. In addition, individual employees are often unable to judge correctly the best procedures to ensure successful implementation of their proposed solutions. If both the choice of problems to address and the implementation of potential solutions are not carefully controlled, agency problems will result in the waste of resources. Moreover, the employees involved become frustrated and develop a reluctance to participate in further TQM efforts when, as with Sterling's accounts payable team, their suggestions are ignored.

Successful TQM organizations establish a process for allocating decision rights that meets three essential objectives. First, the process ensures that individual and team efforts focus on important issues or problems, taking into account relevant interdependencies. Second, it assures that TQM efforts address issues or problems that are important, well-defined, and likely to be solvable.[13] Third, it prevents the corporate hierarchy from interfering with TQM. Sterling addressed team mania by forming a hierarchy of quality committees and adopting a requirement that each quality team both recruit a management sponsor and develop a one-page team chartering document. Below, we analyze the contribution of each of these organizational mechanisms to the effective allocation of decision rights.

Before examining the allocation of decision rights in depth, it is useful to develop more detailed definitions. Following Fama and Jensen in Chapter 7, we break the right to allocate resources to a particular project (or problem-solving effort) into four separate decision-making rights: initiation rights, ratification rights, implementation rights, and monitoring rights. An initiation right is the right to propose that a project be undertaken. A ratification right is the right to approve or reject a project that has been initiated. An implementation right is the right to undertake the project and see that it is effectively integrated into the organization. A monitoring right is the right to monitor a project's implementation and evaluate its success or failure.

Inside an organization, an effective allocation of decision rights controls agency problems by separating initiation and implementation rights (together termed "decision management rights") from ratification and monitoring rights (together termed "decision control rights") by allocating them to different individuals or groups. In other words, an efficient allocation of decision rights separates decision management from decision control, while utilizing valuable specific knowledge. These definitions prove useful in analyzing typical TQM failures and understanding TQM successes. For example, during Sterling's team mania, the right to initiate a problem-solving effort also carried with it the right to ratify the effort. This resulted in large agency costs as individuals worked unchecked on their ideas or problems of choice. At the same time, these individuals were denied implementation rights, with the result that the ideas or problem solutions they developed had little or no impact on the organization. Effective decision control requires monitoring the initiation phase of the process and independent ratification of the proposed TQM project by a person or committee that possesses the relevant specific knowledge of the overall firm interest.

Focusing Resources on Important Problems

Assuring that resources are allocated to important problems without losing valuable specific knowledge requires separating the right to initiate a TQM effort from the right to ratify and monitor the allocation of resources toward that effort. Simply centralizing initiation rights will not be effective because the limited capacity of the human brain makes it impossible for managers to be aware of all problems and the costs they impose on the firm. This means that sometimes the relevant specific knowledge at lower levels of the organization is the awareness that a problem exists. For example, Keating and Wruck (1993) interviewed a Sterling manager who observes:

> It is important to understand that from the top of this organization things look better than they actually are. We aren't over budget, the plant is still producing. The costs of the conflicts are hidden costs. The only people who understand them are people at the grass-roots level.

Solving the decision rights allocation problem, therefore, requires the widespread distribution of initiation rights to take advantage of widespread specific knowledge. Ratification rights must be assigned to individuals or groups with the specific knowledge relevant to assessing both the value of the effort to the organization, and the likelihood that the problem is solvable. The latter requires specific knowledge concerning whether a team of individuals with relevant skills and knowledge can be assembled to both analyze the problem and implement its solution. This generally results in the allocation of ratification rights to individuals or groups with a higher position in the hierarchy than the initiator. Requiring that all TQM initiatives be ratified by a higher-level employee helps ensure that the organization's overall objective is considered. If, for example, a TQM effort is to address a problem crossing functional or departmental lines, it would have to be ratified by an individual (or group) with all the relevant functions or departments under her (or their) purview.

Sterling Chemicals separated decision management from decision control by creating a hierarchy of quality committees, one of which approves each quality initiative. Table 11.3 presents a description of each committee, its membership, and examples of the types of problems it ratifies and monitors. The quality committees are structured in a hierarchical fashion, beginning with department-level committees and culminating in a firm-wide committee. This hierarchy of quality committees, in effect, undercuts the corporate hierarchy by resolving the agency problems emanating from individual managers' narrow, self-interested desire to maintain power.

Initiation rights at Sterling are widespread; anyone in the plant can draw attention to a problem or suggest a TQM project. The ratification and monitoring rights over quality initiatives, however, are assigned to the lowest-level quality committee with the relevant specific knowledge. The result is that work on an issue or problem confined to a single department is ratified and monitored by a departmental committee;

Table 11.3 Sterling Chemicals' Hierarchy of Quality Committees; Each Quality Committee Charters Teams and Monitors the Quality Committees at the Next Lowest Level

Name	Membership	Role	Monitored by	Frequency of meetings	Example of teams chartered[a]
Quality Council (same as Corporate Management Board)	7 members: CEO, all 5 VPs, and Director of Human Resources	Approves policy, sets priorities, monitors results of major quality teams	Board of Directors	Biweekly	• Long-Range Environmental Planning Team • Computer-Aided Manufacturing Team
Plant-Wide Quality Steering Committee	19 members: VP Operations, all 3 Manufacturing Managers, hourly and salaried representatives, all 3 Quality Facilitators	Recommends policy, charters and manages quality teams with interdepartmental issues, identifies quality opportunities, sets plant priorities	Quality Council	At least weekly	• Freeze Protection Team • Vacuum Truck Team • *Pump Failure Team*
Manager-Level Quality Steering Committees	10–15 members each: *in manufacturing*—Manufacturing Manager, Superintendents, other hourly and salaried employees; *in maintenance*—Manager of Maintenance and Engineering, Superintendents, other hourly and salaried employees	Charters and manages quality teams with no interdepartmental issues, identifies quality opportunities	Plant-Wide Quality Steering Committee	Three times a month	• *Accounts Payable Team* • *Scaffolding Team* • Laboratory Measurements Team • Maintenance Scaffolding Team
Superintendent-Level Quality/Staff Committees	6–10 members: *in manufacturing*—Manufacturing Superintendent, Foremen; *in maintenance*—Maintenance Superintendent, Maintenance Supervisors, Foremen	Charters and manages quality teams at the local level, identifies quality opportunities	Manager-Level Quality Steering Committees	Weekly	• Tool Room Team • Equipment Repair Request Form Team

Source: Company documents.

a. Teams listed in italics are discussed in detail in the text.

work on a problem that crosses departmental boundaries is ratified and monitored by a divisional committee; and work on a problem that crosses divisions is ratified and monitored by a corporate-wide committee. If an initiative crossing departmental boundaries is brought before a departmental quality committee, this committee will refer it to the appropriate higher-level committee. Each committee has at least one quality facilitator as a member. Taken together, committee members possess a mix of specific knowledge about the technical and business aspects of issues likely to be raised. To represent specific knowledge at lower levels and to help communicate the criteria used to ratify work on problems to other employees, each committee has several lower-level non-management employees as members.

Assuring That Problems are Well-Defined and the Team has the Right Members

Another important role of the ratification process is to help formulate a well-understood, well-defined objective before work begins. This requires not only defining the problem to be addressed, but determining what can reasonably be expected in terms of outcomes. This reduces waste and increases the likelihood of a successful outcome for at least four reasons. First, a well functioning ratification process forces the clarification of vague, ambiguous, and poorly defined initiatives early on. For example, at Sterling this is accomplished when the relevant quality committee refuses to ratify an initiative and responds with a statement of the request's inadequacies and perhaps recommendations for improvement. Those initiatives that cannot be clarified are dropped before significant costs are incurred. Second, problems that are too large or complex to handle at once can be redefined or broken down into manageable parts, again before significant costs are incurred. Third, once work begins, efforts are sharply focused and the individuals involved have a clear understanding of what is expected. Finally, ratification allows informed individuals or quality committees to consider carefully the assignment of individuals to a TQM effort, taking into account not only expertise in the problem-solving aspects of the effort, but also who will ultimately be responsible for implementing solutions. Such careful selection of team members and definition of the scope of the problem helps curb the natural defensive tendency of individuals; it limits their tendency to deny responsibility, to view the source of a problem as lying outside their team, department, or area, and thereby to lay blame and demands for change on others.

Sterling Chemicals requires the development of a one-page team chartering document as part of its ratification process. As an example, Table 11.4 presents the chartering document for the second pump failure team. Once an idea is initiated, the appropriate quality committee ratifies a preliminary allocation of resources, primarily individuals' time, to work on a one-page team chartering document. Until this chartering document is completed and ratified by the appropriate quality committee, no additional resources are allocated to the effort. Sterling's team charter document identifies the team's sponsor (a member of management), its chairperson (the highest-ranked individual team member), and the other team members. It also contains several paragraphs specifying the problem to be addressed, the scope of the effort, and expected results. Finally, it sometimes proposes deadlines for completing various stages of the project. Often a charter document goes through several rounds with a quality committee before it is ratified. This happens, for example, when the committee is not convinced the problem is important, when the problem is not well defined, when the problem does not appear solvable, or when the appropriate employees have not been recruited into the effort.

Once a chartering document is ratified, the management sponsor and an expert quality facilitator monitor the team's progress and help determine when data analysis is complete. Then each team prepares an action plan describing how and by what date its solutions will be implemented. Like the chartering document, the action plan must be ratified by the appropriate quality committee. If the quality committee does not ratify an action plan, it provides specific instructions telling the team what factors to consider further. Once the action plan is ratified, the team is responsible for its implementation, which again is monitored by the team sponsor and a quality facilitator. If the team runs into opposition, or if the support of someone outside the team is required for successful implementation, the sponsor, facilitator, and ultimately the relevant quality committee become directly involved. Once the solution is implemented and running smoothly, the quality team is disbanded. This assures that TQM teams do not permanently retain decision-making rights and become bureaucratic, inflexible features of the organization.

Table 11.4 Chartering Document for Sterling Chemicals' Pump Failure
Team—53P8/P9 Pump Failures

Purpose of project:	Find cause of why we experience nine failures per year on 53P9's and six per year on 53P8's and develop an action plan for correcting
Team members:	K. Bretz — Chairman
	C. Brown — Engineer
	B. Colianni — Operator
	H. Conrad — Facilitator
	J. Cottingham — Machinist
	R. Devries — Operator
	R. Dougherty — Machinist
	B. Hext — Machinist
	G. Holloway — Machinist
	K. Stinson — Operator
Scope of project:	Meet regularly and use basic tools, data collection, and appropriate statistical methods to accomplish the above purpose. The scope of the team's project efforts should address:
	1. History of pump failures
	2. Comparison of failure with pumps in same or similar service (check BASF New Jersey plant)
	3. Unique characteristics of 53P8/P9 versus pumps in same or similar service
	4. Pump repair procedure
	5. Startup and shutdown procedures
	6. Any other topics the team feels are appropriate
Results expected:	A reduction in failure rate of 53P8/P9
Sponsor:	Plant QSC (Quality Steering Committee)

Source: Company document.

Preventing the Old Hierarchy from Interfering with TQM

To be successful, individuals and teams involved in a quality effort must have the right to cut across or bypass the old hierarchical chain of command. TQM, therefore, requires a mechanism to seize decision rights from uncooperative individuals or groups and assign them to individuals or teams engaged in problem-solving efforts. Allowing TQM teams direct access to management at the level appropriate to the problem at hand is especially effective if the organization's most influential people, including top management, are actively involved. A hierarchy of committees involved in the ratification and monitoring of TQM initiatives and implementation, like that adopted by Sterling, brings with it monitoring of the cooperation or non-cooperation of managers in the traditional corporate hierarchy. This structure makes it difficult for managers to oppose change for narrow or self-interested reasons. Without the support of the committees and ultimately top management, normal human self-interest and defensiveness make it difficult, if not impossible, to transfer the relevant decision rights to individuals or teams involved in the problem-solving effort.

Thus, Sterling's hierarchy of quality committees gives TQM teams the management support necessary to obtain cooperation from resistant areas of the hierarchy. The membership of these committees includes managers with sufficient rank to head off opposition from the established hierarchy at any point in the teams' work. In situations where particular individuals resist implementing suggestions, as in the case of Sterling's accounts payable team, the team can escalate the issue to top management if necessary. In addition, as mentioned earlier, Sterling requires that a member of management agree to sponsor each quality initiative. This management sponsor is accountable for the initiative's success or failure. The fact that each quality effort receives sponsorship from a manager and approval from a quality committee makes it difficult to block its progress.

It was not until after these changes in the allocation of decision rights that the accounts payable team's new policy was implemented. As a result, the number of late invoice payments fell substantially. In 1992 only 2.2% of Sterling's invoices were paid late, compared to 21% in 1988. Also, the work of the scaffolding and pump failure teams described earlier did not occur until after these changes.

11.6 Performance Measurement and Rewards Systems under TQM

As we have seen, implementing TQM effectively requires changing the system for allocating decision-making rights, generally in the direction of greater delegation. Potentially, this creates large agency costs: that is, employees with greater decision rights can use those rights to serve their own, rather than the organization's, interest. The presence of these potential problems makes it desirable for TQM firms to reexamine the two remaining rules of the game: performance measurement systems and systems of rewards and punishments.

TQM Performance Measurement Systems

To encourage individuals to make lasting changes in behavior, management must redefine the organization's objective and communicate the new objective to employees. Performance measurement systems facilitate the communication process because they establish measures that define outstanding performance and set goals for improvement. TQM firms generally make major changes in performance measurement systems, moving away from traditional accounting-based measures toward measures that emphasize the close monitoring of operating efficiency, particularly for tracking progress day-to-day. Common measures include manufacturing cycle time, product failure rates, late delivery rates, order lead times, new product development times, customer complaints and dissatisfaction indices, and waste or scrap rates.

TQM performance measures differ from traditional measures in three important ways. First, they emphasize measuring productivity and quality from the standpoint of the customer. This customer-oriented approach helps prevent an organization from becoming detached and inwardly focused. Second, performance measures to track day-to-day progress are operations-oriented rather than dollar-denominated. Such measures supplement, and sometimes even replace, traditional accounting measures such as product cost, labor rates, material or labor variances, and profitability.[14] This does not mean that TQM organizations are unconcerned with dollar-denominated performance measures, such as product cost, profitability, or value. Rather, these measures are generally viewed as providing weak direction to employees as they make daily decisions. Third, TQM performance measures tend to be more disaggregate and more function- or task-specific than traditional measures, isolating the contribution of particular activities to performance. This helps employees understand what actions they can take to improve overall performance. For example, employees readily understand how their actions affect cycle time or how they can reduce waste or scrap rates. It is difficult to determine, much less communicate, whether and how a particular employee's actions affect aggregate measures such as overall profitability or firm value.

TQM organizations also adopt a new approach to setting standards.

Whereas traditional standards focus on mean overall performance (for example, the average or overall percentage of products without defects, or the average unit product cost), TQM standards are expressed in terms of both mean and variance. The objective is not only achieving a mean level of performance, but improving its predictability through reductions in process variation. For example, the "Six Sigma" standard developed by Motorola requires that the variance in process or product outcomes be low enough that six standard deviations from the mean is still within pre-set control limits (see Harry and Lawson 1992). The C_{pk} index developed by Ford Motor Company sets a similar type of standard, working to assure that outcomes three standard deviations from the mean still meet customer specifications. Standards for measures of means and variance are set aggressively and are revised frequently to make them increasingly challenging. Many TQM organizations also benchmark, comparing their performance to data available on the performance of peer or competitor firms.[15]

The performance measurement philosophy underlying TQM emphasizes the identification and measurement of weaknesses, rather than strengths.[16] This practice helps provide an organizational antidote to the universal human tendency to avoid feedback on personal errors and failures. To most economists, it will seem irrelevant if an organization chooses to report and emphasize, for example, its 4% late deliveries rather than its 96% on-time deliveries. However, in spite of the fact that logically the two measures contain the same information, it is harder for people to deny that a problem exists when weaknesses are the focus of measurement. Individuals focused on a performance measure showing 96% on-time deliveries are more likely to congratulate themselves on outstanding performance than individuals forced to focus on the 4% of deliveries that are failures.

When an organization recognizes and rewards people for finding weaknesses or problems, it becomes very difficult for individuals faced with evidence concerning a new problem or weakness to cover up or avoid it. Such defensive reactions often occur in organizations, particularly when criticisms of the organization are viewed as signs of disloyalty and are, therefore, undiscussable. When honor, recognition, and other rewards are associated with finding new weaknesses, the organization creates a culture that makes it harder for personal and organizational defensiveness to flourish.

TQM Reward and Punishment Systems

For TQM to create lasting improvements in efficiency, it is desirable to establish a system of rewards and punishments that complements the new allocation of decision rights and the new performance measurement system. We define rewards broadly to encompass all types of rewards, both monetary and nonmonetary, including the utility generated by participation in TQM activities (if any), the benefit of making one's job easier and/or safer, public recognition, raises, promotions, bonuses, profit-sharing plans, and equity-ownership programs. All these rewards are valued by employees, and therefore provide motivation or incentives.

The reward system appropriate for a TQM organization is the subject of heated debate. We expect the increased delegation of decision rights to be associated with a strengthening of the relation between rewards (of all types) and organizational performance. Many quality experts, however, advocate completely severing ties between rewards (particularly monetary rewards) and performance. In the following subsections we discuss rewards commonly used by TQM firms. We begin with nonmonetary rewards because we agree with quality leaders on their importance and because their use in TQM programs is widespread. We then tackle the more contentious subject of monetary reward systems.

Participation and Job Improvement

By changing the nature of jobs and the work itself, TQM programs provide rewards to employees. Many employees enjoy participating in the TQM process and utilizing their specific knowledge to solve problems. In addition, to the extent that solving problems makes their jobs easier, safer, or more enjoyable, TQM increases employees' effective compensation (that is, employees receive the same compensation in exchange for a more desirable job). For some employees, working in a TQM environment requires different skills, increased effort, and more stress. Changes in demands placed on employees under TQM will likely lead to turnover in the work force. Such turnover is beneficial if selecting out employees with a distaste for the problem-solving efforts involved in TQM (and selecting in employees who enjoy it) creates value.

Obtaining employee participation will be difficult if the actual or perceived outcome of the TQM efforts is layoffs. Some organizations solve this problem, as did Sterling Chemicals, by guaranteeing that TQM efforts will not lead to layoffs or firings. Obviously, this guarantee is only feasible where major reductions in employment are not necessary or can be handled by attrition, voluntary retirement, or other means. If downsizing is required, firms are often better off employing more centralized approaches to streamlining the organization, such as the currently popular re-engineering efforts, and adopting TQM only after making the required cuts.

Public Recognition

Public recognition for contributing to the firm's quality goals is strongly advocated by quality leaders and widely adopted by TQM companies. For example, Juran (1989, p. 316) identifies recognition, along with other rewards, as an "essential element of motivation for quality," and Crosby (1989, p. 11) advocates recognition as a "necessary component" of TQM. Award ceremonies held to recognize outstanding quality efforts by individuals and teams are common to TQM firms. At such ceremonies, the employees being honored generally receive not only public recognition but a small gift, such as a ring, windbreaker, or plaque. Giving public visibility to quality efforts that identify and remedy problems sends a strong message that such efforts are a valued part of employees' contribution to the firm.

Pay-for-Knowledge Systems

Some TQM organizations use pay-for-knowledge to emphasize the importance of training and learning. Such systems reward employees with increases in hourly wage rates, for example, for first memorizing the steps of a job, then performing the job under supervision, then performing the job unsupervised, then teaching the job to someone else. After completing these four steps for a particular job, employees are encouraged to repeat the process for other jobs, first in their current work team and then in other work teams. Although the monetary rewards associated with pay-for-knowledge programs are generally small, they affect behavior by breaking down the notion of seniority-based wages and emphasizing the importance of learning. Pay-for-knowledge systems are especially valuable in organizations with substantial interdependencies between tasks where flexibility in job assignment or specific knowledge of other jobs improves productivity.

Monetary Pay-for-Performance

As mentioned earlier, monetary rewards are shunned by a number of quality leaders, including Ishikawa, Crosby, and Deming, and by many organizations that adopt their recommendations. For example, one firm we observed included the following paragraph in its internal quality literature (Milliken & Company, Pursuit of Excellence Seminar Notebook, 1991, p. 306):

> We use no financial reward
> - Financial rewards tend to focus people on big changes. We want the many little ideas—not just the few big ones.
> - Financial rewards tend to work against "TEAMS."
> - Less than half of our OFI's [Opportunities for Improvement] are for cost reduction.
> - We believe that ideas and continuous improvement should be a part of every job, every day, and hence, should not have a separate financial reward system.

Other quality leaders take the opposite view. For example, Juran supports tying rewards to performance, and Mizuno emphasizes the importance of sharing the benefits resulting from TQM efforts with employees.

Our analysis and observation lead us to conclude that associating rewards, including monetary rewards, with TQM performance is an important part of encouraging individuals to change their behavior. Juran (1989, p. 211) makes a similar observation:

> The reward system not only serves its basic purpose of rewarding human performance; it also serves to inform all concerned of the upper managers' priorities. If goals are revised but the reward system is not, the result as viewed by subordinates is conflicting signals. Most subordinates resolve this conflict by following the priorities indicated by the reward system.

We find that changing a firm's allocation of decision-making rights and performance measurement system with no change in the structure of the monetary rewards system is likely to make TQM less effective.

The case against monetary rewards made by quality leaders uses two basic lines of argument: first, that money is a poor motivator; second, that numerical measures of performance are flawed and therefore must not be tied to rewards. Below we challenge the validity of each of these arguments.

In arguing against monetary rewards and for nonmonetary rewards, Crosby (1989, p. 11) states:

> For many of the recipients [of the Ring of Quality award], it is literally the biggest moment of their life. Like the rest of the [quality] program, the presentations are treated with dignity and respect. Reactions to the rings and pins has made one thing very clear: cash or financial awards are not personal enough to provide effective recognition.
>
> I do not encourage the carrot-and-stick approach. I always thought that was a dumb idea. People are thinking, caring beings, and they can tell whether you respect them or not. They work for appreciation and the sense of accomplishment they get from doing the job well. They do not work for money. They need it, and it is important, but money is a lousy motivator.

Our observation, however, is that money is not a lousy motivator, but rather that it is an extremely powerful motivator—perhaps too powerful in some circumstances (see also Chapter 8).

Crosby correctly observes that poorly designed and implemented pay-for-performance systems destroy value by rewarding people for doing the wrong things. From this, however, he mistakenly concludes that all forms of monetary pay-for-performance should be abandoned. He fails to recognize that every organization, through implicit and explicit contracts with employees, has a reward system that includes both monetary and nonmonetary rewards. The critical issue is whether or not rewards are associated with contributions to firm value. In addition, although he does not state this explicitly, much of Crosby's argument seems to presume that monetary and nonmonetary rewards are mutually exclusive. Both types of rewards are valued by employees and can be used in combination to provide motivation. Money has the advantage of being a general claim on goods and services that is valued by all employees, and it is easier to vary with performance than some non-monetary rewards such as quality of the work environment.

Deming (1952, 1982) argues that monetary incentive systems are counterproductive because performance cannot be measured accurately and is influenced by factors beyond employees' control. In addition, he argues that monetary incentives destroy teamwork. His argument lumps together all forms of monetary pay-for-performance systems, from individual piece rates to group rewards to profit-sharing and equity ownership plans, analyzing them as though they were identical approaches to compensation.

Clearly, performance is generally measured with a certain amount of error and is influenced by exogenous factors. While the flaws of a particular performance measure must be taken into account when designing a reward system, forgoing the opportunity to tie rewards to any and all performance measures is often inefficient. Adopting pay-for-performance does not necessarily mean establishing a complex system that ties a myriad of disaggregate performance measures to individual rewards. On the contrary, we observe successful TQM firms tying rewards to simple performance measures, including subjective performance evaluations or overall firm profitability (through profit-sharing) or firm value (through employee equity ownership plans). For example, many successful Japanese TQM organizations pay employees annual bonuses based on overall firm performance.

Further, it has long been understood that different types of compensation plans provide different incentives, and are, therefore, inappropriate in some situations. For example, it is easy to see how individually based piece rates can damage efforts to foster quality and teamwork. If teamwork contributes substantially to productivity, rewards based on individual performance destroy value by discouraging cooperation and teamwork. Even worse, rewards based on tournaments (that is, contests in which the highest ranking individual performance is rewarded) can encourage sabotage. Moreover, piece rates encourage employees to trade off quality for increased quantity of output and, therefore, will reduce quality when it is difficult to monitor. In contrast, rewards based on group or team performance directly encourage cooperation (Wageman and Baker 1997). Profit-sharing and equity ownership are group reward systems because they reward employees on the basis of firm-wide performance. Although such group-based compensation programs have potential free-rider problems, they encourage teamwork and do not encourage lower quality.

Unfortunately, their misunderstanding of reward systems leads Crosby and Deming to make a recommendation that damages the very organizations they are trying to help—namely, to reject any and all pay-for-performance systems. The details of design and implementation determine the success or failure of any compensation system. In particular, a well-defined pay-for-performance system can be gutted of its content and productive effects if administered in a way that destroys employees' trust in the system. In effect, this is similar to the destruction of productivity in a lawless society where property rights are weakly enforced and therefore insecure. We use the cases of two companies that have been studied in detail to illustrate this point.

Specifically, we contrast the failure of a piece rate system in an unnamed machine shop described by Roy (1952) with the success of Lincoln Electric's seemingly similar reward system (Fast and Berg 1975). While the compensation system in the machine shop actually reduced productivity, Lincoln's compensation system led it to become the highest-quality producer of arc-welding machines in the world, with a market share of 60%.

Roy's (1952) study seems to confirm the case against monetary rewards. Nominally, the machine shop's piece rate system is founded on the premise that piece work rates will not be changed unless production processes are changed. The shop's management, however, destroys the trust so vital to an effective pay-for-performance system by using trivial excuses to opportunistically reprice a job when employees discover ways to increase output and compensation.[17] In effect, management breaks the pay-for-performance contract with employees to expropriate the value of the increased productivity induced by the increased incentives. Unfortunately, this behavior eliminates the gains it was designed to expropriate. Understanding the actual rules of the game, employees limit their output to avoid the repricing of jobs. The result is the waste of time and resources in what Roy (1952, p. 427) describes as employees' "ceaseless war with management." He estimates the waste from counterproductive behavior induced by the untrustworthy piece rate system at 36% of total output. Quality leaders' experience with manufacturing environments like that of Roy's machine shop has likely played a role in their strong beliefs about the counter productive effects of pay-for-performance systems.

In contrast, Lincoln Electric embeds its pay-for-performance system in a culture of trust and makes it part of a more broadly based reward system. In addition to piece rate compensation, employees receive an end-of-year bonus that depends on cooperation with others, quality, and creativity. Employees also own over 40% of the company's stock. The threat of layoff or unemployment due to productivity increases is eliminated by a promise that after two years of service, employees are guaranteed a job (though not a level of compensation) so long as they live up to company standards.

Lincoln's piece rate system is founded on two important premises. First, piece work prices are never changed unless methods are changed or a new process is introduced. By consistently upholding this promise, management creates an environment of trust in which employees know that productivity will be rewarded, not punished by constantly increasing the "bogey." Subjective merit ratings determine the end-of-year bonus, which, if the company has a good year, doubles compensation. Second, quality is effectively monitored through a program in which employees affix an identifying tag to their output. Products carry a lifetime warrantee, and defects are returned to Lincoln for free correction. If their output has quality problems, employees repair the defects in their output on their own time. Defects are reflected in individual merit ratings which significantly influence compensation.

Defects also affect the employee's bonus directly. "Forgivable" errors result in the employee losing 1% of his or her total annual bonus for each such defect. "Unforgivable" errors result in a loss of 10% of the annual bonus. Although annual total compensation is double the industry average, Lincoln's productivity per worker is five to six times that of its competitors. Thus, the experience of Lincoln Electric contradicts the views of both Crosby and Deming. Its monetary pay-for-performance system encourages employees to improve both productivity and quality and has led it to dominate the industry.

The reward system in the machine shop failed because managers opportunistically expropriated rewards that appeared excessive, while assuming their actions would not affect productivity. Lincoln's 100-year-old system has succeeded because principles opposed to such opportunistic behavior have been elevated to an almost religious status in the organization. Unfortunately, large numbers of pay-for-performance systems tend to be run like the machine shop's reward system rather than like Lincoln Electric's.

Performance Measurement and Rewards at Sterling Chemicals

In day-to-day operations and problem-solving efforts, employees at Sterling use a variety of performance measures, many of which focus on rooting out weaknesses. For example, in the accounts payable area records are kept on the number of late invoice payments. In the manufacturing area product characteristics such as color and density are measured frequently, and events such as pump failures are tracked. In the maintenance area, job completion relative to schedule is an important measure. In the sales area, customer satisfaction is closely followed.

The establishment of performance measures and standards is an important part of any TQM problem-solving effort. Each quality team, as part of its charter, identifies the performance measures appropriate to its efforts. Targets or goals for each performance measure are also identified. The success of the team is measured, at least in part, by the extent to which it is able to achieve the objectives specified in its charter. For example, the pump failure team identified reductions in the failure rate of phthalic anhydride pumps as its performance measure and set as a goal the reduction of failures to a rate at or below that of similar pumps in the plant.

None of the disaggregate performance measures, however, are directly linked to compensation. The compensation of each Sterling employee is composed of a base salary or wage, stock ownership through an employee stock ownership plan (ESOP), and a profit-sharing payout. The performance measures relevant for the reward system, therefore, are a subjective evaluation of individual performance leading to base salary or wage adjustments, appreciation in the firm's stock price, and corporate profitability.

Equity Ownership and Profit-Sharing

After the buyout in 1987, Sterling formed an ESOP that gave all employees the opportunity to buy equity in the company. Under the terms of the ESOP, Sterling matches employee equity purchases $0.60 to the dollar to a maximum of 7% of compensation. Initially, 92% of employees participated. To get 100% participation, management gave a small number of shares to each employee whether or not they bought shares themselves. Prior to its 1988 initial public offering, 17.6% of Sterling's common stock was held by non-executive employees. The rest of the shares were held primarily by managers, directors, and investors in the buyout fund.

In 1988, Sterling implemented a formal profit-sharing program for all employees. Hourly employees agreed to participate, but the plan was not incorporated into union contracts. No competing area employer pays comparable profit-sharing to hourly employees. Profit-sharing payouts are based on earnings before depreciation, interest, and taxes (EBDIT), and are a percentage of base compensation. Under the program, if Sterling achieves its target EBDIT, all employees receive a percentage of their base wage as a profit-sharing payout. In 1992, an hourly employee could earn up to 10% of base in profit-sharing, while top management could earn over 35% of base.

Base Compensation

Base compensation at Sterling is grounded in a philosophy that managers should have substantial "at risk" compensation. The higher an employee's rank in the organization, the lower his or her base compensation is set relative to the market rate. The CEO's salary, for example, is 40%–50% below market. In good years, profit-sharing payouts allow managers to earn substantially more than the market wage. In bad years, they earn considerably less. In contrast, hourly workers receive base compensation equal to the market rate. Profit-sharing payouts to hourly employees put them well above market in good years. In bad years, they earn what they would have earned elsewhere.

An Assessment of Sterling's Reward System

Between 1988 and 1992, Sterling distributed over $95,000 in cash payouts to the average hourly employee through annual profit-sharing, dividends, and the sale of stock in the company's initial public offering (see Jensen and Barry 1992; Keating and Wruck 1993). Table 11.5 summarizes these payments. Profit-sharing distributions ranged from 0% to 20% of base compensation and totaled $17,500 for the average hourly employee. The average hourly employee also received cash distributions of $77,462 through Sterling's employee equity ownership plan. Even after these payouts, as of June 1994, the typical hourly employee holds $70,200 in Sterling equity.

The effectiveness of profit-sharing for hourly employees, however, is

Table 11.5 Dividend Payments and Proceeds from Sale of Stock in Initial Public Offering Received by Average Hourly Employee, 1988–1992

Date	ESOP Payments to Average Hourly Employee[a]	Profit-Sharing Payments to Average Hourly Employee
1987 fiscal year		$2,500
1988 fiscal year		7,000
April 1988	$12,000	
July 1988	1,500	
September 1988	15,000	
October 1988	29,938[a]	
1989 fiscal year	5,265	4,200
1990 fiscal year	7,020	2,800
1991 fiscal year	4,563	1,050
1992 fiscal year	1,755	0
1993 fiscal year	421	0
Total	$77,462	$17,550
Total ESOP and profit-sharing	$95,012	
Value of remaining ESOP shares @ $10	$70,200	

Source: Sterling Chemicals, Inc., annual reports and company documents.

a. With the exception of the $29,938 payment in October 1988, ESOP payments are dividends. In October 1988, Sterling made a public offering of 21% of its common stock at $16 ($15.84 net) per share. At the time of the IPO, the average employee held 9,000 shares of stock through the ESOP. Employees were allowed to sell their ESOP holdings in proportion to the company's offering. Assuming the average employee sold 21% of his holdings, this amounts to 1,890 shares at $15.84 for a total of $29,938. Calculations for distributions following the IPO assume that the average employee continues to hold all shares not sold in the IPO (7,110 shares) and makes no further investment in the company's equity.

a subject of debate at Sterling. Managers hold mixed views on how effective it has been and whether or not it should be continued. They are concerned about the fact that despite its generous payouts, some hourly employees are not content with the plan. For example, scaffolding team leader Gilbert Bills expressed this view on TQM and profit-sharing:

> Morale is critical. The quality program has opened up a better relationship with management than we have ever had before. I am a firm believer in the union movement, but we can't keep things exactly as they've been

for 60 years. The economic environment doesn't let us do that. We have to work together more, and the quality program helps us do that. It lets hourly workers participate more. But the relationship between management and hourly workers isn't perfect yet. We get pennies and they get silver dollars. Profit-sharing is important, but more important is the improvement in our daily living conditions. We now have a safer working environment. And we participate more in decision-making. In fact, it is a bit of a sore spot to talk about profit-sharing these days. The profit-sharing is not really fair.

The dissatisfaction over the profit-sharing plan centers on the fact that the bonus as a percentage of base salary is higher for management than it is for hourly workers. Interestingly, the fact that management base salaries are below market while hourly worker wages are equal to the market has not resolved the conflict.

While concerned about the perceptions of inequity in the plan, most managers believe that profit-sharing has helped improve productivity and foster better union relations, though perhaps not as much or as quickly as they expected. Sterling's director of human resources commented:

Changing the culture is difficult because people's attitudes have to change. I think we've made real strides. In our last labor contract reopener after half a day everyone said, "Let's finish up and go back to work." Usually reopeners drag on for at least three days. Do we have all sweetness and light? No way. But we are starting to sit down and talk about things. We've already made some progress toward more cooperative bargaining. We've also made progress in changing our benefits programs. We show them the data, how much things cost, and they want to help get costs under control.

11.7 Conclusions

Taking an economic and organizational perspective, we have identified two key principles that lie behind effective TQM programs: (1) the effective use of science in everyday decision making by employees at all levels of the organization, and (2) major changes in the three components of the organizational rules of the game. TQM simplifies and systematizes the scientific method so that large numbers of employees with different backgrounds and education levels can be trained effectively.

TQM training builds human capital and provides employees with a foundation that prepares them to participate in a more decentralized organization. Changing the organizational rules of the game to support TQM generally involves the controlled decentralization of decision rights, the adoption of new performance measures, and the implementation of new reward systems that tie both monetary and non-monetary rewards to performance.

More evidence is necessary to test the generalizability of our findings and extend our analysis. It would be useful to conduct a detailed study of companies with failed or withdrawn quality programs to see which, if any, organizational elements necessary for effective TQM are missing. In addition, the effectiveness of TQM cannot be accurately assessed until researchers determine the extent to which failures result from TQM practices per se and the extent to which they are management failures. Organization-wide TQM requires that management undertake strategic decisions and cost control with the same scientific, data-driven rigor they expect of hourly employees. In practice, however, it seems that the use of TQM's philosophy and scientific approach by top management teams and boards of directors is rare.

A remaining unanswered question is why TQM has achieved widespread popularity in the 1980s and 1990s. One can conjecture that TQM spread because of technological changes that made it more feasible. Such changes include, for example, computational, measurement, and communication innovations that have vastly improved performance measurement capabilities. The development of modern manufacturing techniques, such as just-in-time and flexible manufacturing, also seems to be associated with the growth in TQM. Understanding why TQM has spread so rapidly in the last two decades will help us better understand where it works and where it doesn't.

Finally, the future of TQM in America may turn on labor law and organized labor's willingness to be flexible. Moving from job to job within the firm, learning new skills, and earning rewards based on performance are critical to TQM's success and the competitiveness of American firms. Yet such changes are strongly resisted by organized labor. For example, recent rulings by the National Labor Relations Board have forced Polaroid to disband a highly productive 40-year-old labor/management committee, and DuPont to disband seven teams dealing with issues ranging from product development to safety to employee physical fitness (Baird 1993). Returning to Sterling for a final example, that company's Japanese competitors are involving operators in repair and maintenance work. Union work rules thus far have made it impossible for Sterling to do the same, leaving it at a competitive disadvantage.

11.8   Appendix: TQM at Sterling Chemicals

TQM Teams in the Redesigned Organization

Over the five years following the redesign of its decision rights allocation process, 119 quality teams at Sterling have tackled a wide range of problems (for a comprehensive list of quality teams formed at Sterling as of September 1992, see Keating and Wruck 1993). Some of Sterling's TQM applications were quite conventional, for example, addressing inventory control and product quality control. Others—addressing scaffolding requirements, accounts payable processing, absentee control, recycling, and environmental concerns—were more unusual.

Sterling's management does not routinely estimate the costs and benefits of TQM. As a part of our research, we asked management to make such an estimate. Their best estimate of cash flow generated by quality efforts (primarily in the form of cost savings) totals over $8 million per year—almost 20% of Sterling's 1992 earnings before depreciation, interest, and taxes (EBDIT). This does not include the value of many productivity improvements, the value of improved customer relationships, or the cost of employee time spent on TQM efforts. For example, improvements in manpower scheduling led to measurably less waiting for other trades, parts, and equipment, and faster completion of maintenance jobs, but management did not attempt to estimate the value created by this improvement. Sterling's CEO gave another such example of TQM's effects on productivity:

In 1988 we had to shut down the styrene plant to change catalysts. The styrene plant makes over four million pounds of styrene per day, so every day of downtime cost the company a lot of money. An hourly employee suggested that we blow cool air into the reactor to cool down the catalyst faster. To do it, we had to build a temporary duct from a blower to the reactor, but it saved us a day in downtime. Another hourly employee suggested that we overlap shifts by half an hour on each side so that there was no downtime during the shutdown. Everyone agreed to this change in schedule, and it saved us an additional four days. Overall, we broke

Table 11.6 Selected Information on Sterling's Financial Performance, 1987–1993
(dollars in millions)

	Data for Fiscal Year Ended September 30						
	1987	1988	1989	1990	1991	1992[a]	1993
Sales[b]	$412.2	$699.0	$580.8	$506.0	$542.7	$430.5	$518
EBDIT[c]	129.0	340.1	178.8	115.5	78.8	41.5	54
Total debt	129.7	90.8	71.6	69.3	77.3	328.0	284
Profit-sharing payout to hourly employees as a % of wages	NA	20%	12%	8%	3%	0%	0
Stock price range: high/low	NA	NA	$18.75/ 8.75	$8.875/ 5.625	$7.125/ 4.500	$5.125/ $3.875	$5.00/ $3.50

Source: Sterling Chemicals, Inc., annual reports.

a. During 1992, Sterling acquired Tenneco, Inc.'s Canadian sodium chlorate plants for $202 million, which was financed, in part, by $135 million in bank debt and a $20 million line of credit.

b. Sterling enters into a number of long-term profit-sharing contracts, and the profits from these contracts are included in Sterling's sales figures. Sales figures, therefore, do not represent the traditional price per unit times the number of units sold.

c. Calculated on the basis of data presented in Sterling Chemicals, Inc.'s audited annual reports; EBDIT calculations used internally for profit-sharing may differ slightly.

the previous shutdown record by five days and contributed significantly to increased profits.

Sterling's Financial Performance

Table 11.6 presents financial and employment data on Sterling Chemicals. Between 1987 and 1988, Sterling's sales increased from $412.2 million to $699.0 million, and EBDIT increased from $129.0 million to $340.1 million. Outstanding performance in 1988 was in part due to increases in the world price of styrene monomer, which substantially increased Sterling's margins on styrene. By the end of 1988, the company had reduced its debt to $90.8 million from $200.5 million at the time of the buyout, and paid $190.3 million in dividends. The dividend payout was almost 28 times the $6.8 million equity investment made at the time of the buyout.

In 1988, Sterling went public at $16 per share. Recession, coupled with a substantial increase in worldwide styrene capacity, made the period 1989–1993 difficult. In 1992 and 1993 EBDIT totaled only $41.4

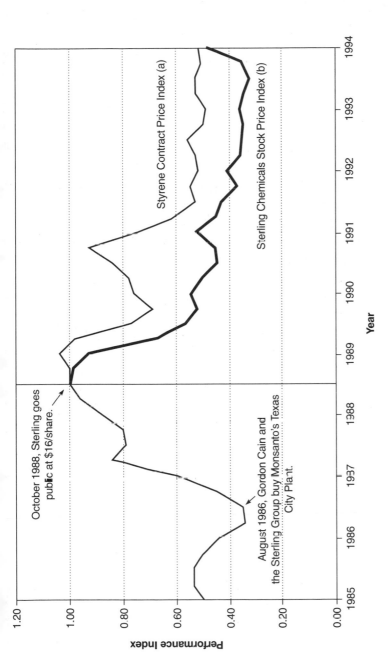

Figure 11.1 Index of Sterling Chemical's stock price performance and styrene price index, January 1985 through March 1994.

(a) The styrene price we use here is the contract price obtained from Sterling Chemicals. This is the price used by parties who have entered into longer-term contracts. It is more relevant to Sterling's situation than the spot price because the majority of Sterling's output is committed through longer-term supply contracts. The styrene contract price index is constructed by deflating the contract price series by the contract price in October 1988.

(b) The stock price index for Sterling Chemicals is constructed by deflating the stock price series by the October 1988 IPO price of $16.

million and $54.1 million, respectively. There were no profit-sharing payouts in either year. Sterling's stock price fell to a low of $3.50 per share. Managers assert that the difficult times made TQM's contributions to performance even more critical.

Analysis of Sterling's stock price performance substantiates the fact that styrene prices play a critical role in the firm's performance. In fact, because of its dependence on styrene prices, Sterling's performance is not directly comparable to other commodity chemical producers. (A financial analyst following Sterling confirms this view.) Sterling's stock price performance is not statistically significantly associated with the performance of the S&P 500 Index, the S&P Chemical Index, or an index we constructed of small publicly traded commodity chemical producers. However, the correlation between Sterling's stock return and percentage changes in styrene prices is a statistically significant 0.71. Figure 11.1 depicts an index of Sterling's stock price performance and a styrene price index. Both are adjusted to equal one in the month of Sterling's public offering. It appears that Sterling's leveraged buyout occurred around styrene price lows and that the company went public at peak styrene price levels. As styrene prices rebounded, so did Sterling's stock, which as of August 1994 traded for about $10 per share.

12 | Divisional Performance Measurement

12.1   Introduction

Our purpose in this chapter is to examine divisional performance measurement methods and related aspects of the rules of the game that govern the behavior of managers. Performance measurement is one of the critical factors that determine how individuals in an organization behave. It is one aspect of what we call the organizational rules of the game, which consist of (1) the performance measurement and evaluation system, (2) the reward and punishment system, and (3) the system for partitioning decision rights among individuals in an organization.

Performance measurement includes the objective and subjective assessments of the performance of both individuals and subunits of an organization such as divisions or departments. Performance evaluation is the process of attaching value weights to various measures of performance to represent the importance of achievement on each dimension.

The reward and punishment system relates the rewards granted to individuals to results measured by the performance measurement system. Rewards and punishments include nonmonetary factors such as honor, attention, and rank, as well as monetary factors such as salary changes and bonuses.

A manager is said to have a decision right if the enforcement and disciplinary powers of the top-level executive office will be used to enforce his ability to take an action. In large organizations, decision rights are more complex than the simple phrase suggests. For example, it is common in such organizations for no single individual to have all the decision rights necessary to undertake a major project. Instead, there is a complex process that brings many people into the decision-making function, a process that breaks the simple notion of a deci-

By Michael C. Jensen and William H. Meckling.

sion right into many components that are allocated to various decision agents. The following is a common breakdown:

1. Initiation right—the right to initiate resource allocation proposals.
2. Notification right—the right to be notified of the actions or proposed actions of others in the organization and the right to provide information or recommendations to the decision process regarding those proposals.
3. Ratification right—the right to review and ratify or veto the resource allocation recommendations of others.
4. Implementation right—the right to implement the ratified resource allocation proposals.
5. Monitoring right—the right to monitor the implementation of ratified proposals, including the rights to measure and evaluate performance and to determine rewards and punishments.[1]

Notification rights differ from ratification rights because the individual does not have veto power over the decisions at issue. Coordination of the individuals who have input into a decision is accomplished through a set of procedures that makes up a large part of what is generally thought of as the management process in an organization. Committees play an important role in coordinating and focusing the input of information into the decision-making process and provide an appeal process to resolve differences of opinion regarding aspects of any decision or project. This process takes on many of the characteristics of an internal court system with its own rules and procedures. Further consideration of the complexity of decision rights and the decision process is left to future work in order to concentrate here on analysis of performance measures.

The three dimensions of the rules of the game are obviously related. The reward and punishment system must coordinate rewards with performance if the performance measures are to have desirable effects on the behavior of an organization's members. Furthermore, the performance measures must be related to the ways in which decision rights are partitioned in an organization. For example, it is less important to measure the way a manager utilizes plant and equipment (e.g., the measurement of return on assets rather than total dollars of profits) if the manager does not influence plant and equipment decisions.

12.2 Specific and General Knowledge

The cost of acquiring and transferring knowledge among decision agents is important to the analysis of performance measurement systems. We define specific knowledge as that knowledge which is costly to transfer among agents and is not easily observable by other agents (in our discussion this means from higher levels in the organization's hierarchy). General knowledge is knowledge that is transferable among agents at low cost or is easily observable by other agents. The terms "specific" and "general" knowledge are used to characterize the two ends of a continuum that measures the cost of transferring knowledge between agents.[2]

Idiosyncratic knowledge of people, machines, organizations, customers, and suppliers, as well as knowledge of time and place, are examples of specific knowledge. This knowledge is difficult or impossible to aggregate; time and place by their very nature are destroyed by aggregation. Specific knowledge is also often obtained at low cost by individuals in an organization as a by-product of other activities, for example, the idiosyncratic knowledge about a machine that its operator gains over time. Prices and quantities are examples of general knowledge that are easily aggregated and are inexpensive to transmit among agents.

Achieving effective utilization of information in decision making is a major problem in organizations. The literature on computers and information systems views the problem as one of finding ways to transfer knowledge relevant to a decision to the agents involved in the decision. This makes sense when the knowledge is general or when the problem is one of discovering new technology that will connect specific to general knowledge. When the relevant knowledge is specific, however, and when the technology (for example, in computing and communications) is unable to lower the cost of transfer substantially, this approach will fail.

The alternative to moving the knowledge is to move the decision rights to those agents who possess the relevant specific knowledge. The cost incurred in this approach to the problem is the cost engendered by the fact that people are self-interested. Therefore, as the decision rights are partitioned out among agents in the organization, self-interested agents will use the decision rights in ways that benefit themselves at the expense of the performance of the organization. This makes it necessary to expend resources to control the costs associated with the inconsistent objectives of agents in the organization—what have come to be called agency costs.

Agency costs include the costs of devising and enforcing contracts with agents, the costs of monitoring the agents' behavior, the bonding costs incurred by the agent to help assure the principal that he or she will not engage in opportunistic behavior, and finally the residual loss, the costs incurred because it is uneconomic to define and enforce contracts perfectly. The residual loss arises because it pays to incur additional monitoring, bonding, and contracting costs only to the point where the improvements in the decision process just pay for themselves. This means that not all counterproductive behavior is eliminated.

12.3   Alternative Divisional Performance Measures

The major categories of performance measurement systems are:

* cost centers
* revenue centers
* profit centers
* investment centers
* expense centers

We shall discuss each of these measurement systems briefly and then turn to an analysis of the conditions under which each one will tend to be an efficient system.

12.4   Cost Centers

There are three alternative forms for a cost center performance measurement and evaluation system:

1. Minimize costs for given output.
2. Maximize output for given total cost.
3. Minimize average costs (with no quantity constraint).

Rules 1 and 2 are logically equivalent, and, conditional on the correct choice of the output or cost constraint, they are consistent with maximizing the value of the firm. Rule 3 is logically inconsistent with maximizing the value of the firm because it motivates the cost center manager to achieve the output that minimizes average cost even though it is different from the value-maximizing level. Figure 12.1 illustrates the

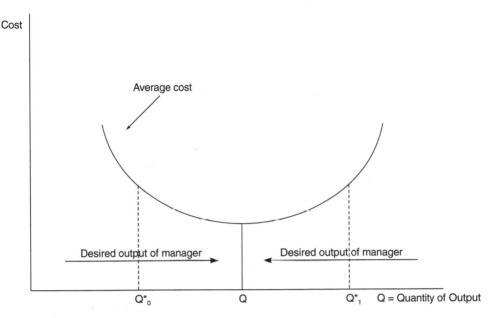

Figure 12.1 Desired output of manager evaluated as a cost center with no quantity constraint. Q^*_0 and Q^*_1 are two alternative optimal outputs.

point for a manufacturing division with a U-shaped average cost function, which is evaluated as a cost center. The figure portrays two alternative optimal output levels, Q^*_0 and Q^*_1, for two alternative sets of demand conditions. Since minimum average cost occurs at output level Q, that is where the divisional manager will choose to operate if he is rewarded for minimizing average costs, and the company as a whole will sacrifice the profits that could have been earned from operating at the optimal level of output.

If the division manager does not have the rights to set the output level unilaterally but has input into the decision, he will tend, other things being equal, to provide a constant source of pressure to move the planned output level closer to Q, the minimum average cost output level. In the situation where optimal output is higher than the minimum average cost point, the manager will tend to take actions that reduce output unexpectedly, for example, claiming machine breakdowns or labor or material shortages (which could have been avoided with better planning). Moreover, if it is difficult for those at higher levels in the hierarchy to distinguish the reasons for these events (because the information required to do so is specific and located in the manufacturing division), it will be difficult to eliminate these counterproductive effects from the system as long as the manufacturing division is a cost center.

Good knowledge of the minimum obtainable cost functions would allow the evaluation mechanism to adjust for differences in quantity of output and therefore to eliminate the problems associated with incentives to game the system on the quantity dimension. The evaluation system would measure performance as deviations from the minimum obtainable cost function. Such knowledge of the cost functions, however, will in general be unavailable or very costly. Standard cost systems are a crude attempt to control for the effects of quantity changes. But they make the correct adjustments only when marginal cost is constant.

Because it reduces measured cost, the cost center manager has incentives to reduce quality below the optimal level as well. This means that cost centers will tend to work better when it is inexpensive to measure both quantity, quality, and the cost functions. For some functions, the measurement of quantity is as difficult as the measurement of quality. Consider, for example, the measurement of the quantity of computer services supplied by a centralized service bureau in a firm. There is no simple, unique way to measure quantity in such a multidimensional environment.

If a division produces different products, the product mix decision will also pose serious difficulties in this structure because the relative amounts of each product to be produced must be decided outside of the division and given to the cost center divisional manager as a constraint that must be met. This is another example of the necessity to control the quantity decision for a cost center manager.

The general principle in assigning decision rights is to colocate the decision rights and the relevant specific knowledge. The cost center manager is given decision rights over the factor input decisions, operating procedures, technology, and so on, all of which generally require a great deal of knowledge that is specific to the local situation. The advantages of this system, when it can be implemented, come from the specialization it induces. The cost center manager can focus on increasing the efficiency of the production process without distractions caused by changes in demand conditions that would affect him if revenues were included in the performance measure.

Our earlier discussion illustrates the interrelation between the choice of performance measure and the allocation of decision rights. The discussion indicates that cost centers will tend to work better when the optimal quantity and product mix decisions are made outside the division. When it is expensive to measure quantity and quality and when the knowledge required to make the optimal quantity and product mix decisions is specific and inaccessible to those higher in the hierarchy, it will be difficult to operate the division as a cost center. This situation is addressed below.

12.5   Revenue Centers

Revenue centers are the logical complement to a cost center. The performance measure in such centers is total revenue, and they have many of the same problems and advantages as cost centers. They can take one of three logical forms:

1. Maximize total revenues for a given price.
2. Maximize total revenues for a given quantity of unit sales.
3. Maximize total revenues (with no quantity constraint).

Again, the first two of these options are logically the same, and, for the correct choice of price or quantity, are consistent with maximizing the value of the firm. The revenue center manager cannot be allowed to determine the quantity, or he will simply go to the quantity where revenue is maximized (the point where marginal revenue is zero). As long as marginal costs are positive this will exceed the profit-maximizing quantity.

The product mix decision is a particular problem in revenue centers because the additivity of revenues from different product lines increases the probability that the measurement will evolve to total revenues from all products. If so, other things being equal, the manager will substitute sales efforts from lower-priced to higher-priced products at the expense of overall profits. In this situation, a better performance measure is total dollars of gross margin defined as the difference between total revenues and total variable costs.

The advantage of the revenue center is that the manager can specialize on the marketing and sales effort without concern for the factors that influence production cost. To do so the manager will generally be given decision rights over those issues involving marketing and sales which require considerable knowledge that is specific to the local level but not the rights to decide on quantity or product mix. This means that if the knowledge required to make the quantity and product mix decision is available at low cost at higher levels in the hierarchy, the revenue center structure will tend to work better.

12.6   Profit Centers

A divisional profit center is evaluated on the difference between its revenues and costs as defined by the measurement system. "Profit center" is a term that strictly describes the performance measurement system, but it is also widely used to describe a divisional structure in which the profit center manager is given a broader set of decision rights. Profits can be (and are) used as a measure of performance in divisions in which the manager is given a limited set of decision rights as well as in divisions in which managers are given a broad set of decision rights. We use the term here to describe a system in which a division's performance is measured by its profits.

If the knowledge required to make the product mix, quantity, and quality decisions is specific to the division and therefore costly or impossible for managers at higher levels in the hierarchy to obtain, the profit center can be an effective performance measurement system. In these cases it is desirable to use profits as a performance measure in conjunction with an assignment of decision rights over factors such as the product mix, quantity, and quality.

The profit center structure, however, has its own serious problems. It is well known that maximization of profits for each division does not lead to maximum profits for the firm as a whole, except in the special circumstance in which there are no interdependencies between divisions. These interdependencies can take the form of:

- interdependencies introduced when one or more divisions buys the product of another, and therefore the price paid by the buying division affects its costs and pricing decisions (the transfer pricing problem);[3]
- interdependent demands (e.g., Pontiac and Oldsmobile, or film and cameras) where demand for one or more of the firm's products depends on the policies for the other products (e.g., pricing, quality, or technology); or
- interdependent supply or cost functions where the cost of producing a product depends on the production decisions for other products (e.g., gasoline and kerosene, since more gasoline production means less kerosene obtained from a barrel of crude oil).

To the extent that interdependencies between centers are major, profit center performance measurement can induce serious suboptimal behavior on the part of divisional managers. One solution to the interdependencies induced by the transfer pricing problem is for corporate headquarters to set a transfer price equal to the marginal cost of the producing division at the optimal quantity of output. This requires top management to know both the revenue and cost functions of the product in detail (in order to determine the optimal output level in each period and the marginal cost at the optimal output level). If the information required to know both revenue and cost functions is specific to the operating divisions, it will be difficult for top management to set the optimal transfer price. When close substitutes for the good being traded internally are traded in outside competitive markets, the optimal transfer price is the outside market price.

There is no simple solution to the problems caused by interdependencies in demand or cost functions.[4] If these interdependencies are serious and there is no simple way to coordinate the actions of the two divisions, one solution is to merge them into one division, with the profit measure applied only to the sum of the two divisions rather than to either separately.

12.7 Investment Centers and EVA

Investment centers are a variation on the profit center structure in which the manager is evaluated on the relation between profits and the assets used to generate them. They tend to be desirable when the profit center manager is given decision control over the amount of assets used in the activity and when the costs associated with asset utilization are important.

As such, investment centers are performance measurement systems which take into account the efficiency of asset utilization. They are important when managers of the division have the specific knowledge required to decide on the optimal level of investment, and are given or acquire decision rights over investment and asset levels, and when the costs of asset utilization are important. It has historically been common for organizations to take asset utilization into account by using rate of return measures such as return on assets (ROA) or return on equity (ROE). Both of these measures are highly susceptible to gaming and tend to provide counterproductive incentives when managers have decision rights over the level of investment or assets. Again, as is true for cost centers and revenue centers, the objective function in an investment center can take one of three forms:

1. Maximize the percentage return on assets for given total assets.
2. Maximize total assets for given total percentage return.
3. Maximize total percentage return on assets (with no constraint on total assets).

Forms 1 and 2 can be consistent with maximizing the value of the firm if the constraints on total assets or total percentage return are chosen correctly, and this can work if top management has the relevant specific knowledge to set the correct constraints. However, a common form for this objective function to take is the unconstrained version, 3, and this is inconsistent with maximizing the value of the firm. A manager evaluated on maximizing the total percentage return on assets has incentive to reduce assets to the point where the firm owns no assets other than the single asset whose returns are greatest. This, of course, is not consistent with maximizing value or wealth. A 100% return on $1,000 of assets is $1,000, while a 30% return on $100,000 of assets is $30,000. EVA (Economic Value Added)[5] is an alternative performance measure that does not have this critical fault.

EVA is defined as net cash flow in a period less a capital charge which is the cost of capital times the dollar value of the assets employed in the business. This "residual income," as it used to be known in the accounting literature, has none of the disadvantages mentioned above concerning return on asset or equity measures. It is total dollars of net cash inflow less the total dollar charges for capital used in the business and is an appropriate number to maximize. EVA also has the advantage of revealing to managers the real cost of the capital used in a business. Accounting statements reflect the cost of the debt capital used in a business in the accounting reports, but not the equity capital. This causes managers regularly to think that equity has no cost. EVA accounting statements show a loss when net cash flows are not sufficient to cover the full cost of an organization's capital.

Because EVA is a flow measure, it does not solve the capital value problem. This means that if the future annual EVA of a project is sufficiently large, it will pay a company to take a project whose early years' EVA is negative. Market value, the discounted present value of net cash flows less the investment required to generate them, is the appropriate value to maximize. Thus, while EVA is the best flow measure of performance currently known, it is not the universal answer to the search for the perfect performance measure. Perfect measures of capitalized value will never be found because value is never something that can be known perfectly until *after* a project has run its course to completion and shutdown.

12.8 Expense Centers

A division organized as an expense center is the private equivalent of the classic public bureaucracy.[6] The division generally produces services for the rest of the organization, and the consuming units are not charged for the services they consume. An organization's internal administrative services such as human resources, patent, and public relations services are commonly organized as expense centers.

Consider a division which negotiates a budget allocation from a central budget office at the beginning of each year and simultaneously makes a commitment on the quantity of services that will be provided. Figure 12.2 portrays the demand for the division's services from the rest of the organization. This curve plots the marginal value to the organization as a whole of the division's output at various levels. For simplicity, we assume the service is produced with no fixed costs and marginal costs given by the schedule in Figure 12.2. The profit-maximizing output level, Q^*, is the point where the marginal production cost of the service equals the demand price at the marginal benefit to the organization of an additional unit of the good or service.

If the manager of the expense center in Figure 12.2 is motivated to maximize the size of the division (perhaps because compensation is determined by a system such as the Hay system in which compensation schedules reward jobs with larger budgets and more people), the equilibrium output level will be Q in Figure 12.2. For simplicity the figure assumes that the relevant measure of size in the objective function of the divisional manager is the quantity of output. The point Q is determined under the assumption that the budget office can estimate reasonably well the value to the organization of the division's total output but has poor knowledge of the costs and benefits of individual units of output. This means the budget office will never authorize a budget for the division which exceeds the division's total value to the organization. Q then is the maximum quantity that can be produced by the division subject to the constraints that (1) its total budget does not exceed the total

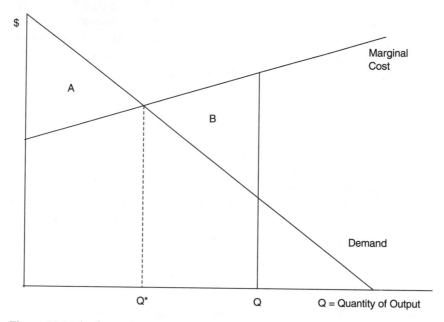

Figure 12.2 The firm value maximizing level of output, Q*, for an internal service center organized as an expense center and the center's optimal output level, Q.

value of its output to the organization (the area under the demand curve) and (2) its total cost of producing the output (the area under the MC curve) does not exceed its budget. Graphically, this is the quantity at which area A equals area B. The manager of the center wants to produce as much as possible, and the total value of the center to the organization rises as the promised output rises. Therefore the budget increases with increases in the promised level of output. The manager cannot produce more than Q, however, with the maximum total budget the budget office is willing to give him at that level of output. Thus such expense centers will tend to be too large since Q is greater than Q*, the output level that maximizes the value of the organization as a whole.

The tendency of an expense center to overproduce is exacerbated by the fact that the consumers of the center's product are not charged for the services they consume. Therefore, consumers have no incentives to compare the cost of the services they consume with the value of the services to them. In addition, if the budget office attempts to cut the center's budget, the center will be able to obtain support from the consumers of its output to oppose such cuts. The center director reacts to budget cuts by threatening cuts in the most highly valued rather than the marginal services, and this also motivates the center's users to lobby against such cuts. The fact that the users of the service do not pay for the output they consume also means they will tend to demand services of too high a quality.

12.9 Internal Chargeback Systems and Decentralization of Part of the Control Function

Consider a situation where the knowledge required to evaluate the performance of a division that provides services or products to other units of an organization is

- not easily observable from higher levels in the hierarchy,
- specific (that is, costly to transfer among agents), and
- located among users of the division's output.

In this situation it can be desirable to transfer some of the control function to the users of the division. This can be done by instituting a charge system in which the users pay for the output of the producing division. When consumers must pay for a good or service rather than receiving it at no cost, they have incentives to compare the benefits of the goods with the prices they must pay for them. This will cause them to consume less of the goods or services than when they are supplied at no cost, thereby reducing the overconsumption problem engendered by the expense center structure.

If a chargeback system is to be effective as a decentralized control mechanism, the users must also have decision rights that give them effective choices: for example, the right to purchase the good outside, to produce it themselves, or to buy it from another division that has gone into competition to produce and supply the good internally. Given these decision rights, a buying division also has incentives to compare the quality and prices of the goods offered by the supplying division to that which they can obtain from other suppliers or by making it themselves. This constant evaluation will then be reflected in the buyer's decision to purchase or not to purchase from the supplying division. This right to choose to buy elsewhere provides great incentive for the buying division to monitor the hard-to-assess qualities of the product of the supplying division, and it will be able to use its specific knowledge of those qualities in its monitoring. In such a system the higher levels in the hierarchy have decentralized much of the monitoring of the supplying division to its customers. The overall divisional monitoring function can then be accomplished at higher levels in the hierarchy by measuring the profits of the producing division, thus freeing the monitor from many of the details associated with measuring and evaluating dimensions such as the quality and quantity of output.

Divisions that deal with the ultimate consumer are dealing with the most effective chargeback system, namely, markets. Internal charge-back systems can be used with any of the performance measures thus far described. In each case there are benefits to be obtained by soliciting the help of the buyers of the division's output in the monitoring function.

Chargeback systems work better the smaller are the agency costs with the managers of the buying divisions—that is, the easier it is to evaluate and motivate the buying managers to act in a way that closely reflects the organization's objective function, and the smaller are the internal monopoly powers of the supplying division. Unfortunately, there are strong forces that tend to exacerbate the monopoly problem while at the same time substantially reducing incentives for users to make effective use of their specific knowledge regarding the quality and quantity of the output of the producing division. One source of such pressure is what we have labeled the "locus of uncertainty" problem.

12.10 The Locus of Uncertainty Problem

Organizations that institute chargeback systems as part of a decentralized control mechanism commonly inhibit the functioning of those systems by disabling an important part of the choice set faced by managers buying the services of the selling division. They do so by constraining the choices of the customers of the internal seller through such devices as line budgets or "funny money" allocations that cannot be spent on anything other than the good or service in question. Computer services are a good example. It is common for computer funds in the budgets of buyers of a centralized internal computer supplier to be constrained for use in purchases from the central facility only. Since the funds allocated in such line budgets have zero opportunity cost to the managers, the managers' purchase decisions do not reflect their assessment of the value of the service relative to other uses of the funds. This means that the purchasing decisions of users do not reflect their evaluation of the quality and quantity of the services supplied by the central facility in comparison to that available from alternative suppliers or from their own production of the service. Thus, one of the major benefits deriving from the introduction of a chargeback system, the revelation of such specific knowledge possessed by users, is lost to the organization.

In every organizational situation in which a chargeback system is used, there is an individual who must bear a great deal of uncertainty in order for the organization to receive the benefits of the chargeback system. This is the person responsible for the budgets of both the selling and the buying divisions. The problem surrounds the fact that at the beginning of the year the same monies allocated to the selling division for use in the production of the service must also be allocated to the buying divisions. If the buying divisions choose to spend the resources on goods and services other than those forecast by the selling division for its product, the budget officer will experience a deficit. The deficit arises because the monies for production of the good have been committed (if they can be undone easily, the problem goes away) and therefore have in effect been spent twice if the users choose to spend them on producing the good themselves or to purchase other goods and services. If the evaluation mechanism faced by the budget officer is not flexible enough to allow for these deficits, the budget officer has incentives to collaborate with the pleadings of the supplying division to make it a monopoly by forbidding the expenditure of funds allocated for its product on anything else. This is accomplished by line budget allocations. Such constraints destroy much of the benefits of the chargeback system.[7]

Centralized restriction of choices through line budgets makes sense when problems of measuring the performance of users make it difficult to ensure that buying division users are generally reflecting the value of the good to the entire organization in their decisions. Such restrictions, unfortunately, are also widely used when there is no benefit to the organization and when they generate considerable costs. In these cases, the perversion of incentives reflects the "locus of uncertainty" problem.

12.11 Choice of Performance Measure

The choice of a performance measure requires a theory that predicts when one performance measure will dominate another. Our goal is the construction of a theory of the determinants of performance measurement that enables one to predict when a division will be organized as a profit center, cost center, investment center, revenue center, or expense center.

The choice between an expense center and the other options is essentially the choice over whether to monitor the division directly from higher in the hierarchy. This option will be more attractive when it is easier to evaluate the performance of the division from higher levels of the hierarchy, and when it is difficult to decentralize the monitoring function to users of the output of the division. It is, for example, sometimes difficult to identify a set of users who could be charged for the output of the unit. Such users must be individuals whose valuation of the center's output is equal to the value to the organization as a whole. The output of the patent services group in a large organization is an example where this condition is unlikely to be satisfied. If the scientists in the lab are given the decision rights on patent services and are charged for them, it is likely the organization will consume too little of the service. On the other hand, since the lag between the decision on the patent and disclosure issues (a substitute for patent acquisition) is so long, it is difficult to give the decision rights to the manufacturing or marketing divisions, who are unlikely to have the scientific expertise to keep up with the multitude of developments in the lab and to foresee the commercial applicability of that subset which should be protected with patents or disclosure. They will tend to focus their attention instead on the struggle to contain the usual day-to-day emergencies in the firm's current markets. In short, it will be difficult in many organizations to decentralize the monitoring of such services. In these situations the major alternative is to organize the supply of such services as an expense center and monitor its performance directly. It will tend to have all the problems of expense centers, but the costs of these problems might nevertheless be the lowest attainable among all alternative organizational structures.

In general, a cost center will be more desirable the lower is the cost of obtaining good information on:

- quantity
- quality
- correct output mix
- cost functions

Profit centers will tend to be more desirable the higher are the above costs and:

- the easier it is to identify the correct revenues for the division,
- the smaller are interdependencies in cost and demand functions between divisions, and
- the smaller are internal monopoly problems

Profit centers will tend to work best when they are combined with a rights assignment that decentralizes part of the monitoring function of the center to its customers through a chargeback system that gives those customers effective alternatives and thereby provides potential or actual competition for the profit center.

Investment centers and EVA will tend to be more desirable the more capital-intensive is an activity and the harder it is to identify optimal divisional asset investments from higher in the hierarchy.

Notes

1. The Nature of Man

1. We use the word "man" in the chapter title as a non-gender-specific reference to human beings. We have attempted to make the language less gender-specific because the models being discussed describe the behavior of both sexes. We have been unable to find a genderless term for use in the title which has the same desired impact.

2. When one takes into account information costs, much behavior that appears to be suboptimal "satisficing" can be explained as attempts to maximize subject to such costs. Unfortunately, "satisficing" (a much misused term originated by Herbert A. Simon [1955]) does not suggest this interpretation.

3. The original temporary law was made permanent in 1975, with safety being cited as a primary reason.

4. Moreover, in 1987 the law was changed to allow states the option of raising the speed limit to 65 mph on interstate highways outside highly populated areas, and later extended to certain non-interstate highways.

5. Obtained in private communication with the Federal Communications Commission.

6. REMM is not meant to describe the behavior of any particular individual. To do so requires more complete specification of the preferences, values, emotions, and talents of each person. Moreover, individuals respond very differently to factors such as stress, tension, and fear, and in so doing, often violate the predictions of the REMM model. For purposes of organizational and public policy, many of these violations of REMM "cancel out" in the aggregate across large groups of people and over time—but by no means all. For a brief discussion of a Pain Avoidance Model (PAM) that complements REMM by accommodating systematically nonrational behavior, see Jensen (1994).

7. The word "need" has meaning only when used in the conditional sense. For example: An individual needs X cubic liters of air per hour in order to live. This statement, or others like it, does not imply, however, that individuals are willing to pay an infinite price for that air.

8. See Hayek (1945, 1977).

9. For example, it is common practice in rent-controlled areas for new tenants to make higher-than-market-price payments to old tenants and/or landlords for furniture or minor improvements they have no use for to get the right to rent the apartment for a below-market rate.

10. In particular, employment or wage discrimination against women implies profit opportunities for new firms that can therefore hire superior women at market rates. Such profits can be shared with the employees through profit sharing or partnership structures.

11. For an account of the role of corporate restructuring in addressing both the U.S. and worldwide problem of industrial overcapacity, see Jensen (1993).

12. The "tough love" movement and twelve-step programs such as AA for treating substance dependence are designed to provide help while insisting that individuals maintain their personal responsibility for their fate.

13. Plato, *Laws* 739c, ff., and 942a, f., as cited by Karl Popper (1950, p. 102).

14. Maslow (1943, p. 370).

15. "So far, our theoretical discussion may have given the impression that these five sets of needs are somehow in a step-wise, all-or-none relationship to each other . . . This . . . might give the false impression that a need must be satisfied 100 per cent before the next need emerges. In actual fact, most members of our society who are normal, are partially satisfied in all their basic needs and partially unsatisfied in all their basic needs at the same time. A more realistic description of the hierarchy would be in terms of decreasing percentages of satisfaction as we go up the hierarchy of prepotency.

  "As for the concept of emergence of a new need after satisfaction of the prepotent need, this emergence is not a sudden, salutatory phenomenon but rather a gradual emergence by slow degrees from nothingness." Maslow (1943, pp. 388–389).

16. The income elasticity of demand describes how an individual's consumption of a good changes with a given change in income. It is the percentage change in the quantity of a good demanded by an individual divided by the percentage change in the individual's income (holding all prices and quantities of other goods constant).

17. Economists call such goods "necessities" and "luxury" goods. They are defined by their income- or wealth-elasticity of demand.

18. See Peltzman (1974, pp. 15–16), and Wardell, Hassar, Anavekar, and Lasagna (1978). Hansen (1982) reviews the literature on the effectiveness of the FDA drug regulation procedures, and Kaitin, Kenneth, Bryant, and Lasagna (1993) provide data indicating that the average rate of new drugs approved has not changed through 1990.

19. See Henderson (1977).

20. Buchanan and Tullock (1965).

21. See, for example, Jensen (1986a, 1988, 1989a, 1989b) and Lang, Poulsen, and Stulz (1994); see also Blanchard, Lopez-de-Silanes, and Shleifer (1994) and the references therein.

22. See Becker (1968, 1973) on crime and marriage.

23. See Downs (1957) and Buchanan and Tullock (1965) on political choice; Niskanan (1971) on bureaucracies.

24. See Alchian and Demsetz (1972), Arrow (1964a), Williamson (1970, 1975), Milgrom and Roberts (1992), and Chapters 3 and 4 of this volume.

2. Self-Interest, Altruism, Incentives, and Agency Theory

1. To some extent, this non-optimal behavior can be incorporated into REMM by recognizing that individuals' visions of the world and their ability to act or react depend on various factors (such as the intensity of emotions) that have the power to change, if only temporarily, their perception of "goods." Such an expanded model could explain deviant behavior as the result of maximizing actions in situations where an individual's perceptions of the world are systematically different, or more constrained, than normal. Abraham Zaleznik suggested this constrained maximization view of deviant behavior. Weick's (1983) survey of the effects of stress on the behavior of humans describes behavior that is consistent with such a view.

2. See LeDoux (1994) and the references therein, and the September 1992 *Scientific American* special issue on the brain.

3. For example, in large sample surveys, almost no one ranks himself or herself below the 50th percentile of their peers. For discussion of these phenomena see Schwert (1993), Chapters 8 and 9 of this volume, and and the references therein.

4. See Peck (1978) and Argyris (1991, 1993). Consistent with this, there is some evidence that those behaving according to the REMM model live more successful lives. See Larrick, Nisbett, and Morgan (1993).

5. Jensen and Meckling 1976 (Chapter 3 of the present volume). The agency article was written at the same time that we were working on early versions of "The Nature of Man" (Chapter 1), and in a sense this latter paper is the foundation of our work on agency. Although "The Nature of Man" has been widely circulated over the years, it remained unpublished because it seemed to be such a straightforward summary of 200 years of work in economics. Yet the puzzle has been that the paper has generated considerable controversy, similar to that represented in Brennan's article. The reasons, I now see, go to the heart of the conflict between science and views on the perfectibility of human beings that emanate from religious preachings as well as the secular views that come from other branches of the social sciences, and policy advocates.

6. See Thaler and Shefrin (1981). Richard Thaler was a colleague at Rochester at the time he did this original work, and although I always found it interesting, I failed for more than a decade to see the generality and the importance of this self-control issue.

7. One branch of opposition to some of this analysis came from those who believed that conflicts of interest exist, but are completely resolved by markets and competition.

3. Theory of the Firm

1. We do not use the term "capital structure" because that term usually denotes the relative quantities of bonds, equity, warrants, trade credit, and so on, which

represent the liabilities of a firm. Our theory implies that there is another important dimension to this problem—namely the relative amount of ownership claims held by insiders (management) and outsiders (investors with no direct role in the management of the firm).

2. Reviews of this literature are given by Peterson (1965), Alchian (1965, 1968), Machlup (1967), Shubik (1970), Cyert and Hedrick (1972), Branch (1973), Preston (1975).

3. See Williamson (1964, 1970, 1975), Marris (1964), Baumol (1959), Penrose (1958), and Cyert and March (1963). Thorough reviews of these and other contributions are given by Machlup (1967) and Alchian (1965).

Simon (1955) developed a model of human choice incorporating information (search) and computational costs which also has important implications for the behavior of managers. Unfortunately, Simon's work has often been misinterpreted as a denial of maximizing behavior, and misused, especially in the marketing and behavioral science literature. His later use of the term "satisficing" (Simon 1959) has undoubtedly contributed to this confusion because it suggests rejection of maximizing behavior rather than maximization subject to costs of information and of decision making.

4. See Meckling (1976) for a discussion of the fundamental importance of the assumption of resourceful, evaluative, maximizing behavior on the part of individuals in the development of theory. Klein (1976) takes an approach similar to the one we embark on in this chapter in his review of the theory of the firm and the law.

5. See Coase (1937, 1959, 1960), Alchian (1965, 1968), Alchian and Kessel (1962), Demsetz (1967), Alchian and Demsetz (1972), Monsen and Downs (1965), Silver and Auster (1969), and McManus (1975).

6. Property rights are of course human rights, that is, rights which are possessed by human beings. The introduction of the wholly false distinction between property rights and human rights in many policy discussions is surely one of the all-time great semantic flimflams.

7. See Berhold (1971), Ross (1973, 1974a), Wilson (1968, 1969), and Heckerman (1975).

8. Given the optimal monitoring and bonding activities by the principal and agent.

9. As it is used in this chapter, the term "monitoring" includes more than just measuring or observing the behavior of the agent. It includes efforts on the part of the principal to "control" the behavior of the agent through budget restrictions, compensation policies, operating rules, and the like.

10. As we show later, the existence of positive monitoring and bonding costs will result in the manager of a corporation possessing control over some resources which he can allocate (within certain constraints) to satisfy his own preferences. However, to the extent that he must obtain the cooperation of others in order to carry out his tasks (such as divisional vice presidents) and to the extent that he cannot control their behavior perfectly and costlessly, they will be able to ap-

propriate some of these resources for their own ends. In short, there are agency costs generated at every level of the organization. Unfortunately, the analysis of these more general organizational issues is even more difficult than that of the "ownership and control" issue because the nature of the contractual obligations and the rights of the parties are much more varied and generally not as well specified in explicit contractual arrangements. Nevertheless, they exist, and we believe that extensions of our analysis in these directions show promise of producing insights into a viable theory of organization.

11. They define the classical capitalist firm as a contractual organization of inputs in which there is "(a) joint input production, (b) several input owners, (c) one party who is common to all the contracts of the joint inputs, (d) who has rights to renegotiate any input's contract independently of contracts with other input owners, (e) who holds the residual claim, and (f) who has the right to sell his contractual residual status."

12. By "legal fiction" we mean the artificial construct under the law which allows certain organizations to be treated as individuals.

13. For example, we ordinarily think of a product as leaving the firm at the time it is sold, but implicitly or explicitly such sales generally carry with them continuing contracts between the firm and the buyer. If the product does not perform as expected, the buyer often can and does have a right to satisfaction. Explicit evidence that such implicit contracts do exist is the practice we occasionally observe of specific provision that "all sales are final."

14. This view of the firm points up the important role that the legal system and the law play in social organizations, especially the organization of economic activity. Statutory laws set bounds on the kinds of contracts into which individuals and organizations may enter without risking criminal prosecution. The police powers of the state are available and are used to enforce performance of contracts or to enforce the collection of damages for non-performance. The courts adjudicate conflicts between contracting parties and establish precedents which form the body of common law. All of these government activities affect both the kinds of contracts executed and the extent to which contracting is relied upon. This in turn determines the usefulness, productivity, profitability, and viability of various forms of organization. Moreover, new laws as well as court decisions often can and do change the rights of contracting parties ex post, and they can and do serve as a vehicle for redistribution of wealth. An analysis of some of the implications of these facts is contained in Jensen and Meckling (1978), and we shall not pursue them here.

15. For use in consumption, for the diversification of his wealth, or more important, for the financing of "profitable" projects which he could not otherwise finance out of his personal wealth. We deal with these issues later in the chapter after having developed some of the elementary analytical tools necessary to their solution.

16. Such as office space, air conditioning, thickness of the carpets, friendliness of employee relations, and so forth.

17. And again we assume that for any given market value of these costs, F, to the firm the allocation across time and across alternative probability distributions is such that the manager's current expected utility is at a maximum.

18. At this stage when we are considering a 100% owner-managed firm, the notion of a "wage contract" with himself has no content. However, the 100% owner-managed case is only an expositional device used in passing to illustrate a number of points in the analysis, and we ask the reader to bear with us briefly while we lay out the structure for the more interesting partial ownership case where such a contract does have substance.

19. The manager's utility function is actually defined over wealth and the future time sequence of vectors of quantities of non-pecuniary benefits, X_t. Although the setting of his problem is somewhat different, Fama (1970b, 1972) analyzes the conditions under which these preferences can be represented as a derived utility function defined as a function of the money value of the expenditures (in our notation F) on these goods conditional on the prices of goods. Such a utility function incorporates the optimization going on in the background which defines $\hat{X}$ discussed above for a given F. In the more general case where we allow a time series of consumption, $\hat{X}_t$, the optimization is being carried out across both time and the components of X_t for fixed F.

20. This excludes, for instance, (a) the case where the manager is allowed to expend corporate resources on anything he pleases, in which case F would be a perfect substitute for wealth, or (b) the case where he can "steal" cash (or other marketable assets) with constant returns to scale—if he could the indifference curves would be straight lines with slope determined by the fence commission.

21. Point D defines the fringe benefits in the optimal pay package since the value to the manager of the fringe benefits, F^*, is greater than the cost of providing them, as is evidenced by the fact that U_2 is steeper to the left of D than the budget constraint with slope equal to -1.

   That D is indeed the optimal pay package can easily be seen in this situation since if the conditions of the sale to a new owner specified that the manager would receive no fringe benefits after the sale, he would require a payment equal to V_3 to compensate him for the sacrifice of his claims to V^* and fringe benefits amounting to F^* (the latter with total value to him of $V_3 - V^*$). But if $F = 0$, the value of the firm is only $\overline{V}$. Therefore, if monitoring costs were zero, the sale would take place at V^* with provision for a pay package which included fringe benefits of F^* for the manager.

   This discussion seems to indicate there are two values for the "firm," V_3 and V^*. This is not the case if we realize that V^* is the value of the right to be the residual claimant on the cash flows of the firm and $V_3 - V^*$ is the value of the managerial rights, i.e., the right to make the operating decisions which include access to F^*. There is at least one other right that has value which plays no formal role in the analysis as yet—the value of the control right. By control right we mean the right to hire and fire the manager, and we leave this issue to a future paper.

22. The distance $V^* - V'$ is a measure of what we will define as the gross agency

costs. The distance $V_3 - V_4$ is a measure of what we call net agency costs, and it is this measure of agency costs which will be minimized by the manager in the general case where we allow investment to change.

23. I^* is the value-maximizing and Pareto-optimum investment level which results from the traditional analysis of the corporate investment decision if the firm operates in perfectly competitive capital and product markets and the agency cost problems discussed here are ignored. See Debreu (1959, chap. 7), Jensen and Long (1972), Long (1972), Merton and Subrahmanyam (1974), Hirshleifer (1958, 1970), and Fama and Miller (1972).

24. Each equilibrium point such as that at E is characterized by $(\hat{\alpha}, \hat{F}, \hat{W}_T)$ where $\hat{W}_T$ is the entrepreneur's post-investment financing wealth. Such an equilibrium must satisfy each of the following four conditions:

$$(1) \quad \hat{W}_T + F = \overline{V}(I) + W - I = \overline{V}(I) - K,$$

where $K \equiv I - W$ is the amount of outside financing required to make the investment I. If this condition is not satisfied there is an uncompensated wealth transfer (in one direction or the other) between the entrepreneur and outside equity buyers.

$$(2) \quad U_F(\hat{W}_T, \hat{F}) / U_{W_T}(\hat{W}_T, \hat{F}) = \hat{\alpha},$$

where U is the entrepreneur's utility function on wealth and perquisites, U_F and U_{W_T} are marginal utilities, and $\hat{\alpha}$ is the manager's share of the firm.

$$(3) \quad (1 - \hat{\alpha})V(I) = (1 - \hat{\alpha})[\overline{V}(I) - \hat{F}] \geq K,$$

which says the funds received from outsiders are at least equal to K, the minimum required outside financing.

(4) Among all points $(\hat{\alpha}, \hat{F}, \hat{W}_T)$ satisfying conditions (1)–(3), (α, F, W_T) gives the manager highest utility. This implies that $(\hat{\alpha}, \hat{F}, \hat{W}_T)$ satisfy condition (3) as an equality.

25. *Proof.* Note that the slope of the expansion path (or locus of equilibrium points) at any point is $(\Delta V - \Delta I)/\Delta F$, and at the optimum level of investment this must be equal to the slope of the manager's indifference curve between wealth and market value of fringe benefits, F. Furthermore, in the absence of monitoring, the slope of the indifference curve, $\Delta W/\Delta F$, at the equilibrium point, D, must be equal to $-\alpha'$. Thus,

$$(2) \quad (\Delta V - \Delta I)/\Delta F = -\alpha'$$

is the condition for the optimal scale of investment, and this implies that condition (1) holds for small changes at the optimum level of investment, I'.

26. Since the manager's indifference curves are negatively sloped we know that the optimum scale of the firm, point D, will occur in the region where the expansion path has negative slope, i.e., the market value of the firm will be declining and the *gross* agency costs, A, will be increasing and thus, the manager will not minimize them in making the investment decision (even though he will mini-

mize them for any *given* level of investment). However, we define the *net* agency cost as the dollar equivalent of the welfare loss the manager experiences because of the agency relationship evaluated at $F = 0$ (the vertical distance between the intercepts on the Y axis of the two indifference curves on which points C and D lie). The optimum solution, I', does satisfy the condition that net agency costs are minimized. But this simply amounts to a restatement of the assumption that the manager maximizes his welfare.

Finally, it is possible for the solution point D to be a corner solution, and in this case the value of the firm will not be declining. Such a corner solution can occur, for instance, if the manager's marginal rate of substitution between F and wealth falls to zero fast enough as we move up the expansion path, or if the investment projects are "sufficiently" profitable. In these cases the expansion path will have a corner which lies on the maximum value budget constraint with intercept $\overline{V}(I^*)-I^*$, and the level of investment will be equal to the idealized optimum, I^*. However, the market value of the residual claims will be less than V^* because the manager's consumption of perquisites will be larger than F^*, the zero agency cost level.

27. The careful reader will note that point C will be the equilibrium point only if the contract between the manager and outside equity holders specifies with no ambiguity that they have the right to monitor to limit his consumption of perquisites to an amount no less than F''. If any ambiguity regarding these rights exists in this contract, then another source of agency costs arises which is symmetrical to our original problem. If they could do so the outside equity holders would monitor to the point where the net value of *their* holdings, $(1-\alpha)V-M$, was maximized, and this would occur when $(\partial V/\partial M)(1-\alpha)-1 = 0$, which would be at some point between points C and E in Figure 3.3. Point E denotes the point where the value of the firm net of the monitoring costs is at a maximum, i.e., where $\partial V/\partial M-1 = 0$. But the manager would be worse off than in the zero monitoring solution if the point where $(1-\alpha)V-M$ was at a maximum were to the left of the intersection between BCE and the indifference curve U_3 passing through point B (which denotes the zero monitoring level of welfare). Thus if the manager could not eliminate enough of the ambiguity in the contract to push the equilibrium to the right of the intersection of the curve BCE with indifference curve U_3, he would not engage in any contract which allowed monitoring.

28. If we could establish the existence of a feasible set of alternative institutional arrangements which would yield net benefits from the reduction of these costs, we could legitimately conclude that the agency relationship engendered by the corporation was not Pareto-optimal. However, we would then be left with the problem of explaining why these alternative institutional arrangements have not replaced the corporate form of organization.

29. The monitoring and bonding costs will differ from firm to firm depending on such things as the inherent complexity and geographical dispersion of operations, the attractiveness of perquisites available in the firm (consider the mint), and so on.

30. Where competitors are numerous and entry is easy, persistent departures from profit-maximizing behavior inexorably lead to extinction. Economic natural selection holds the stage. In these circumstances, the behavior of the individual units that constitute the supply side of the product market is essentially routine and uninteresting, and economists can confidently predict industry behavior without being explicitly concerned with the behavior of these individual units.

When the conditions of competition are relaxed, however, the opportunity set of the firm is expanded. In this case, the behavior of the firm as a distinct operating unit is of separate interest. Both for purposes of interpreting particular behavior within the firm as well as for predicting responses of the industry aggregate, it may be necessary to identify the factors that influence the firm's choices within this expanded opportunity set and embed these in a formal model (Williamson 1964, p. 2).

31. Assuming there are no special tax benefits to ownership nor utility of ownership other than that derived from the direct wealth effects of ownership such as might be true for professional sports teams, race horse stables, firms that carry the family name, and so forth.

32. Marris (1964, pp. 7–9) is the exception, although he argues that there exists some "maximum leverage point" beyond which the chances of "insolvency" are in some undefined sense too high.

33. By limited liability we mean the same conditions that apply to common stock. Subordinated debt or preferred stock could be constructed that carried with it liability provisions; that is, if the corporation's assets were insufficient at some point to pay off all prior claims (such as trade credit, accrued wages, senior debt, and so on) and if the personal resources of the "equity" holders were also insufficient to cover these claims, the holders of this "debt" would be subject to assessments beyond the face value of their claim (assessments which might be limited or unlimited in amount).

34. Alchian and Demsetz (1972, p. 709) argue that one can explain the existence of both bonds and stock in the ownership structure of firms as the result of differing expectations regarding the outcomes to the firm. They argue that bonds are created and sold to "pessimists" and stocks with a residual claim with no upper bound are sold to "optimists."

As long as capital markets are perfect with no taxes or transaction costs and individual investors can issue claims on distributions of outcomes on the same terms as firms, such actions on the part of firms cannot affect their values. The reason is simple. Suppose such "pessimists" did exist and yet the firm issues only equity claims. The demand for those equity claims would reflect the fact that the individual purchaser could on his own account issue "bonds" with a limited and prior claim on the distribution of outcomes on the equity which is exactly the same as that which the firm could issue. Similarly, investors could easily unlever any position by simply buying a proportional claim on both the bonds and the stocks of a levered firm. Therefore, a levered firm could not sell at a different price than an unlevered firm solely because of the existence of such differential expectations. See Fama and Miller (1972, chap. 4) for an excellent exposition of these issues.

35. Corporations did use both prior to the institution of the corporate income tax in the United States, and preferred dividends have, with minor exceptions, never been tax-deductible.

36. See Kraus and Litzenberger (1973) and Lloyd-Davies (1975).

37. And if there is competitive bidding for the firm from potential owner-managers, the absentee owner will capture the capitalized value of these agency costs.

38. The spectrum of claims which firms can issue is far more diverse than is suggested by our two-way classification—fixed versus residual. There are convertible bonds, equipment trust certificates, debentures, revenue bonds, warrants, and so on. Different bond issues can contain different subordination provisions with respect to assets and interest. They can be callable or non-callable. Preferred stocks can be "preferred" in a variety of dimensions and can contain a variety of subordination stipulations. In the abstract, we can imagine firms issuing claims contingent on a literally infinite variety of states of the world such as those considered in the literature on the time-state-preference models of Arrow (1964b), Debreu (1959), and Hirshleifer (1970).

39. An apt analogy is the way one would play poker on money borrowed at a fixed interest rate, with one's own liability limited to some very small stake. Fama and Miller (1972, pp. 179–180) also discuss and provide a numerical example of an investment decision which illustrates very nicely the potential inconsistency between the interests of bondholders and stockholders.

40. The portfolio diversification issues facing the owner-manager are brought into the analysis in Section 3.5 of this chapter.

41. See Smith (1976) for a review of this option pricing literature and its applications, and see also Galai and Masulis (1976), who apply the option pricing model to mergers and corporate investment decisions.

42. Although we used the option pricing model earlier to motivate the discussion and provide some intuitive understanding of the incentives facing the equity holders, the option pricing solutions of Black and Scholes (1973) do not apply when incentive effects cause V to be a function of the debt/equity ratio as it is in general and in this example. Long (1974) points out this difficulty with respect to the usefulness of the model in the context of tax subsidies on interest and bankruptcy cost. The results of Merton (1974) and Galai and Masulis (1976) must be interpreted with care since the solutions are strictly incorrect in the context of tax subsidies and/or agency costs.

43. The numerical example of Fama and Miller (1972, pp. 179–180) is a close representation of this case in a two-period state model. However, they go on to make the following statement on p. 180: "From a practical viewpoint, however, situations of potential conflict between bondholders and shareholders in the application of the market value rule are probably unimportant. In general, investment opportunities that increase a firm's market value by more than their cost both increase the value of the firm's shares and strengthen the firm's future ability to meet its current bond commitments." This first issue regarding the

importance of the conflict of interest between bondholders and stockholders is an empirical one, and the last statement is incomplete—in some circumstances the equity holders could benefit from projects whose net effect was to reduce the total value of the firm, as they and we have illustrated. The issue cannot be brushed aside so easily.

44. Myers (1975) points out another serious incentive effect on managerial decisions of the existence of debt which does not occur in our simple single decision world. He shows that if the firm has the option to take future investment opportunities, the existence of debt that matures after the options must be taken will cause the firm (using an equity value maximizing investment rule) to refuse to take some otherwise profitable projects because they would benefit only the bondholders and not the equity holders. This will (in the absence of tax subsidies to debt) cause the value of the firm to fall. Thus (although Myers does not use the term) these incentive effects also contribute to the agency costs of debt in a manner perfectly consistent with the examples discussed in the text.

45. Black and Scholes (1973) discuss ways in which dividend and future financing policy can redistribute wealth between classes of claimants on the firm.

46. Black, Miller, and Posner (1974) discuss many of these issues with particular reference to the government regulation of bank holding companies.

47. In other words, these costs will be taken into account in determining the yield to maturity on the issue. For an examination of the effects of such enforcement costs on the nominal interest rates in the consumer small loan market, see Benston (1977).

48. To illustrate the fact that it will sometimes pay the manager to incur "bonding" costs to guarantee the bondholders that he will not deviate from his promised behavior, let us suppose that for an expenditure of b of the firm's resources he can guarantee that project 1 will be chosen. If he spends these resources and takes project 1 the value of the firm will be V_1-b, and clearly as long as $(V_1-b) > V_2$, or alternatively $(V_1 - V_2) > b$, he will be better off, since his wealth will be equal to the value of the firm minus the required investment, I (which we assumed for simplicity to be identical for the two projects).

On the other hand, to prove that the owner-manager prefers the lowest-cost solution to the conflict, let us assume he can write a covenant into the bond issue which will allow the bondholders to prevent him from taking project 2, if they incur monitoring costs of m, where $m < b$. If he does this his wealth will be higher by the amount $b-m$. To see this, note that if the bond market is competitive and makes unbiased estimates, potential bondholders will be indifferent between:

(i) a claim X^* with no covenant (and no guarantees from management) at a price of B_2,

(ii) a claim X^* with no covenant (and guarantees from management, through bonding expenditures by the firm of b, that project 1 will be taken) at a price of B_1, and

(iii) a claim X^* with a covenant and the opportunity to spend m on monitoring (to guarantee project 1 will be taken) at a price of B_1-m.

The bondholders will realize that (i) represents in fact a claim on project 2 and that (ii) and (iii) represent a claim on project 1 and are thus indifferent between the three options at the specified prices. The owner-manager, however, will not be indifferent between incurring the bonding costs, b, directly, or including the covenant in the bond indenture and letting the bondholders spend m to guarantee that he take project 1. His wealth in the two cases will be given by the value of his equity plus the proceeds of the bond issue less the required investment, and if $m < b < V_1 - V_2$, then his post-investment-financing wealth, W, for the three options will be such that $W_i < W_{ii} < W_{iii}$. Therefore, since it would increase his wealth, he would voluntarily include the covenant in the bond issue and let the bondholders monitor.

We would also like to mention, without going into the problem in detail, that similar to the case in which the outside equity holders are allowed to monitor the manager-owner, the agency relationship between the bondholders and stockholders has a symmetry if the rights of the bondholders to limit actions of the manager are not perfectly spelled out. Suppose the bondholders, by spending sufficiently large amounts of resources, could force management to take actions which would transfer wealth from the equity holder to the bondholders (by taking sufficiently less risky projects). One can easily construct situations where such actions could make the bondholders better off, hurt the equity holders, and actually lower the total value of the firm. Given the nature of the debt contract, the original owner-manager might maximize his wealth in such a situation by selling off the equity and keeping the bonds as his owner's interest. If the nature of the bond contract is given, this may well be an inefficient solution since the total agency costs (i.e., the sum of monitoring and value loss) could easily be higher than the alternative solution. However, if the owner-manager could strictly limit the rights of the bondholders (perhaps by inclusion of a provision which expressly reserves all rights not specifically granted to the bondholder for the equity holder), he would find it in his interest to establish the efficient contractual arrangement since by minimizing the agency costs he would be maximizing his wealth. These issues involve the fundamental nature of contracts, and for now we simply assume that the bondholders' rights are strictly limited and unambiguous and that all rights not specifically granted them are reserved for the stockholders—a situation descriptive of actual institutional arrangements. This allows us to avoid the incentive effects associated with bondholders potentially exploiting stockholders.

49. If the firm were allowed to sell assets to meet a current debt obligation, bankruptcy would occur when the total market value of the future cash flows expected to be generated by the firm is less than the value of a current payment on a debt obligation. Many bond indentures do not, however, allow for the sale of assets to meet debt obligations.

50. While this is true in principle, the actual behavior of the courts frequently involves the provision of some settlement to the common stockholders even when the assets of the company are not sufficient to cover the claims of the creditors.

51. If under bankruptcy the bondholders have the right to fire the management, the

management will have some incentives to avoid taking actions which increase the probability of this event (even if it is in the best interest of the equity holders) if they (the management) are earning rents or if they have human capital specialized to this firm or if they face large adjustment costs in finding new employment. A detailed examination of this issue involves the value of the control rights (the rights to hire and fire the manager), and we leave it to a subsequent paper.

52. Kraus and Litzenberger (1973) and Lloyd-Davies (1975) demonstrate that the total value of the firm will be reduced by these costs.

53. These include only payments to all parties for legal fees, professional services, trustees' fees, and filing fees. They do not include the costs of management time or changes in cash flows due to shifts in the firm's demand or cost functions discussed later in this chapter.

54. Which, incidentally, exist only when the debt has some probability of default.

55. Our theory is capable of explaining why in the absence of the tax subsidy on interest payments, we would expect to find firms using both debt and preferred stocks—a problem which has long puzzled at least one of the authors. If preferred stock has all the characteristics of debt except for the fact that its holders cannot put the firm into bankruptcy in the event of nonpayment of the preferred dividends, then the agency costs associated with the issuance of preferred stock will be lower than those associated with debt by the present value of the bankruptcy costs.

However, these lower agency costs of preferred stock exist only over some range if as the amount of such stock rises the incentive effects caused by their existence impose value reductions which are larger than that caused by debt (including the bankruptcy costs of debt). There are two reasons for this. First, the equity holder's claims can be eliminated by the debtholders in the event of bankruptcy, and second, the debtholders have the right to fire the management in the event of bankruptcy. Both of these will tend to become more important as an advantage to the issuance of debt as we compare situations with large amounts of preferred stock to equivalent situations with large amounts of debt because they will tend to reduce the incentive effects of large amounts of preferred stock.

56. One other condition also has to hold to justify the incurrence of the costs associated with the use of debt or outside equity in our firm. If there are other individuals in the economy who have sufficiently large amounts of personal capital to finance the entire firm, our capital constrained owner can realize the full capital value of his current and prospective projects and avoid the agency costs by simply selling the firm (i.e., the right to take these projects) to one of these individuals. He will then avoid the wealth losses associated with the agency costs caused by the sale of debt or outside equity. If no such individuals exist, it will pay him (and society) to obtain the additional capital in the debt market. This implies, incidentally, that it is somewhat misleading to speak of the owner-manager as the individual who bears the agency costs. One could argue that it is the project which bears the costs since, if it is not sufficiently profitable to cover all the costs (including the agency costs), it will not be taken.

We continue to speak of the owner-manager bearing these costs to emphasize the more correct and important point that he has the incentive to reduce them because, if he does, his wealth will be increased.

57. We continue to ignore for the moment the additional complicating factor involved with the portfolio decisions of the owner, and the implied acceptance of potentially diversifiable risk by such 100% owners in this example.

58. We continue to ignore such instruments as convertible bonds and warrants.

59. Note, however, that even when outsiders own none of the equity, the stockholder-manager still has some incentives to engage in activities which yield him non-pecuniary benefits but reduce the value of the firm by more than he personally values the benefits if there is any risky debt outstanding. Any such actions he takes which reduce the value of the firm, V, tend to reduce the value of the bonds as well as the value of the equity. Although the option pricing model does not in general apply exactly to the problem of valuing the debt and equity of the firm, it can be useful in obtaining some qualitative insights into matters such as this. In the option pricing model $\partial S/\partial V$ indicates the rate at which the stock value changes per dollar change in the value of the firm (and similarly for $\partial B/\partial V$). Both of these terms are less than unity (cf. Black and Scholes 1973). Therefore, any action of the manager which reduces the value of the firm, V, tends to reduce the value of both the stock and the bonds, and the larger is the total debt/equity ratio, the smaller is the impact of any given change in V on the value of the equity, and therefore, the lower is the cost to him of consuming non-pecuniary benefits.

60. This occurs, of course, not at the intersection of $A_{S_0}(E)$ and $A_B(E)$, but at the point where the absolute value of the slopes of the functions are equal, i.e., where $A'_{S_0}(E) + A'_B(E) = 0$.

61. On the average, however, top managers seem to have substantial holdings in absolute dollars. A survey by Wytmar (*Wall Street Journal*, August 13, 1974, p. 1) reported that the median value of 826 chief executive officers' stock holdings in their companies at year end 1973 was $557,000, and it was $1.3 million at year end 1972.

62. These diversification effects can be substantial. Evans and Archer (1968) show that on the average for New York Stock Exchange securities approximately 55% of the total risk (as measured by standard deviation of portfolio returns) can be eliminated by following a naive strategy of dividing one's assets equally among 40 randomly selected securities.

63. The work of Myers (1975) which views future investment opportunities as options and investigates the incentive effects of the existence of debt in such a world where a sequence of investment decisions is made is another important step in the investigation of the multiperiod aspects of the agency problem and the theory of the firm.

64. Becker and Stigler (1972) analyze a special case of this problem involving the use of nonvested pension rights to help correct for this end game play in the law enforcement area.

65. By our colleague David Henderson.

66. This also suggests that *some* outside debtholders can protect themselves from "exploitation" by the manager by purchasing a fraction of the total equity equal to their fractional ownership of the debt. All debtholders, of course, cannot do this unless the manager does so also. In addition, such an investment rule restricts the portfolio choices of investors and therefore would impose costs if followed rigidly. Thus the agency costs will not be eliminated this way either.

67. Consider the situation in which the bondholders have the right in the event of bankruptcy to terminate his employment and therefore to terminate the future returns to any specific human capital or rents he may be receiving.

68. See Fama (1970a) for a survey of this "efficient markets" literature.

69. See Jensen (1969) for an example of this evidence and references.

70. Ignoring any pure consumption elements in the demand for security analysis.

71. Again ignoring the value of the pure consumption elements in the demand for security analysis.

4. Specific and General Knowledge and Organizational Structure

1. Harris et al. (1982) also recognized this principle.

2. Like Hayek, economists have generally taken the costs of information transfer to be prohibitively large, and, therefore, have taken the distribution of knowledge as given. They have analyzed extensively the effects of "information asymmetry" (as it is known in the principal/agent literature) on contracting relations. Williamson (1975) in his study of institutions defines the concept of "information impactedness" to deal with the organizational implications of transactions where information is "known to one or more parties but cannot be costlessly discerned by or displayed for others" (p. 31). Explicitly recognizing the costs of transferring knowledge is more useful analytically.

3. See, for example, Arrow (1964a). An excellent counterexample is Alchian and Allen (1983, and earlier editions dating back to 1969).

4. Including the right to sell the rights in output that an individual or firm creates with the resource.

5. It follows that the values established in exchanges are values of bundles of rights, not prices of physical objects. Property whose use is restricted by regulatory constraints or private covenants will sell at different prices from identical property with full use rights. Goods are sometimes alienated illegally, for example, theft, black markets, drugs, and prostitution. When the police powers are not 100 percent effective, rights are not 100 percent secure, and the lower value of such rights will reflect the probability that the rights will be taken (either illegally, or legally through political action such as confiscation or nationalization).

6. In the absence of externalities or monopoly, of course. But externalities are themselves a result of an incomplete definition and assignment of rights. See Coase (1960).

7. Customs and mores, not embodied in law, also confer decision-making powers

and constraints on individuals or groups, especially in primitive societies. The social sanctions imposed on those who take actions in violation of social or group norms can have substantial impact on the decision rights of individuals, which is separate from formal legal sanctions of the state. Alternatively, individuals sometimes possess decision-making powers without having legal rights in those resources, for example, possessors of stolen goods. Those engaged in illegal activities themselves employ threats of physical violence to preserve powers.

8. See Crook (1990) for an excellent survey.

9. Alienability includes the right to sell or transfer alienability itself.

10. See Rubin (1978) for a description and analysis of the nature of the franchise contract. Like so much of the literature on franchises, this analysis ignores the critical role of alienability in the functioning of this organizational form.

11. We can assume that the right is optimally assigned within each level in the hierarchy.

12. Assuming the CEO does not have agency problems with himself or herself (see Thaler and Schefrin 1981).

13. Mrs. Fields' Cookies is an example of a firm experiencing technological development that made it possible for headquarters to obtain detailed and timely information on store operations and to provide very detailed day-by-day, even hour-by-hour directions on operating decisions in its company-owned stores (see Richman 1987).

14. J. C. Penney's investment in satellite communications which provided the firm with closed-circuit TV made it possible to decentralize much of the store purchasing decisions from corporate headquarters to the local store managers. The TV system made it possible for central buyers in New York to display and "market" the goods to local store managers, who could then utilize their specific knowledge of local tastes and fashions to stock their stores (see Gilman 1987).

15. Chapter 7 provides further discussion of the breakdown of the decision process into initiation, ratification, implementation, and monitoring rights.

16. This could occur when there are external effects on other parts of the organization that cannot be incorporated in the manager's performance measure, but can be incorporated in the performance measure at a higher level of the organization.

17. The "every tub on its own bottom" budgeting systems of some universities are examples of variable performance-related budgets.

5. Organization Theory and Methodology

1. The use of the term "positive" in this context has had the unfortunate effect of linking accounting researchers who have been engaged in the effort to develop "positive" theories with "logical positivism," a school of thought in philosophy which has been controversial. The proposal to focus on positive theories of accounting does not commit those who propose it to logical positivism.

2. And often involve the result of other individuals' maximization process.

3. This conjecture, of course, is a positive theory and capable of being tested.

4. See Zimmerman (1977).

5. See Hansmann (1980, 1981) and Fama and Jensen (1985) as well as Chapters 6 and 7 of this volume for several recent attempts to understand where nonprofit organizations survive and why.

6. For a number of studies that address these issues see Watts (1977), Watts and Zimmerman (1978, 1979), Leftwich (1983), and Holthausen (1981).

7. Chapter 12 offers the beginning elements of such a theory.

8. Understanding why the FASB and the SEC behave as they do and their effects on accounting requires a positive theory of the political process—another difficult area which is experiencing great scientific progress. The research on financial reporting evidences an understanding of this, and I shall ignore these political/regulatory issues here.

9. See, for example, Williamson (1964, 1975, 1979, 1981), Arrow (1964a, 1974), Alchian (1950, 1969, 1981), Alchian and Demsetz (1972), Pejovich (1969), Furubotn and Pejovich (1973), Jensen and Meckling (1979), Lazear (1979), Lazear and Rosen (1981), Klein, Crawford and Alchian (1978), Harris and Raviv (1978), Harris, Kriebel, and Raviv (1982), Fama and Jensen (1983a, 1983b, 1985), Fama (1980), Smith and Warner (1979), Chandler (1962, 1977), Chandler and Daems (1980), Daems (1978), Hansmann (1980, 1981), Demsetz (1982), Reagan and Stulz (1986), Marvel (1982), Meckling (1976), Mayers and Smith (1981, 1982a, 1982b), and Chapters 3 and 4 of this volume.

10. See, for example, Benston (1963, 1975a, 1975b, 1979–1980), Watts (1977, 1981), Watts and Zimmerman (1978, 1979, 1982a), Hagerman and Zmijewski (1979), Leftwich, Watts, and Zimmerman (1981), DeAngelo (1981a, 1981b), Collins, Rozeff, and Dhaliwal (1981), Holthausen (1981), Zmijewski and Hagerman (1981), Dhaliwal (1980), Lilien and Pastena (1982), Bowen, Noreen, and Lacey (1981), Healy (1985), Dhaliwal, Salamon, and Smith (1982), Jarrell (1979), and Lys (1982). Useful reviews of this literature are provided by Holthausen and Leftwich (1982), Zimmerman (1980), and Watts and Zimmerman (1982b).

11. "A connection, tie, or link between individuals of a group, members of a series, etc." *Webster's New World Dictionary* (1978).

12. See Meckling (1976) Chapter 1 for a discussion of alternative models of man as the elementary unit of analysis. Sociobiologists, however, find it useful for analysis of some questions to view the gene as the elementary maximizing entity. See Hirshleifer (1978) and Dawkins (1976) and the references therein for discussions of this alternative model.

13. "In general, no one department should be responsible for handling all phases of a transaction, and if possible, the division of responsibility should keep operations and custodianship separate from accounting." Stettler (1977, p. 56).

14. Philosophers have a precise definition of tautology. I use the term here more loosely and more in accord with its use in the social sciences.

15. I am left with questions; for example, why don't we organize our thoughts

about the family through the double-entry tautology? Perhaps someday these issues will be better understood.

16. For some interesting applications of this approach see Smith and Warner (1979), who use it to explain covenants in bond indentures; Mayers and Smith (1981, 1982a, 1982b), who examine contracting and organizational practices in the insurance industry; and Leftwich (1983), who examines the private contractual specification of accounting procedures. Holthausen (1981) uses the approach to derive hypotheses about management decisions to change depreciation methods. His tests indicate that the data are not consistent with the hypotheses.

17. Alchian (1950) long ago argued for the use of the natural-selection principle in economic analysis.

18. Some representative but far from exhaustive references are Spence and Zeckhauser (1971), Ross (1973, 1974a), Raviv (1979), Harris and Raviv (1978), Mirrlees (1976), Harris and Townsend (1981), Townsend (1979), Holmstrom (1979), and Shavell (1979). Demski and Kreps (1982) review the accounting-related literature in this area.

19. See, for example, Myers (1977), Smith and Warner (1979), Fama (1980), Holthausen (1981), Mikkelson (1981), Leftwich (1981, 1983), Mayers and Smith (1981, 1982a, 1982b), Watts and Zimmerman (1982a, 1982b), Fama and Jensen (1985), and Chapters 3, 6, and 7 of this volume.

6. Agency Problems and Residual Claims

1. This definition of agency costs first appears in Chapter 3.

2. See Chapter 7. See also Fama and Jensen (1985).

3. See, for example, Arrow (1964b) or Fama (1976, chaps. 7 and 8).

4. See Reagan and Stulz (1986) for an analysis of risk sharing between internal agents and residual claimants and for references to the related literature.

5. See, for example, Fama (1978).

6. See Furubotn and Pejovich (1973); and Jensen and Meckling (1979).

7. The details of the argument are given in Chapter 2.

8. However, in partnerships and closed corporations, some mechanisms for resolving conflicts among residual claimant decision makers (for example, buyout rules) are required.

9. In Chapter 7, we discuss how the diffusion of information among decision agents influences the survival of organizational forms. For simplicity, we have ignored these issues here.

10. Mayers and Smith (1982a) argue that insurance itself is a way to purchase monitoring.

11. See DeAngelo (1981b).

12. See Fama and Jensen (1985).

13. See Thompson (1978).

14. Because policy premiums are included as business receipts, the latter are a larger fraction of total receipts for insurance companies than for banks. Never-

theless, comparison of the business receipts of corporate and mutual insurance companies is relevant.

15. See Mayers and Smith (1981) for additional hypotheses regarding contract structures in the insurance industry.

16. Hansmann (1980) analyzes the nonprofit organization in detail, but he tends to attribute the nonprofit form more to the nature of products than to the agency problems of donations. He treats donors as customers and looks for product characteristics that would make for "contract failure" in a for-profit framework. For example, charity is delivered to third parties, and the customer (donor) has difficulty verifying delivery. Hansmann also argues that the nonprofit form is attractive for high technology goods (because the customer has difficulty verifying quality) and public goods. However, his approach predicts wider dominance for nonprofits (for example, all high technology or public goods) than is observed. The hypothesis that the nonprofit form is related to donor financing is more promising.

17. See Hansmann (1980).

18. The role of specific knowledge is discussed in Chapter 7.

7. Separation of Ownership and Control

1. Alchian (1950) is an early proponent of the use of natural selection in economic analysis. For a survey of general issues in the analysis of organization, see Chapter 5 of the present volume.

2. See Smith (1776); Berle and Means (1932); and Chapter 3 of the present volume.

3. See Chapter 3.

4. See Jensen and Meckling (1979).

5. The terms "public corporation" and "close corporation," which are common in the legal literature, are not used here. "Closed corporation" seems more descriptive than "close corporation." The term "public corporation" best describes government-owned corporations such as Amtrak and the TVA. In contrast, what we call "open corporations" are private organizations.

6. This definition of agency costs comes from Chapter 3.

7. Specific information is closely related to the notions of "information impactedness" and "bounded rationality" discussed in Williamson (1975, 1981). Hayek (1945) uses specific information to discuss the role of markets in complex economies. See also Sowell (1980). Our analysis of the relations between specific information and efficient decision processes owes much to ongoing work with William Meckling.

8. See, for example, Arrow (1964b) or Fama (1976, chaps. 6 and 7).

9. In contrast, the analysis predicts that when venture equity capital is put into a small entrepreneurial organization by outsiders, mechanisms for separating the management and control of important decisions are instituted.

10. These propositions are developed in Chapter 6.

11. See Alchian and Demsetz (1972).

12. See Weber (1947); Blau (1956); Simon (1962); and Williamson (1975, 1980). The historical development of hierarchies in open corporations is analyzed in Chandler (1977) and Chandler and Daems (1980).

13. The separation of decision management from decision control that we emphasize is reflected in the auditing profession's concern with allocating operating and accounting responsibility to different agents. For instance, it is recommended that an agent with responsibility for billing should not have a role in receiving or recording customer payments. See, for example, Horngren (1982, chap. 27) or Stettler (1977, chaps. 4 and 8).

14. See Fama (1980).

15. Decision functions can be delegated in two general ways: (1) joint delegation to several agents (as in a committee), or (2) partitioning and delegation of the parts to different agents. Boards of directors are examples of the former approach; decision hierarchies are examples of the latter.

16. Monitoring from the takeover market is emphasized in Manne (1965).

17. See Herman (1981, chap. 2) for data on the characteristics of corporate boards.

18. See Fama (1980).

19. For example, Horngren (1982, p. 911) describes the role of the audit committee of the board (generally composed of outside board members) as a collector and conduit of information from the internal mutual monitoring system: "The objective of the audit committee is to oversee the accounting controls, financial statements, and financial affairs of the corporation. The committee represents the full board and provides personal contact and communication among the board, the external auditors, the internal auditors, the financial executives, and the operating executives."

20. See Herman (1981, chap. 2).

21. Ibid.

22. See Herman (1969) for documentation of such lack of interest. For example, he describes situations where in more than a decade only four depositors in total attended the annual meetings of two savings and loan associations, and other situations where management did not even bother to collect proxies.

23. See Chapter 6. See also Hansmann (1980) for a general discussion of nonprofits.

8. Compensation and Incentives

1. A partial list of some of this work includes Coase (1937), Alchian and Demsetz (1972), Williamson (1975), Stiglitz (1975), Holmström and Tirole (1987), the papers at the May 1987 Yale conference in honor of Ronald Coase, and Chapters 3, 4, 6, and 7 of this volume.

2. See, for example, Hart and Holmström (1987) and the 142 references therein.

3. See Hamner (1975) and Beer et al. (1984) for a summary of the problems associated with merit systems.

4. General Motors vice president Roy Roberts offers a refreshing alternative view

that underscores the inherent ambiguity of words like *fair* and *equal:* "To treat people fairly you have to treat people differently." (Quoted in Schlesinger 1988.)

5. See Lawler (1973), p. 123.
6. Fast and Berg (1975).
7. In particular, they find that the R-squares of cross-sectional earnings-profile regressions rise from .36 to .74 in Company A, and from .34 to .85 in Company B.
8. See Baker (1988) and Gibbs (1989) for a more thorough discussion of the comparative-statics results.
9. See Jensen (1989b).
10. Average equity holdings of the management team in Kaplan's (1991) sample of 76 buyouts in the 1980–1986 period is 36.7%.
11. Deutsch (1986) comments on the growing prevalence of "dual-track promotion ladders" as a means of keeping technical employees from losing incentives and leaving organizations.
12. These three situations, graphically represented by the cases where the hierarchical output relations intersect one or more times, are identical, or do not intersect, are mutually exclusive and exhaustive.
13. Some behaviorists might argue that the pre-tenure period is one in which new members are indoctrinated into the culture of the organization, and that after tenure is awarded incentives are no longer necessary for motivation. Although indoctrination or training is important for other reasons, the problem faced by many institutions with unproductive senior faculty, many of whom devote considerable energy and effort to outside activities, seems inconsistent with the argument that apprenticeship substitutes for incentives in an organization.
14. If turnover is really important in these organizations, however, it is hard to explain why these firms provide for no turnover among those who are promoted. There seems to be a trend to increasing the partner turnover in accounting and law firms, as more partners are asked to leave.
15. In fact, Company B subsequently dropped the bottom two performance categories.
16. Artificially imposing costs to affect monitoring incentives is similar to the tendency of individuals to impose costs on themselves by placing a bowl of peanuts across the room to raise the cost of consumption or by a joining a Christmas, health, or diet club where costs are borne from violating a precommitment. Thaler and Shefrin (1981) provide a model to explain this and other puzzling behavior using the notion of conflicts between two inner selves in each individual, the "planner" and "doer." The planner acts as the monitor for the doer, and executes decisions that limit the actions of the doer that tend to be short-term-oriented at the expense of long-term goals of the individual.
17. Conference Board (1985).
18. In intertemporal settings, the level of compensation is the expected present value of the future stream of payoffs.

9. Performance Pay and Top-Management Incentives

1. This is calculated from column 5 of Table 9.2 as 893 + .0020 × (−400,000), where .0020 is the estimated pay-performance sensitivity for a CEO owning the 73-firm sample median of 0.16% of his firm's common stock.

10. CEO Incentives

1. The median CEO in our sample holds stock worth $2.4 million. The average 1988 salary and bonus for the CEOs in our sample was roughly $1 million. At a real interest rate of 3%, the present value of the salary and bonus for the next five years to retirement (the average for the sample) is $4.6 million. Thus total lifetime wealth from the company is $7 million.
2. See Gibbons and Murphy (1990, p. 30-S).
3. See Warner, Watts, and Wruck (1988, p. 461) and Weisbach (1988, p. 431).
4. For more detail on these tests, see Chapter 9.
5. Data on hourly and salaried workers come from the Michigan Panel Study on Income Dynamics. The sample includes 21,895 workers aged 21 to 65 reporting wages in consecutive periods. See McLaughlin (1989).
6. *Wall Street Journal,* March 21, 1986.
7. The accompanying tables (Tables 10.3 through 10.6) present estimates of pay-for-performance sensitivities for only a fraction of the CEOs in our full survey. Readers who would like a copy of the full 430-company survey, along with a detailed technical appendix fully describing our methodology, can write to Professor Kevin J. Murphy at the University of Southern California, Dept. of Finance and Business Administration, Los Angeles, CA 90089-1421.

11. Science, Specific Knowledge, and Total Quality Management

1. For an overview see March and Garvin (1986). A small sampling of such work includes works by quality leaders Crosby (1979, 1989), Deming (1952), Ishikawa (1985), Juran (1989), Mizuno (1988), and Suzaki (1987) and research conducted by Ernst & Young/American Quality Foundation (1992), Feigenbaum (1991), Garvin (1988), Jaikumar (1989), and Kantor and Zangwill (1993).
2. It appears that quality rhetoric has been helpful in reducing resistance to organizational change. Eccles and Nohria (1992) discuss the role that rhetoric plays in accomplishing organizational change.
3. Jensen (1993) argues that TQM is one of the technological forces behind the third industrial revolution.
4. In addition to their own research, studies surveyed by Baldwin and Clark (1992) include Garvin (1988) on the effects of TQM in the U.S. and Japanese room air conditioning industry, Clark and Fujimoto (1991) on investments in organizational capabilities supporting new product development in U.S. and Japanese automobile manufacturers, and Jaikumar (1989) on investments in

organizational capabilities supporting flexible manufacturing technology in the U.S. and Japan.

5. The plant produces stryrene monomer, acrylonitrile, tertiary-butylamine, lactic acid, sodium cyanide, acetic acid, and plasticizers. Monsanto sold the plant as part of an effort to exit certain commodity chemicals businesses and enter consumer businesses. The best known transaction associated with this effort was Monsanto's $2.75 billion acquisition of G.D. Searle in 1985. Monsanto used the proceeds from the sale of the Texas City plant and other similar transactions to repay debt incurred in the Searle acquisition. Chandler (1993) analyzes the restructuring of the chemical industry that occurred in the 1980s.

6. Experiments conducted by psychologists, behavioral economists, and experts in organizational behavior provide evidence that individuals systematically make decisions based on wrong theories. In the organizational behavior area, Argyris (1990, 1992) provides evidence that managers often make decisions based on invalid, untested theories which they are unaware they hold. Thaler (1991) presents a collection of behavioral economics articles documenting systematic "quasi-rational" behavior. Larrick, Nisbett, and Morgan (1993) provide evidence that cost-benefit reasoning is a learned behavior that improves individual decision making once mastered.

7. When discussing the application of science in decision making, we are not referring to the so-called "scientific management" developed in the early 1900s by F. W. Taylor. Taylor's approach emphasized reliance on Industrial Engineering methods (such as time and motion studies) to set work standards and improve efficiency.

8. Argyris (1992) argues that while TQM programs tend to move organizations in the right direction, they are not always successful in overcoming organizational defensive routines.

9. See, for example, Stigler and Becker (1977), who describe habits as an efficient approach to decision making when information collection is costly and the environment is reasonably stable.

10. For example, Juran (1989, p. 264) encourages managers to "delegate to the work force to the maximum extent possible." Other examples are presented in Ishikawa (1985, p. 62), Suzaki (1987, pp. 216–217, 222–224), Mizuno (1988, p. 11), and Juran (1989, p. 293).

11. While Jensen and Meckling (Chapter 4) do not specifically address the potential value of team-based problem-solving, they do argue that one of the reasons firms exist is that "bringing diverse knowledge together to bear on decisions significantly expands the opportunity set because no one person is likely to possess the set of knowledge relevant to a particular decision."

12. As economists, we cannot subscribe to the theory proposed by Crosby (1979) that quality is literally free. Experience indicates, however, that in many situations the benefits of TQM far outweigh its costs.

13. In other words, employees' efforts must be directed toward a clear objective function that is closely coordinated with that of the organization. Our findings are consistent with extensive research on teamwork by Hackman (1986), who

identifies four conditions supporting effective self-managed teams: (1) a clear, engaging direction, (2) an enabling team structure (sufficient effort, knowledge, and skills, and appropriate task performance strategies), (3) a supportive organizational context (the reward system, the education system, and the information system), and (4) available expert coaching.

14. See, for example, Dixon, Nanni, and Vollmann (1990), Kaplan and Norton (1992), Lynch and Cross (1991), and Hall, Johnson, and Turney (1991).

15. Not all firms that benchmark also practice TQM. Data for benchmarking are sometimes obtained from consultants, and sometimes firms agree to cooperate with one another. Cooperation generally occurs between firms which are not direct competitors, but which have similar processes or approaches so that each can learn from the other's practices.

16. For example, Schneiderman (1988) recommends measuring the rate at which remaining problems are eliminated from a process or product. Rather than reporting yields of 99.7% (i.e., 99.7% of products made correctly), it would be reported that the process is creating 300 defective parts per million. Effort is then focused on efficiently driving the number of defective parts downward.

17. Under the machine shop's system, minimum compensation is set at 85¢ per hour. Once employees exceed quota, they earn a piece rate per additional unit produced. Employees classify jobs into two categories: "stinker" and "gravy" jobs. Stinker jobs are priced such that without extraordinary effort it is impossible to meet quota. On stinker jobs, employees "goldbrick," exerting little effort and opting for the minimum hourly compensation. Gravy jobs are priced such that it is possible to meet quota. Employees observe that once they begin to earn $1.25 an hour or more, management reprices gravy jobs. Employees then restrict output so that the $1.25 limit is not breached and pressure others to do the same.

12. Divisional Performance Measurement

1. In Chapter 7, Fama and Jensen discuss initiation, ratification, implementation, and monitoring rights, and how their assignment can reduce agency costs.

2. The importance of the costs of transferring knowledge was suggested by our reading of Hayek's (1945) article "The Use of Scientific Knowledge in Society." Although he used the terms "scientific" and "particular" knowledge, we believe that the concept of specific and general knowledge defined in terms of cost of transferring knowledge between agents captures the important dimensions of Hayek's discussion of the role of knowledge. Williamson (1975) uses the term "information impactedness" to characterize a similar phenomenon. That term, however, does not suggest a continuum in which the costs of information transfer can vary, and this seriously constrains the effectiveness of the analysis. The notion of "asymmetric information" widely used in the principal/agent literature (see, for example, Harris, Kriebel, and Raviv 1982) deals with the same issue and has the same problem.

3. See Hirshleifer (1964).

4. See Hirshleifer (1964).
5. EVA is a registered trademark of Stern Stewart & Co. See Stewart (1991) for a detailed description of EVA and its uses.
6. See Niskanen (1968).
7. See Baker and Monsler (1995) for a case dealing in part with the Locus of Uncertainty problem.

References

Alchian, Armen A. 1950. "Uncertainty, Evolution and Economic Theory." *Journal of Political Economy* 58, no. 3 (June), pp. 221ff.

—— 1965. "The Basis of Some Recent Advances in the Theory of Management of the Firm." *Journal of Industrial Economics* (November), pp. 30–44.

—— 1968. *Corporate Managment Behavior and Property Rights.* Economic Policy and the Regulation of Corporate Securities, American Enterprise Institute Symposium, Washington, D.C., pp. 183–201.

—— 1974. *Some Implications of Recognition of Property Rights and Transaction Costs.* First Interlaken Conference on Analysis and Ideology, June 1979. Economics and Social Institute, ed. Karl Bruner. The Hague: Nyhoff.

—— 1981. "Property Rights, Specialization and the Firm." Corporate Enterprise in a New Environment. Essays in honor of Neil Jakoby, ed. J. F. Weston. ITT Publishers.

Alchian, Armen A., and Allen, W. R. 1969. *Exchange and Production: Theory in Use.* Belmont, Calif.: Wadsworth.

—— 1983. *Exchange and Production: Competition, Coordination, and Control.* Belmont, Calif.: Wadsworth.

Alchian, Armen A., and Demsetz, Harold. 1972. "Production, Information Costs, and Economic Organization." *American Economic Review* 62, no. 5 (December), pp. 777–795.

Alchian, Armen A., and Kessel, R. A. 1962. "Competition, Monopoly, and the Pursuit of Profits," in *Aspects of Labor Economics,* ed. H. Gregg Lewis, pp. 157–182. Princeton, N.J.: National Bureau of Economic Research.

American Quality Foundation. 1992. "The International Quality Study: Best Practices Report and Automotive, Health Care, Computer, and Banking Industry Reports." New York: Ernst & Young and the American Quality Foundation.

Argyris, Chris. 1990. *Overcoming Organizational Defenses.* New York: Allyn and Bacon.

—— 1991. "Teaching Smart People How to Learn." *Harvard Business Review* (May-June), pp. 99–109.

—— 1992. "The Next Challenge for TQM: Overcoming Organizational Defenses." *Journal for Quality and Participation* (March), pp. 26–29.

—— 1993. *Knowledge for Action: A Guide to Overcoming Barriers to Organizational Change.* San Francisco: Jossey-Bass.

Arrow, Kenneth J. 1964a. "Control in Large Organizations." *Management Science* 10 (April), pp. 397–408.

——— 1964b. "The Role of Securities in the Optimal Allocation of Risk Bearing." *Review of Economic Studies* 31, no. 86 (January), pp. 91–96.

——— 1974. *The Limits of Organizations.* New York: Norton.

Atkinson, T. R. 1967. "Trends in Corporate Bond Quality," in *Studies in Corporate Bond Finance 4.* New York: National Bureau of Economic Research.

Baird, Charles W. 1993. "Are Quality Circles Illegal? Global Competition Meets the New Deal." Briefing Paper no. 10. Washington, D. C.: Cato Institute.

Baker, George P. 1988. "Incentives in Hierarchies: Promotions, Bonuses, and Monitoring." Harvard Business School Working Paper no. 88-023. Boston: Harvard Business School.

Baker, George P., Jensen, Michael C., and Murphy, Kevin J. 1988. "Compensation and Incentives: Practice vs. Theory." *Journal of Finance* 43, no. 3 (July), pp. 593–616. (Chapter 8 of this volume.)

Baker, George P., and Monsler, Karin B. 1995. "San Francisco Bay Consulting." Harvard Business School Publishing, Case no. 9-195-096.

Baldwin, Carliss Y., and Clark, Kim B. 1992. "Capabilities and Capital Investment: New Perspectives on Capital Budgeting." *Journal of Applied Corporate Finance* 5, no. 2, pp. 67–82.

Baumol, W. J. 1959. *Business Behavior, Value and Growth.* New York: Macmillan.

Becker, Gary S. 1957. *The Economics of Discrimination.* Chicago: University of Chicago Press.

——— 1968. "Crime and Punishment: An Economic Approach." *Journal of Political Economy* 76 (March/April).

——— 1973. "A Theory of Marriage: Part I." *Journal of Political Economy* 82 (July/August).

Becker, Gary S., and Stigler, George J. 1972. *Law Enforcement, Corruption, and Compensation of Enforcers.* Conference on Capitalism and Freedom (October).

——— 1974. "Law Enforcement, Malfeasance, and Compensation of Enforcers." *Journal of Legal Studies* 3 (January), pp. 1–18.

Beer, Michael, Spector, Bert, Lawrence, Paul R., et al. 1984. *Managing Human Assets.* New York: The Free Press.

Benston, George J. 1963. "The Role of the Firm's Accounting System for Motivation." *The Accounting Review* (April), pp. 347–354.

——— 1975a. "Accountants' Integrity and Financial Reporting." *Financial Executive* 43 (August), pp. 10–14.

——— 1975b. "Accounting Standards in the U.S. and U.K.: Their Nature, Causes and Consequences." *Vanderbilt Law Review* 28 (January), pp. 235–268.

——— 1977. "The Impact of Maturity Regulation on High Interest Rate Lenders and Borrowers." *Journal of Financial Economics* 4, no. 1.

——— 1979–1980. "The Market for Public Accounting Services: Demand, Supply and Regulation." *The Accounting Journal* II, 1 (Winter), pp. 1–46.

——— 1985. "The Self-Serving Management Hypothesis: Some Evidence." *Journal of Accounting and Economics* 7 (April), pp. 67–84.

Berhold, M. 1971. "A Theory of Linear Profit Sharing Incentives." *Quarterly Journal of Economics* 85 (August), pp. 460–482.

Berle, Adolf A., and Means, Gardiner C. 1932. *The Modern Corporation and Private Property*. New York: Macmillan.

Black, F., Miller, M. H., and Posner, R. A. 1974. "An Approach to the Regulation of Bank Holding Companies." Unpublished Manuscript, University of Chicago.

Black, F., and Scholes, M. 1973. "The Pricing of Options and Corporate Liabilities." *Journal of Political Economy* 81, no. 3, pp. 637–654.

Blanchard, Oliver, Lopez-de-Silanes, and Schleifer, Andre. 1994. "What Do Firms Do with Cash Windfalls?" *Journal of Financial Economics* .

Blau, Peter M. 1956. *Bureaucracy in Modern Society*. New York: Random House.

Boulding, Kenneth E. 1962. *Conflict and Defense*. New York: Harper & Row.

Bowen, R. E., Noreen, E. W., and Lacey, J. 1981. "Determinants of the Corporate Decision to Capitalize Interest." *Journal of Accounting and Economics* 3 (August), pp. 151–179.

Branch, B. 1973. "Corporate Objectives and Market Performance." *Financial Management* (Summer), pp. 24–29.

Brennan, Michael. 1994. "Incentives, Rationality, and Society." *Journal of Applied Corporate Finance* (Summer).

Brickley, James A., and Dark, Frederick H. 1987. "The Choice of Organizational Form: The Case of Franchising." *Journal of Financial Economics* 18 (June), pp. 401–420.

Buchanan, James M., and Tullock, Gordon. 1965. *The Calculus of Consent: Logical Foundations of Constitutional Democracy*. Ann Arbor: University of Michigan Press.

Chandler, Alfred D., Jr. 1962. *Strategy and Structure*. Cambridge, Mass.: MIT Press.

——— 1977. *The Visible Hand: The Managerial Revolution*. Cambridge, Mass.: Harvard University Press.

——— 1993. "Chemicals and Electronics: Winning and Losing in Post-war American Industry." Unpublished manuscript, Harvard University.

Chandler, Alfred D., Jr., and Daems, Herman. 1980. *Managerial Hierarchies: Comparative Perspectives on the Rise of the Modern Industrial Enterprise*. Cambridge, Mass.: Harvard University Press.

Chase, Dennis J. 1975. "Foregrounding the News." *Reason* (August).

Clark, Kim B., and Fujimoto, T. 1991. *Product Development Performance: Strategy, Management and Organization in the World Auto Industry*. Boston: Harvard Business School Press.

Coase, Ronald H. 1937. "The Nature of the Firm," *Economica* 4, pp. 386–405. Also published in Coase (ed.), *Readings in Price Theory*. Homewood, Ill.: Irwin, pp. 315–331.

——— 1959. "The Federal Communications Commission." *Journal of Law and Economics* II (October), pp. 1–40.

——— 1960. "The Problem of Social Cost." *Journal of Law and Economics* III (October), pp. 1–44.

——— 1964. "Discussion." *American Economic Review* 54, no. 3, pp. 194–197.

Collins, Daniel W., Rozeff, Michael S., and Dhaliwal, Dan S. 1981. "The Economic Determinants of the Market Reaction to Proposed Mandatory Accounting

Changes in the Oil and Gas Industry: A Cross Section Analysis." *Journal of Accounting and Economics* 3, no. 1 (March), pp. 37–71.

Conference Board. 1985. *Top Executive Compensation.* New York: Conference Board.

Copeland, D. G., and McKenney, J. L. 1990. "Airline Reservations Systems: The Lessons from History." *MIS Quarterly* 12, no. 2, pp. 352–370.

Coughlan, Anne T., and Schmidt, Ronald M. 1985. "Executive Compensation, Management Turnover and Firm Performance: An Empirical Investigation." *Journal of Accounting and Economics* 7, no. 1–3 (April), pp. 43–66.

Crook, C. 1990. "Perestroika: And Now for the Hard Part." *The Economist*, April 28, pp. 1–22.

Crosby, Philip B. 1979. *Quality Is Free.* New York: McGraw-Hill.

———— 1989. *Let's Talk Quality.* New York: McGraw Hill.

Cyert, R. M., and Hedrick, C. L. 1972. "Theory of the Firm: Past, Present and Future: An Interpretation." *Journal of Economic Literature* 10 (June), pp. 398–412.

Cyert, R. M., and March, J. G. 1963. *A Behavioral Theory of the Firm.* Englewood Cliffs, N.J.: Prentice-Hall.

Daems, Herman. 1978. *The Holding Company and Corporate Control.* Amsterdam: Martinus Nijhoff.

Davidson Consultants. 1984. *Wage and Salary Administration in a Changing Economy.* Chicago: Dartell Press.

Dawkins, Richard. 1976. *The Selfish Gene.* Oxford: Oxford University Press.

DeAlessi, L. 1973. "Private Property and Dispersion of Ownership in Large Corporations." *Journal of Finance* (September), pp. 839–851.

DeAngelo, Linda E. 1981a. "Auditor Independence, 'Low Balling,' and Disclosure Regulation." *Journal of Accounting and Economics* 3, no. 2 (August), pp. 113–127.

———— 1981b. "Auditor Size and Audit Quality." *Journal of Accounting Perspectives* 3, no. 3 (December), pp. 183–200.

Debreu, Gerard. 1959. *Theory of Value.* New York: John Wiley & Sons.

Deci, Edward 1972. "The Effects of Contingent and Non-Contingent Rewards and Controls on Intrinsic Motivation." *Organizational Behavior and Human Performance* 8.

Deming, W. Edwards. 1952. *Elementary Principles of the Statistical Control of Quality,* rev. 2nd ed. Tokyo: JUSE.

———— 1982. *Quality, Productivity and Competitive Position.* Massachusetts Institute of Technology Center for Advanced Engineering Study, Cambridge, Mass.

Demsetz, Harold. 1967. "Toward a Theory of Property Rights." *American Economic Review* 57 (May), pp. 347–359.

———— 1969. "Information and Efficiency: Another Viewpoint." *Journal of Law and Economics* 12 (April), pp. 1–22.

———— 1982. *Economic, Legal, and Political Dimensions of Competition.* Amsterdam: North-Holland.

———— 1988. "The Theory of the Firm Revisited." *Journal of Law, Economics and Organizations* 4, pp. 141–162.

Demski, Joel S., and Kreps, David M. 1982. "Models in Managerial Accounting." *Supplement to Journal of Accounting Research.*

Deutsch, Claudia. 1986. "Holding on to Technical Talent." *New York Times,* November 16.

Dhaliwal, D. 1980. "The Effect of the Firm's Capital Structure on the Choice of Accounting Methods." *The Accounting Review* 55 (January), pp. 78–84.

Dhaliwal, D., Salamon, G., and Smith, E. D. 1982. "The Effect of Owner versus Management Control on the Choice of Accounting Methods." *Journal of Accounting and Economics* 4 (July), pp. 41–53.

Diamond, P. A. 1967. "The Role of Stock Market in a General Equilibrium Model with Technological Uncertainty." *American Economic Review* 57 (September), pp. 759–776.

Dickens, William T., Katz, Lawrence, Lang, Kevin, et al. 1987. "Employees, Crime, Monitoring and the Efficiency Wage Hypothesis." NBER Working Paper. National Bureau of Economic Research.

Dixon, J. Robb, Nanni, Alfred J., and Vollmann, Thomas E. 1990. *The New Performance Measurement Challenge.* Homewood, Ill.: Dow-Jones-Irwin.

Downs, Anthony. 1957. *An Economic Theory of Democracy.* New York: Harper & Row.

Eccles, Robert G., Nohria, Nitin, and Berkley, James D. 1992. *Beyond the Hype: Rediscovering the Essence of Management.* Cambridge, Mass.: Harvard Business School Press.

Ehrenberg, Ronald G., and Milkovich, George T. 1987. "Compensation and Firm Performance." NBER Working Paper #2145. National Bureau of Economic Research.

Evans, J. L., and Archer, S. H. 1968. "Diversification and the Reduction of Dispersion: An Empirical Analysis." *Journal of Finance* (December).

Fama, Eugene F. 1970a. "Efficient Capital Markets: A Review of Theory and Empirical Work." *Journal of Finance* 25, no. 2 .

―――― 1970b. "Multiperiod Consumption-investment Decisions." *American Economic Review* 60 (March).

―――― 1972. "Ordinal and Measurable Utility," in Michael C. Jensen (ed.), *Studies in the Theory of Capital Markets.* New York: Praeger.

―――― 1976. *Foundations of Finance.* New York: Basic Books.

―――― 1978. "The Effects of a Firm's Investment and Financing Decisions on the Welfare of Its Security Holders." *American Economic Review* 68, no. 2 (June), pp. 272–284.

―――― 1980. "Agency Problems and the Theory of the Firm." *Journal of Political Economy* 88, no. 2 (April), pp. 288–307.

Fama, Eugene F., and Jensen, Michael C. 1983a. "Agency Problems and Residual Claims." *Journal of Law and Economics* 26, no. 2, pp. 327–349. (Chapter 6 of this volume.)

―――― 1983b. "Separation of Ownership and Control." *Journal of Law and Economics* 26 (June), pp. 301–325. (Chapter 7 of this volume.)

―――― 1985. "Organizational Forms and Investment Decisions." *Journal of Financial Economics* 14, pp. 101–119.

Fama, Eugene F., and Miller, M. 1972. *The Theory of Finance*. New York: Holt, Rhinehart, and Winston.

Fama, Eugene F., and Schwert, G. William. 1977. "Asset Returns and Inflation." *Journal of Financial Economics* 5 (November), pp. 115–146.

Fast, Norman, and Berg, Norman. 1975. "The Lincoln Electric Company." Harvard Business School case no. 376–028. Boston: Harvard Business School.

Feigenbaum, A. V. 1991. *Total Quality Control* (1st ed., 1951). New York: McGraw-Hill.

Forbes. 1991. "Pay Is Not a Motivator." *Forbes,* May 27, 1991, pp. 212.

Friedman, Milton. 1970. "The Social Responsibility of Business Is to Increase Its Profits." *New York Times Magazine,* September 13, pp. 32 ff.

Fuchsberg, Gilbert. 1992a. "Quality Programs Show Shoddy Results." *Wall Street Journal,* May 14, 1992.

——— 1992b. "Total Quality Is Termed Only Partial Success." *Wall Street Journal,* October 1, 1992.

Furubotn, E. G., and Pejovich, S. 1972. "Property Rights and Economic Theory: A Survey of Recent Literature." *Journal of Economic Literature* 10 (December), pp. 1137–1162.

——— 1973. "Property Rights, Economic Decentralization, and the Evolution of the Yugoslav Firm, 1965–1972." *Journal of Law and Economics* 16 (October), pp. 275–302.

Galai, D., and Masulis, R. W. 1976. "The Option Pricing Model and the Risk Factor of Stock." *Journal of Financial Economics* 3, no. 1/2, pp. 53–82.

Garvin, David. 1988. *Managing Quality: The Strategic Competitive Edge*. New York: Free Press.

Gibbons, Robert, and Kevin J. Murphy. 1989. "Agency Theory and the Determinants of Executive Compensation." Working Paper. Rochester, N.Y.: University of Rochester.

——— 1990. "Relative Performance Evaluation for Chief Executive Officers." *Industrial and Labor Relations Review* (February).

Gibbs, Michael J. 1989. "Promotions, Compensation, and Firm Organization." Ph.D. dissertation, Department of Economics, University of Chicago.

Gilman, H. 1987. "J.C. Penny Decentralizes Its Purchasing: Individual Stores Can Tailor Buying to Needs." *Wall Street Journal,* May 8.

Gitlow, Howard S., and Gitlow, Shelly J. 1987. *The Deming Guide to Quality and Competitive Position*. Englewood Cliffs, N.J.: Prentice-Hall.

Hackman, J. Richard. 1986. "The Psychology of Self-Management of Organizations," in M. S. Pallack and R. O. Perloff (eds.), *Psychology and Work: Productivity, Change, and Employment*. Washington, D. C.: American Psychology Association.

Hagerman, R., and M. Zmijewski. 1979. "Some Economic Determinants of Accounting Policy Choices." *Journal of Accounting and Economics* (August), pp. 141–161.

Hakansson, N. H. 1974a. "Ordering Markets and the Capital Structures of Firms with Illustrations." Institute of Business and Economic Research Working Paper no. 24. Berkeley, Calif.: University of California.

—— 1974b. "The Superfund: Efficient Paths Toward a Complete Financial Market." Unpublished.

Hall, Robert W., Johnson, H. Thomas, and Turney, Peter B. 1991. *Measuring Up: Charting Pathways to Manufacturing Excellence.* Homewood, Ill.: Business One Irwin.

Hamner, W. Clay. 1975. "How to Ruin Motivation with Pay." *Compensation Review* 7, pp. 17–27.

Hansen, Ronald W. 1982. "The Relationship between Regulation and R&D in the Pharmaceutical Industry: A Review of Literature and Public Policy Proposals," in *The Effectiveness of Medicines in Containing Health Care Costs: Impact of Innovation, Regulation, and Quality.* National Pharmaceutical Council.

Hansmann, Henry B. 1980. "The Role of Nonprofit Enterprise." *Yale Law Journal* 89, no. 5 (April), pp. 835–901.

—— 1981. "Nonprofit Enterprise in the Performing Arts." *Bell Journal of Economics* 12, no. 2 (Autumn), pp. 341–361.

Harris, M., and Raviv, A. 1978. "Some Results in Incentive Contracts with Applications to Education and Employment, Health Insurance, and Law Enforcement." *American Economic Review* 68 (March), pp. 20–30.

Harris, M., and Townsend, R. 1981. "Resource Allocation Under Asymmetric Information." *Econometrica* 49 (January), pp. 33–64.

Harris, M., Kriebel, C. H., and Raviv, A. 1982. "Asymmetric Information, Incentives and Intrafirm Resource Allocation." *Management Science* 28, no. 6 (June), pp. 604–620.

Harry, Mikel J., and Lawson, J. Ronald. 1992. *Six Sigma Producibility Analysis and Process Characterizations.* Reading, Mass.: Addison-Wesley.

Hart, Oliver D. 1983. "The Market Mechanism as an Incentive Scheme." *Bell Journal of Economics* 14 (Autumn), pp. 366–382.

Hart, Oliver D., and Holmström, Bengt. 1987. "The Theory of Contracts," in Truman Bewley (ed.), *Advances in Economic Theory.* Cambridge: Cambridge University Press.

Hayek, Freidrich A. 1945. "The Use of Knowledge in Society." *American Economic Review* 35, no. 4 (September).

—— 1977. "Planning our Way to Serfdom." *Reason* (March).

—— 1979. *The Political Order of a Free People.* Chicago: University of Chicago Press.

Hayes, Robert H. 1985. "Strategic Planning Forward in Reverse?" *Harvard Business Review* 63, no. 6, pp. 11–19.

—— 1986. "Too Much Dictating from the Top: Why Strategic Planning Goes Awry." *New York Times,* April 20.

Healy, Paul. 1985. "The Effect of Bonus Schemes on Accounting Decisions." *Journal of Accounting and Economics* 7, pp. 85–107.

Heckerman, D. G. 1975. "Motivating Managers to Make Investment Decisions." *Journal of Financial Economics* 2, no. 3, pp. 273–292.

Henderson, David R. 1977. "Coal Mine Safety Legislation: Safety or Monopoly?" Rochester, N.Y.: University of Rochester.

Herman, Edward S. 1969. "Conflict of Interest in the Savings and Loan Industry," in Irwin Friend (ed.), *A Study of of the Savings and Loan Industry.* Washington, D.C.: Federal Home Loan Board.

———— 1981. *Corporate Control, Corporate Power.* Twentieth Century Fund Study. New York: Cambridge University Press.

Hirshleifer, Jack. 1958. "On the Theory of Optimal Investment Decisions." *Journal of Political Economy* (August), pp. 329–352.

———— 1964. "Internal Pricing and Decentralized Decisions," in Robert K. Jaedicke, Charles P. Bonini, and Harvey M. Wagner (eds.), *Management Controls: New Directions in Basic Research.* New York: McGraw-Hill.

———— 1970. *Investment, Interest, and Capital.* Englewood Cliffs, N.J.: Prentice-Hall.

———— 1978. "Competition, Cooperation, and Conflict in Economics and Biology." *American Economic Review* 68, no. 2 (May), pp. 238–243.

Holmström, Bengt. 1979. "Moral Hazard and Observability." *Bell Journal of Economics* 10 (Spring), pp. 74–91.

———— 1982. "Moral Hazard in Teams." *Bell Journal of Economics* 10 (Autumn), pp. 74–91.

Holmström, Bengt, and Tirole, Jean. 1987. "The Theory of the Firm," in R. Schmalensee and R. Willig (eds.), *Handbook of Industrial Organization.* New York: North Holland.

Holthausen, Robert W. 1981. "Evidence on the Effect of Bond Covenants and Management Compensation Contracts on the Choice of Accounting Techniques: The Case of the Depreciation Switch-Back." *Journal of Accounting and Economics* 3 (March), pp. 73–109.

Holthausen, Robert W., and Leftwich, Richard W. 1982. "The Economic Conse quences of Accounting Choice: Implications of Costly Contracting and Monitoring." Center for Research in Security Prices Working Paper No. 87. Chicago: University of Chicago Graduate School of Business.

Horngren, Charles. 1982. *Cost Accounting: A Managerial Emphasis.* Englewood Cliffs, N.J.: Prentice-Hall.

Initiative Committee for National Economic Planning. 1975. "The Case for Government Planning." *New York Times,* March 16.

Ishikawa, Kaoru. 1985. *What Is Total Quality Control? The Japanese Way.* Englewood Cliffs, N.J.: Prentice-Hall.

Jaikumar, Ramchandran. 1989. "Japanese Flexible Manufacturing Systems: Impact on the United States, Japan and the World Economy." *International Journal of Economic Theory and Policy* 2, pp. 113–143.

Jarrell, G. A. 1979. "Pro-Producer Regulation and Accounting for Assets: The Case of Electric Utilities." *Journal of Accounting and Economics* (August), pp. 93–116.

Jensen, Michael C. 1969. "Risk, the Pricing of Capital Assets, and the Evaluation of Investment Portfolios." *Journal of Business* 42, no. 2, pp. 167–247.

———— 1975. "Tests of Capital Market Theory and Implications of the Evidence." In *Is Financial Analysis Useless? Proceedings of a Seminar on the Efficient*

Market and Random Walk Hypotheses (The Financial Analysts Research Foundation, 1975). Reprinted in J. L. Bicksler (ed.), *Handbook of Financial Economics* (North-Holland, 1979).

——— 1983. "Organization Theory and Methodology." *Accounting Review* 50 (April). (Chapter 5 of this volume.)

——— 1986a. "Agency Costs of Free Cash Flow: Corporate Finance and Take-overs." *American Economic Review* 76 (May), pp. 323–329.

——— 1986b. "The Takeover Controversy: Analysis and Evidence." *Midland Corporate Finance Journal* (Summer). Reprinted in John Coffee, Louis Lowenstein, and Susan Rose-Ackerman (eds.), *Knights, Raiders, and Targets: The Impact of the Hostile Takeover* (Oxford University Press, 1988), and in Joel M. Stern, G. Bennett Stewart III, and Donald H. Chew (eds.), *Corporate Restructuring and Executive Compensation* (Ballinger, 1989), pp. 3–43.

——— 1988. "Takeovers: Their Causes and Consequences." *Journal of Economic Perspectives* 2, no. 1 (Spring), pp. 21–48.

——— 1989a. "Active Investors, LBOs, and the Privatization of Bankruptcy." *Journal of Applied Corporate Finance* 2, no. 1 (Spring), pp. 35–44.

——— 1989b. "Eclipse of the Public Corporation." *Harvard Business Review* 67, no. 5 (September-October), pp. 61–74.

——— 1993. "The Modern Industrial Revolution, Exit and the Failure of Internal Control Systems." *Journal of Finance* (July), pp. 831–880.

——— 1994. "Self-Interest, Altruism, Incentives, and Agency Theory." *Journal of Applied Corporate Finance* 7, no. 2 (Summer). (Chapter 2 of this volume.)

Jensen, Michael C., and Barry, Brian K. 1992. "Gordon Cain and the Sterling Group (A)." Harvard Business School case no. 9–492–021. Boston: Harvard Business School.

Jensen, Michael C., and Meckling, William H. 1976. "Theory of the Firm: Managerial Behavior, Agency Costs, and Ownership Structure." *Journal of Financial Economics* 3, no. 4 (October), pp. 305–360. (Chapter 3 of this volume.)

——— 1978. "Can the Corporation Survive?" *Financial Analysts Journal* (January-February).

——— 1979. "Rights and Production Functions: An Application to Labor-managed Firms and Codetermination." *Journal of Business* 52, no. 4 (October), pp. 469–506.

——— 1992. "Specific and General Knowledge, and Organization Structure," in Lars Werin and Hans Wijkander (eds.), *Contract Economics*. Oxford: Basil Blackwell, pp. 251–274. Reprinted in *Journal of Applied Corporate Finance* (Fall 1995). (Chapter 4 of this volume).

——— 1994. "The Nature of Man." *Journal of Applied Corporate Finance* (Summer). (Chapter 1 of this volume.)

Jensen, Michael C. and Murphy, Kevin J. 1990a. "Are Executive Compensation Contracts Structured Properly?" Working Paper. Boston: Harvard Business School.

——— 1990b. "Performance Pay and Top Management Incentives." *Journal of Political Economy* 98, pp. 225–264. (Chapter 9 in this volume.)

Johnson, W. Bruce, Magee, Robert P., Nagarajan, Nandu J., et al. 1985. "An Analysis of the Stock Market Price Reaction to Sudden Executive Deaths: Implications for the Managerial Labor Market." *Journal of Accounting and Economics* 7 (April), pp. 151–174.

Juran, J. M. 1989. *Juran on Leadership for Quality*. New York: Free Press.

Kaitin, Kenneth I., Bryant, Natalie R., and Lasagna, Lewis. 1993. "The Role of Research-Based Pharmaceutical Industry in Medical Progress in the United States." *Journal of Clinical Pharmacology* 33 (May), pp. 412–417.

Kantor, Paul B., and Zangwill, Willard I. 1993. "Toward a Theory of Continuous Improvement." Working Paper. Chicago: University of Chicago Business School.

Kaplan, Robert S. 1982. *Advanced Management Accounting*. Englewood Cliffs, N.J.: Prentice-Hall.

Kaplan, Robert S., and Norton, David P. 1992. "The Balanced Scorecard-Measures that Drive Performance." *Harvard Business Review* (January-February), pp. 71–79.

———— 1991. "Staying Power of CBOs." *Journal of Financial Economics* 29, no. 2, pp. 287–313.

Kaufman, Henry. 1989. "Bush's First Priority: Stopping the Buyout Mania." *Washington Post,* January 1.

Keating, Scott A., and Wruck, Karen H. 1993. "Sterling Chemicals, Inc.: Quality and Process Improvement Program." Harvard Business School case no. 9–439–026. Boston: Harvard Business School.

Kensinger, J. W., and Martin, J. D. 1991. "Financing Network Organizations." *Journal of Applied Corporate Finance* 4, no. 1, pp. 66–76.

Kiechel, W. 1982. "Corporate Strategists Under Fire." *Fortune,* December 27.

Klein, Benjamin, Crawford, Robert, and Alchian, Armen A. 1978. "Vertical Integration, Appropriate Rents, and the Competitive Contracting Process." *Journal of Law and Economics* 21, no. 2 (October), pp. 297–396.

Klein, W. A. 1976. "Legal and Economic Perspectives on the Firm." Unpublished manuscript. Los Angeles: University of California.

Kohn, Alfie. 1988. "Incentives Can Be Bad for Business." *INC* (January), pp. 93–94.

Kraus, A., and Litzenberger, R. 1973. "A State Preference Model of Optimal Financial Leverage." *Journal of Finance* (September).

Krueger, Alan, and Summers, Larry. 1988. "Efficiency Wages and the Inter-Industry Wage Structure." *Econometrica* 56 (January).

Kruse, Douglas L. 1987. "Profit Sharing and Employment Variability: Microeconomic Evidence." Department of Economics, Harvard University.

Lang, Larr, Poulsen, Annette, and Stulz, Rene M. 1994. "Asset Sales, Firm Performance, and the Agency Costs of Managerial Discretion." *Journal of Financial Economics* 37, no. 1, pp. 3–37.

Larner, R. J. 1970. *Management Control and the Large Corporation*. New York: Dunellen.

Larrick, Richard P., Nisbett, Richard E., and Morgan, James N. 1993. "Who Uses the Cost-Benefit Rules of Choice? Implications for the Normative Status of Microeconomic Theory, Organization Behavior and Human Decision Processes." Unpublished manuscript.

Lawler, Edward E. III. 1971. *Pay and Organizational Effectiveness: A Psychological View.* New York: McGraw-Hill.

———— 1973. *Motivation in Work Organizations.* Monterrey, Calif.: Brooks/Cole.

Lazear, Edward P. 1979. "Why Is There Mandatory Retirement?" *Journal of Political Economy* 87, no. 6 (December), pp. 1261–1284.

Lazear, Edward P., and Rosen, Sherwin. 1981. "Rank-Order Tournaments as Optimum Labor Contracts." *Journal of Political Economy* 89 (October), pp. 841–864.

LeDoux, Joseph. 1994. "Emotion, Memory, and the Brain." *Scientific American,* June, pp. 50–57.

Leftwich, Richard. 1981. "Evidence of the Impact of Mandatory Changes in Accounting Principles on Corporate Loan Agreements." *Journal of Accounting and Economics* 3, no. 1 (March), pp. 3–36.

———— 1983. "Accounting Information in Private Markets: Evidence for Private Lending Agreements." *The Accounting Review* (January).

Leftwich, Richard, Watts, Ross L., and Zimmerman, Jerold L. 1981. "Voluntary Corporate Disclosure: The Case of Interim Reporting." *Journal of Accounting Research,* Supplement to vol. 19, pp. 50–77.

Lewellen, Wilbur G. 1971. *The Ownership Income of Management.* New York: Columbia University Press.

Lilien, S., and Pastena, V. 1982. "Determinants of the Intramethod Choices in the Oil and Gas Industry." *Journal of Accounting and Economics* (December).

Linden, Dana W., and Contavespi, Vicki. 1991. "Incentivize Me Please." *Forbes,* May 27, pp. 208–212.

Lintner, J. 1965. "Security Prices, Risk, and Maximal Gains from Diversification." *Journal of Finance* 20 (December), pp. 587–616.

Lloyd-Davies, P. 1975. "Risk and Optimal Leverage." Unpublished manuscript, University of Rochester.

Long, J. B. 1972. "Wealth, Welfare, and the Price of Risk." *Journal of Finance* (May), pp. 419–433.

———— 1974. "Discussion." *Journal of Finance* 39, no. 12, pp. 185–188.

Lotka, Alfred J. 1956. *Elements of Mathematical Biology.* New York: Dover.

Lynch, Richard L., and Cross, Kelvin F. 1991. *Measure Up! Yardsticks for Continuous Improvement.* Cambridge, Mass.: Basil Blackwell.

Lys, Thomas. 1982. *Selection of Accounting Procedures and Implications of Changes in Generally Accepted Accounting Principles: A Case Study Using Oil and Gas Accounting.* Rochester, N.Y.: University of Rochester.

Machlup, F. 1967. "Theories of the Firm: Marginalist, Behavioral, Managerial." *American Economic Review* (March), pp. 1–33.

Manne, H. G. 1962. "The 'Higher Criticism' of the Modern Corporation." *Columbia Law Review* 62 (March), pp. 259–284.

—— 1965. "Mergers and the Market for Corporate Control." *Journal of Political Economy* (April), pp. 110–120.

—— 1967. "Our Two Corporate Systems: Law and Economics." *Virginia Law Review* 53 (March), pp. 259–284.

—— 1972. "The Social Responsibility of Regulated Utilities." *Wisconsin Law Review* V, no. 4, pp. 995–1009.

March, Artemis, and Garvin, David. 1986. "A Note on Quality: The Views of Deming, Juran, and Crosby." Harvard Business School case no. 9–687–011 and Teaching Note no. 5–691–022. Boston: Harvard Business School.

March, J. G., and Simon, H. A. 1958. *Organizations*. New York: John Wiley and Sons.

Marris, R. 1964. *The Economic Theory of Managerial Capitalism*. Glencoe, Ill.: Free Press of Glencoe.

Martin, Kenneth J., and McConnell, John J. 1988. "Corporate Performance, Corporate Takeovers, and Management Turnover." Working Paper. West Lafayette, Ind.: Purdue University.

Marvel, Howard P. 1982. "Exclusive Dealing." *Journal of Law and Economics* 25, 1 (April), pp. 1–25.

Maslow, A. H. 1943. "A Theory of Human Motivation." *Psychological Review* 50 (January), pp. 370–396.

Mason, E. S. 1959. *The Corporation in Modern Society*. Cambridge, Mass.: Harvard University Press.

Mayers, David, and Smith, Clifford W., Jr. 1981. "Contractual Provisions, Organizational Structure, and Conflict Control in Insurance Markets." *Journal of Business* 54, no. 3 (July).

—— 1982a. "On the Corporate Demand for Insurance." *Journal of Business* 54, no. 3 (July), pp. 407–433.

—— 1982b. "Toward a Positive Theory of Insurance," in Ernest Bloch and Paul Wachtel (eds.), *Salomon Brothers Center for the Study of Financial Institutions*. New York: New York University Graduate School of Business Administration.

McLaughlin, Kenneth J. 1987. "The Quit-Layoff Distinction in a Joint Wealth Maximizing Approach to Labor Turnover." Ph.D. dissertation, University of Chicago.

—— 1989. "Rigid Wages?" University of Rochester Working Paper. Rochester, N.Y.: University of Rochester.

McManus, J. C. 1975. "The Costs of Alternative Economic Organizations." *Canadian Journal of Economics* VII (August), pp. 334–350.

Meckling, William H. 1976. "Values and the Choice of the Model of the Individual in the Social Sciences." *Schweizerische Zeitschrift fur Volkswirtschaft und Revue Suisse d'Economie Politique et Statistique* (December).

Medoff, James L., and Abraham, Katherine G. 1980. "Experience, Performance, and Earnings." *Quarterly Journal of Economics* 95 (December), pp. 703–736.

Merton, R. C. 1973. "The Theory of Rational Option Pricing." *Bell Journal of Economics and Management Science* 4, no. 1, pp. 141–183.

—— 1974. "On the Pricing of Corporate Debt: The Risk Structure of Interest Rates." *Journal of Finance* 29, no. 2, pp. 449–470.

Merton, R. C., and Subrahmanyam, M. G. 1974. "The Optimality of a Competitive Stock Market." *Bell Journal of Economics and Management Science* (Spring), pp. 145–170.

Meyer, Herbert H. 1975. "The Pay-for-Performance Dilemma." *Organizational Dynamics* 3.

Mikkelson, Wayne H. 1981. "Convertible Calls and the Security Returns." *Journal of Financial Economics* 9, no. 3 (September), pp. 237–264.

Milgrom, Paul, and Roberts, John. 1992. *Economics, Organization, and Management.* Englewood Cliffs, N.J.: Prentice-Hall.

Milkovich, George T., and Newman, Jerry M. 1987. *Compensation.* Plano, Tex.: Business Publications.

Miller, M. H., and Modigliani, F. 1966. "Some Estimates of the Cost of Capital to the Electric Utility Industry, 1954–57." *American Economic Review* 48 (June), pp. 333–391.

Millikin and Company. 1991. "Milliken Pursuit of Excellence Seminar Notebook." Millikin and Company.

Mirrlees, J. 1976. "The Optimal Structure of Incentives and Authority Within an Organization." *Bell Journal of Economics* 7, no. 1 (Spring), pp. 105–131.

Mizuno, Shigeru. 1988. *Company-wide Total Quality Control.* For Asian Productivity Organization, Hong Kong: Nordica International.

Modigliani, F., and Miller, M. H. 1958. "The Costs of Capital, Corporate Finance, and the Theory of Investment." *American Economic Review* 48 (June), pp. 261–297.

—— 1963. "Corporate Income Taxes and the Cost of Capital: A Correction." *American Economic Review* (June), pp. 433–443.

Monson, R. J., and Downs, A. 1965. "A Theory of Large Managerial Firms." *Journal of Political Economy* (June), pp. 221–236.

Murphy, Kevin J. 1985. "Corporate Performance and Managerial Remuneration: An Empirical Analysis." *Journal of Accounting and Economics* 7 (April), pp. 11–42.

—— 1986. "Incentives, Learning, and Compensation: A Theoretical and Empirical Investigation of Managerial Labor Contracts." *Rand Journal of Economics* 17 (Spring).

Myers, Stewart C. 1975. "A Note on the Determinants of Corporate Debt Capacity." Unpublished manuscript. London: London Graduate School of Business.

—— 1977. "Determinants of Corporate Borrowing." *Journal of Financial Economics* 5, no. 2 (November).

Niskanan, William A., Jr. 1968. "The Peculiar Economics of Bureaucracy." *American Economic Review* 58 (May), pp. 293–305.

—— 1971. *Bureaucracy and Representive Government.* Aldine-Atherton.

Noreen, Eric W., and Wolfson, Mark A. 1981. "Equilibrium Warrant Pricing Models and Accounting for Executive Stock Options." *Journal of Accounting Research* 19 (Autumn), pp. 384–398.

O'Keefe, Mary, Viscusi, W. Kip, and Zeckhauser, Richard J. 1984. "Economic Contests: Comparative Reward Schemes." *Journal of Labor Economics* 2 (January), pp. 27–56.

Pareto, Vilfredo. 1935. *The Mind and Society.* New York: Harcourt, Brace.

Peck, M. Scott. 1978. *The Road Less Traveled.* New York: Simon & Schuster.

Pejovich, S. 1969. "The Firm, Monetary Policy and Property Rights in a Planned Economy." *Western Economic Journal* 7, no. 3 (September), pp. 193–200.

Peltzman, Sam. 1974. *Regulation of Pharmaceutical Innovation.* American Enterprise Institute.

Penrose, E. 1958. *The Theory of the Growth of the Firm.* New York: Wiley.

Popper, Karl. 1950. *The Open Society and Its Enemies* (2nd ed.). Princeton, N.J.: Princeton University Press.

Postrel, S., and Rumelt, R. 1992. "Incentives, Routines, and Self-Command." *Industrial and Corporate Change* 1, pp. 397–425.

Preston, L. E. 1975. "Corporation and Society: The Search for a Paradigm." *Journal of Economic Literature* 13 (June), pp. 434–453.

Raviv, A. 1979. "The Design of an Optimal Insurance Policy." *American Economic Review* 69 (March), pp. 84–96.

Reagan, Patricia B., and Stulz, Rene M. 1986. "Risk Bearing, Labor Contracts, and Capital Markets." *Research in Finance* 6, pp. 217–232.

Richman, T. 1987. "Mrs. Fields's Secret Ingredient." *Inc.,* October.

Risher, Howard. 1978. "Job Evaluation: Mystical or Statistical?" *Personnel* (September-October).

Rogers, David. 1989. "Grass-Roots Issue: Congress's Pay Raise, Slated for Next Week, Stirs a Spirited Debate." *Wall Street Journal,* February 1.

Ross, S. A. 1973. "The Economic Theory of Agency: The Principal's Problems." *American Economic Review* 62 (May), pp. 134–139.

——— 1974a. "The Economic Theory of Agency and the Principle of Similarity," in M. D. Balch et al. (eds.), *Essays on Economic Behavior under Uncertainty.* Amsterdam: North-Holland.

——— 1974b. "Options and Efficiency." Rodney L. White Center for Financial Research Working Paper no. 3-74. Philadelphia: University of Pennsylvania.

Roy, Donald. 1952. "Goldbricking in a Machine Shop." *American Journal of Sociology* 57, pp. 427–442.

Rubenstein, M. 1974. "A Discrete-Time Synthesis of Financial Theory, Parts I and II." Institute of Business and Economic Research, Working Papers no. 20 and 21. Berkeley: University of California.

Rubin, Paul H. 1978. "The Theory of the Firm and the Structure of the Franchise Contract." *Journal of Law and Economics* 21 (April), pp. 223–233.

Sabo, Richard S. 1984. *What Is the Lincoln Incentive Management System?* Cleveland: Lincoln Electric Company.

Salop, Joanne, and Salop, Steven. 1976. "Self-Selection and Turnover in the Labor Market." *Quarterly Journal of Economics* 90 (November), pp. 619–627.

Schlesinger, Jacob M. 1988. "GM's New Compensation Plan Reflects General Trend Tying Pay to Performance." *Wall Street Journal,* January 26.

Schonberger, Richard. 1986. *World Class Manufacturing.* New York: Free Press.

Schwert, G. W. 1993. "Mark-up Pricing in Mergers and Acquisitions." Rochester, N.Y.: University of Rochester.

Scitovsky, T. 1943. "A Note of Profit Maximisation and Its Implications." *Review of Economic Studies* 11, pp. 57–60.

Sharpe, W. F. 1964. "Capital Asset Prices: A Theory of Market Equilibrium under Conditions of Risk." *Journal of Finance* 19 (September), pp. 425–442.

Shavell, S. 1979. "Risk Sharing and Incentives in the Principal and Agent Relationships." *Bell Journal of Economics* 10 (Spring), pp. 55–73.

Shubik, M. 1970. "A Curmudgeon's Guide to Microeconomics." *Journal of Economic Literature* 8 (June), pp. 405–434.

Silver, M., and Auster, R. 1969. "Entrepreneurship, Profit, and Limits on Firm Size." *Journal of Business* 42 (July), pp. 277–281.

Simon, Herbert A. 1955. "A Behavioral Model of Rational Choice." *Quarterly Journal of Economics* 69, pp. 99–118.

—— 1959. "Theories of Decision Making in Economics and Behavioral Science." *American Economic Review* (June), pp. 253–283.

—— 1962. "The Architecture of Complexity." Proceedings of the American Philosophical Society.

Slater, Philip. 1980. *Wealth Addiction.* New York: Dutton.

Smith, Adam. 1937. *The Wealth of Nations* (1776; ed. Edwin Cannan, 1904). Reprint: New York: Modern Library.

—— 1991. *The Theory of Moral Sentiments.* Indianapolis: Liberty Press.

Smith, Clifford W., Jr. 1976. "Option Pricing: A Review." *Journal of Financial Economics* 2, no. 1/2, pp. 3–52.

Smith, Clifford W., Jr., and Warner, Jerold B. 1979. "On Financial Contracting: An Analysis of Bond Covenants." *Journal of Financial Economics* 7 (July), pp. 117–161.

Sowell, Thomas. 1980. *Knowledge and Decisions.* New York: Basic Books.

Spence, M., and Zeckhauser, R. 1971. "Insurance, Information and Individual Action." *American Economic Review* 61, no. 2 (May), pp. 380–387.

Stelzer, Irwin M. 1994. "Pricing Health Care: There Is No Health Care Crisis." *Wall Street Journal,* January 25.

Stettler, Howard P. 1977. *Auditing Principles.* Englewood Cliffs, N.J.: Prentice-Hall.

Stewart, G. Bennett. 1991. *The Quest for Value: A Guide for Senior Managers.* New York: Harper Business.

Stewart, G. Bennett, and Glassman, David M. 1988. "The Motives and Methods of Corporate Restructuring: Part II." *Journal of Applied Corporate Finance* (Summer).

Stigler, George J., and Becker, Gary S. 1977. "De Gustibus non est Disputandum." *American Economic Review* 67, pp. 76–90.

Stiglitz, Joseph E. 1975. "Incentives, Risk, and Information: Notes Toward a Theory of Hierarchy." *Bell Journal of Economics* 6 (Autumn), pp. 552–579.

——— 1986. "Theories of Wage Rigidity," in James L. Butkiewicz, Kenneth J. Koford, and Jeffrey B. Miller (eds.), *Keynes' Economic Legacy.* New York: Prager.

Suzaki, Kiyoshi. 1987. *The New Manufacturing Challenge: Techniques for Continuous Improvement.* New York: Free Press.

Sykes, Charles J. 1992. *A Nation of Victims: The Decay of the American Character.* New York: St. Martin's Press.

Thaler, Richard H. 1991. *Quasi Rational Economics.* New York: Russell Sage Foundation.

Thaler, Richard H., and Shefrin, H. M. 1981. "An Economic Theory of Self-Control." *Journal of Political Economy* (April).

Thompson, Rex. 1978. "Capital Market Efficiency, Two-Parameter Asset Pricing and the Market for Corporate Control: The Implications of Closed-End Investment Company Discounts and Premiums." Ph.D. dissertation, University of Rochester, Graduate School of Management.

Townsend, R. M. 1979. "Optimal Contracts and Competitive Markets with Costly State Verification." *Journal of Economic Theory* 21 (October), pp. 265–293.

U.S. Department of Commerce. 1987. *Franchising in the Economy, 1986–1987.* Washington, D.C.: Government Printing Office.

U.S. Securities and Exchange Commission. 1940–41. *Survey of American Listed Corporations, Parts 1–7.* New York: Securities and Exchange Commission (For Work Projects Administration).

Vancil, Richard. 1987. *Passing the Baton: Managing the Process of CEO Succession.* Boston: Harvard Business School Press.

Wageman, Ruth, and Baker, George P. 1997. "Incentives and Cooperation: The Effects of Task and Reward Interdependence on Group Performance." *Journal of Organizational Behavior* 18, pp. 139–158.

Walsh, James P. 1988. "Top Management Turnover Following Mergers and Acquisitions." *Strategic Management Journal* 9 (March-April).

Walton, Mary. 1986. *The Deming Management Method.* New York: Dodd, Mead.

Wardell, William M., Hassar, Mohammed, Anavekar, Sadanand N., et al. 1978. "The Rate of Development in New Drugs in the United States, 1963 through 1975." *Clinical Psychology and Therapeutics* 24, no. 2 (August).

Warner, Jerold B. 1975. "Bankruptcy Costs, Absolute Priority, and the Pricing of Risky Debt Claims." Unpublished manuscript, University of Chicago.

Warner, Jerold B., Watts, Ross L., and Wruck, Karen H. 1988. "Stock Prices and Top Management Changes." *Journal of Financial Economics* (January-March).

Watts, Ross L. 1977. "Corporate Financial Statements, A Product of the Market and Political Processes." *Australian Journal of Management* 2 (April), pp. 53–75.

————— 1981. "The Political Economics of the Determination of Accounting Standards," in R. Hoyt (ed.), *The Relationship of Accounting Theory to the Standard Setting Process*. Faculté des Sciences de l'Administration, Université Labal.

Watts, Ross L., and Zimmerman, Jerold L. 1978. "Towards a Positive Theory of Determination of Accounting Standards." *The Accounting Review* 53 (January), pp. 112–134.

————— 1979. "The Demand for and Supply of Accounting Theories: The Market for Excuses." *The Accounting Review* (April), pp. 273–305.

————— 1982a. "Agency Problems, Auditing and the Theory of the Firm: Some Evidence." *The Accounting Review* (July), pp. 273–305.

————— 1982b. "Positive Theories of the Determination of Accounting Procedures." Unpublished manuscript, University of Rochester.

————— 1986. *Positive Accounting Theory*. Englewood Cliffs, N.J.: Prentice-Hall.

Weber, Max. 1947. *The Theory of Social and Economic Organization*. Glencoe, Ill.: Free Press.

Weick, Karl E. 1983. "Stress in Accounting Systems." *Accounting Review* 58, no. 2 (April).

Weisbach, Michael S. 1988. "Outside Directors and CEO Turnover." *Journal of Financial Economics* (January-March).

Weitzman, Martin L. 1984. *The Share Economy: Conquering Stagflation*. Cambridge, Mass.: Harvard University Press.

Whitehead, Alfred N., and Russell, Bertrand. 1910. *Principia Mathematica*. Cambridge: Cambridge University Press.

Williamson, Oliver E. 1964. *The Economics of Discretionary Behavior: Managerial Objectives in a Theory of the Firm*. Englewood Cliffs, N.J.: Prentice-Hall.

————— 1970. *Corporate Control and Business Behavior*. Englewood Cliffs, N.J.: Prentice-Hall.

————— 1975. *Markets and Hierarchies: Analysis and Antitrust Implications*. New York: Free Press.

————— 1979. "Transaction-Cost Economics: The Governance of Contractual Relations." *Journal of Law and Economics* 22, no. 2 (October), pp. 233–261.

————— 1981. "The Modern Corporation: Origins, Evolution, Attributes." *Journal of Economic Literature* (December), pp. 1537–1568.

Wilson, R. 1968. "On the Theory of Syndicates." *Econometrica* 36 (January), pp. 119–132.

————— 1969. "La Décision: Agrégation et Dynamique des Ordres de Préférence," in Wilson (ed.), *Editions du Centre National de la Recherche Scientifique*. Paris: Centre National de la Recherche Scientifique.

Wruck, Karen H., and Jensen, Michael C. 1994. "Science, Specific Knowledge and Total Quality Management." *Journal of Accounting and Economics* 18, pp. 247–287. (Chapter 11 of this volume.)

Zimmerman, Jerold L. 1977. "The Municipal Accounting Maze: An Analysis of

Political Incentives in Studies in Measurement and Evaluation of the Economic Efficiency of Public and Private Nonprofit Institutions." Supplement to *The Journal of Accounting Research* 15, pp. 107–144.

—— 1979. "The Costs and Benefits of Cost Allocations." *The Accounting Review* (July), pp. 504–521.

—— 1980. "Positive Research in Accounting," in R. D. Nair and T. H. Williams (eds.), *Perspectives on Research*. Madison: University of Wisconsin.

—— 1993. "Non-traditional Accounting Systems, Ch. 10," in *Accounting for Decision Making and Control*. Rochester, N.Y.: University of Rochester.

Zmijewski, M., and Hagerman, R. 1981. "An Income Strategy Approach to the Positive Theory of Accounting Standard Setting/Choice." *Journal of Accounting and Economics* 3 (August), pp. 129–149.

Acknowledgments

Chapter 1: The Nature of Man

The first draft of this chapter was written in the early 1970s. Since then it has been used annually in our course on Coordination and Control at both Rochester and Harvard. We are indebted to our students for much help in honing these ideas over the years. An earlier version of some of the ideas presented here appeared in William H. Meckling, "Values and the Choice of the Model of the Individual in the Social Sciences," *Schweizerische Zeitschrift fur Volkwirtshaft und Statisik/Revue Suisse d'Economie Politique de Statistique* (December 1976).

This research has been supported by the Managerial Economics Research Center, University of Rochester, and the Division of Research, Harvard Business School. We are grateful for the advice and comments of many people, including Chris Argyris, George Baker, Fischer Black, Donald Chew, Perry Fagan, Donna Feinberg, Amy Hart, Karin Monsler, Kevin Murphy, Natalie Jensen, Steve-Anna Stephens, Richard Tedlow, Robin Tish, Karen Wruck, and Abraham Zaleznik.

Chapter 2: Self-Interest, Altruism, Incentives, and Agency Theory

This research has been supported by the Division of Research, Harvard Business School. I am indebted to many individuals for comments and discussions over the years that have helped me understand these issues. Although they bear no responsibility for the views expressed herein, I am grateful to Chris Argyris, George Baker, Donald Chew, Perry Fagan, Donna Feinberg, Gerald Fischbach, Jack Gabarro, Richard Hackman, Steven Hyman, William Meckling, Steve-Anna Stephens, Richard Thaler, Karen Wruck, the participants in the Mind, Brain, Behavior initiative at Harvard University, and my former colleagues at the University of Rochester.

Chapter 3: Theory of the Firm

An earlier version of this chapter was presented at the Conference on Analysis and Ideology, Interlaken, Switzerland, June 1974, sponsored by the Center for Research in Government Policy and Business at the University of Rochester, Graduate School of Management. We are indebted to F. Black, E. Fama, R. Ibbotson, W. Klein, M. Rozeff, R. Weil, O. Williamson, an anonymous referee, and to our colleagues and members of the Finance Workshop at the University of Rochester for their comments and criticisms, in particular G. Benston, M. Canes, D. Henderson, K. Leffler, J. Long, C. Smith, R. Thompson, R. Watts, and J. Zimmerman.

Chapter 4: Specific and General Knowledge and Organizational Structure

This research has been supported by the Managerial Economics Research Center, University of Rochester, and the Division of Research, Harvard Business School. We are grateful for the comments and criticisms of George Baker, Robert Eccles, Lars Werin, and Karen Wruck.

Chapter 5: Organization Theory and Methodology

This chapter is drawn from my Plenary Lecture to the American Accounting Association in 1982. I am indebted to Charles Christenson, Robert Kaplan, and to my colleagues George Benston, Andrew Christie, Ann Coughlan, Martin Giesel, Clifford Holderness, John Long, William Schwert, Clifford Smith, René Stulz, Jerold Warner, and especially Ross Watts, William Meckling, and Jerold Zimmerman for their comments and suggestions.

Chapter 6: Agency Problems and Residual Claims

This chapter is a revision of parts of our earlier paper, "The Survival of Organizations" (September 1980). In the course of this work, we have profited from the comments of R. Antle, R. Benne, F. Black, F. Easterbrook, A. Farber., W. Gavett, P. Hirsch, R. Hogarth, C. Holderness, R. Holthausen, C. Horne, J. Jeuck, R. Leftwich, S. McCormick, D. Mayers, P. Pashigian, M. Scholes, C. Smith, G. Stigler, R. Watts, T. Whisler, R. Yeaple, J. Zimmerman, and especially A. Alchian, W. Meckling, and C. Plosser. Financial support for Eugene Fama's participation came from the National Science Foundation. Michael Jensen was supported by the Managerial Economics Research Center of the University of Rochester.

Chapter 7: Separation of Ownership and Control

This chapter is a revision of parts of our earlier paper, "The Survival of Organizations" (September 1980). In the course of this work we have profited from the comments of R. Antle, R. Benne, F. Black, F. Easterbrook, A. Farber, W. Gavett, P. Hirsch, R. Hogarth, C. Holderness, R. Holthausen, C. Horne, J. Jeuck, R. Leftwich, S. McCormick, D. Mayers, P. Pashigian, M. Scholes, C. Smith, G. Stigler, R. Watts, T. Whisler, R. Yeaple, J. Zimmerman, and especially A. Alchian, W. Meckling, and C. Plosser. Financial support for Eugene Fama's participation came from the National Science Foundation. Michael Jensen was supported by the Managerial Economics Research Center of the University of Rochester.

Chapter 8: Compensation and Incentives

This research was supported by the Division of Research, Harvard Business School, the Managerial Economic Research Center, University of Rochester, and the John M. Olin Foundation. The authors would like to thank Michael Beer for helpful discussions leading up to this paper, and Robin Cooper, Natalie Jensen, Kenneth Merchant, Richard Ruback, Robert Simons, and Richard Vancil for comments on an early draft; these people should not be held responsible for the authors' opinions or possible errors.

Chapter 9: Performance Pay and Top-Management Incentives

We have benefited from the assistance of Stephanie Jensen, Natalie Jensen, Mary Rojek, and Mike Stevenson and from the comments of Sherwin Rosen, George Baker, Carliss Baldwin, Ray Ball, Gary Becker, Joseph Bower, James Brickley, Jeffrey Coles, Harry DeAngelo, Robert Gibbons, Gailen Hite, Clifford Holderness, Robert Kaplan, Steven Kaplan, Edward Lazear, Richard Leftwich, John Long, Jay Lorsch, John McArthur, Paul MacAvoy, Kenneth McLaughlin, Kenneth Merchant, Andrall Pearson, Ronald Schmidt, G. William Schwert, Robert Simons, Jerold Warner, Ross Watts, and Jerold Zimmerman. This research was supported by the Division of Research, Harvard Business School; the Managerial Economics Research Center, University of Rochester; and the John M. Olin Foundation.

Chapter 12: Divisional Performance Measurement

This chapter is based on a presentation at the Harvard Colloquium on Field Studies in Accounting, June 18–20, 1986. This research was supported by the Division of Research, Harvard Business School, and the Managerial Economics Research Center, University of Rochester.

Index